VOICES
FROM THE
ATTIC

The Williamstown Boys in the Civil War

5/24/18

Best wishes,

Carleton Young

CARLETON YOUNG

William James Morris
Holding Company

Voices From the Attic: The Williamstown Boys in the Civil War

Copyright ©2015 Carleton Young

Published by William James Morris, Inc.
Syracuse, Indiana

ISBN: 978-0-9968430-0-3 (paperback)
ISBN: 978-0-9968430-1-0 (ebook)

Cover image and design: Kirk DouPonce, DogEarred Design
Interior design and typeset: Katherine Lloyd, The DESK

Introduction

THE LETTERS
IN THE ATTIC

Even after a century and a half, the Civil War continues to fascinate and intrigue, as demonstrated by the rows of books in the Civil War section at book stores. Historians have calculated that more than 50,000 books have been written about the Civil War, or about one per day ever since the war ended in 1865. I certainly never expected to be adding to this vast corpus, but I believe that we have something unique to contribute.

After my father passed away in 2002, I helped to clear out a lifetime's worth of accumulated possessions from his house in Pittsburgh. Tucked away in the attic was a very old wooden box, jammed full of envelopes and other papers. With so much to sort through and throw away, there was no time to examine it, so it was placed in the "keep" pile destined for my sister's garage and quickly forgotten.

A few months later, my sister and brother-in-law said I might want to look at the box because it contained some letters from the Civil War. As a high school history teacher, I was immediately interested. Shortly thereafter, my wife, Carol and I invited a fellow history teacher with a great interest in the Civil War, Edd Hale, and his wife Nancy to get together at our house to explore the box.

We spent the rest of the evening in amazement as we paged through hundreds of letters, mostly from two Civil War soldiers, as well as many hand written orders, officer commission papers, and other documents. The letters, in their original envelopes, were mostly addressed to someone named Chester Martin in Williamstown, Vermont by two soldiers named William Henry Martin and Francis Smith Martin.

To help in deciphering what we had just found, we called on Edd's friend, Bill Lutz, a retired math teacher who had seemingly read most of those 50,000 Civil War books and had visited many of the battlefields and other sites mentioned in the letters. His encyclopedic knowledge of the war would prove invaluable as we tried to interpret the references to people and places contained in the letters.

The five of us began meeting weekly to read the letters together. Edd scanned them and made a CD for each of us. Then we divided the letters up to read individually during the week in order to have a few rough drafts transcribed enough to go over at the weekly meeting. It proved to be a very slow process because of the difficult handwriting, particularly that of Henry, who often became increasingly sloppy as a letter progressed. Toughest of all were the letters that used cross-writing. To save paper, the author would turn the letter sideways and begin writing across the lines he had just written, creating a jumbled mess of frequently illegible words in both directions.

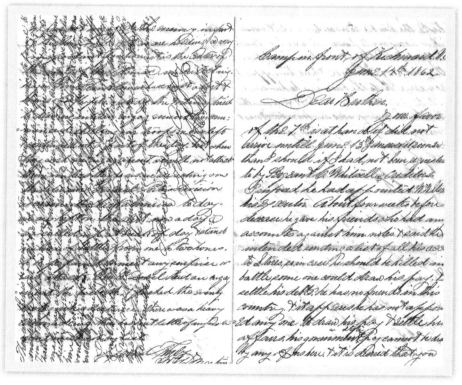

Page 1 of a folded letter is to the right and page 4 to the left.
To conserve paper, Henry sometimes turned the page sideways and used cross-writing.

In our group meetings we would try to fill in words and phrases that the initial reader had been unable to figure out. Sometimes we would spend several minutes staring at one word or phrase, suggesting possibilities, until someone had a flash of insight. It took several years to go through the letters of the two soldiers in this way and then we took several more years to go back through the early letters, trying again to decipher passages that we couldn't figure out the first time.

We also visited Vermont to search for more information about the Martin family and others mentioned in the letters. Although we saw and learned a lot on our first trip, as explained further in the Afterword, we were disappointed by our inability to find any photographs of the people we had come to know so well. I was thus especially pleased to discover Paul Zeller's *The Second Vermont Volunteer Infantry Regiment, 1861-1865*. After ordering this book, I turned first, as always, to the index to look for any references to people named Martin. This time, my mouth dropped open as I read "Martin, Pvt. Francis S." followed by two page listings. One of the pages was in bold ink, indicating a photograph. We celebrated that night at Edd and Nancy's house as we looked at Francis, standing on one leg, with the stump of his left leg exposed beneath his cut-off pants.

The photograph of Francis was in a collection at the University of Vermont, and it came originally from a fascinating, hand-written journal by Dr. Henry L. Jane. As a Civil War surgeon, Dr. Jane had taken photographs of those he had operated on and written case studies of how the surgeries had turned out. Each page included a photograph, neatly trimmed and glued to the page, along with a description of the patient's wounds and treatment.

Before our return trip to Vermont, we sent letters to people from the Williamstown area with the last name of Martin, seeking assistance with our research. That mailing brought us a reply from Winnie Martin, whose deceased husband had been very interested in family history. Since he was from another branch of the family, none of their photographs would be of use to us, but Winnie did have an old genealogical record entitled "*George Martin of Salisbury, Mass. and His Descendants*." Besides giving us a great deal more genealogical information on the Martin family, the entry on Francis also mentioned that prior to the war he had written a regular feature for the *Vermont Watchman*, published in Montpelier, called "Williamstown News."

At the state public records office in Montpelier, we found that old copies of the *Vermont Watchman* were available on microfilm and began reading through them. One article of interest was the obituary for Francis, which stated that during the war Francis had continued writing for the newspaper as a war correspondent under the pseudonym "Conscript." We eventually found twelve such articles.

We had found everything we wanted - except a picture of Henry. We tried the University of Vermont, the Vermont Historical Society, and various collections of photographs from the brothers' two regiments, the Second and Fourth Vermont, but without success. Finding a photo of Henry was seeming hopeless until I looked back at the website on Vermont in the Civil War (vermontcivilwar.org) and went through the photographs of soldiers in the Fourth Vermont Infantry. In the photographs owned by collector John Gibson, the name William Henry Martin had been added. We now had our picture of Henry, and it was time to break out the champagne again.

Through researching these letters, I learned a great deal about the Civil War soldiers of Williamstown, Vermont and about my own family history. But why publish yet one more Civil War book? The reason lies primarily in the historical significance of the letters. Although many soldiers recorded their experiences in letters and diaries, the Martins' letters stand out not only in number but in depth and breadth of analysis. When marching through Confederate territory, they carefully observed the agriculture, economy and lifestyles of the South, drew comparisons to their native Vermont, and reflected on how slavery had shaped Southern society. After fighting in battles, rather than glossing over the horrors of war (as soldiers commonly did) so as not to frighten or upset their family members back home, these two brothers carefully recorded their experiences. Furthermore, they served in what would become one of the most prestigious and renowned units in the war, the Old Vermont Brigade. They witnessed and helped to make history, and then they preserved that history in their surprisingly detailed and insightful letters. After 150 years, their letters do much more than tell us about one family and town; they are a valuable source of firsthand information on America's great Civil War.

Chapter 1

CEDAR CREEK

(October 20, 1864)

The surgeon wiped a knife twice across his bloodstained apron. With a sense of both exhaustion and despair in his voice, he uttered just one word to the orderlies: "Next." Francis Martin was already being carried to the surgeon's tent. As he stared forlornly at the ever-growing stacks of amputated arms and legs that they were passing, the events of the last several days flashed through his mind. A day and a half had passed since Francis had again been shot in battle. He remembered the intense fighting that had preceded being hit in the leg and, carried from the field, the excruciating ambulance ride, the cold and the pain as he lay on the frigid ground all night waiting for a surgeon to see him.

As he was placed on the table, Francis's mind whirled. *Were they really going to take his leg?* He had seen that happen so often before to others with similar injuries. *No! It could not be. What would happen to the family farm? Surely this could not be God's will.* The surgeon took just a cursory glance at the leg wound and then spoke to the orderlies rather than directly to Francis. He would not know if the leg could be saved until he had a better look. As a result, Francis would not know if he still had his left leg until he woke up after the examination.

As the chloroform began to take effect, Francis realized that he didn't even know if the Union side had won the battle. Mixed reports overheard from other wounded soldiers as he lay in agony overnight had only left him further confused.

That October morning the previous day was chilly and clear as, in the predawn light, Jubal Early's Confederate forces stealthily crept toward the Army of the Shenandoah camped at Cedar Creek, Virginia. If Early's surprise assault succeeded, General Sheridan's army might be driven from the Valley, and the fast-approaching election of 1864 might greatly favor Democrats and peace candidates.

Sheridan's army of 30,000 men included, within the Sixth Corps, the now-renowned Vermont Brigade whose veterans had seen much hard fighting and hard marching from the start of the war. Their tenacity and courage in battle were seldom surpassed. Their willingness to stand when others ran had made them almost legendary. Before this day ended, they would have a chance to again prove themselves in combat.

Private Francis S. Martin, known to his family and friends as Frank, was among the men of the Second Vermont Infantry to spring to duty. Frank had enlisted late. Poor health had kept him at home, but he strongly believed that people should do their God-ordained duty, and he saw helping to bring about a Union victory was clearly the morally correct course of action. Having been with the Second Vermont for just over a year, he had seen far less fighting than his brother, Henry, who had been in the war practically from the beginning. Six months earlier they had fought together in the Battle of the Wilderness. Never before had Vermont soldiers endured such desperate fighting. The Vermont Brigade suffered over 1000 casualties as they helped to stop the advance of General Longstreet's corps at the crossroads of the Orange Plank and Brock roads. Their resolve had played a considerable role in avoiding another defeat to General Lee's army. Both brothers had been among the casualties: Frank was shot in the neck, and his brother was even more severely injured. Recovering quickly, Frank had rejoined his unit at Cold Harbor a month later and was a seasoned veteran by the time of the battle at Cedar Creek.

The first day did not start well for the Federal forces. General Early surprised them with an early morning attack, and Union forces began rapidly moving backward. When the Confederate advance finally reached them, the Vermont Brigade once again lived up to its reputation, holding its lines against the Confederate onslaught as others were retreating around them. So impressive was the rebuff that General Gordon described the Vermont Brigade to Early as a "granite wall," a most appropriate metaphor for troops from granite-producing areas such as Frank's hometown of Williamstown. Eventually, however, they had no choice but to fall back and become aligned with the rest of the Union forces. Later that morning, after General Sheridan arrived and rallied the troops, the course of the battle swung and the Confederates were the ones moving backwards. The Vermont Brigade was out front in the pursuit. For Frank, though, the war was about to end. As he and his comrades pursued the fleeing rebels, Frank stopped to help a wounded comrade. After doing what he could, he rose to rejoin the rest of his company, but suddenly, a Minié ball tore into his left leg, shattering the bones above his ankle.

Eventually Francis reached the battlefield hospital. Now, before succumbing to the chloroform vapors, his mind raced back over the last three years of the war.

It had often looked as though the Confederates might win the war, but he was certain that this could not be God's plan. That was why he had enlisted. Now, suffering from a serious injury, he concluded that this situation too, as bleak as it appeared, must also be part of God's plan. Perhaps he had been wounded because he was needed at home. With a badly injured leg, or even with an artificial leg in place, he would find a way to help his aging mother and father on the farm. It was time to return to Williamstown.

Chapter 2

WILLIAMSTOWN, VERMONT

Williamstown, located within ten miles of the geographic center of the state, was a fairly typical village in Vermont. The village was about six miles south of Barre and twelve miles south of the state capital, Montpelier. In 1860, nearly 1,400 people lived in the town and surrounding hillsides. This small community provided more than its share of young men for the Civil War: more than 140 soldiers, many of whom were killed or wounded in battle or died in prison camps or from disease.

Years earlier, just two months after the conclusion of the Revolutionary War, 76 men and women drew up a charter establishing the township of Williamstown. The township was six by six miles in size, following a pattern which would be used extensively in the Northwest Territories of the newly formed nation. The history of this small town might have been significantly different if one early resident had succeeded in an ambitious attempt to have the University of Vermont situated in Williamstown. Instead, the university went to Burlington and Williamstown remained just another small farming community.

Aaron Martin, a veteran of the Revolutionary War from Windham, Connecticut, was one of the earliest settlers in Williamstown. Born in 1742, he was a direct descendant of Susannah Martin, who had been hanged as a witch in Salem exactly fifty years earlier. Martin built his log cabin on the east side of town, and then, to hold his claim, he had three of his children (ages 10, 14 and 16) live in it for the winter. In the spring, he was able to move the remainder of his extensive family to Williamstown. This included his wife, Eunice, and the remainder of his 15 children. In a time of high infant and child mortality, surprisingly all 15 lived to adulthood and all but one married and had children, making the Martin name quite ubiquitous in this small community. Aaron and Eunice ultimately had 122 grandchildren.

One of those grandchildren, Chester Martin, was born in 1795 and married

Betsey Smith in 1822. They had four children: Caroline, George, Francis, and Henry. Like most people in the area, Chester and Betsey were farmers. This part of Vermont produced a variety of crops that provided both food and cash: a wide variety of grains, fruits, vegetables, berries, maple syrup, livestock, and dairy products. Another contributor to the local economy was granite. By the end of the nineteenth century, Barre was known as "the granite capital of the world," with many large quarries located in the short stretch between South Barre and Williamstown. Small, independent producers began selling granite early in the nineteenth century, although the great surge in production would not begin until the decade after the Civil War.

The Chester Martin family, though perhaps not wealthy, was relatively prosperous. One hint of this fact is that Caroline, born in 1825, attended a boarding school in the 1840s. At a time period when women's education lagged far behind that of men, this would have been considered an unnecessary expense by most rural families. It is perhaps surprising that the Chester Martin family sent their daughter to an expensive school, even though in many other ways they fit the stereotype of excessively frugal New Englanders.

An old photo of the Chester Martin house
Courtesy of Williamstown Historical Society

Caroline attended the Select Family School for Young Ladies in Hanover, New Hampshire. This private school, housed in what is now Webster Hall on the Dartmouth campus, was actually more expensive than Dartmouth. (Caroline's receipts show expenses of almost $250 per year at a time when tuition, room, and board at Dartmouth totaled $165.) The school's purpose, as explained in a brochure from this time, was "to combine the regular systematic discipline of school with religious and moral instruction, and the care and comforts of a home." A contemporary of Caroline, Susan Coolidge, later became a very popular author of children's stories and one of her books, *What Katy Did at School,* was based on life at the Select Family School.

The school was run by one Mrs. Peabody, the widow of a Dartmouth professor. She was known for keeping such a tight leash on her charges that the students at all-male Dartmouth nicknamed her school "the nunnery." When the girls took their weekly walk to a local bathhouse, soap and towels in hand, rowdy Dartmouth boys would line up and yell bawdy comments as the group walked past them. The curriculum at the school included "all the branches of a thorough English education, with Latin, French, German, and Italian languages, Music, and Natural Sciences." In her letters home, Caroline often complained about trying to keep up with the demanding academic workload, yet her grade reports show scores of "Excellent" for every class in each term that she attended.

After graduation, Caroline moved home and was soon engaged to a lawyer named Denison Smith, whose practice was in nearby Barre. They married in 1849. Her newspaper obituary, written the next year after Caroline's death at the age of 24, refers to her as "one whose departure is truly mourned" and highlights her "benevolent spirit, her great amiableness and Christian courtesy" that had won her such a large number of friends. "Though unusually gifted by nature, she was not simply admired. In the relations of wife, daughter, and sister, she was eminently an ornament and a blessing."

Caroline was preceded in death by her brother, George. Little is known about him except that he died at the age of seven in 1836. Neither the death certificates nor the obituaries for George or Caroline list a cause of death, but since there are no accounts of an accident in the local newspapers, they likely both died from a fever or disease. The two remaining brothers, Francis, born in 1833, and Henry, born in 1838, would later serve in the Vermont Brigade.

In mid-nineteenth century America, formal public education generally ended at the elementary level. For the more affluent, a private secondary academy might follow. By the time Henry had entered adolescence, Barre Academy was the closest such school. Barre Academy had been founded by Jacob Spaulding, a Dartmouth graduate who served as principal and taught Latin and Greek. It opened its doors in 1852 and soon had an enrollment of over 300 students, about half female, from more than 25 states. Its founding statement said that "an attempt will be made to excite in the scholar a love of right-doing, and to awaken within him a sense of his obligations to himself, to his parents, and to his Creator." The three-year course of study had an ambitious curriculum that included courses in algebra, trigonometry, history, physiology, geography, astronomy, botany, chemistry, rhetoric, philosophy, geology, and political economy. Several of Williamstown's future Civil War soldiers attended Barre Academy along with Henry during the 1850s. Francis, however, entered Kimball Union Academy, a boarding school in Meriden, New Hampshire that remains in operation today, a year before Barre Academy opened and did not transfer closer to home when the opportunity arose. Many of his Williamstown cousins from the Smith and Bass families attended Kimball Union as well. Two of Betsey Martin's brothers had attended Dartmouth, and acquiring a good education was clearly important to this family.

In the 1850s a new industry arose nearby. Two brothers, George and Edwin Colby, began processing willows to be weaved into such items as baby carriages, demijohn whiskey bottles, and baskets. As this business grew rapidly and diversified, Chester Martin realized that his low land farm with a stream running through it was quite suitable for growing willows. Along with his sons Francis and Henry, both unmarried and living at home, Chester began to cultivate this new cash crop. By 1864, the farm was producing about four tons of willows and transporting them the twenty-five miles to what was then known as Colbyville, just a short distance from where Ben and Jerry's ice cream factory sits today in Waterbury.

Barre Academy
Courtesy of David Rumsey Map Collection

When the war began, the army began purchasing some of the Colbys' products and the increased demand caused them to operate two shifts, day and night. Unfortunately, as more young men went off to war, the Colby brothers struggled to find enough workers to operate their factory and had to reduce the amount they were purchasing from local farmers. Nevertheless, Chester Martin continued to accumulate wealth through the willows and other ventures. In the 1850 census, his estate had been valued at $5,700; by 1870, it had grown to $12,180, a rather large sum for a rural Vermont farmer.

After being harvested, the green willow reeds had to be stripped of their bark.

At first this work was done tediously by hand, by members of the Martin family along with local young men and women who they employed. Since Chester was in his late sixties during the war, his enlisted sons, in their letters home, often encouraged him to find help with the farm work. As more and more young men left for the war, however, the Martins faced the same labor shortage as the Colbys. Chester could have started selling the willows unstripped for less profit. Instead, he invested in a machine to assist the process.

No railroad came to Williamstown until 1888. Prior to that, the closest railroad stop was 13 miles away at Montpelier Junction. Therefore, all crops being shipped out of the area had to be hauled to this junction first. Much of the harvest was consumed locally, but during the war, Francis and Henry encouraged their father to sell his products for the war effort since prices were rising so rapidly. They also often asked their parents to send them extra items such as butter because they could sell it at a good price to other soldiers in camp.

While Chester never seems to have involved himself in politics or to have held political office, members of his extended family certainly did. Levi Smith, Betsey's father, was at one time Williamstown's treasurer; Darius Pride, husband of Betsey's sister, Sally, was at various times town clerk and town treasurer. Across the road from the Martins lived Ebenezer Bass, who was related to them in two ways. His mother was Chester's aunt, Polly Martin; after his first wife died, Ebenezer married another of Betsey's sisters, Lucy. Bass served the community as a judge and was chosen as a state senator in the 1840s. He also held a commission as a general in the Vermont militia, and Chester held a commission as a major, but it appears that neither of them saw any active service. Many of the Williamstown boys of the 1860s, on the other hand, were about to see more military action than they ever could have imagined.

Chapter 3

CAMP LIFE
AT THE CAPITAL

After secessionists fired on Fort Sumter on April 15, 1861, President Lincoln immediately called for loyal troops to put down the rebellion, and Vermont responded by forming its First Infantry Regiment. Composed initially of men from the existing state militia, it quickly added many eager new recruits. On May 2, less than three weeks after Lincoln's appeal, the companies reported at Rutland. The regiment was mustered into the U.S. Army on May 8 and departed for Fort Monroe, Virginia the next morning.

The regiment received its first actual taste of combat in an unfortunate episode on June 10. Intending to surprise the Confederates at Big Bethel, Virginia with an early morning attack, Federal forces marched through the night. Approaching the Confederate fortifications in the dark, the inexperienced soldiers inadvertently became entangled in a friendly fire battle that not only resulted in casualties but alerted the Confederates to the impending attack. Although they outnumbered the Confederates by four to one, the Federal assault was easily repulsed. Among the 76 Federal casualties, one soldier was from the First Vermont.

The unit returned home in early August, having completed its three-month term of service, but what many had expected to be a short-lived rebellion had not ended. Two weeks later the troops received their pay and the unit was disbanded. By then, however, it was clear that more soldiers would be needed, and for a longer duration, to put down the growing insurrection.

Vermont had already begun to assemble more regiments in June. The Second Volunteer Infantry Regiment, the first Vermont unit to enlist for three years, arrived in Washington, D.C. on June 25 and, with minimal training, fought at Bull Run on July 21. Several days after this shocking first defeat for Federal forces, the Third Vermont arrived at the capital.

By August, additional regiments were forming, including the Fourth and the Fifth. The original advertising on recruiting posters for the Fourth announced that it was creating a 100 man Company A as a Zouave unit to be commanded by John E. Pratt. Pratt hoped to have the entire regiment wear the distinctive Zouave uniforms. Although recruits poured in, interest in the Zouave concept gradually waned, probably as a result of the much higher expense associated with these units. The Fourth Vermont Regiment soon boasted 1,048 men. One of them was twenty-two-year-old William Henry Martin of Williamstown, who enlisted on August 19, 1861.

The regiment was officially mustered in on September 21 for a three-year enlistment. Henry was placed in Company B, as were nearly all the men from Orange County, and was appointed its orderly sergeant. By the end of September, the Second through Sixth Regiments formed the "Vermont Brigade." Later known as the "Old Brigade," it remained unbroken to the end of the war and gained a well-deserved reputation for its courage and valor. It also would suffer more casualties than any other brigade.

As Henry had never traveled so far from home before, departing for the war must have seemed like the beginning of a great adventure. He wrote a letter home on September 11 detailing the start of his journey:

> We left Chelsea Saturday last and arrived at Brattleboro about dark. We had a pleasant journey. The people of Chelsea hired teams and carried us to South Royalton. There we found a good dinner and after dinner we listened to a numbre of speeches then took our place in the cars with two other companies. ... We had not been in Camp only a very short time before we received a telegraphic dispatch to leave for the seat of War but the Col. remanded the dispatch but expect to go tomorrow. We have not received all of our equipments, but expect them before we leave. ... I have abandoned all hopes of visiting home while at Brattleboro.

Two weeks later, on September 26, he described his memorable journey by rail and steamboat.

> My journey was seemingly a very long one. We left Brattleboro Sept 21st eight PM & arrived at New Haven six AM. There we took a steamer for Jersey City, N.J. by way of Long Island Sound. Then we went by cars to Philadelphia and arrived there at nine PM where we found a full table waiting for us. After supper, we again took the cars for Baltimore. We passed through Haver De Grace a noted place for secessionists, but now under the controll of the government and arrived at Baltimore at half past eleven AM. There we left the cars and marched through the city to the next station where we

were to embark for Washington. We passed through the streets where the Mass men were mobbed, but we did not have any trouble. Some would bid us good bye and others would wish us to bring back Jef's scalp, others would cry out hurrah for Davis &c. After dinner we took the cars for Washington.

At 1 a.m. on September 24, the Fourth Vermont finally arrived at Washington, D.C.

William Henry Martin
Courtesy of John Gibson Collection

We left the cars and marched to a place called the Soldiers Rest. There we stacked arms, ate supper, and spread our blankets and slept the rest of the night. In the morning we were detailed to unload the baggage cars. After dinner we received orders to march to our encampment about 3/4 of a mile from the city of Washington. There we joined a large army of forty thousand men. I never saw such a sight before. There were a number of thousand Cavilry, flying artilery & Infantry. The cavilry were on drill when we arrived. They attracted considerable attention. Their chargeing at full speed accompanied with the flying artilery . . . was a grand sight.

Initially, the Fourth Vermont was stationed at Camp Advance, about one mile west of the Chain Bridge. The encampment was given its name by eager, if unrealistic, enlistees who had anticipated a quick advance on Richmond. In two weeks they advanced only a few miles west as they were transferred to the much larger Camp Griffin. Located on land owned by Robert E. Lee's father, it is now part of McLean Central Park (not far from Central Intelligence Agency headquarters). This camp would be their home for the next five months.

From the moment the Fourth left Vermont, rumors had suggested that they were about to be sent into a major engagement. In his early letters Henry often forwarded these rumors as if he believed they were likely to occur. As the stay in camp turned from weeks to months, he began to relay these rumors with a more cynical attitude. On November 9 he wrote:

Today the camp rumor is that we are to moove to Fortress Monroe. What the next one will be I know not.

Although the daily routine at Camp Griffin consisted largely of troop drills and eating, Henry found much to write home about. As he continued in his November 9 letter:

We have daily Brigade drills & practice in firing by Company & Regiment. We also practice in firing at will, that is to load & fire as fast as possible. After a few rounds the smoak becomes very thick so that a person can not see any distance a head.

In an earlier letter, on October 8, Henry described in detail his own personal duties, as orderly sergeant, on a typical day.

At Revillee, roll call and march the Co. to breakfast. At half past six is Surgeon's Call and all of the sick that are able are marched to the doctors to get excused or take medecine. At half past seven is Police Call. The police are the guard that were on duty the day before and their duty is to sweep all the grounds in the camp. At nine is guard mounting. They are marched to the center of the Regiment. There formed as in dress parade. At ten I call out the company, call the roll and drill 1 1/2 hours. Then come home, wait untill dinner, march the "co" to their meals. Call them out again at three, call the roll, drill 2 hours, then form in to ranks for dress parade. Then the orderlies are called to the front & center to report if any are absent with out any cause. They are reported to the Officer of the day and looked up and put in to the guard house. At half past eight roll call & at nine tattoo & retire. We have two blankets, India ruber & wollen, which makes very comfortable in warm weather.

The drills of tens of thousands of soldiers became over time a very impressive display. As Henry explained in November:

We are now encamped on an excellent parade ground which is occupied daily by Infantry, artilery & Cavilry. You would go a great distance to see our daily drills which are sometimes Battalion or Regtal or Brigade composed of the command of Gen Brooks. ... We have not received orders to moove yet. The circulateing report is that we shall soon.

But no such order was forthcoming yet; rather, the drills continued unabated. On Sunday mornings, inspections were held. Henry described them for his mother in a letter on December 4.

The hour set is nine A. M. Evry man shoulders his knapsack & marches out in line of battle & then they wheel to the right & open ranks. The Colnel & Lieut Colnel inspect the soldiers guns & if a speck of dirt is found on or in them they are liable to be marched to the gd. house. Our clothes are to be clean & evry man well washed. His knapsack is laid uppon the ground, opened & looked over by the Colnel. Some of the men do not wash as often as they should so the Colnel is very particular. If a man does not look clean he will pull down his collar & satisfy himself. Next in order is the inspection of the tents & streets. Evry thing has to be in good order inside, the streets are swept evry day & evry bit of mud, sticks or filth of any kind is carried across the lines. It is no small job to clean our swoards, guns and boots.

In early January, Henry complained about just how rigorous these inspections could be. Due to recent heavy rains, the soldiers drilled and walked in deep mud throughout the camp.

Yesterday the company saw hard times on inspection. In the morning they were inspected by the Coln. and sent in to reclean themselves and equipments & after services return. Which they did. When the Coln. came arround he ordered six of the rear rank men to the guardhouse & all of the front rank to their quarters to clean their equipments & be inspected again at dress parade. Such neatness as is required in the army surpasses anything I ever saw before. Everything has to glisten but men are to be pitied if they are not clean when inspected by Col. Stoughton. For the past few days it has rained & the boys being compelled to drill & fire blank cartridges. So you can see what circumstances we have to labor under and keep clean.

Henry also observed that meals and drills sometimes were held at very irregular hours:

Yesterday we rose at half past four AM and drank our coffee, drilled 1 hour, ate breakfast composed of hard crackers, fried pork and soft bread. At ten oclock we commence drill and are recalled at 1/2+11 AM then we wait untill one PM eat our dinner composed of pea soup, hard or soft bread and coffee. At three we have battalion drill, return at five, eat supper at six, composed of tea & bread or crackers.

Williamstown families regularly sent packages of food and supplies to their loved ones, and transportation to camp was so speedy that sometimes even perishable goods could be sent. Henry wrote from camp in November:

I received the box you sent last Sunday. The butter & blanket were thankfuly received. They came in good condition. Henry Smith & Charles Lynde received their cheeses last night the reception of which rejoiced their hearts.

Sometimes the gifts exceeded what the recipients could use.

The box of quilts, socks & mittens came into camp today, & the most of these have been distributed among the soldiers from Wmtown. They were all pleased with the articles sent. But they cannot contrive how they are to carry all these comfortables when we moove.

Henry also described the Williamstown boys' deep gratitude for these boxes from friends and loved ones:

They remind me of home. I have not been to the cook tent for a number of days. All the articles arrived in good condition & very fresh. All of the Williamstown boys met the other day & ate one of the chicken pies. They filled a large tent & all spoke in high terms of the thoughtful friends at home.

Another way for the army to get food was by foraging in the countryside. This could lead to small skirmishes, as Confederate forces were scattered around the Federal camps near the capital. When Henry first arrived, he observed that "we are in sight of four different camps & one Rebel Batery." Occasionally, Federal forces were sent out to engage the enemy. Henry was part of one such attempt, as he explained in a letter of October 9:

We were ordered this morning at 3 AM to pack our knapsacks to be in readiness to march at break of day. We were all excited in expectation of a battle. The cannon were flying by our camp at full speed and evry thing was done with dispatch. Evry man was ordered to have 40 rounds of cartridges & 24 hours rations. At 6 oclock the signal of one cannon from the fort was given and evry man formed into line. The roll called and arms inspected. Then we started and marched four miles and were drawn into line of battle and waited about 1/2 hour. Then we received orders to march in to the woods which we did. Then we were ordered to detail a number of choppers from our company to obstruct a road & clear a range for our guns before night. We had cut about one hundred acres of chestnut, oak, sasafrass, and other trees. Then we commenced making preparations to camp for the night so we felled a number of trees and built a good fire which bid fair to be a pleasant emcampment for the soldiers. But to our surprise just at dark we were ordered to march in another direction. So we shoulderd our guns & blankets & marched with in a mile of Lewinville Mill where we were expecting an attack from the Rebels. So we were placed in line of battle and ordered not to fire a gun untill ordered & to spread our blankets uppon the ground in line of battle. Evry man had his gun loaded and within reach at moments warning. The officers all slept under a chestnut tree on the left of the Co. and evry man expected an attack before break of day but the rebils retired before morning so our expectations were not realized. The most of the men were perfictly cool and preserved good order. I suppose that General McClellan was expecting a great battle. He was present to see us form. We were placed on the right of the post of honor and sustained by Sherman's battery. We were to receive the first attack. The number of men on the ground when we arrived was 20,000 besides McCall's Divs and a number of other regiments & batteries the total no. estimated was 50,000 & strange to say in the morning we could not see only a few regiments of Infantry & two or three hundred cavelry but the woods were filled with men. So you see that our Generals are shrewed in secreeting their men if nothing more.

Nine days later Henry wrote:

We remain in the same camp where I last wrote. We have had a number of blighted expectations of attacks from the Rebils. They drove in our pickets but would not give an attack. We have taken a number of droves of cattle & a number of Prisoners besides other articles. Shermans Batery was inspected yesterday by General McClelland & Staff. They fire shells into the rebil quarters which spread consternation among the troops. They were in such haste to get out of their range that they left equipment & letters in large numbers. Our troops followed them a number of miles. We have to day sent out six companies scouting with instructions of taking posession of the ground abandoned. We do not expect any resistance of any account before we arrive at Menassas Junction.

Danger was ever-present, and a sudden attack could befall anyone who ventured out into the countryside or was posted on picket duty. Henry wrote on November 25:

Today our cavilry went beyond their bounds & were surprised & attacked by a superior force & lost twelve men & a number of wounded. Also a number of our neighboring pickets have been shot by the enemy.

A day later, he added:

The President & Gen McClelland reviewed over 75,000 troops. The review was ten miles from camp & only four miles from the enemy who were drawn up in the line of battle all day. They drove in our pickets yesterday & shot two men. Today the whole of the Vt Brigade have gone out with one hundred army waggons foraging. It seems to me it is a large party for that business & I presume they will have a fight before they return.

Six P. M. The foraging party who I mentioned is now returning laden with hay, corn &c. The souldiers have not arrived yet. The cavilry were attacked.

During the first week of December, Henry found himself again in a potentially dangerous situation:

Last friday myself & company went out forageing & came very near having an engagement. We marched to Viena & drove in the enemies pickets & took four of them prisoners. We were posted on independence hill to support the batery. We had not been there long before Gen. Hancock sent word to Gen. Brooks, that he was expecting trouble & wished him to sustain him. Soon after a large number of Cavilry came up & were posted in the woods. Soon after another lot came & were posted in the same place. There we remained untill night when we received orders to moove so we started all supposing for home. But we took another road to support Gen. Hancock who was trying the enemies pluck but as he advanced the enemy retired so we received orders to return & arrived at camp 1 p.m. One hundred teems accompanied us & returned sixty of them loaded with corn the rest with oats & hay. Also an excelent yoke of oxen girthing eight feet & a number of hogs & horses, carages &c. [&c was used rather than etc.].

The small engagements around the Federal camps continued as 1861 came to a close. Writing on December 18, Henry reported:

The Brigade was called out to assist the Bucktails in making an attack. We left camp at about two oclock P.M. in distinct hearing of our cannon & as we drew nearer the musketry mingled with the cannon. But the enemy were repulsed before we arrived. They fled in great haste leaving guns, blankets and other articles. So the victors returned once overloaded with spoil. It is the first victory of any account gained on the Potomac. There were over fifty rebels killed & a number wounded. The Bucktails lost ten men. We traveled a distance of twelve miles & back before eight oclock.

The enemy are troubling our pickets considerable & we are expecting to advance on them this week in the direction of Leesburg.

A Vermont Brigade foraging party leaving Camp Griffin
Courtesy of Vermont Historical Society

Although some soldiers were being injured and killed in the vicinity of the camp, the health issues within the camp were of greater concern. Since so many of the young men had never been far from home and came from somewhat isolated towns and villages, they often lacked any immunity to the diseases that ran rampant through the camp. Henry's parents doubtless inquired often about his health. In early October he reported to them:

My health has been generaly good. I have had some slight attacks of diareha oweing to the change of climate and watter & all of the souldiers that have kept away from the Sutlers & eaten temperately have enjoyed good health. Some will over load their stomacks with evry change of food & the consequence is disintary. I have gained in flesh a number of pounds.

A month later, the situation had deteriorated greatly. Henry wrote on November 9:

There is a great amount of sickness in the Regt. Charles Lyndes eyes have become very bad but are improveing. John Green is a little unwell. Fay is on the Sick list, also Deck Jones, Cosgrove, Frank Flint but not very sick. Newel Carleton is quite sick with tyfoid feever but we hope he will soon be better. The Measles & mumps are prevailing extensively. Many of the souldiers are haveing what the Drs. call acclimating feever. We have all had a hard diarea which has generaly benefited the men but in some cases it has assumed a Chronic form.

Considering that the Vermont Brigade ultimately suffered a staggering casualty rate of 38%, it is somewhat remarkable that all the men mentioned in this letter except Newell Carleton survived not only their initial camp illnesses but their entire war experience. Newell, a classmate of Henry's from Barre Academy, did not improve from his fever as Henry had hoped. In late November, Henry informed his parents that Newell's fever had gotten progressively worse over a three-week period:

> As soon as he was confined to his bunk I had him mooved to my tent where it was stiller & more spare room. He remained there about two weeks & received as good care & attention as could be given him under the circumstances. He was not in his right mind nights. He constantly spoke of his Father & he was finaly remooved to the Hospital where he received prety good care but he grew worse evry time his feever changed & last Saturday night at about eight P.M. he died. He was not at any time in great pain but his feever seemed to ware him down very rappidly

Not knowing how to deal with the death of a hometown friend, Henry decided to collect ten dollars each from several of the Williamstown boys in order to raise the $95.00 needed to have the body embalmed, so it would "keep a year or more," and transported back home. Under Henry's plan, Mr. Carleton would then reimburse the families of those who had contributed. Henry was very disappointed to hear that Mr. Carleton was not happy with the arrangements, because his son's body was returned without his army uniform. Mr. Carleton's anger should not have been directed at the boys from Williamstown, but rather at one of the unscrupulous Army figures whose behavior Henry often bemoaned. For example, Henry did not have a good impression of his company captain, James Platt. In an earlier letter he had written:

Captain James Platt

> Our Captain has prooved a rascal and the first Lieut is his brother in law so they are about alike. They have not given us our full rations & have shown out their bad sides. They like the pay without the labor.

Now Henry had another reason to dislike Captain Platt. Henry had seen to it that Newell Carleton's body had been properly dressed in his uniform, but the captain had removed the uniform for his own purposes.

Henry struggled to adjust to the immoral behavior and rough language of many of the new people he encountered. Thomas P. Lowry, in *The Story the Soldiers Wouldn't Tell*, explains that wherever any army was encamped during the war, large numbers of prostitutes soon assembled. Gambling was also widespread among both officers and the common soldiers, and use of vulgar language was routine. Shortly after arriving at camp, Henry assured his mother that he hoped

> *to keep myself unspotted from the evils of army life & temptations. The souldiers are generaly very thoughtless & profane but I trust they are improoving. I am doing my best to check all evil & have a few supporters. Gambling has prevailed to some extent but I have finaly succeed to put a stop to it and evry man I find gambling I order him to the guard house. The Williamstown boys do finely and are respected for it.*

Some Williamstown boys, according to Henry, even improved their morals while in the army:

> *Deck Jones is a very steady man in the army so is Cosgrove. A life in the Army tends to make wild boys sober men.*

Concerning Newell Carleton, Henry now affirmed that

> *he sustained a good moral character while in the Army. I will assure you that it takes a strong man not to be turned by the temptations of Army life. Almost evry man in camp is steeped in profanity. Our Colnel is a very profane man so are all of the officers in the Regiment but one. There are but few redeaming characters in the Regiment.*

Along with the deteriorating moral situation, health conditions also continued to decline in the camp. On December 4, Henry explained how dire the situation had become.

> *Tomorrow we expect to moove our encampment. Where we are it is very unhealthy & the most of the Regt are unfit for duty. Only 25 in Co. B. are reported for duty. The camp is to be in the woods which will be very pleasant. We expect to winter there. Dr. Phelps is here for the purpose of ascertaining the true condition of the Vt. troops. He reports only 1500 men fit for duty in the Vt. Brigade.*

Charles Lynde, one of Henry's cousins from Williamstown, was sent home briefly in December due to health problems.

> *The Surgeon told him it would be of no use for him to remain any longer because he would be blind if he did not go where he could be better cared for.*

Lynde's family was prominent in Williamstown. His grandfather, Cornelius Lynde, had been apprenticed into the clothing trade after his parents died. During the Revolutionary War, he enlisted in the army and rose to the rank of lieutenant. After the war, he helped to survey the land around Williamstown and then decided to purchase a section for a family farm.

In the very early stages of the Civil War, Major Isaac Lynde, one of Cornelius Lynde's sons and an uncle to Charles Lynde, received a fair amount of notoriety. Stationed in New Mexico, he surrendered his fort to a reportedly inferior Confederate force in July 1861. Henry wrote home in December to inform his parents about Major Lynde's arrival in the capital:

> *Major Lynde is now at Washington trying to get an investigation of his conduct. As soon as he arrived he sent for Fred to come and see him.*

Fred Lynde, Major Lynde's son, was another of the Williamstown boys in the Fourth Vermont. While stationed near Washington, D.C., Henry was able to do a good bit of sightseeing, sometimes with Charles and Fred, who had just a few years earlier been his classmates at Barre Academy. Henry was often awed by the sights:

> *We went into the Capitol & feasted our eyes untill dinner time. Such splendor is beyond description. Such life like paintings of the Pilgrims, of Washington, Miles Standish & wife. Also statues of marble, the Progress of Civilization. Everything as natural as life. The Senate Chamber's one of the most splendid rooms I ever saw. A person needs one whole day to see what there is to be seen in the Capitol alone. They need to be posted on history to be able to*

Chain Bridge over the
Potomac River
Courtesy of Library of Congress

understand half what they see. Such splendid marble as is used for pillars & floors & statuary. Also sandstone is worth going a great distance to see.

Charles Lynde
Courtesy of Vermont
Historical Society

To reach the city from camp, they had to walk four miles from camp to the Chain Bridge and cross the Potomac to Georgetown. Here they caught an omnibus to a residence called the Avenue House where one of Henry's older cousins, Chauncey Smith, boarded. Born in 1802, Chauncey had grown up in Williamstown and was just three years younger than his Aunt Betsey, Henry's mother. In 1831 Chauncey moved to Washington, Vermont, about seven miles east of Williamstown, to take the position of Postmaster. That same year he married Stella Jane Hale of Chelsea. In 1833 their son, Nathan, was born. In the mid-1840s, Chauncey transferred within the Post Office from Washington, Vermont to Washington, D.C., where he served as Bond and Register Clerk. Nathan returned to Vermont to attend Norwich University in 1850 then practiced law in Wisconsin. At the outbreak of the Civil War he became a first lieutenant in the Twelfth Wisconsin Infantry. Stella died in 1857, and when Chauncey hosted Henry he was living alone at the Avenue House Hotel on Pennsylvania Avenue. Chauncey's parents had remained in Williamstown, and both died just prior to the war. Chauncey was also closely related to the Lynde family. The mother of Charles Lynde, Dolly Smith Lynde, was Chauncey's sister. It is therefore possible that Henry had previously met Chauncey if he had visited Williamstown; however, he certainly did not know him well prior to arriving with his regiment in Washington.

On one visit, Chauncey treated Henry to a dinner that he described in a letter home as being far better than camp food, consisting of "potatoes, Fish, Steak, bread and Pudding." Henry had little free time on this visit, but the city's scenery captured his interest and he returned to visit his cousin whenever the opportunity afforded itself.

On another day, Henry visited an earthwork fortification in Arlington that had been built by Vermonters:

I got permission from the Colonel to visit Fort Ethan Alen- an earthwork of great size and built by the Vt. boys. It is a sight worth going a great distance

Chauncey Smith in 1868
Courtesy of Williamstown
Historical Society

to see, the guns are of the best kind. There are twenty four there now but a number more could be supplied in case of necessity. It commands six miles arround. It has thrown shells to Limmsville. There is quite a contrast between those pieces at Montpelier & some of Ethan Alens guns which would almost admit a mans body. It has a trench ten feet deep & ten wide. These trenches are commanded by small guns raking the whole line. Just outside there are craged trees fastened in the ground & so interwoven that it would seem impossible for a man to crawl through & if they should be so fortunate they could not cross the trench. There is a Regiment of regulars there now. They live in baracks built of large logs & covered with dirt. It is supposed to be bomb proof & I should think it would be. Next are the magazines. They are built in the same maner only a little more secluded. There is a gait on the back side & a bridge to cross the trench which can be raised in case of an attack. ... After looking about as much as we liked we went past Ft. Morsey another Ft - named after some Vt.er & built by our boys& finaly wanderd home.

Abraham Lincoln also ventured out one day to visit Fort Ethan Allen. The fort never became a battleground during the war, however, as the only attack came later from north of the city. (Remains of the fort can still be viewed at Fort Ethan Allen Park in Arlington.)

The Vermont Brigade remained at Camp Griffin until March 1862. During this time in winter quarters, skirmishing continued, the health of many soldiers deteriorated further, and rumors continued to circulate that the army would soon move out. On January 4, Henry wrote:

We were expecting to have had a chance at the enemy but time has passed. There are men on picket firing every night but the enemy do not advance. We have got the enemy prety well pinned in on the right. Gen Banks is advancing and cutting off the retreat in that direction. On the left Gen McDowell fastens them & the centre is occupied by Gen Hancock & Brooks. The supposed plan is to drive the enemy down upon us & hem them in so they cannot retreat in any direction. We would be glad to receive them any day.

By the end of the month, Henry was actually enjoying his stay at camp but also realizing that it could not go on like this much longer.

I never spent a winter so comfortably before. My hands were never so free from calouses as now. I have become so accustomed to traveling that a march of fifteen or twenty miles does not fatigue me but very little. But I expect to soon see harder times. From what I can learn from the signes of the times is that we are soon to start for Manassas as soon as the ground freezes hard enough so that they can transport the artilary. Many of the regiments on our left have been ordered to send all extra baggage such as blankets knapsacks & officer's trunks to Washington & they are provided with small tents to accommodate only two men & those are to be carried on our backs. This looks to me like something. Also cannon is being transported across Chain Bridge. Fifty pieces crossed last week. ... At the grand review by McClelan, as he was riding past the second regiment, he told them that they should go home next fourth of July.

Henry believed that the muddy conditions were the main reason why they had not yet started marching south to Richmond. He also realized that Northerners were anxious to see some movement. He wrote in early February:

Up to this date we have not received orders to advance the mud being bottomless. But I suppose the country is anxious to have us advance. Let the circumstances be what they will.

Also, around this time Isaac Lynde returned for a visit to the camp, having spent the last several weeks attempting to defend his actions out west.

Major Lynde came into camp yesterday (Thursday) to see Fred. He will return on Saturday to Washington. He has grown old very fast. Since he was last at Williamstown his hair is as white as snow. He is trying to get a hearing so as to be in condition to offer his services to the country.

Major Lynde, 57 years old at this time, was unsuccessful at obtaining a hearing to clear his name. A West Point graduate, Lynde had served in the Mexican

Postwar photograph of Isaac Lynde
Courtesy of Williamstown
Historical Society

War and been promoted to major in 1855. At the start of the Civil War, Lynde was ordered to command Fort Fillmore in New Mexico. As Confederate forces grew in the area, Lynde decided that his position at the fort was no longer tenable and attempted to move all of the men and women to Fort Stanton. Traveling in July with temperatures exceeding 100 degrees, the marchers encountered numerous difficulties. Lynde's exhausted expedition eventually staggered upon a Texan battalion of about 250 in a strong defensive position. Believing that they were in no condition to fight a battle, Lynde surrendered, and the 540 soldiers under his command were paroled.

Lynde was widely criticized for his actions in Washington and was dismissed from the army. He sought an official court-martial hearing in order to explain his actions but was rebuffed in this request and in his attempts to meet with President Lincoln, who could gain nothing by intervening in this dispute.

As the war continued, Isaac Lynde refused to give up on restoring his honor, and he was not without important connections. In particular, Brigadier General Frederick Dent, a close associate of General Grant throughout the war and in the years that followed, was both Grant's brother-in-law and Isaac Lynde's son-in-law. Grant and Dent had graduated together from West Point in 1843, and five years later Grant married Dent's sister. In 1852, Dent married Isaac Lynde's oldest daughter (and another of Henry's many Williamstown cousins), Louise. Through the efforts of Grant and Dent, President Johnson reinstated Lynde for one day in 1866 and his military record was cleared of any misconduct. Almost a century and a half later, a Williamstown resident discovered that Lynde's biography in the West Point *Register of Graduates* stated that he had surrendered "to an inferior force of insurgents." A review was requested, and in 2010 the wording was altered to say that Lynde had surrendered "to invading Confederate forces."

During his visit to their camp, Henry learned from Major Lynde the viewpoints of many of those in power in the capital:

> *He says that congress feels very anxious to have something done soon if ever. Gen Rice says unless there be some important moove made soon our*

Louise Lynde Dent
Courtesy of Williamstown
Historical Society

Brigadier General Frederick T. Dent
Courtesy of Williamstown Historical Society

cause will be without hope. He thinks France and England will declare war & acknowledge the confederacy. He also thinks those highest in command are in favor of the south. There is one thing certain. We have laid still a long time. Last Dec. the ground was settled, the leaves off the trees, the weather comfortable & one of the best of times to advance but the cry was to advance in February when the ground was frozen. The time has come & as any one that was acquainted with the camp would have predicted [we have] impassable roads at this season. We cannot stir for a number of weeks.

As the soldiers remained in camp, the ravages of disease, which Henry attributed primarily to the rainy winter weather, continued to intensify. In late February he wrote:

When we left Brattleboro it [the 4ᵗʰ Vermont Regiment] numbered 1100 strong able bodied men. Over sixty have died of disease, many discharged & a great number sick. Our company numbered one hundred & one now ninety & only thirty six privates for duty. A number of the other boys are not very well. Almost evry one of them are troubled with jaundice. They will be as yellow as yellow paint.

A sick soldier might be sent to the hospital, which, from Henry's description, did not sound like a particularly desirable place in which to recover.

I have visited the hospital a number of times & it is not a very pleasant place to call at. Almost evry foot of ground is occupied with sick men afflicted with almost evry disease. The pneumonia is the worst disease we have here and is almost sure death. They suffer a great deal.

I see sights that would make any one of you at home shudder. Almost every morning will be seen outside the hospital a corpse of some fellow soldier lying uppon an iron bedsted out of doors coverd by his blankets. There to remain untill the next day without a watcher to see that no harm befalls the remains. Finaly the corpse is dressed and placed in a pine coffin ready for burial. Then the captain of the company to which he belongs & all of his officers & eight or twelve men who carry their pieces reversed & four or six for barers, march to the hospital - where the chaplin makes a prayer & then the remains are put into an ambulance & carried to the grave. On arriving at the briggade burying ground the corpse is laid in the grave & if a private six shots are fired,-if a non commissioned officer a voley of thirteen &c-all of these scenes we become familiar with & think but little of.

Burial of a Second Vermont soldier at Camp Griffin
Courtesy of Special Collections, University of Vermont Libraries

In the meantime, the Union soldiers continued to have dangerous encounters with the Rebels:

Today two regiments of our cavilry had a brush with the enemy. The result of which I have not ascertained. They commenced in the morning & have been skirmishing all day. They have brought in thirteen prisoners. One of their captains and sergts were wounded and brought in.

Soldiers expressed discontentment about their inaction, indicating that they would rather have a major engagement than an occasional small skirmish. Henry wrote home in mid-February:

We still remain at Cp. Griffin so you can see how many expectations we have & how few realized. The soldiers remark quite often that they will not have a chance of seeing a rebel while in the army. But they are a little mistaken for they can see rebel deserters most any time they wish. Last week our cavalry brought in thirteen & today three hundred deserted & were received inside Gen McCall s lines & sent to Washington.

Henry was apparently feeling very optimistic at this point because word of a major victory by General Burnside in the Outer Banks of North Carolina had just swept through the camp. After his successful movement through Hatteras Inlet, Burnside took Roanoke Island on February 7. The news that Union forces in the East had won an actual battle reached Camp Griffin a week later. Henry wrote to his brother:

I wish you could have been here last night so as to have heard the cheering on the reception of the great success of the Burnside Expedition. ... The adjutants had the companies called up while he read the charming news & such hardy cheering I guess you never heard. It was a relief to evry man. On our right and left we could hear the different regts exulting over the defeat of the enemy.

The strategy for victory was becoming clear to Henry: Richmond was to be surrounded and then crushed by the invading Federal forces. He wrote on February 22:

We are now enjoying the good news resulting from the great victories won by the Federal troops. There are reports in circulation that the enemy is on the point of evacuating Manassas but such news is almost too good to believe. There is one thing true. That Jeff Davis must feel not a little concerned for his future fate. He is being well cornered. ... Gen McCall has gone to Centervill with 15000 troops (so reported). Also Captain Ayer & battery have succeeded in getting in rear of the forces at Leesburg who have been waching Gen Banks movements so that the only way for them to escape is to cross the Blue Ridge Mountains. Everything looks like an onward moove soon.

Five days later, Henry wrote home again:

*Yesterday we received orders to be ready to march at a moments warning &
to take three days rations. This afternoon we rec'd orders to take one woolen
blanket & rifles & leave every thing else in our tents. Also Gen McClellen
crossed the Potomac with one hundred thousand men last night. We are
expecting to encounter the enemy before we return.*

On March 4, Henry wrote that the Vermont Brigade was still in camp:

*Ere this date you must have received by last letter - written in haste expecting
every moment to be ordered to march but up to this date the order has not
been given. We were to be in readyness to go to aid Banks if he received much
resistance in crossing the river. Fortunately he was able to do his own work
without assistance.*

A week later the Vermont Brigade finally began to move. Henry did not have
time to write about it until March 19:

*One week ago we were a sickly discontented lot of soldiers but today it is the
opposite. Hundreds that were excused by the Surgeon & truly unfit for duty
[but now] the change is mirackulous. One week ago yesterday we received
orders at two A. M. to be ready to march. At four we started & marched in
the rain to Fairfax & encamped for the night. Our clothes wet to our bodies
& no chance to dry them. But the next morning found us all well without
taking cold - or stifening our joints very much. ...We remained there three
days & were reviewed by Maj Gen McClelan. The next morning we received
orders to march previous to which we had read to us Gen McClelan s message which you must have seen in the papers ere thus. Then we left Fairfax
a beautiful but deserted place & marched in a hard rain & encamped five
miles from Alexandria. We were a great deal wetter than before & its being a
cold rain we did not get much sleep that night. I did not take cold - but it was
a rather hard time. I will assure you we are expecting evry day to be orderd to
march to Alexandria and embark for some where.*

In Henry's next letter, ten days later, they had arrived at that "somewhere," but
as part of a strategy far different than what Henry had envisioned.

Chapter 4

THE PENINSULA CAMPAIGN

After much prodding by the President and many delays, General McClellan finally unveiled his plan to defeat the Confederacy. Rather than march to Bull Run to avenge the defeat from the previous summer, or to Centreville, then south to Richmond, McClellan instead devised an amphibious operation on the Virginia Peninsula. By invading from the east, he could avoid the Confederate defenses north of Richmond. On March 17, 1862, a massive force of 121,500 men, along with horses, supplies, and weapons, set sail from Alexandria. The army arrived safely at Fort Monroe, and McClellan initiated his plans to advance up the peninsula. On March 29, Henry finally had time to write to his brother and describe his journey from Alexandria to Old Point Comfort, the land area around Fort Monroe:

It has been some time since you received a letter from me, but circumstances would not permit me to write sooner. Last sunday we marched from our camp near Alexandria & embarked on board a vesel named Baltimore & set sail for Old Point Comfort & arrived there at six o clock P.M. Tuesday night. Then we landed & spent the night in a comfortable store shed outside the fort.

The fort had once been home to Robert E. Lee. As Lieutenant of Engineers, he had lived there for three years in the early 1830s and aided in completing the fort's construction. Such an imposing, moat-surrounded fortress was a very welcome sight to Henry:

Finally after riding down the bay we came in sight of the only fortification truly formidable & seemingly impregnable. It is built of stone & cannon mounted in every place provided for them. The walls are about twenty feet high & a trench fifteen or twenty feet wide & eight or ten deep & can be filled with water if necessary. The inside is beautiful adorned with peach & other fruit trees & flowers. The soldiers are kept very neat - their clothes clean, shoes blacked, equipments glistening - quite a contrast from those in the field. We are a black looking lot of soldiers exposed to evry passing blast of wind - but our health is good not with standing our exposure & privations. The next morning we marched to Hampton - staid overnight & the next morning we started for Yorktown but after marching fourteen miles we found the bridges burnt & the enemy so strong that it would not be prudent to advance further - so we retreated a mile planted our bateries & encamped for the night. The next morning we marched back to Newport News & are here still. Expecting every day to advance uppon Yorktown & Bethel. The enemy are strongly fortified & we expect hard fighting.

We had only about six hard crackers for breakfast & two days rations. We marched fourteen miles & back on that amount of food & such a hungrey lot of boys I never befor saw. This great blunder was on account of the quarter master's not doing his duty.

Although it had been a difficult march, there had been one sight of great interest. McClellan's plans had been complicated by the appearance of the *Merrimack* (or CSS *Virginia*) earlier that month. The Confederate ironclad demonstrated its superiority over old wooden ships in the Battle of Hampton Roads on March 8. The next day the Union's counterpart, the *Monitor*, arrived and neutralized its opponent in their epic battle. The panic in the capital after the *Merrimack's* early successes, followed by the *Monitor's* ability to force it into the harbor and away from the Federal ships, had given the *Monitor* instant fame. Now Henry had a firsthand look at this ironclad just weeks after its famous encounter:

I also saw the little Monitor anchored near the fort. It is an inferior looking thing for one so noted for execution. It looks like a raft with a tub on top of it. I have seen the vesels that were sunk & burnt or their remains that were engaged with the Merrimac. She has been out today but has not come near our vessels. (We are ready to meet her any day.)

Monitor (on left) battles the Merrimack

Henry explained that he had to keep this letter short because he was writing inside one of the small, open-ended tents that the soldiers carried with them, as rain was pouring down around them.

Although the next goal was to take Yorktown, General McClellan believed that this famous Revolutionary War site was far more heavily defended than was actually the case. Confederate General John B. Magruder, with only about 15,000 men to defend the lower peninsula, established a defensive line along the Warwick River, extending across the peninsula from Yorktown in the north to the James River in the south. By using such elaborate ruses as marching his men in circles in view of McClellan, Magruder convinced the northern general that a large army was defending the town. McClellan decided to lay siege to Yorktown rather than risk using his army, numbered in six figures, in an all-out attack.

Siege cannon and most of the Army of the Potomac moved toward York-town on April 5. The Fourth Corps, however, was ordered to advance along the James River side of the peninsula and establish a position between Yorktown and Williamsburg, helping to block any possible escape route for Magruder's army. McClellan believed that by encircling and destroying Magruder in this way, he could then continue unmolested up the peninsula to face the main Confederate army led by General Joseph Johnston outside Richmond. Although the Vermont Brigade was part of the Sixth Corps for most of the war, it was initially attached to the Fourth Corps. On April 4, as part of General William "Baldy" Smith's division, the Vermont Brigade moved out, leading the Fourth Corps. The first line of Confederate defenders they encountered was a rather weak line of defense, intended only to slow down any Union advance as stronger fortifications were being constructed near Williamsburg. Writing home on April 10, Henry described the initial movement up the peninsula:

> We left Newport News last Saturday morning for Richmond. We started at six A.M. & marched a number of miles without encounterring any of the Rebils. Finally we discovered a fortification at Ship Point on the James River so we were drawn up in line of battle in the woods after which we advanced in front of the enemy. After arriving within range of [the] enemies guns we divided three companies to the left & the rest to advance upon the centre earthworks. At the word we took double quick step & charged the fortifications but the enemy fled at our approach after firing a few rounds. Our company was the first to enter the fort. We had to wade through the mud up to our knees & some of them in water up to their waists. The enemy had very

comfortable quarters & left in a great hurry leaving many things; books, cakes just ready for the oven & a hundred bushel of grain. We encamped there for the night & took a number of prisnors & one army waggon loaded with provisions.

Rebels at Young's Mill similarly offered just token resistance before giving up their position, which they had maintained for almost a year, and retreating to the Warwick River.

The next morning we started on in the rain & arrived at Warwick where we found the enemy strongly intrenched just across the Warwick Crick. We advanced within half of a mile of their fortifications & halted for the night & planted a number of our bateries & commenced shelling the enemy & learning the position & strength of the enemy. The next day we were ordered out scouting. Soon we came up to the crick. About five hundred yards across there were the enemies skirmishers so we placed ourselves behind trees & commenced firing at evry man we could see. To what effect I do not know. They returned our shots occasionally but did not hit any of our company. They were within talking distance & some of the boys had quite a talk with them. Some were saucy others civil. They said they should certainly whip us if we had any other General but McClelan. We are becoming accustomed to the sound of shells & balls. We were within reach of the guns from the fort & had quite a number of shells & shot fall near by. They made sad work of the trees but did not wound any of our men. But we have not attacked yet, the enemy being very strong & entrenched strongly between the James & York River. We have moved out of range of the enemies guns & are now within four miles of Yorktown. I hope that Gen McClelan will prove as success-ful as Washington was at the same place. Probably befor the arrival of this letter we shall have encountered the enemy. It is reported that the enemies strongest hold is here & all of the army of Manassas Gap. It is very rainy weather thus far & the roads very bad. We have been quite short of food for a number of days.

It had rained every day since they had left on April 4, making movement dif-ficult on the mud-caked roads. Supplying the troops was a bigger problem than expected, and the Fourth Corps was put on half rations throughout this campaign. Finally, on April 10 (the day when Henry wrote the letter quoted above), the rain stopped.

Vermont Boys Taking Possession of Rebel Fortifications and Barracks at Young's Mill
Sketch by Larkin Mead; Courtesy of Vermont Historical Society

The poor condition of the roads was one reason why McClellan concluded that he could not quickly advance on Richmond and instead concentrated on the siege of Yorktown, to be followed by a more methodical move up the peninsula. McClellan was also concerned that the Confederates were strengthening their fortifications in the area of Dam No. 1, located at about the midpoint of the Confederate defensive line between the James and York Rivers. McClellan therefore authorized General Smith, who believed that the defenses along the Warwick River were less formidable than McClellan was assuming, to attempt a limited probe into that defensive line. As a result, on April 16, Henry was involved in his first actual battle. Henry's company was one of those selected from the Vermont Brigade to cross the river in an early morning attack on the fortified defenses at Dam No. 1. Two days later Henry described the experience:

> *The 16th was a memorable day in my experience & the first time I ever faced cold lead from an enemies guns. The night before we were ordred to be in light marching order & to start early in the morning. So we started at four AM. ate our breakfast & started about seven & marched about a mile & halted. There the Colonel told us we were about on the point of meeting the enemy & wished us to be self posessd & obey evry order & remember that much was depending upon our conduct. That our State expected evry man to do his duty and the eyes of our country & of the world were upon us so we must do our best. Then we marched across the field to a piece of woods in front of the enemy. We halted & Co. B & G were ordered off as skirmishers so we entered the woods & marched along to the edge of the woods in front of the fortifications.*

We were very shy & advanced within five hundred yards of the fort. We surprised them. They were having a guard mounting & knew nothing of our approach untill the Colnel (Stoughton), after the boys were secreted behind the trees, fired a signal gun & the battle commenced in earnest. The moment the Colonel fired the whole line of skirmishers opened uppon the fort which was answerd by a shell from a large cannon bursting a short distance from us. Then Captain Ayres Batery opened & such a roaring I never before heard but it did not continue long as our company would at the moment the gunners appeard to load pick them off so fast that they could not man their guns, but our shots drew the enemies sharp shooters & evry few moments they would fire voley after voley. But fortunately none of us were hit. Soon our gunners aimed so accurately as to dismount their cannon & finaly they dismounted evry one of their guns. We were out untill noon & were relieved by other companies. About four oclock we were ordered to charge the breastworks which was tried by four companies. As soon as they left the woods voley after voley were fired at our men but the most went over our heads, but there being a stream of water thirty rods wide we could not cross so we retreated on hands & knees & strange to say only two were killed & six wounded. Our Colonel led the charge flourishing his swoard & encouraging his men on & not a man flinched from his duty. It was a desperate charge I will assure you in face of thousands of rebils. We lost only eight or ten killed & wounded out of our regiment. The other regiments suffered fearfuly & the enemy must have lost hundreds as our shot and shells were kept bursting over their rifle pits. The third Regiment mounted the brestworks on the right flank but could not hold their position for want of support & were obliged to retreat. It is reported that we have a worse place to take than Fort Donalson & we are making great preparations to bombard the fortifications. We work night and day fortifying. You will see an account in the papers when this reaches you. The Brigade has done itself great honor & have received great praise from our Generals. None of the Williamstown Boys have been hurt as yet. We are expecting evry day to renew the attack. There are fifty cannon mounted to operate on this one fort. I never expected to feel as I did on the occasion. After the first few shots I felt perfectly self posesed & ready to go any where orderd. The bulets and shells were very plenty & evry man did his duty. This is a hasty outline of what occurd but I must close & if spared to survive another battle I shall write as soon as possible.

General McClellan had arrived at about noon and had personally authorized sending the soldiers of the Third Vermont across the river. They were to signal for reinforcements if there was an opportunity to quickly take the rebel fortifications, but otherwise were to return rather than instigate a major engagement. Although they attempted to call for reinforcements, their attempts to communicate across the river were marred by confusion and no reinforcements were sent. Confederate reinforcements, on the other hand, did arrive, and their counterattack forced the Vermonters back across the river. The Vermont Brigade suffered over 200 casualties at Dam No. 1. Although they had failed to force the Confederates out, the Federal forces established their own position and set up fortifications along the Warwick River. They remained in that position for the next two weeks. Henry described the situation in a letter of May 3:

> The roads leading to Yorktown & vicinity are filled with teams drawing ammunition, mortars, siege guns & rations. The road for miles is cordyroyed so that our teems can pass without sinking out of sight in mud. You cannot imagine what it is to see mud. When we advanced from Newport News there was artilary baggage wagons passing in such numbers that those in the rear were finally compelled to stop. In some instances the mules would get into mud so deep that it was impossible for them to get out alone & it was necessary for to draw them out by the neck. We are now hoping to see no more such times & if successful here trust will not. We are now encamped in fine woods where the ground is as level as a floor & but little rubish or shubery. It is a delightful spot & one cannot realise that he is so near an enemy if allowed could throw shells among us & drive us away. But they are not allowed to show even a head without being shot at. Yesterday an officer on a horse was seen by our sharpshooters & shot from his horse. Their works are very strong & improving evry day. I expect that only a few days more will elaspe before our guns will open upon them. There is a great deal of skirmishing along the lines & some lives lost. The other day the 2nd Regt. lost three skirmishers were shot by sharp shooters. Two of them were instantly killed. The Adjutant General from Vt. is here providing a way by which our wounded & dead may be carried to Vermont. If successful it will be great consolation to the boys. It seems hard to have them left here. The woods are filled with graves.

McClellan, believing that the Confederate forces outnumbered his own, braced for the big offensive. He brought in so much artillery that Henry predicted "his shell will meet from the James & York Rivers." Henry explained further:

> We are expecting McDowell & Banks this afternoon. The baloon ascends twice a day to watch the movements of the enemy & if they should undertake to whip McDowell we shall attack immediately. It will be an awful day when battle opens.

Henry's expectations were not fulfilled, partly because of the successes of "Stonewall" Jackson in the Shenandoah Valley. Fearing for the safety of his own capital, President Lincoln decided to keep McDowell's First Corps protecting Washington rather than joining McClellan for the assault on Richmond. Furthermore, an all-out attack on Yorktown became unnecessary. On May 4, a day after Henry's letter, an observation balloon reported that the Confederate earthworks were now empty. Confederate troops were moving back toward Richmond. General Johnston had been skeptical about the defensive line at the Warwick River and would have preferred to pull all troops back to the Richmond defenses earlier. He had temporarily yielded to Magruder, General Lee, and Jefferson Davis, and he supported slowing McClellan's advance. In mid-April Johnston arrived with his forces and assumed command of the defenses along the Warwick River. By late April, however, his own observation balloons were reporting the Union artillery power and troop strength, and other sources of intelligence also indicated that the assault was about to begin. He thereby ordered the withdrawal toward Richmond, which occurred late at night on May 3.

The military use of observation balloons was not an entirely new idea. France had deployed a balloon as early as 1794, during the French Revolution, in the Battle of Fleurus. Balloons had not gained general acceptance by the time of the Civil War, but Northerner Thaddeus Lowe developed a proposal and presented it to Treasury Secretary Salmon Chase, who arranged for a meeting between Lowe and Lincoln. His demonstration of floating about 500 feet above the capital and sending a telegraph signal to the ground below persuaded Lincoln to establish the U.S. Balloon Corps. Later in the campaign, Henry again noted their use:

> *The baloon ascends two or more times every day. It annoys the enemy very much. They try to bring it down with their cannon but to no efect. The Baloonist is enabled to see all their works and the position of the troops, of any change of position. There is a telegraph wire attached so that evry thing seen is transmited immediately to Gen McClelland.*

Gas generators inflate
Lowe's balloon at the
Gaines farm
Courtesy of Library of Congress

After the observation balloon reported that the fortifications at Yorktown were unmanned, Henry credited McClellan's strategy with this success:

Last sabath morning we were called up earlier than usual & the news came that the fortifications were evacuated & immediately we were ordered to occupy their works & we were surprised at the strength of their works. Evry approach was commanded by strong brestworks of the most formidable character. But McClellans skill was to much for them & they left in great haste leaving tents, comisary stores &c.

When McClellan learned that Johnston was moving back toward Richmond, he sent troops in pursuit to try to disrupt the retreat. The mud was also slowing Johnston's movements, so with Federal cavalry gaining on him, he decided to leave a part of his force, under General Longstreet's command, in a defensive position near Williamsburg to await the Union advance. There the Confederates had established a line of 14 earthworks flanking a central fortification called Fort Magruder. The Battle of Williamsburg began on May 5 with an early morning attack by General Hooker (who would acquire his sobriquet of "Fighting Joe" in this battle) into the center of the Confederate line at Fort Magruder. After some early success, Confederate reinforcements arrived and Hooker's division began to be forced back. In another part of this spread-out battlefield, General Smith had learned from a local slave that two redoubts on the Confederate left were unoccupied and could be reached by crossing a nearby dam. He responded by sending General Hancock's brigade to seize those two redoubts, which he accomplished early in the afternoon. From his new position, Hancock believed he could take the remaining redoubts between himself and Fort Magruder if Smith sent reinforcements. Smith agreed and twice tried to send the Vermont Brigade to join Hancock. General Sumner was in command, however, and both times decided instead to keep them in place to protect his center, although there was no discernible threat to that position. Instead of attacking, Hancock remained in a defensive position and successfully warded off an assault by Jubal Early's brigade and D. H. Hill's division. Early was wounded twice in this attack. Hooker, still fighting in the center of the line, was reinforced by Philip Kearny's division in mid-afternoon and began pushing the rebels back. Overnight the Confederates abandoned the Williamsburg defenses and continued their withdrawal to Richmond. Federal casualties totaled 2,283 to 1,682 for the Confederates. A week after the battle, Henry explained:

We pursued them [from Yorktown] so closely that many prisoners were taken & quantities of baggage. Our cavelry was a terror to them numbering about eleven thousand men. Finally we arrived at Williamsburg where they made a stand & we had a terrible battle on Monday in the rain & a fiercer fight was never fought. Fort McGruder was charged four times & repulsed. But for some unaccountable reason their attention was drawn in another direction & so Gen Hancock s Brigade crossed a dam & sudenly apperd on their left flank & a fierce strugle ensued. The enemy charged uppon them twice & made them retreat. But oweing to the coolness of our men we [were] invincible. Our men would wait untill the enemy were within ten rods of them when they would deliver a sure & deadly fire cutting whole ranks. Still they advanced untill within reach of each other with their guns when a dash was made & they flew for their lives, with grapeshot & canister from Whellers & Mots Bateries killing great numbers. Their loss was very great - hundreds of dead strewed on the ground. Generals, Colonels, Majors, Captains & privates were numbered with the dead. Our loss was great. None of the Vt. boys were wounded. It took two days to bury the dead & evry house in Williamsburg was filled with wounded. The Rebils were tenderly cared for & very thankful. On the eighth we started on & found the road strewed with waggons & everything else & numbers of dead Rebils who are hotly pursued by cavelry, infantry & shell all along the river by our gun boats. They have been so closely pursued that they have not been able even to obstuct our road or make a stand of any importance.

Though Henry was pleased with the victory, the reality of war was proving quite different from what he had anticipated. What made the brutality at least palatable was that things seemed to be advancing militarily and the end was within sight. Once they took Richmond, just a short distance ahead, the Confederacy would quickly crumble.

I have seen enough of war but I have duties to perform & trusting in the Lord to protect and keep me, I go forward. It seems that the war cannot last long. Our men are superior fighters. Especially the New Englanders.

Tomorrow morning we start again & expect to find fortifications on the Chickihomina River. We are only two days march from Richmond where I expect an awful fight.

General McClellan had also viewed Williamsburg as a great victory over the supposedly superior numbers of the enemy. But more significantly, this Union victory delayed McClellan long enough that Johnston could get most of his army back to Richmond, where they could dig in behind the formidable defenses Lee had been laboring to create. As Henry had predicted, the next line of Confederate defenses was positioned just across the Chickahominy River. As the Fourth

Vermont approached, Henry found himself in a rather harrowing situation. He wrote on May 23:

Your letter of fifteenth came to hand being five days on the road. Since my last we have changed our position a number of times. The day we left New Kent Ct House we came very near being taken prisoners by the enemy. The Colonel lost the Brigade & wandered almost into the enemies lines. We drove in their pickets & came very near being surrounded but fortunately we just escaped them. Our absense caused considerable alarm & the whole of Smith's Division & a regt. of calvilry were sent to our rescue. But we were fortunate enough to get out alone & was the cause of taking seven hundred prisoners. We encamped at Cumberland Landing on the Pamunky River. With one hundred thousand troops it was quite a populous city. As far as the eye could reach nothing could be seen but tents, artillery & cavalry.

Even in the midst of such peril, Henry, ever the tourist, continued to pay close attention to the sights that he encountered:

The next morning the mass began to move & in a short time the field was nearly vacated. We mooved up the river to Lee s Landing very near the residence of George Washingtons wife before her conection with him. It is one of the most splendid situations I have seen since I have been in Va. There is a very large plantation & numberless slaves of all complexions. They were all of good expressions & say that their time of bondage is nearly ended. Every man has been drafted in this vicinity, their negros left in charge. The fences as we pass along the roads are lined with slaves cheering us on. ...

The corn is two inches high; the trees green & leaves full grown; cherries turning; peaches, pairs & apples as large as tame cherries; clover in blossom & knee high; wheat headed out. Everything is thriving indicating a distinct supposition of our ever coming this way. The inhabitants are well protected & their property respected. It must be true that no army ever before passed through a country before without leaving it desolate.

Not only were they cheered on by slaves, but word was spreading among the soldiers that little resistance would be ahead as the Confederates realized that they could not defend their capital.

We are now north of Richmond & eleven miles from the city. We have joined McDowell s Corp. Our pickets joined us last night & the enemy are evacuating Richmond & it is reported that the North Carolinians are being sent home. One of General Brookes Aids went within four miles of Richmond yesterday

& met nothing formidable. Tomorrow morning all expect to advance. Our balloons are so in such good positions that they can see the streets of Richmond. A paper was found by Capt. Reed (the Aid). Jeff warned his men not [to] come in contact with New England soldiers. They have proved to be the best in the army.

Henry had experienced enough combat in this campaign, however, that he could not be so optimistic:

We are expecting to see Richmond before another week closes & I hope it will be without much blood shed. But I fear it will not be the case.

Blood would be shed within the week, but not in the all-out assault on Richmond that Henry had anticipated in his May 23 letter from "Camp Near Hanover Court House." Although the invading Federal army numbered about 105,000 men compared to Johnston's 60,000 defending Richmond, General McClellan accepted intelligence reports indicating that he was badly outnumbered. As a result, the movement toward Richmond came to a standstill and the following weeks were marked by small skirmishes rather than the titanic struggle that might have brought the war to an early conclusion. The Fourth Vermont changed locations several times in the next days. Around the same time, Henry learned that another cousin, George Smith, had enlisted in the regular army, and he was not pleased with that decision. On May 25, writing from "Camp Near Richmond Va," Henry explained:

I fear George will repent of his Enlistment. I suppose he is bound for five years & it will be very doubtful whether he gets a Lieutenancy. Recruiting officers tell large stories. I will wish him success.

We are constantly on the moove. Yesterday we marched two miles toards Richmond & encamped. Over night our right wing went within four miles of their capital but did not deem it proper to hold their position. We are within five or six miles of that place. I expect soon to see one of the most bloody battles ever fought on this continent.

When General McClellan was informed that Confederate forces were moving toward Hanover Court House, he had two concerns. Not only would this make it more difficult to bring in reinforcements from McDowell's army as he still desired, but a large enough Confederate army in that location could even conceivably threaten the right flank of McClellan's army. Consequently, he sent Federal troops to intercept the Confederates on their way to Hanover Court House. In the ensuing battle, the greatly outnumbered Confederates were forced to retreat. This battle took place just four days after Henry's letter from that location, but

Henry did not take part in it. By that time, the Vermont Brigade had moved south to Gaines' Mill, near the Chickahominy, and was encamped on Dr. Gaines' farm.

With McClellan seemingly preoccupied with the positioning of his right flank, General Johnston, detecting an opportunity for the Confederates, launched an attack on McClellan's left flank. Since Confederates had earlier destroyed the bridges, the two Federal corps south of the Chickahominy River were isolated from the three corps north of the river. The resulting Battle of Seven Pines occurred on May 31. The Vermont Brigade, now attached to the newly formed Sixth Corps, was part of the three corps north of the river. Henry was therefore not part of this battle either and was instead employed building pontoon bridges to connect the two parts of the army. He wrote to Frank two days later from "Camp Near Cold Harbor, Virginia," on Monday, June 2, to update him on the campaign:

Another week has passed. Our division has not been engaged with the enemy. We are within talking distance of each other. Our pickets are but few rods apart. Saturday night our pickets crossed the Chicahomina Crick. They had to ford the stream where the water was up to their necks & stand in water all night up to their knees. We were obliged to set up all night in readiness to receive an attack. At three A. M. we were ordered out & marched down to the crick to support our Engineer and Pioneer Corps in placing the pontoon and trestle bridges across the stream in face of the rebels. They offered no resistance & if they had it would have been of no avail - we have over thirty cannon commanding their position. So you see it would have been destruction to their cannon if they had shown their heads. They are supposed to be evacuating. They are moving their troops somewhere. One of their baggage wagons were seen passing in an opening by Captain Mott. He cited one of his cannon & fired. The shell struck underneath the wagon blowing it to pieces. He is a fine marksman & can land a shot where ever he wishes. He saved the day at Williamsburg by his promptness & deadly fire. His battery was charged uppon but his grape and cannister mowed them by hundreds. He destroyed a whole regiment. There was hardly a man left to tell the tale.

The long day of fighting at Seven Pines (or Fair Oaks) was somewhat inconclusive. The South failed to break through the Federal lines and ultimately withdrew. Union casualties numbered 5,031 as opposed to 6,134 for the Confederates. Among those casualties was General Johnston, and as a result, Robert E. Lee now assumed command of the Army of Northern Virginia.

Henry was close enough to hear the barrage of artillery fire, and based on what he was hearing from others, he believed this to be an overwhelming victory for his side:

*Last Saturday was an awful day for the rebels. They attacked our lines on
the left & were handsomely whipped. Their loss must have been greater than
at Williamsburg. The firing commenced about one P.M. fought untill dark.
There was an incessant firing from cannon and muskets. They drove the
enemy four miles. Took one battery, horses & all & payed them off in their
own coin. The rebels fought bravely giving only inch by inch. But it is impossible for southern men to fight like a northener. When they are handsomely
whipped they will not give up but are ready to renew the fight at the first
command. One of the rebel prisoners said their officers admit that our men
are superior [at] one thing. That is when repulsed in a charge or engagement
our men can be rallied but theirs are all fire for the dash but if repulsed
cannot be rallied. Yesterday Gen Keys took five hundred prisoners & one
general. They were surrounded the night before. Everyday deserters come in
all stating great want and destitution. They are ragged and dirty.*

A spirit of optimism must have filled the Union camps as Henry also inac-
curately reported a great naval victory in which Federal gunboats, including the
Monitor, supposedly had cleared the way to Richmond.

*Last Saturday Fort Darling was surrendered. Our gunboats silenced their
guns & compelled them to surrender all their guns & accessories. & Yesterday our gunboats went to Richmond. It is reported that Gen McClelland
gives them three days to surrender which they had better do if our mortar
fleet has got where they can reach them. Our gunboats are terrible things.
Their guns carry so large shells if one explodes near a line of men there will be
few if any that will escape unharmed. At West Point a shell burst in the midst
of a company & killed or wounded all but twelve or fifteen men.*

In actual fact, Fort Darling, located on Drewry's Bluff just seven miles from
Richmond on the James River, had not surrendered but instead repulsed the Union
attack. It would not fall until 1865.

Henry continued his letter the next day, but his excitement was somewhat tem-
pered, perhaps due to a combination of the difficult labor in which his company was
engaged and the receipt of better information about the battle. On June 3 he added:

*Our company being called out to help build a bridge I did not have time to fin-
ish my letter. The men had a hard days labor. They left just before dinner &
worked hard in mud & water untill ten oclock P.M. without supper. Finally
we sent to camp & had our supper brought down to us. After it was eaten they
labored untill two A.M. & were relieved. The swamp is a hard one to make*

roads in. There are three streams each about twenty rods apart. It is a very bad place to attempt to make a crossing.

The result of Saturday's fight was satisfactory but our loss was very great - reported to be four thousand men. We drove them at every point. They resisted every inch of ground. The fight enabled us to cross 40,000 men. Our position is commanded by 132 guns. It is supposed to be the place where the rebels will try to break our lines. We occupy the center & shall not see much fighting if either flank can carry their positions. ... The boys a fort night ago were talking of being in Vermont next fourth of July but I fear they will be disappointed. The raising of more men looks rather suspicious to me. I can hear heavy cannonading before Richmond. They appear to be shelling some place. The shots are not quite as frequent as last Saturday. I took out my watch and counted seventeen shots in a minute. That fire was kept up from 1 p.m. to dark. McClellen says bomb shells are cheaper than men. ... The thermometer stood at 105 yesterday noon. The rebils tried to plant a batery this morning commanding our location but were defeated by the eagle eyes of our artillerymen. I suppose the enemy are efectively surrounded & our forces are pressing on their rear. Yesterday afternoon I heard the engine whistle supposed to be on the Richmond road. Our hospitals are full of sick and wounded. Many are dying of feavers.

Besides this update on the progress of the war, Henry also enclosed a thoughtful souvenir for his brother, "a piece of a sesesh [secessionist] Colnels gold lace taken from his dead body at Williamsburg."

General McClellan claimed a great victory at Seven Pines yet became even more convinced that he must avoid rashly attacking the Confederate forces close to Richmond, and instead had to build defensive positions of his own. In Henry's next letter, on June 14, he admitted that very little had happened in the past two weeks.

We have not engaged the enemy in front of Richmond yet. We are holding a very important position. It is the center of the Army of the Potomac under acting Major General Franklin. We have built a fort & strings of rifle pits. Yesterday the enemy tried to draw us into an engagement. They commenced shelling our troops on our left & continued it a part of the day. But when they wish an engagement we will not attack them unless they do us. We are acting on the defensive. General Porters division is crossing the Chickhominia today. We are kept on the alert now adays and are called up at the break of day and stand in line of battle from one to two hours to be prepared to meet any surprise or early attack. General McDowel had an engagement the

twelveth & pushed the enemy back such a distance. There was a heavy can-
nonading. There has but little if any note occurred since I wrote my last.

The lull in the action gave Henry time to deal with some of the financial issues
that always seemed to be on his mind. For one thing, he had promised Charles
Whitwell that he would settle his financial affairs were the sergeant to fall in
battle. Whitwell died from the wounds he had received at Williamsburg, and it
was now time to honor that promise. Henry asked his brother to try to ascertain
Whitwell's debts and to investigate how to draw his back pay in order to fulfill
those debts. Henry had a personal debt on his mind too: he had lent money to a
soldier named Riley Mardin, from nearby Brookfield, and was not receiving the
agreed-upon repayments. This problem would trouble Henry and his family for
the next several years.

Henry also pointed out that another local boy, Frank Flint, was fortunate
to have been sent home early from camp for health reasons, rather than to have
needed medical attention in the midst of a military campaign.

The accommodations for sick & wounded soldiers are very poor. Our being so
constantly on a moove will not permit the Surgeon having suitable hospitals.
The wounded at the battle in front of Richmond could not be cared for for
three days after the battle because of the great numbers. The dead were so
numerous that they could not bury them before they mortified & they were
obliged to burn the bodies by hundreds. ...The weather is becoming extremely
hot & sickness is beginning to prevail to considerable extent.

Frank Flint's discharge for chronic diarrhea kept him out of the remainder
of the war. He returned home and became a conductor for the Vermont Central
Railroad.

Henry wrote home again a week later, on June 21, and reported that the big
battle still had not occurred:

Another week has passed. It has been a very short one. The time here slips
aways so fast that it is almost impossible to number the days. The ten months
which I have been in the service of the United States are very short ones to
look back upon. Nearly one year of my servise has expired a longer term than
I expected to serve when I left home. I think it probable that I shall serve my
time of enlistment should my life and health be spared.

I suppose you are expecting evry day to hear of an awful fight at Rich-
mond. I do but McClelland is a wise General & will not strike till he can
crush them.

While they waited, defenses continued to be prepared and more small skirmishes were fought. The Sixth Corps crossed to the south of the Chickahominy and established its camp on the Golding farm, very close to Confederate pickets across the field. Under General Smith's orders, all regiments were required to be awake and in line of battle by 3:00 every morning because of the possibility of an attack. If it did not come by sunrise, the exhausted soldiers were assigned labor duties for the day.

> *We are daily expecting an attack or to advance. Day before yesterday we expected to have made an advance & made evry necessary preparation but the order was countermanded. We rise every morning at three oclock & stand in line of battle. There is daily a great deal of cannonading & shelling going on but little damage is done & few lives lost.*

Henry accepted the workload and sleep deprivation as necessary precautions. He explained further in his June 14 letter:

> *We are now in face of a very formidable enemy. Strong in numbers a concentrated force &c. strong fortifycations daily growing stronger but we are not lying still. We are building brestworks, rifle pits, mounting siege guns, & prepairing to meet almost any emergency. Our left wing is in sight of the steeples of Richmond and our Siege guns can reach the enemy at their capital. Last Wednesday P.M. about four oclock the enemy made an attack on our left. Oweing to some disasters Gen. McClelland was informed of their intentions & prepared a trap for them. He ordered the pickets to retreat at the approach of the enemy & on arriving at a certain spot were ordered to open right & left, discharge their pieces. The enemy came as expected two or three Brigades strong. Our men conformed to the orders & retired on the approach of the Rebels. They were sure of entering our lines but to their great surprise the bushes were filled with cannon which caused many a heart to bleed for the friends killed on that spot. The grape and canister mowed them like grass & killed & wounded four hundred men. The enemy turned & fled as usual when they made the attack. The cannon did not fire more than a dozen shots. Some of the Generals thought the battle of Richmond had commenced in earnest but it proved to be other wise.*

Health conditions also continued to plague the soldiers as they fought and labored in the summer heat of Virginia:

> *It is becomeing quite sickly, this hot weather mostly Diareha. ...I purchase all the Oranges & lemons I can find. We are very short of vegetables & many*

of the soldiers are having the skurvy. One felow had it so hard that his teeth were so loose that they could be pulled out with the fingers. My health continues good. The weather extremely hot.

Henry expressed some uncertainty as to whether the Federal forces would be advancing or facing a Confederate counterattack. Within a few days he knew the answer, in the form of a week of fighting like nothing he had seen before. The Seven Days Battle, in which General Lee led the Confederate forces in an offensive against McClellan's army, occurred from June 25 through July 1. McClellan first attempted a movement on June 25, hoping to launch his attack before Stonewall Jackson could arrive from the Shenandoah Valley and be a factor. The Battle of Oak Grove, in which McClellan wished to secure land that would enable him to move his siege guns closer to Richmond, gained very little against the Confederate defenses. The next day, Lee's offensive began, aiming to overpower the remaining Federal forces north of the Chickahominy. Lee had hoped to overwhelm the opposition with help from Jackson's men, but Jackson arrived later than Lee had planned. The Union lines withstood the rebel attack at Mechanicsville and established a defensive position close to the river. Given the chaotic set of movements, it is understandable that Henry seemed unclear about what was happening when he wrote home on June 26, the same day when Confederates were attacking north of the river:

We have had quite lively times for the past two days. Yesterday our left wing advanced two miles & took up a position on a hill within sight of Richmond & fortified themselves. Have planted large siege guns that can knock many a steeple or spire to the ground. The enemy fought hard to keep them back but to no avail. Our men were compelled to return once to their old position but being reinforced drove them back & maintain their position. We built a fort last night out side of our pickets. Three thousand men did the work. The enemy did not like it very well but did but little harm - made one attack & was repulsed by our pickets alone. There is considerable shelling going on every day. We have had a number of skirmishes since my last.

The next day, Henry found himself in the midst of heavy fighting. Confederate forces mostly concentrated on attacking the Fifth Corps, still north of the river, at the Battle of Gaines' Mill. The Federal lines eventually were pushed back and a retreat was ordered across the river after dark, using the recently built bridges. South of the Chickahominy, General Magruder had only about 25,000 men, but McClellan had been confused by Magruder's movements. The same day as Gaines' Mill, Magruder attacked the Sixth Corps at Garnett's farm. The Federal forces faced a strong artillery attack starting at about 4 p.m. Early in the evening Magruder's forces finally attacked, hitting Hancock's men hard. The Fourth and Sixth Vermont were among the regiments sent to reinforce Hancock. Darkness eventually brought an end to the fighting that had resulted in 368 Federal and 461 Confederate casualties. When the Seven Days were finally over and Henry had time to write on July 5, he described the different battles in which he had taken part.

> Fearing you would be very anxious about my welfare I take the first opportunity to send you a letter. We have had one of the hardest times we have seen since I enlisted. When I wrote you last I spoke of hard fighting at Mechanicsville. It was an artilery fight. Gen. Porter lost only sixty men. The next day he was ordered to retreat & not resist the enemy only to cover the retreat so as to allow the baggage & artilery trains to get out of the way. The next morning the retreat commenced, the enemy rushing on with great fury. But we being able to pick our own positions we could resist any force. The rebils would come upon us by thousands & be mowed down by the hundreds making breastworks of human bodies. They were sure of success.

The Sixth Corps turned back the Confederate attacks at Garnett's Farm on June 27 and the adjacent Goldin's Farm on June 28; however, McClellan viewed the defeat at Gaines' Mill, north of the Chickahominy, combined with these continuing attacks south of the river as evidence that he was indeed badly outnumbered. Smith's division was selected to act as part of the rearguard as the rest of the Army of the Potomac retreated to the James River and the protection of the Union gunboats. Lee pursued the Federal army and the next day, on June 29, Henry was once again in the midst of an enemy attack, this time at Savage's Station. When they arrived earlier in the day, joining Sumner's Second Corps, the Vermont Brigade witnessed the mass destruction of food and military supplies that was taking place to avoid letting them fall into enemy hands. There was also a large group of wounded and sick soldiers near the station hoping to be transported out. Late in the afternoon, Magruder attacked.

> Our marching had to be done in the night & so we did not get any sleep for six days except a little in the daytime. ... Sunday morning we were on the retreat. We were the last division to leave the position we held. The enemy were aware of our movements & as soon as we were ready to start we were welcomed by shell after shell interspersed with solid shot. The Colonel immediately got us into a hollow where we were less exposed. But the enemy having perfect range would burst their shell over our heads. The pieces in many instances grasing our backs but killing no one.

Other regiments were not so fortunate and casualties began to mount. Late in the day, in the midst of heavy thunderstorms, the Vermont Brigade was ordered to attack into the heavily defended woods where Confederate forces were concentrated. They proceeded to fire at each other at close range.

> *Sunday night our Brigade had a severe fight but they drove the enemy at evry point. Gen Brooks was wounded in the knee & Mart Burnham shot through the head & killed instantly. The rest of the Wmstown boys are all right but Don P Nichols who is supposed to be taken prisoner. He could not stand the march & fell out. The 5th Regt. was cut to pieces. One company lost all its officers but one Sergeant & all its men but sixteen. The Regt. has only eight companies. They were exposed to a cross fire & grape & canister but they took the batery & brought off all the wounded. After dark we commenced the retreat & marched all night without halting once.*

The Vermont Brigade suffered 439 casualties that day, more than any other brigade. Historians consider the battle a stalemate, with about 1,500 casualties on both sides. Henry's information on his fellow Williamstown boys was not totally accurate. Martin Burnham survived and was captured by the Confederates. He and Don P. Nichols were both paroled and sent to the hospital at Camp Parole in Annapolis to recuperate; both later deserted. As Federal troops continued their long retreat, they were forced to leave behind 2,500 wounded and sick soldiers who could no longer be transported.

Wounded Soldiers at Savage's Station

Savage's Station was "an exciting spot to be in but nothing to be compared with what followed" for Henry. By early Monday afternoon, most of the Union army had cleared the bottleneck at the White Oak Swamp Bridge and was continuing towards the James River. Lee decided to attack the Federal forces located between White Oak Swamp and Glendale with the bulk of his army in order to secure the Glendale crossroads. Stonewall Jackson was to march from Savage's Station and drive out the soldiers remaining before him, then continue to Glendale. When Jackson arrived at White Oak Swamp, he found the bridge destroyed but Union troops placed just across the swamp. Perhaps exhausted from his movements and battles of the previous two weeks, Jackson made no attempt to attack but instead stealthily placed his guns in range of the Union defenders. The Sixth Corps, acting as the Union's rearguard, suddenly found itself the target of Jackson's artillery attack. After having marched through the night, many were resting when the surprise afternoon barrage began:

> *After light we halted & took a position in a field. About four o'clock we were all asleep & to our great surprise we were awakened by the whising of solid shot & bursting shell. Six bataries opened upon us at once. Each batary having six guns. We were surprised I will assure you & all of us started for the woods. The shells did not kill any of our men - a great wonder. Many were knocked down. They came so near them some of our bataries suffered very much, killing almost evry horse & sixty men. There was a scene of confusion for a while. Horses without riders, men running in evry direction. You can imagine for yourself what a sight it must have been. We soon ralied & formed a line to resist an attack but our battaries being on hand silenced the enemy very quick.*

Rearguard at
White Oak Swamp

Because they held their position at White Oak Swamp, the Sixth Corps deprived General Lee of having Stonewall Jackson flanking the Federal army at Glendale (or Frayser's Farm), just a few miles away. Jackson made no attempt to cross at White Oak Swamp until the next day, after the Federal position had been abandoned. General William B. Franklin, on the other hand, was able to release 10,000 of his men from the Sixth Corps to march south and aid significantly at Glendale against Longstreet's and A. P. Hill's divisions. Jackson's surprisingly unaggressive behavior at White Oak Swamp and the disjointed Confederate attack at Glendale added up to a missed opportunity for a clear Confederate victory. Instead, the 8,000 casualties were about evenly divided between the two sides, and McClellan's retreat continued. Lee had one remaining place to attack the retreating Union Army, and that was Malvern Hill.

The Sixth Corps again marched through the night, and the exhausted troops arrived at Malvern Hill early in the morning on July 1. Without breakfast or rest, they were immediately deployed along the strong defensive lines established by the Army of the Potomac. As it turned out, the many Confederate attempts to directly break through those defenses did not involve the woods adjacent to Western Run where the Vermont Brigade was placed. As a result, Henry did not seem to view Malvern Hill as being a particularly significant engagement as he concluded his letter on the Seven Days. In reality, Lee's army had made several failed assaults on the Federal defenses and sustained severe casualties, losing 5,355 men in a clear Union victory. After the battle, rather than go on the offensive and counterattack Lee, McClellan chose to continue the retreat to Harrison's Landing.

> At eleven P.M. we left that spot (White Oak Swamp) & marched till day-light next day & arrived at City Point one mile from Fort Darling. There we formed a line to resist a cavelry charge but they did not dare to come on. Next we mooved down to another point near whare President Harrison was born. It is a splendid mansion. We are now under the cover of our gun boats & hope to stay here a while. I saw the Monitor yesterday. It threw a number of shells at the enemy & drove them back. We have received great reinforcements. They have gone on to the rear of Richmond to take our places & let us have a little rest. We are all exhausted & our numbers thinned remarkably.

The Seven Days Battle had come to a close, although that may not have been clear to Henry at this time. Lee had forced McClellan's army into a retreat. Nevertheless, the Army of the Potomac remained large, intact, and a dangerous threat to Richmond. The Confederates had suffered heavy casualties and had missed several opportunities to strike a decisive blow against the invading army. Writing home a week and a half after Malvern Hill, Henry seemed run down, although not necessarily discouraged:

> My health continues but am very tired. & The weather is extremely hot. It tells on the men. Many of [them] faint when on duty & many are sun struck. I supose

it will be very sickly before the close of another month. Uncle Sam works us very hard at this time. We do not receive any news papers lately that let us know what is going on. We are daily receiving reinforcements & various rumors are in circulation that foreign powers will put an end to this strife soon if possible.

In the weeks that followed at Harrison's Landing, rather than dwelling on the battles in which he had just been engaged, Henry began thinking about the family farm and commodity prices. In particular, he wondered if the army's need for goods would positively impact the price of what his family was producing. He wrote to Francis on July 21, responding to a letter that he had finally received after two weeks of no news from home:

Evry mail but the last was a disappointment to me. I had waited almost two weeks but I will excuse all delays as you must be very busy at the present time. I suppose you are just commencing haying in earnest. I hope you will have good success using the mowing machine. You must keep it in perfect repair & not try to mow in rough or bogy places. If you do it will give you plenty of trouble. ... Is the hay crop as good as last. I suppose it will be about as good as usual on the meadows, only a little late. Is beef going to sell high this year at Vermont. I should suppose it might. It takes a great amount to supply this army & such a waste would make folks at home grumble. Are horses high or low. I should suppose there would be a very quick sail for them. Horses can not stand hardly one campaign without being totaly worn out. Calvary & Artilary horses are on the jump evry day. I am rejoiced to hear that you had so good luck peeling willows & that they hold out so well in weight. I suppose they will sell as well as last year. I see a great many of them used in the Army as a covering for Whiskey & evry other kind of licker bottles & demajohns. ... I have but little war news to write. We are very busy building fortifications of a very formiable character. They extend the whole length of our picket lines or front on this point. Cannon are to be placed all along the line as thick as they can be worked. Over one hundred have been planted ready & as many more will be before the week expires. The soldiers are worked very hard sent out some times twice a day to dig in the trenches. They complain biterly thinking it most to hard to fight as they did while on the retreat & then what remains of them be compelled to labor so hard on fortifications when in the rear there are thousands of men doing nothing but drill. Our Brigade does not number over eight hundred well men for duty. We are a mere handful of men. I have wondered what Vermont will do after raising three or four more Regiments. With this shatered Brigade our numbers sick & well are not three thousand men. It is reported here that the ninth Regiment is coming here & join this Brigade. I hope they will come soon.

... Our gunboats are daily engaged with the enemy. The little gun boat Teaser came through the Blockade the other day & lay under Darling. Our gun boats saw her and went up under her guns. Took her in defianse of all they could do. It came down to Newport News when we were there & threw a few shells at us doing no harm. ... Mardin has gone to the hospital & perhaps will get a discharge so look out for him. I saw Eldon Tildin yesterday. His health is not very good. Has not recovered from the retreat yet. John Clough lost one finger in that engagement at Savage Station. He is at Baltimore. Don P. Nichols is supposed to be a prisoner at Richmond. Henry Smith & Chester Clark are excused by the Surgeon. Diareha is prevailing extensively. ... Many of the Officers are seeing so much of the reality of war that they are anxious to get out of it. Lieut. Colnel Worthen & Adjutant Faxon have resigned & gone home.

Despite losing a finger and being discharged, John Clough later re-enlisted and was captured at Spotsylvania. He was sent to Andersonville prison camp, but managed to escape early in 1865. After returning home, Clough began to drink heavily and eventually his wife left him, claiming abuse. Many years later, Clough committed suicide by cutting his throat with a knife.

As for the *CSS Teaser* to which Henry referred, it had fought in the Battle of Hampton Roads in March. At this point it was laying mines in the James River as well as transporting a balloon that was used to identify the positioning of McClellan's troops at Harrison's Landing. On July 4, in an engagement with the *USS Maratanza*, the *Teaser's* boiler was blown up by a shell, and the ship was abandoned. The ship was recommissioned as the *USS Teaser* and fulfilled many later roles, assisting Burnside's December invasion across the Rappahannock and participating in the coastal blockade of Virginia and Maryland.

As the men wondered what to expect next in the Peninsula Campaign, a rumor spread about a new strategy for taking Richmond

It is conjectured here that General Pope is to come down in rear of Richmond take it & drive the enemy down upon our fortifications.

The conjecture was incorrect. Although Henry did not know it yet, General Halleck was being recalled from the western campaign and was appointed the new General-in-Chief on July 23. The army remained at Harrison's Landing, but in a letter to Francis on August 1, Henry indicated that the Confederates were not totally leaving them alone, despite their strong defensive position:

Last night about half past twelve A. M. I was sudenly awakened by the booming of the heavy cannon along the banks of the river. The enemy had planted three batteries to shell our transports. They were planted and discovered last

night by our baloon. It was very dark & they working hard preparing to give us a fair welcome. But to their surprise our gunboats & siege guns opened simultaneously & the report is that it made them leave their work in great haste. The hundred & two hundred pound shells can not be otherwise than a terror to any troops. When they lodge in the ground they leave holes large enough to take in our old cart body. A number of Rebel gunboats appeared & our ever vigilant gunboats were ready to meet any thing that might come upon them. Our troops were immediately under arms & ready to meet any imergency but they did not dare to pick out us. We do not expect they will try very hard to drive us from our position. It is defended so well by nature that with our improvements, if I may so term it, for I suppose nature cannot be improved by man only for some purpose. Gen. Porter's mortar fleet is reported to be in the James River. I wish you could have seen the mortar shells rush through the dark, the fuse burning & finally exploding resembling a star. The cannon would belch forth fire enough to light the darkness all around. The Rebils killed three men. They threw a great many shells. There has but little transpired since my last but this last event.

Henry also appears to have believed McClellan's numerous protestations that his army had been badly outnumbered throughout this campaign:

It is evry able bodied man's duty to come forward at this great crisis. Otherwise we shall be overpowered by overwhelming numbers. We have withstood twice our number all summer but it cannot be expected we can always. I hope there will be no delay in sending forward men.

When he wrote home again, on August 11, Henry realized that they would not be remaining at Harrison's Landing much longer. A few days earlier, McClellan had sent General Hooker to reclaim Malvern Hill and hoped, by showing some success, to convince Halleck to leave the army on the peninsula instead of entirely abandoning McClellan's larger strategy. But when Hooker met strong resistance, rather than risk a possible defeat, McClellan ordered him back to Harrison's Landing. This move helped to confirm Lee's suspicion that McClellan no longer posed a threat to Richmond, and that the Army of the Potomac would soon move off the peninsula to link up with Pope's army. Henry's account indicates he was accepting McClellan's analysis of their situation:

We expect to evacuate tomorow morning. The Rebils are at Malvern Hill about thirty six miles from our camp in overwhelming numbers. Last Tuesday our forces under Gen. Hooker surprised the enemy who were fortifying on that hill, surrounded them & slaughtered them in great numbers. Our

gunboats did terrible execution. We captured a large number of prisoners &
a number of cannon. The next day we were ordered out with two days rations
to keep the enemy from outflanking Gen Hooker. We remained there two
days but were not attacked & returned home. The weather was extremely
hot. We laid out without tents or blankets. The ground is now occupied by
the enemy. I hope we shall not be obliged to march all the way to Ft. Monroe.
It is nearly ninety miles from here & I fear we have got to cover the retreat
again. Our bagage has gone to the landing today. We anticipate a ride up the
Rapahanoc. ... [Frank Cosgrove] has returned to recruit for this regiment.
The Colonel sends one man from each company. We are hoping they will
have good luck & it will be a good chance for anyone, better than to join a
new regiment. They will have the benefit of the experience of the old soldiers
& share the honors of the old vetern Brigade. They will have an easier time
& better fed because the Quartermasters department is well established &
every thing goes on regularly. I hope the Williamstown boys will enlist & join
our company. Tell evry man that has good health that it is his duty to come
out here & help us in time to save the country.

Frank Cosgrove may not have been a very convincing recruiter. He had just
been in the hospital with severe diarrhea before being sent home to recruit. Cosgrove continued to have health problems and was finally granted a disability
discharge the next year. He never fully regained his health and died in 1872.

On August 14 Henry started a letter home. In the opening section he said,

We are waiting in suspense to know what the next move will be. We have
packed all of our baggage & it has been carried down to the landing &
loaded onto the transports. & All the teams load with rations calculated to
last us six days. Some think if Pope deceives the enemy enough so as to draw
the greater part of their forces away from Richmond, then McClelelan will
rush his force to the rear & enter Richmond & hold it. One thing is evident -
that some great move is on foot to meet the enemy who are trying to anialate
both armies before we can get reinforcements. I trust they will not be success-
ful in their attempt. ... We have just received orders to be ready to march at
daybreak - two days rations. The mail is closed & this letter will be laid aside
& finished the first chance I can get to send it.

McClellan's grand strategy to end the war quickly had failed. After four months
of fighting and a combined 36,000 casualties, the Peninsula Campaign ended. Under
Halleck's orders, the Army of the Potomac began moving north to join up with Pope.
More than a week passed before Henry could complete his letter.

Chapter 5

"INCESSANT FIGHTING" IN MARYLAND

The Army of the Potomac began its retreat from the Peninsula Campaign by abandoning Harrison's Landing and marching back to Fort Monroe. Between August 22 and 27, Henry completed his letter from a week earlier and added two more letters as he recounted his experiences on this march. Just as Henry had feared, the Vermont Brigade was assigned as part of the rearguard covering the retreat. Due to the immensity of the retreating army and its supplies, the Vermont Brigade did not leave Harrison's Landing until Saturday, August 16, four days after the vanguard had departed. The baggage train ahead of them alone spanned twenty-five miles. On Sunday they crossed the Chickahominy using a pontoon bridge. They then continued their 80-mile march, retracing many of their steps of the early campaign.

> *Last Saturday we left Harrison's Landing - the last troops to leave. ... You have seen an account of our retreat from Harrisons Landing in the papers but one from one so nearly conected & having taken a part in it may be interesting to you if it is told. We left Harrison's Landing at about four P.M. & marched to Charles City Court House & encamped for the night. We feasted on roast corn & marched at break of day to the Chicahomine & crossed on a pontoon bridge an eighth of a mile long. Just at the mouth of the river our gunboats were placed along the banks of the river to defend our retreat forces. The next morning we started for Williamsburg & arrived there about three P.M. & reviewed our old battle grounds. It was nothing but the hand of providence that enabled Gen. McClelland to see their weak point & take advantage of it as he did. One of the rebil engineirs taken prisoner said that McClelland on arriving befor Yorktown instantly saw their only weak point & commenced work there. & it was useless for them to resist. It was a point that would [have] taken them a year to have*

discovered, so he said. The next day we marched to Yorktown. Arrived there about noon. Encamped for the night. I visited the old town & saw many old buildings occupied by the Revolutionary Generals as head Qts. There I saw large cannon mounted on evry batary or fort. Had it not been for the skill of our Gen. our whole army could have been sacreficed & the place not taken. The river was commanded by heavy Columbiads. From the Glouster side & Yorktown the enemy were obliged to leave all their works whole with their cannons to man them. The town was full of peach trees bending to the ground with their burden. In fact, the whole road on our march was shaded by peach, pear & apple trees. This is a fruit country. The next morning we marched to Great Bethel. Stoped for the night. There was but little to be seen there. The next day we marched to Hampton & stoped there two days & marched to Fortress Monroe. Arrived three P.M. & waited untill the next day about four P.M. when we embarked on the Empire City. Next we pushed out to sea & anchored there. ... We have had an awful march of over eighty miles. Many were worn out by it but had to march along the best they could. I was providentially favored & was well & marched through. I am very tired but my health is good. ... The report here is that Gen. McCleland has been deprived of his command. I hope not. We are expecting to see rough times befor snow flies & to see a speedy crushing of this rebellion. & It seems to me that a war of extermination will be necessary because the rebils are becoming so barbarous towards Pope's men.

The voyage at sea did not begin pleasantly for Henry, although it soon improved:

We left there [Hampton] Saturday & landed at Alexandria yesterday P. M. I had a sick time the first day the sea being so rough. But after a smart vomit I was relieved so that the roughest waters would not in the least affect me. ... I had a very pleasant trip up the Potomac. I had a very good view of Mt. Vernon & Ft. Washington.

While on board the steamboat, Sergeant Martin was informed that he had earned a promotion:

The Colonel called me down to his state room & said he wished me to report to the Capt. of Co. A as 2nd. Lieut. Also gave me some instructions & praise. He says it was something I have earnt in the different engagements & duty in camp.

Company A of the 4th Vermont shortly before Henry was reassigned
Courtesy of Vermont Historical Society

Although Henry seemed proud of the promotion, he also could not help but be concerned about the expenses involved in taking his new position:

> *I wish you could send me twenty five dollars as my necessary expenses in rigging anew will be large. It will take a months wages certain. I have got to buy a suit of clothes, swoard, sash, valise &c. of which cost heavy.*

A receipt saved from that time period shows that Henry ended up paying $72 for his sword (plus $1.50 to have his name engraved on it), $7.50 for the sword belt, and $25 for an ivory-handled Colt revolver. This total of $106 would be the equivalent of about $2,500 today.

After the boat docked at Alexandria, Henry took on a new role, serving as a provost guard:

> *We are expecting to go to Fredricksburg very soon. Our first destination was Aquia Crick but for some reason we were landed at Alexandria. Today I am on Provost Guard - a new business for me. I never saw so many drunken men before in my life. The streets & roads are lined with men dead drunk. The city is nearly deserted by citizens & the windows broken by the drunk soldiers. Many new troops have arrived & come to the seat of war. Their ranks are full & make a great show beside our thinned ranks. It seems strange that our numbers should be so small. Our regiments are not much*

larger than two or three companies of new troops. The new are anxious to fight but those that have seen service dread the future. They do not know what is for their good. We shall take matters cooly & stand in face of danger but are not so full of energy as the new men.

While the Army of the Potomac was slowly moving back toward its capital, General Pope's newly formed Army of Virginia was facing scattered attacks from their opponents. Jackson attacked one part of Pope's army at Cedar Mountain on August 9. When Longstreet began another engagement against Pope, Jackson used the opportunity to circle around and destroy Pope's supply depot at Manassas Junction on August 26. Henry reported on August 27:

Today a brigade of our troops took the cars and rode to the seat of war & were surprised & taken prisoners. Pope is retreating. All the contrabands are flocking to this city for protection. ... Pray for me that I may be kept & if called to face dangers on the field of battle I may be equal to whatever may be required of me - that my health may be preserved & I return once more to my home.

Pope was not retreating as Henry had been informed, but was attempting to locate and pursue Jackson. When he finally did so, Pope prepared for the battle, which took place on the familiar grounds of Bull Run on August 29. Thinking he had Jackson on the run, Pope attacked again the next day, not realizing that Longstreet's divisions had arrived. The result was another devastating defeat for the Union army, which began retreating from Bull Run toward Washington, D.C. just as it had done a year earlier. Second Bull Run, however, saw five times more casualties than the first encounter—about 20 percent of the combatants on both sides.

Henry did not have to worry about his courage this time, though, because he wasn't there. Although the Sixth Corps had arrived at Alexandria with orders to assist Pope's army, it had waited until all its supplies, horses, and ammunition had arrived and then marched out on August 29, proceeding very slowly. Although the men came within a few miles of Bull Run, they moved on toward Centreville and missed the entire battle. Historian Paul Zeller has noted that it had taken them fifty hours to arrive at this point, but only seven hours to return to their starting point in Alexandria. Some have concluded from this evidence that McClellan was less than enthusiastically supportive of Halleck and Pope's strategy and may actually have been doing what he could to thwart it. In his September 3 letter home, Henry, still strongly supporting McClellan, explained some of what had taken place:

We went to Manassas Junction & came very near having a part in the three days fight which you must have heard about. We have been having some of the most desparate bloody fighting that has occured since the commencement of this war. & The unequald Pope would have lost his whole army if it had not been for McClelland & his brave troops. They say that Pope plans no retreat. It seems very true. Last Friday about noon we were ordered to march with three days rations & went nearly to Fairfax & encamped. The next morning we resumed our march & about four P.M. we arrived at Centerville. But there being a very hard fight taking place on the old Bull Run ground we were ordered on & should [have] taken a part in the fight. But McDowel did not maintain his position at the Gap & let Gen. Longstreet & Lee in with heavy reinforcements. So the day was lost & we marched back to Centerville & took up a position in the old works.

Jackson was baged - cut off from all supplies & reinforcements. He had been in this condition for two days before we arrived & had our General done his duty we should [have] closed in upon him & taken evry thing he had. But as it is, he, Jackson, is in front of our fortifications at Harper's Ferry & Chain Bridge with one hundred thousand men. But we have hope as Gen. McClelland has taken command of the whole forces in Virginia. Not a day has passed since the fifteenth of Aug. without a battle & today the cannon are booming in the direction of Vienna. We have lost Gen. Carney, one of the most daring efitient officers in the service. Also Gen. Stevens & another. I do not remember his name. All good generals. Our officers are slaughtered in great numbers by sharpshooters. One of Hooker's Regts. went into battle with one hundred & forty men & returned with sixty men only. It has been nothing but slaughter on both sides. We have lost over twenty thousand men. When will this horrid work be stopped? Many think the day will be decided before another month expires. Jackson, I trust, will never return to Richmond & their only hope is to whip us before we get reinforcements. But I trust we shall be able to withstand any force brought against us. It appears to be the plan to let them come up to our fortifications arround Washington & let them spend their strength. ... This war is growing more & more desparate every day. The men are becoming hardened & fight like demons. Hardly a man expects to come out of battle alive so he goes determined to do all the execution he can. Some of the new men run at first fire & of course loose more men than if they stood up to the mark. Times look dark now but I trust a bright future is before us & hope & pray it may dawn soon. ...You would hardly know the boys. They are so black & care worn. They have not had hardly one good nights rest since the tenth of last March.

In the aftermath of Second Bull Run, Pope was exiled to the West to fight the Sioux, and McClellan now clearly controlled his army again. The next move was to attempt to locate the Confederate forces, which seemed intent on invading the North. Henry wrote a letter to Francis on September 12, describing the movements after Second Bull Run:

Your favor of Sept. 5 came to hand after we commenced our march for Jackson. Last Saturday we left Alexandria and marched to Darnestown just outside of Washington City. Arrived there about 2 P.M. Encamped in a field. Sunday we rested untill about 4 P.M. when we resumed the march & went about six miles on the road to Poolsville. We are passing through a delightful county. The roads are macademized & level. The farms & residences beautiful but all show the effects of slave labor. The men & women are very fat & indolent. Many strong secesh. At Barnsville our cavilry had a skirmish & many of the citizens joined the enemy & took part in the fight but they repented when they met our vetren cavilry. They could not stand a charge & were taken prisoners, wounded & killed. The old troops are better than new. Our generals will not trust them when exposed to danger. There is a new Regt. in Hancock's Brigade. But yesterday we were expecting a fight & advanced upon the enemy. But they gave away after exchangeing a few shots with our skirmishers. One man in the 3 Regt. was killed by Rebil Cavilry. Thus the anticipated [fight] ended & we took up a position. Then Hancock sent for his new men. Hancock's Brigade is in Smith's Division composed of Maine & Pennsylvania troops. Today we are intending to advance a little further. Perhaps will engage the enemy. We have heard that Jackson is in Pennsylvania & if our Generals are shrewd enough for him I am glad to hear it & I trust he will never see Virginia again. I suppose Gen. Wool is striking hard for his rear. His men are very destitute but will get supplies in abundance when he reaches Penn. He touchs nothing in Maryland without paying for it. He considers them all right.

Maryland resembles Vermont especially the part near Harpers Ferry. The roads are lined with fruit - peaches, apples, pears, quinces - the gardens & fields full of watermelons & evry thing that grows in Vermont gardens under high cultivation but here without any at all. The brooks are lined with grapevines full of ripe grapes. This is the only county I have seen preferable to Vt. Don't be disappointed if you do not hear from me as often as usual as we are on the march evry day & have no chance to write or send letters. This I wrote on my knee & perhaps it will not get to Washington for some days to come. Continue to write as usual & I shall get them some time. ... Our

Brigade is growing smaller evry day. The 5 Regts. do not number over 1400 men. The marches are so hard for the boys that the best, strongest men are obliged [to] fall out beside the road & get along the best they can. We have very poor medical attendance. The men are left to die beside the road alone.
My health continues good.

One day later (September 13), a somewhat more significant letter, wrapped around three cigars, was discovered by Federal soldiers at an abandoned Confederate campsite. General Lee's Special Order No. 191 revealed his planned troop movements through Maryland, including a proposed attack on Harpers Ferry. Lee had again daringly divided his invading army of 55,000. McClellan could see that he was closer to some of these Confederate forces than they were to each other. If he moved quickly with his massive army, he could overwhelm each portion of the Confederate force, ending the rebellion in the east. But McClellan did not move as quickly as some later analysts would have preferred. Concerned by intelligence reports indicating that Lee's combined forces were as much as twice his own, as well as Halleck's worries that the Special Order was a trick designed to trap the Army of the Potomac, McClellan moved his army cautiously, giving Lee time to bring much of his army back together.

South Mountain, the name for the Blue Ridge Mountains once they cross into Maryland, extended between McClellan and Lee. Having learned of McClellan's approach, Lee sent forces to try to block the mountain passes and thereby give the Confederates more time to reassemble their army. McClellan attacked to open up the passes for troop movement and to split the Confederate forces. General Burnside commanded the right wing, combining the First Corps under General Hooker and the Ninth Corps under General Jesse Reno, and attacked at Turner's Gap and Fox's Gap to the north. General Franklin's Sixth Corps, including the Vermont Brigade, attacked further south at Crampton's Gap. Both phases of this attack, which occurred on September 14, are known as the Battle of South Mountain. Confederate Major General Lafayette McLaws deployed just 2,100 men to defend Crampton's Gap against an approaching force of 12,800. The Confederates were positioned with infantry at the top of the mountain, artillery halfway down, and cavalry with more infantry toward the base, stationed behind a stone wall. They watched nervously for three hours as General Franklin moved his forces into position and carefully organized the attack. When it finally came, the Fourth Vermont led the charge across an open field toward the stone wall. The badly outnumbered Confederates retreated up the hill and were able to briefly hold on to the higher elevations before being overwhelmed.

Crampton's Gap

During the charge up the hill, a lieutenant in the Fourth Vermont took actions that earned him the Medal of Honor. First Lieutenant George Hooker, brother-in-law of financier James Fisk, rode ahead of his men and came upon a group of 116 Confederates. He ordered them to surrender, thereby singlehandedly capturing the entire Sixteenth Virginia regiment and its colors. The Sixth Corps suffered 533 casualties at Crampton's Gap to 887 for the Confederates. The fighting proved more difficult for the Federal forces in the two northern passes. Although Turner's Gap remained in Confederate control after nightfall, Lee decided that it was futile to try to hold these positions and ordered his men to retreat. They had served their purpose of delaying McClellan's advance, but now Lee needed them to help save his army.

Two days after the Battle of South Mountain, Henry described the fighting at Crampton's Gap in a letter home, written from "Camp near Burkittsville, Md":

Last Saturday we drove the enemy from Fredrick & crossed the mountains to Jeferson. Sunday morning the enemy attacked our right wing commanded by Gen Burnside. The attack was not commenced by us so our Generals prepared for them. We mooved forward within a mile of the mountain where the enemy had chosen an excellent position. It was the side of the mountain as steep a hill as where the poplars grow down by the cold hollow. It was well wooded. There is no place on your farm steeper. There was a heavy force secreted behind fences & trees & we had to drive them away under disadvantagerous circumstances and on top was a batery - also one on the side hill. Our Brigade was ordered forward & when we came in sight the shells began to fly. We marched about one-fourth of a mile & came to a vilage under the mountain. But the enemy did not let us alone but continued their work regardless of the inhabitants there or within two or three hundred yards. Finaly we arrived at the foot of the mountain & the bulets began to fly the whole length of the Regt. Immediately A, B, G are deployed as skirmishers & returned fire. Next we were ordered to advance into the open field which exposed us to a galling fire but soon the Regt. formed & started to charge. I gave the order to my skirmishers to double quick & kept in advance & on the left of the Regt. the shells & balls began to fly like hail. But our course was forward - let the circumstances be what they might. A solid shot struck within a foot of the Capt. of Co. F, covered him with dirt but did him no harm. But our line was kept perfect paying attention to nothing but their business. On arriving within a few rods of the enemy they broke & run but most of them gave themselves up as prisoners & over a hundred were taken. But we did not stop but rushed over the mountain & took up a position there which we have held ever since. We routed a great force of the enemy & all the next day the Rebils came in & gave themselves up numbering over 1,000 & officers of evry rank. On our right there was a slaughter averageing in killed ten Rebs to one Fed. - wounded one in six. The roads were lined with the dead. Luck favored us. We lost only two instantly killed & twelve wounded some mortaly. None of the Wmtown boys were hurt. Evry man conducted himself as men should. Not one turned but with a cheer pressed forward. We took a large number of knapsacks filled with all their clothing & evry thing else - also one cannon. We were favored by providence who directed the Gens. to strike at the weak point. A whole Brigade was double quicking up the mountain to surprise the enemy. We drove but had to disperse in evry direction to save their lives. Sunday we whiped them at evry point & slaughtered them by thousands. McClelland's men are the ones to take the brunt of all the battles. Evry day they are engaged but have never been whipped. ... Today we are not on the march but under marching orders to be in readiness to receive an attack from the enemy encamped in sight. But up to this time they have not appeared. On our right there was a severe fight. Have not heard the result. How long is this incesant fighting to continue? Ever since we left Washington the cannon have been booming on our right & left. A severe fight evry day. We are now on the Blue Ridge Mountains & within seven miles of Harpers Ferry. ... From what little I can learn we are doing good business & will crush the enemy soon. We must be patient & wait the Lord's appointed time. I trust the enemy will be shown their weekness & quit this slaughter. It is nothing else. I was never before exposed to such a galling fire. Many a bulet whistled seemingly very close to my head. But I did not feel any like dodging but felt perfectly cool & self posessed. Still you know it is a hard place to stand in. But trusting in the Lord to protect me, I go forward where ever I am ordered.

As it turned out, they were ordered to march to Antietam, where, just a day after he wrote of feeling overwhelmed by the bloodshed, he would be part of the bloodiest single-day battle of the war. The fighting started at dawn on September 17. Lee had been able to bring together an army of about 40,000 to face the attack that McClellan was finally willing to unleash. McClellan had 70,000 men, and the number would soon grow to almost 90,000. But that numerical advantage was somewhat offset by the ever-cautious general's decision to keep part of his army back in reserve, poised to counterattack the hoards of phantom rebels in whom "the Young Napoleon" so fervently believed, based on his intelligence reports. At approximately 5:30 a.m., Hooker's First Corps attacked down the Hagerstown Turnpike in an attempt to gain possession of the high ground around the Dunker Church. The Sixth Corps did not arrive from Burkittsville for another four and a half hours, and by that time the carnage was already well underway. Hooker's attack against Jackson's forces on Lee's left flank was stopped and then followed by disjointed charges by both sides across Miller's cornfield and around the Dunker Church. Heavy casualties mounted on both sides; by 7:30 a.m. Hooker had already suffered 2,500 casualties, and he achieved very little gain before becoming a casualty himself (shot in the foot). Mansfield's Twelfth Corps, approaching in a tight formation to Hooker's left, took particularly high casualties from the Confederate artillery. Two divisions from the Second Corps, under Sedgwick and French, mounted an attack to the left of the Twelfth Corps to take some of the pressure off them. Sumner, the Corps commander, leading Sedgwick's division himself, lost contact with French's division and launched an ill-fated attack on his own at about 9:00 a.m. After facing a strong artillery barrage, followed by a charge of three Confederate divisions from different directions, Sedgwick's division took 2,200 casualties and finally retreated.

When French's division was finally located, Sumner, on instructions from McClellan, ordered them to attack into the center of the Confederate lines in order to reduce the pressure on the Federal forces fighting in the West Woods. The woods were located to the right of the cornfield, where so many lives would be lost this day. Sumner's attack was against the division of D. H. Hill. Although Sumner had more than twice as many men, Hill positioned himself in a strong defensive location along a sunken road now remembered as "the Bloody Lane." French initiated the attack at about 9:30 a.m. Wave after wave of soldiers was sent forward and cut down by the intense Confederate fire from their tactical position. French's division of 5,700 men sustained 1,750 casualties in this attack. Between 10:00 and 11:00, in the midst of this fighting, the Sixth Corps finally arrived after a march from Burkittsville that had started at 5:30 a.m. They were ordered immediately into battle to support Union forces in the East Woods. French was beginning to give way as Confederate forces engaged in a counterattack, but, according to Henry, the Sixth Corps arrived just in time to "save the day" for the Union. In a letter to his father a week later, on September 24, Henry recalled:

One week ago last Sunday we had a fight at Berketsville a town at the foot of the Blue Ridge. The enemy had taken up a position at the foot of the mountain behind the fences & in the woods, a very strong position but we over come all obstacles & drove them in evry direction & took up a position the other side of the mountain & remained there untill Wednesday morning when we started for the battleground near SharpsBurg. Our Corps arrived just in time to save the day. We arrived about ten A.M. crossed the stream after which the battle was named, forded it & passed over to the right where the hardest of the fighting was going on & a part of our Division engaged the enemy & held them at bay. The enemy were determined to break the lines & charge upon our bataries seemingly as long as they had any men left. Certainly hardly a man escaped that charged upon our cannon. Next we were orderd down to the centre & drove the enemy from the field & took up a position there ready to repell any attack from [the] enemy. All this time the enemy were shelling us from two bataries. But a few shots took effect.

Franklin's Sixth Corps, 12,000 strong, established a position from which it might have launched a major attack on the beleaguered Confederate defenses. When Sumner refused to allow this charge, Franklin tried appealing directly to General McClellan to permit it. The Sixth Corps could have united with over 10,000 nearby troops from the Fifth Corps and 3,500 cavalry for the attack. McClellan, however, sided with Sumner, determining that it would not be prudent to initiate such an attack at that time. The Vermont Brigade remained in its position, about 170 yards from the Bloody Lane, for the next 48 hours. It was exposed to artillery shells, but no actual combat, for the remainder of the battle.

My company was orderd to the front as skirmishers. We deployed & advanced to the brow of the hill within about four hundred yards of the enemy. We halted & layed down to watch the moovements of the enemy. Soon we began to draw the shots of the enemy sharpshooters also some from their cannon, grape & canister shot & shell. The dirt flew in evry direction but Providentialy none of us were hit but a few in the Regt. were but none of the Williamstown boys. There we lay in sight of the enemy. Could see evry moove they made with their cannon. Four of our bataries were playing as smart as they could. The shells burst over the cannons killing horses & men but still they maintained their position till about night leaveing the ground coverd with the dead & wounded. The enemy were determined to whip us that day at whatever loss of life & Officers & men would fight untill shot down. It was the most desperate & fatal battles fought on this continent. The loss on both sides was enormous.

From this position Henry witnessed a great deal of killing as the battle raged on through the day and reinforcements arrived on both sides:

Regt. after Regt. were cut to pieces. The Irish Brigade went into battle with nearly two thousand men & came out with between six & seven hundred. One company had thirty eight & came out with only seven men. The battle was fought with the old troops principaly.

The battle continued throughout the day in a largely disjointed and uncoordinated fashion. Lee managed to move his troops into new positions well enough to overcome the numerical superiority of McClellan's massive army, which failed to break through Lee's defensive lines. However, Lee's attempt to invade the Union through Maryland had also failed, and, having lost almost one-third of his army, he began preparing to retreat south. McClellan's Fifth and Sixth Corps had done very little in the battle and could have spearheaded a new assault; however, he chose not to attack the next day and gave Lee the opportunity to withdraw.

Henry reported graphically on the carnage left behind after the bloodiest battle ever held on the American continent up to that point:

After the battle was the worst of sights. Evry house was filled to the brim as thick as they could lye. Still there was not room & all the barns were filled in the same way. Still there was lack of room. Nearly one hundred had to lye out of doors many remained on the field three days. Many did not have their wounds dressed for two days. Their wounds in some instances became magety – the dead had to be piled in heaps & burned as it was impossible to bury them. The enemy left all of their wounded on our hands when they retreated. The Rebil soldiers are getting a little sick of war but they cannot help themselves. They undergo evry imaginable privation dirty raged shoeless & no food to eat except green corn, potatoes &c.

The combined total of casualties was about 23,000. Listed among them was Lieutenant William Henry Martin. He had been injured early on but refused to take himself out of the fighting. Two days after the battle, the Sixth Corps was sent on a short-lived, token pursuit of Lee's army, but Henry was sent in another direction:

I was a little unfortunate as we were forming line of battle to charge if necessary. I ran a bayonet into the top of my foot just below the instep. That night I went to the hospital had my wound dressed. The next morning I was caried to another in the rear & remained untill last monday morning when

I left for Fredrick & arrived there too late to take the cars. The next day at three P.M. I started for Washington & arrived there about ten P.M. stayed in Soldiers rest & next morning I went up to the Avenue House & saw Mr Chauncy Smith. He invited me to stop with him untill my foot was well which offer I accepted thankfuly. My foot is not very badly hurt & is getting better evry day. The bayonet entering among the cords makes my foot very sore but not a dangerous wound so I do not wish you to be alarmed about me. I am in good hands. Mr Smith is very kind & says he is very glad to have me stop with him. My health is good but am very tired of it. ... All the Hospitals are full. Almost evry house is one. The old capital is nearly full & still there are more to come. Where is the room for them. ... I begin to long to see the end of this strife. Too many of our best young men are being sacreficed. This war has turned to slaughter the like has never been known before.

While he was recovering in Washington, writing each day from September 25 to 27, Henry composed a letter to Francis. In this letter he explained the aftermath of the injury further, while showing little interest in explaining how exactly this self-inflicted accident had occurred:

I hurt my foot about twelve o cloak but knowing my services might be needed before night as we are expecting the enemy to attack us evry moment. I would not leave the field. You know that evry man ought to be at his post then if ever as a person does not <u>closely</u> engage the enemy many times in a whole <u>year.</u> We are many times threatened. I have left my story. About ten P.M. my foot was so sore that I could hardly walk but I hobbled down to the barn where our Regt.'s wounded were left & stoped over night. The next morning I had my foot dressed. About eight I was sent with the rest of wounded in an ambulance to a house about a mile from the battleground. There they were so kind as to give me a bed in a small room with a dozen other wounded. Rather crowded but the whole house was the same & many had to lye out of doors. The next day I went down stairs & the cook told me I might stay with him. I gladly accepted. He gave me good food & did evry thing possible to make me comfortable. It was a dreadful place to stay. The house so crowded the wounded suffering so much, the amputation of limbs &c. The last was not so bad because they were under the influence of cloroform. I saw one limb taken off. It was done very quick. First the flesh was cut down to the bone the laps turned back then the bone was sawed off. The arteries and veins tied, the laps turned back & sewed together then bound up & kept wet in cold water.

Henry's drawing of an
amputation

I remained there untill Monday morning when I got a chance to ride to Fredrick in a government teem. I passed through Boonsville a pleasant little town filled with wounded. From there to Midletown. That was also full of the same. From there to Fredrick a beautiful place as large as Montpelier. There was evidence of great wealth. From there to the station. But being a little too late I stoped over night at a private house & slept in a <u>bed</u>. Next day at three I took the cars for Washington. Arrived at Baltimore about dark. Changed cars & arrived at Washington about eight P.M. Being late I stoped at the Soldier's Rest. Next morning I went to the Avenue House & met Mr. Smith at the door. He invited me to stop & I did. He had me take breakfast then showed me to his room where I now am enjoying myself.

Avenue House, where Henry convalesced with the aid of Chauncey Smith, was located on Pennsylvania Avenue between Seventh and Eighth Streets, just three short blocks from Ford's Theater. Its location would place it today across the street from the National Archives and adjacent to the United States Navy Memorial. Built in 1851, Avenue House sat above several shops operating at ground level. In 1885 the hotel site was converted into the first Saks Clothing Store, several years before Saks decided to relocate to Fifth Avenue in New York. In 1862, however, this location served as an excellent home base as Henry, despite his foot injury, managed to be a capital tourist once again. Thomas Lowrey demonstrates in *The Story the Soldiers Wouldn't Tell* that Washington at the time contained great contrasts of both splendor and debasement. The area now known as the Federal Triangle, which would have included Avenue House along its northern perimeter, "was then thirteen blocks of vice, a dense warren of low saloons, boisterous brothels, and hideouts for pimps, thieves, and pickpockets," Lowrey wrote. Washington's *Evening Star* reported that there were 450 officially registered houses of prostitution in the city in 1862. Henry either did not notice or chose not to relate any sordid details about the city, however:

Washington is a beautiful city. The publik buildings built of marble. The President's house & the grounds are the height of splendor. I can not describe them but you can not imagine too much. The Capitol dome is nearly finished. I wish you could see the building. It is now filled with wounded soldiers & on some accounts I think them more profitable occupants than congress men. The emancipation question creates considerable excitement here espetially among the negroes. It is generaly approved by the people of Washington.

I do not conjecture the result south but matters can not be much worse. One thing is certain - we are freeing ourselves of an awful curse & I trust by so doing we shall have the Lord on our side. There are some fine looking negroes some nearly as white as our people. Very inteligent capable men. I do not blame their masters for dislikeing to lose them so bad as they will hafto stir themselves & do something themselves. As it is the men & women are large fat & indolent. The negro does all their work so they stand & look on. They clothe the Rebil army. Their uniform is made of flax woven by the slave. A good uniform for an officer costs one hundred dollars.

Henry greatly enjoyed this break from the slaughter that he had been witnessing. On Friday, September 26, he added to his letter:

This morning is a pleasant one. The air is braceing & just warm enough. We breakfast about eight. Had potatoe, bisquit, fritters, cold bread, chicken, steak, coffee &c. We dine at three. Had yesterday halibut, potatoes, roast beef, cabbage, pickled beet, bread, pie & peaches. For tea about eight - warm toast, baked apples, cake, tea &c. So you see we have a variety. Mr. Smith says he intends to go to Vermont about Thanksgiving time if his business will permit. If he does I hope yours or Fathers & Mothers (I will pay an extra expense) hospitality will not fall short toards him. His has not toards me. I should have had a lonesome time if it was not for him. It seems like a seckond home & a very pleasant one because it is at Washington. Mr Smith is very busy at the present time making out a book [of] some kind for the Post Office department. He has got an excelent situation & I suppose is well paid for his services & I judge him worth a handsome property. He is growing gray but as sociable as ever. He takes a deep interest in the masonic lodges. How did he get into the Post Office Department? Major Lynde & wife passed through this place on their way to Fredricksburg to see their daughter. There her husband is in the southern army. Perhaps the Major will join him. On one side you will see a map. I have marked out some of my wanderings.

Mary, Isaac Lynde's second oldest daughter, married a soldier whom she had met at a western fort where her father was stationed, just as her older sister had done. Major Norman Fitzhugh was from Virginia, however, and when the war began he returned to fight for the Confederacy when called by his governor. Because he opposed secession, Fitzhugh agreed to enlist only if the word "volunteer" was removed from his oath. He then joined the Ninth Cavalry and became part of Jeb Stuart's staff, serving as Assistant Adjutant General to General Stuart. Henry's comment indicates that he may have accepted the accusations of some that his Uncle Isaac's surrender had been the result of southern sympathies. After the war, Isaac Lynde lived with the Fitzhughs in Florida until his death in 1886.

On Saturday the 27th, Henry concluded his letter to Francis:

> *Today my foot feels much better & shall return to my regiment before many days. The wound is healing fast - the soreness nearly gone. I took a walk this morning. I visited the [Smithsonian Institution] containing the curiosities. They are of the choicest specimens of birds, snakes, bears, sharks, turtles, aligators, fish of evry description, monkeys, paintings & statues & foreign presents brought from Japan & China by Com. Perry & in fact evry thing one could think of. I was very much interested in the curiosities. It is quite a lively time here. Troops are coming in. The rattle of army waggons besides many people from the north are here caring for their friends. I have not room to write more.*

Henry attended church with Chauncey on Sunday, and the next day he described the service in a letter to his parents:

> *There was not a very full congregation. Mr. Smith says there never is that the people of the city are very slack in attending divine service. In the evening the minister gave a lecture to young men. It was a good one. His text was taken from the pasages relating to King David & his son Absolum. He thought the young men were coming up in that fast disipated way & it was proving the ruin of not them alone but the country. His remarks were apt & truthful.*

On Tuesday, Henry was still enjoying his stay in the capital. He had also satisfied his curiosity about Chauncey's salary, reporting to his parents that Chauncey earned $1,600 a year in his postal clerk position.

> *Today is market day & the farmers evry one that has any thing for sale is apparently anxious to be on hand. The teems began to arrive about three A.M. with hay, apples, fruit of evry kind &c the market is full. After breakfast I took a walk. Also stoped and had my ambrotype taken which I will send in this letter. I wish you would have a case purchased so that it may be kept. I thought you would like to see how much a year has changed my countenance. I think there are but few that have changed less. I have been providentially favored with good health so that I have not grown old as fast as many. Some are so changed in their countenance as that you would hardly know them. They are, so far as looks are concerned, ten years older than when they left home.*
> *There is a great moovement among the new troops. The report is that one*

hundred & fifty thousand have passed over the Baltimore & Ohio railroad towards Harpers Ferry. Also that a very strong force has gone down towards Bull Run. I expect to hear before many days of hard fighting some where. I hope a decisive battle. If we can get a strong force in their rear we can do them great harm & in case of their defeat. If the General in command is a good one he will make short work of their baggage trains & retreating forces. These little air castles, if I may so term them, have been many time formed but we have never been able, thus far, to carry them out. For some reason after a battle when we have defeated the enemy our forces are to much exausted to follow them up & other Gens. placed in the most important commands hardly without lifting a finger, give up their positions & frustrate all our plans so that the little old army has all the work to do. There is some one to be greatly blamed for keeping Col. Miles in any command what ever. He had been courtmartialed & deprived of his command all summer untill the last battle. But I suppose the leak outs are ordered seemingly to get the north fairly awake, to let the Benedict Arnolds show themselves, to let the south have a fair trial of their strengths & make the people truly sick at heart of war.

Dixon Miles, a career military officer, was accused of being drunk during the First Battle of Bull Run (where he and his men had been kept in reserve). Although he was exonerated because he had taken the alcohol under doctor's orders, his reputation was badly damaged. Henry apparently did not find it appropriate that Miles was then given the rear area command of Harpers Ferry. When Jackson attacked this valuable strategic position on September 15, Miles surrendered after offering a feeble defense of his post. Over 12,000 men were captured. Miles himself was killed by a shell shortly after ordering the surrender. A court of inquiry that later investigated his conduct in the battle declared it to be "incapacity amounting almost to imbecility."

The next evening Henry started a letter to Francis, which he mistakenly dated as Wednesday, September 31, and which spanned the next five days. He had spent Wednesday once again casually walking around the city:

After breakfast I went up to the Post Office department. Read the news which was little of importance. Gen. McClelland's official report of the two last battles stating our loss in killed & wounded at about fifteen thousand. That of the enemy over twenty. We also took in the Antietam engagement fourteen thousand stands of arms. Also thirteen cannon. We lost more. They also think the enemy desparate to get hold of some forage some where even at great risks. They say the army is not inactive but little is known of their moovements. From the P.O. I took an omnibus & rode down to the Navy yard where extensive business in the war line is being carried on. Evry building is filled with workmen, some casting cannon, others finishing them, some filling shells, casting, making gun cariages, rifling cannon, repairing gunboats & in fact, almost evry thing was being done. Also a lot of the old cannon taken at Norfolk were there. Some new mortars four feet in diameter. I saw one of the fifteen inch shells to be used in the new moniters. I hope there never will be any of the kind thrown at me. They are filled with musket balls. The yard is very pleasantly situated. There are a great many buildings & work shops in abundance. The horse railroad was finished to there today. It is a great improvement to the omnibus. You can ride miles for five cents.

After dinner I went up to a hospital to see some of the wounded & sick which are doing well. I steped to the door & saw companies of citizens drilling themselves [as]homeguards. I hope to see them go forth if called upon.

There were more places to visit the next day, including the Treasury Department where a former Williamstown friend, James Delano, was working as a clerk.

This new month I trust will be an eventful one for hostilities cannot, with justice to the soldiers, be continued longer. The rainy season commences next month rendering army moovements very hard & improfitable. This morning papers state firing to have been heard in the direction of Winchester. No news of importance. I went up to the Treasury dept. Saw Mr. Delano. I inquired about the Ainsworth boys. Henry has stoped business. Charles is not doing much. He has lost a great deal in one way & another. Also is dissipated. He says Josh Hatch is becoming quite a noted man west & has occupied prominent public position. I did not stop long. He is coming down after he finishes his days labors. I went past the President's house. Also the statue of Andrew Jackson. He is mounted on his dashing steed. It is a splendid thing. The grounds arround are beautifuly laid out in walk &c. The trees are full grown, the shrubery beautifuly trimmed, seats under all the pleasant shades &c. Tomorrow I intend visiting the President's east rooms. Mr. Smith says it is an elegant one. The yard in front is three sided. A road runs around it. You can imagine with what taste the yard would be arranged. There is any quantity of weeping willows here. They are a splendid tree. I would like to see them growing in Vermont.

Friday brought the planned visit to the White House:

Another pleasant morning has dawned upon us. The breezes are warm & the heat of the sun causes the sweat to flow freely. We have not had a frost yet. I visited the President's house. The east room is dashing & magnificent. Two chandaliers with any number of lights & hundreds of dangling pearls such as you have seen attached to centre table lamps making a splendid show. Certainly in the night. The curtains, looking glasses, carpets & furniture was obtained regardless of cost.

On Saturday, Henry indulged himself in an additional big-city experience:

This morning I took a bath for the first time in a public bath house. It surpassed natures bath conveniences. I enjoyed it much & have decided if I ever happen this way again I shall call. I supose you have tried them yourself. ... I visited the Patent Office building this afternoon & saw as usual at such places evry thing & still did not see hardly over half. There were models of all the inventions from what time I do not know. I saw the swoard worn by Washington while in the service. Also his suit worn the day of his resignation. Also his camp chest used during all his campaigns. Also presents of Turkish sabers, guns & Japanise saddle, bridle &c. All very rich. Many of their silk suits. On the whole one can little imagine what there is to be seen - so much of evry thing is there exhibited. ... The morning papers state that Jef threatens to raise the black flag if the emancipation bill is put in force. Also that he is impressing thousands in Virginia from the vacinity formerly occupied by our forces but they say they will not fire a gun. Also own that their army is becoming demoralized. I am sorry to hear that the nine months troops have not been officered by experienced men. Men that have been tried & shown themselves equal to their tasks. But, I see that they are all new & it is generaly the case & to us their gunnery is quite amusing.

Henry finally concluded his long letter on Sunday:

After I retired last night Mr. Smith brought me a letter from you containing two drafts. I was glad to receive a letter from you while here but it was more than I expected. I have decided to return tomorrow or next day to Hagerstown. As for geting a leave of absence about Thanksgiving time I doubt my being able. If we continue in the field it will be impossible except in case of sickness. We are closely confined to our business but there is nothing known without trying which I will do.

Henry had enjoyed this break from the war, but it was now time to rejoin his regiment. He had intended to leave on Monday, October 6, but he was persuaded to remain in the capital one more day. In his next letter home, he also expressed his view of the significance of the Emancipation Proclamation on September 23:

At the urgent request of Mr. Smith I stop till tomorrow morning. It was my intention to have left today. He wished me to remain & visit some Vermonters. Last night I attended the evening service. The minister is a native of Vermont. I do not recollect his name. His text was about God's course towards the ancient city of Ninivah. I think it was that place. Certainly it was the one which Jonah prophesied against. He considered that God did carry out the course he said he would. The dreadful sin was repented of or destroyed leaving it a new city. He also considered we were going through nearly the same process of cleansing & trusted that the people were coming to see the enormity of their crimes & repent in time to save the nation. One thing was certain - destruction or an unparalled future are before us and are finaly striking at the root of the rebelion by the abolishing of slavery - the acknowledged cause of the war. After service we called upon a Miss Caroline Buck formerly from Chelsea. Perhaps you used to know her. She is an old maid living to benefit others. She is very kind to the sick soldiers, visits them & sends them many luxeries. She is quite agreeable & is well posted in army moovements &c.

Miss Buck was not the only female acquaintance to whom Henry had been introduced, but he chose not to mention the others in his detailed accounts of his Washington visit to his parents. A few days after Henry's return to his regiment, Chauncey sent him a letter:

I drop you a line this morning principally to say that I have received a small bundle for you, and shall send it up so soon as may safely be. It came by "Express" and I presume is from your parents, and presume it contains light articles of clothing, as the bundle is light. I shall go down to the government storehouse and push it along this evening, or soon as possible.

Have no news to mention, either from home, about this city, or from any friends. Have not seen Nellie or Hattie since you left, but doubt not they were _well_ pleased with our "call".

Hattie Coyle was the twenty-one-year-old daughter of a wealthy merchant in Washington, D.C. Now that Henry was back in camp, he could finish (on October 11) the letter home that he had started on October 6:

Today I am sitting in my tent a mile out of Hagerstown. I arrived yesterday morning. I left Washington Wednesday about eleven A. M. & arrived at Fredrick about nine P.M. There I spent the night. The next day I took a pasage on the stage for my regiment. It was about twenty miles. The entire road was macademised as the most of the roads are in the state. The people are very old fashioned in dress & in their ways of performing their labor. But, they sow their grain with a machine & cut it with one also. Let the machine remain out of doors the remainder of the season. They have large stone barns & log houses. They use horses for all purposes. They are very large averaging twelve & fourteen hundred lbs. a piece. They plough with three abreast & drive them with one rain just as our government teemsters drive six horses or mules. Their daughters are generly plain looking. In fact I have hardly seen a handsome girl in the whole state. On arriveing at Hagerstown I found evry hotel full & was troubled to get lodgeing for the night. The reason is that so many citizens are comeing here to see the old battleground at Sharpsburg. It is a money making time for some. I suppose it is not the case evry where. The next morning I went to the Regt. They were all glad to see me back. They heard that I had got to lose my foot. I find the old soldiers a hard looking set of men - dirty, black, worn out fellows. I should think it would frighten the recruits. About eleven P.M. the Brigade was called out to be ready to resist an attack of the enemy cavilry which had crossed at Williamsport but they did not come. Still we had to be ready & slept on their arms all night.

Henry was referring to Jeb Stuart's cavalry raid, which had instead occurred at Chambersburg, destroying a significant amount of army supplies at the railroad depot. Stuart also left with 1,200 of the Union army's horses.

The Vermont Brigade was experiencing some unwanted changes. The Twenty-Sixth New Jersey Infantry became a part of their brigade, so it no longer consisted solely of proud Vermonters. Also, it lost its commander as General Brooks was promoted to command the First Division of the Sixth Corps. Henry commented on these changes in a letter home from Hagerstown on October 20:

It has been some time since I have received a letter from home. My last was from Frank acknowledgeing the receit of my ambrotype &c. I cannot see the reason why we cannot receive regular mails as we are located only one half mile from the railroad from Harisburg, Pen. - a safe line & only a short distance from Washington.

I suppose cold weather has commenced in earnest. We think it has here. We suffer considerable nights but nothing as bad as last year. At this time we have not had any frosts yet but the dews are very heavy, nearly equal to a shower. Our acommodations are not as good as last year. We have nothing but small tents that hold four men. The tents are the ones they started with last spring but we hope we shall be permitted to go into baracks soon. It is talked of if we remain here this winter, we shall have easy times. The only duty our Brigade & City guard all numbering about two hundred men a day. We have been strengthened considerable by the arrival of recruits. Also a Jersey Regt. has joined the Brigade. It is nearly as long as our whole Brigade. The men appear very green to us & appear to think they can do as they please. They have been in the habit of running the guard & it was my fortune to have them to deal with. Twice I was called up to the Gens. & told that the men persisted in disregarding the guard & was told to put a stop to it. So I went up to the posts where they troubled & instructed my guard to load his piece & shoot the first man that would not halt when told. Which would be justifyable for a guard is not to be trifled with. But to my gratification, I had no more trouble.

Today we received information that General Brooks was promoted Major General & to command Slocum's Division. All the officers of the Brigade met to see what present to make him & concluded to raise one hundred dollars to a Regt. What they will do with it I do not know. The men feel sorry to loose him, not withstanding his rigid discipline. He has prooved himself a wise officer. We fear we shall not get another one as good. We have got a new Chaplain. His name is Roberts from Chelsea. I believe he was methodist preacher. I hope he will do more than our old one has. It was as well to be without as to have a man that did nothing.

A letter arrived from Chauncey, dated October 22, informing Henry about the progress of his package and also mentioning that he had "not seen Hattie or Nellie since your call, but I presume both are well, and would send a world of 'good wishes' if they knew I was writing." He also reported that large numbers of soldiers were arriving every day in the city. The belief among local residents was that a great Confederate army must be forming nearby. Chauncey assumed that the Army of the Potomac would soon be on the move to meet them and that, as a result, Henry would miss the package. The Vermont Brigade remained stationary, however, and spent the week engaged in various reviews. Henry described the week to his brother on October 24.

I wrote Father & expected to get a letter from some of you before this but we have had only one mail since that brought me one from Mr. C. Smith. I can not imagine why we are so neglected about our mail matters. When we were on the Chickahomnia & only five or six miles from Richmond we had our daily mail but since we have retired from the dangerous position of the front they seem to think we do not need any mail. It seems to me that I shall have a big mail when it gets along. Certainly it has been a long time accumulateing.

This week has been a week of reviews. Sunday a Brigade by Gen. Brooks for the last time. Tuesday the Brigade was reviewed by Major Generals Franklin & Smith. Thursday a Division Review by the same Generals. The Division was not much larger than one Brigade last fall. It created considerable curiosity on the part of the inhabitants in the vicinity. It is expected that Gen. Smith is to command this Corps. Franklin to command the right wing of McClelland's army. Brooks to command Slocums old Division. We are all sorry to have him leave as we see no one to fill his place. Certainly Col Whiting is not & Colnel Stoughton is to young & ambitious & Col. Lord I think the best but doubt his geting it. What we want now is the ablest men of the nation. We are passed the pomp & show of war & want nothing but substantial. Our Lieut. Colnel is quite sick at Hagerstown. He is very young & hardly fited to fill the important position he now occupies. His rule during the absence of the Colnel has been unsatisfactory to the Officers of the Regiment & Brigade very partial & tyrannical. The major is incompetent to fill his position & I think it probable he will be invited to resign. They were greatly disgusted with him at the review. I do not wish to have the above get out as coming from me. Colnel Lord returned to his Regt this morning. He was hartily cheered by his men. He has been away for a long time. The report is that the twelveth Regiment is to join this Brigade. I hope it will.

The Williamstown boys are generaly well. Charles Lynde is the poorest of them. He is troubled with the chronic diareha. That is the worst thing we can have as no medicine will take least affect. If they could go home they might get better. But the exposure & food is very bad.

Although Henry ruled out Colonel Henry Whiting as an appropriate replacement for General Brooks—probably because many Vermont soldiers believed he acted cowardly during battles—Whiting was nevertheless chosen as the new commander of the Vermont Brigade.

The regiment was still in the vicinity of Hagerstown on October 28; however, Henry's letter to Francis indicated that they were about to move out.

Yours bareing date October 23 was received yesterday Oct. 27 coming very direct from home. This is the second one received since I joined my Regt. That was one from Father bareing date Oct. 8. I suppose there must be a number of letters some where on the road. The most of our stuff goes to Harpers Fery - Hagerstown being off the principal army roads.

Yesterday I received a letter from Mr. C. Smith & enclosing a bill of the bundle which he has forwarded to me. It has not arrived yet. I have received the box sent last Aug. containing tea, sugar &c. It came to hand just the night we received orders to march to Centerville but I was a little fortunate in being so that I could save all. I put all except a haversack full into our mess chest. That sent, the rest of the boxes had to be disposed of as circumstances would permit. Much was sold. The remainder put in haversacks. On the whole I think it unwise to send boxes in warm weather or when we are not stationed at a permanant camp. Last night we received [orders] to be in readiness to march at an early hour on the morow but the time has come & passed but we are still here but may moove before night or in the course of a day or two. Mr. Smith said it was expected we should advance soon & that troops had been arriving evry day since I left. Also that he saw Denison Martin's son from the twelvth Vt. The Regt. is camped back of the Capital on Capital hill. They are enjoying good health. It reported that our General has been trying to get them to join our Brigade. I hope they will as we want nothing but Vermonters with us.

Dennison Martin's son, Carlos Martin, saw his term with the Twelfth Vermont end just after the Battle of Gettysburg. For a bounty of $315 he soon rejoined the war effort, this time with the Eighth Vermont, and remained with them for the rest of the war.

Three days later Henry added, "We are at Williamsport but leave for Boonsboro tomorrow & from there I do not know where. Some say to South Carolina & some to Washington." As it turned out, they were heading back to Virginia. Lee had again divided his army, with Jackson back in the Shenandoah Valley. McClellan was hoping that the Army of the Potomac could engage Longstreet's corps alone. Henry wrote to Frank on November 4 from Snicker's Pass, Virginia, describing their movement:

We are again on the march for Richmond. We left Hagerstown last month to Wmport. First day marched from there to Boonsboro, twelve miles. Next morning to Berlin, six miles below Harpers Fry. Stoped over night & next morning took up our march into old Virginia. We all dreaded entering the state again. The usual welcome-the booming of cannon was distinctly heard. Fighting commenced three days ago & has not ceased yet. First our men were driven but yesterday we drove them regained our old ground & still hold it. Today we marched fifteen miles or more to reinforce at this pass. We were hurried up as fast as possible for the enemy tried to break our line but did not make out. The enemy are reported to be in very strong force here & Gens. Jackson & Lee are concentrating their entire force here. They are in a close place & it will be a miricle if they get to Richmond as soon as we do. I hope that we shall be able to hold these here while other columns advance on their capitol. I suppose before many days there will be a general battle.

While marching through Maryland I noticed many nice conviences & buildings. The barns are built of stone, in many instances being better than their houses. Their women are all homely & many are extensive slave owners. Their children lasy & feel very important. Many are very ignorant & extremely old fashioned. Their work is done in the old way still they use a great deal of machinery. All their grain is sowed by machine & rept by the same. Ground planted to corn is loosened by a cultivator or first the corn is cut & then the cultivator run between the rows & then it is ready for the sowing machine. The grain is up now & looks finely. Also the weather is very fine being warm. But, strange to say, these expensive machines are not housed at all but left where last used. One thing I noticed worth imitating - they are ovens for baking bread or any thing else. They are built out of doors in some convenient place & there all the baking is done & well done too.

It seems to be our luck to visit all our old battle grounds & to see what we have done seems miraculous. At Burketville nothing but generalship could have carried that mountain. But I hope not to retrace our steps from Richmond as we did before.

Two days later Henry added:

We are now on our way to Thorofare Gap making forced marches. Fighting has been going on day & night but we have not been engaged yet. Today news came that the enemy were recrossing at Williamsport. It shows a desparate condition of their affairs. Heavy firing is heard on our left.

On November 6, the army paused and Henry had time to begin what became a long letter to his father from "Camp Near White Plains & Cramptons Pass on Manassas Gap Railroad":

We have at length arrived at the Gap we started for. We arrived today 1 P.M. We have marched over 75 miles since the first of November. I never had an easier march before. It is on account of the cool weather & hardly a man thinks of falling out on account of fatigue. The enemy continues to retreat as we advance & probably will untill they reach Richmond. What force they have left in the Shanandoah I do not know but I hope it is a large one & we shall effectualy cut them off from Richmond. Evry thing seems to work well. Our soldiers are rather hard on the secesh & unmanageble. In one instance they were insulted by a secesh woman by slamming the door in their faces so down came the door & almost evry thing in the house was taken. Also their *sheep & hogs. I could not blame them much. Also a number of hives of honey were taken tonight. ... I like Captain Pratt very much. He is kind & obliging but I have had to be in command of the company for a long time. He is acting Major. Our Liut. Colnel is sick & gone home so we have only our field officers in command of the Regiment.*

Two days later, on November 8, Henry added more about their upcoming plans and the jockeying for position among the officers. Ironically, he was not yet aware that a day earlier Lincoln had altered both the chain of command and the upcoming battle plans by relieving General McClellan of his command.

We are now within one hours ride of Washington. We expect to march tomorrow morning. I expect towards Culpeper as we are acting as reserve. We are not hurried along as those in front. Franklin's Corp is very large & composed of Smiths - Couches & Brooks Divisions. All of which have been reinforced by one or two Regiments to each Brigade. It seems that when the enemy hear of Franklin's approach they retire. It is an excelent time for campaigning. The weather is rather cold & yesterday it snowed all day but today it is quite warm. Evry night we encamp in the woods & so have plenty of wood to keep us warm. Still we suffer some. The country is pleasant but the people are strong secesh.

Yesterday we received a new Brigade Commander Gen. Howe. I saw him this morning about some men from my company in the guard house. He appeared very polite & kind. I was much pleased with him. Colonel Stoughton commands a Brigade in Brook's Division & takes one of his aids from this Regiment. Also Gen. Brooks takes two with him making a number of vacancies. My Captain had the promise of Majors berth today.

Also there is a vacancy of a Captain in Co. E & there will be another soon if my Captain gets it. Captain Platt has been working for it a long time & if he dont get it he will resign. It will not be much regreted. Thus you see how ambitious men act when disappointed. Its rumerd the Lieut. Colonel will not come back again. He was not very well liked by the line officers. He is not twenty one years of age yet. He has not as old head on his sholders as his brother - consequently more boyish but very smart. ... At your request I will tell all I know about the Williamstown Volunteers. The Wilsons are good soldiers & healthy but are not so strong minded as they should be. Henry Smith & the Clarks do well & are regardless of all evil influences & in good health. The rest are about the same as to health but principles I do not wish to say any thing about. Billy is looking well & enjoys the life much. A number of the boys in the Sixth Regiment are in the hospitals. George Howard of the third Regt. has been promoted 2nd Lieut. He was color barer for a long time.

A short addition on November 9 was written from "Camp near New Baltimore. Six miles from Warrenton & the same distance from the Orange & Alexandria Railroad":

At seven A.M we started for our present destination & arrived about two P.M. The weather is very cold but when marching we keep warm. We passed through Thoroughfare Gap, passed down Ford mountain to the right of Pond Mt. The mountains are very steep and rocky. The people are very strong sesech & will take none but Richmond money but we are supplied. Quite a lot was found on the dead rebils.

Gen. Sigel left here last night. Also a report is curant that McClelland is superseded by Burnside. If so I fear we are lost & soon shall suffer a terrible defeat.

The rumor was soon confirmed. General Burnside had previously rejected Lincoln's offer to command the army, but faced with the prospect of seeing General Hooker take command, Burnside relented. On November 10, McClellan gave his farewell address to the Army of the Potomac in New Baltimore. Henry reported the events of the day:

This morning we received orders to be ready to go on picket at half past twelve P.M. so we prepaired for it. Next came the order to fall in immediately to Cheer McClelland which we did & such hearty cheers you do not often hear but he appeared very sober. His eyes looked very red & as he rode along the lines he appeard to a deep interest in his old army & Officers & afterwards we learned the reason why. It was his last review of his men who had done so much under him. His successor Burnside rode immediately behind him. Also nearly all of the Generals of his old army. It is quite a sight to see the Chief Commander of the army & Staff Composed of Generals, Colnels, Majors, Captains & down to privates. Also a body guard of five hundred or a thousand cavilry & evry thing, shining horses prancing, bands playing &c but why he should be superceded just in the middle of a moove I can not imagine but as Sen. Foot says I hope rebil property shall no longer be protected. The democrats say it is because he is one of their party. This party spirit is in our men & it seems to rage very extensively evry whare.

Regardless of whether McClellan's dismissal was for military or political reasons, the Army of the Potomac was about to invade Virginia with a new plan and under new leadership.

Chapter 6

FREDERICKSBURG

In an attempt to make the Army of the Potomac less unwieldy and more efficient, General Burnside reorganized it into three Grand Divisions, each consisting of two corps, under the leadership of Sumner, Hooker, and Franklin. William "Baldy" Smith moved up to head the Sixth Corps in Franklin's Left Grand Division. Smith in turn was replaced by Albion P. Howe as commander of the Second Division, within which the Vermont Brigade was now under Colonel Henry Whiting as its previous leader, William T. H. Brooks, took command of Smith's First Division.

Despite Burnside's changes, for the common soldier disorganization and confusion remained a part of everyday life, as Henry explained in a November 14 entry within the long letter that he had started on November 6:

> *After the review the new General was anxious to see us drill so we had a Batalion Brigade drill which was not very agreeable to us. We were kept there untill twelve & dismissed at half-past. We were ordered on picket. We went out about six miles. It was very cold. We were expecting the rebel Gurilas, but they did not come during the night. It was extremely cold the next morning. I breakfasted at a house. It was a rather coarse one. They had no wheat flour, consequently, no bread, but very good hoecake. For meat musty ham. Coffee I should think parched corn, for sweetening honey. They were destitute of coffee, Sugar, & salt. Their butter was very poor like all Virginia butter. They are destitute of salt to an alarming extent. Two bushels of salt were sold a short time since for one hundred dollars. Sugar for 26 a lb. They complain biterly & curse the*

General William F. Smith
Courtesy of Library of Congress

Yankees so much the harder. Also our cavilry take all the horses they can find
& appropriate them for their own use. About nine we received information
that we should be relieved at one P. M. One P.M. came but no relief & nine
P. M. came & no relief so we prepared for another night. But about ten we
were ordered into camp. After marching about two miles we came to a picket
line. The Officer of the picket had neglected to inform us of the change in the
line which he should have done & we should have returned to camp in good
season. So you can see how we fare some times. We lost two nights sleep.

As usual, Henry was also observing the local people and customs and making comparisons to his home state:

I wish you could come down to Virginia & see how old fashioned the people
are. The remotest corners of Vermont are no comparison and they are all very
hombly. Also they ride horseback invariably even the women. I saw a man &
his mother on the same horse. It was quite a curious sight & even the poor-
est have two or three slaves. The owners are fat, tyrannical & lazy. It is not
strange they dislike being changed by the North. Slavery will of its self lead to
despotic rule in a short time.

When he finally concluded his letter the next day, Henry indicated some second thoughts about the quality of McClellan's performance, yet he displayed little optimism about the appointment of General Burnside:

One unaccountable delay was made at Antietam. Why did McClelland not
follow up that retreating army who were in great confusion as it has since
proved to be the case & take their common baggage & the like has occurred a
number of times.

Last night I received a letter from Francis. I was glad to learn that you
had finished cutting willows. I hope you will dispose of them more readily
than this year & probably will if the war is closed but I do not think it can
be for years to come. I hope Burnside will follow up his success if he has any.

Burnside was under pressure from President Lincoln to succeed quickly, because January 1, 1863—the date when the Emancipation Proclamation would go into effect—was rapidly approaching and for political reasons a military victory prior to that event was most desirable. Without immediate military success, the proclamation might appear to be an act of desperation taken out of weakness. Burnside responded with a plan under which the army feigned making a forward movement between Lee and Jackson into the Shenandoah Valley and then instead moved quickly towards Fredericksburg, planning to cross on pontoon bridges that would be secretly moved into the area as the army arrived. After crossing the Rappahannock, the army could proceed toward Richmond. Lee would be forced into trying to catch up with the Army of the Potomac and would have no choice but to attack into the defensive positions that Burnside would establish. The strategy could succeed, but only if the timing was right and everything fell into place as planned.

Henry's next letter, written to Francis, attested to the speed at which the army was moving toward Fredericksburg, although he was unaware of Burnside's overall strategy. The letter began on November 16 at "Camp Near Catlets Station, Virginia," the location where, prior to Second Bull Run, Jeb Stuart had audaciously attacked and gained possession of General Pope's supply depot and absconded with Pope's personal baggage including his dispatch book. Intelligence from that book had helped to convince Lee to attack Pope.

> *I acknowledged the receit of your last letter in my last to Father. It arrived before we took up our march for Aquia Crick. The next morning we left New Baltimore at six A.M. & marched to Catlets Station where General Popes baggage was taken. It is not much of a place, only a house & Railroad Depot. It seems strange that he should have not guarded his rear better. It must have occasioned great rejoicing among the Rebils. The march was a hard one of fifteen miles. We encamped about three P.M. & then the usual forrageing parties started out killing hogs, sheep, cattle hens turkeys ducks gease & robing beehives & evry thing they could lay their hands on. Old Col Whiting tried to prevent it but could not. I favor the Soldiers in takeing all they can find. By protecting their property we are ading to the leangth of this rebelion. If a Union man give him a quartermasters [certificate] & he can get his pay of Uncle Sam but not leave any thing to support of the enemy.*

Two days later, Henry added a few lines from "Camp Near Elktown, Va":

> *Another days hard march & within twelve miles of Fredricksburg. Nothing of intrest occured during the day. The country is very desolate & rather swampy. The usual depredations were committed after dark.*

The next entry, on November 20, was from "Camp Near Stafford Court House":

> *Yesterday we arrived at the above destination. It is within three or four miles of Aquia Crick & the Potomac River. What we can be here for I cannot immagine. To day the report is that the enemy are in strong force at New Baltimore. If we have got to fight the enemy front & rear I guess we shall have hard times*

but trusting in the ability of our General Franklin that he will bring us out all right we rest easy. Let our position be ever so precarious. We have been soldiers long enough not to borrow any trouble under any circumstances. During the last campaign we have been destitute of news. It seems hard but I trust all for the best. The old saying is that while in ignorance is peace & security. Some have said that we were going to Galveston Texas under Banks. I should like to go there for some reasons, one is we should not see as hard fighting there as here.

You spoke of my coming home to Thanksgiving which I would gladly do & a little expected to be able to then but now it is past all hope as another campaign is well advanced & nothing but sickness or a resignation would let me off. It is with me as with all the rest. The only thing that keeps us in the service is a duty we owe to our country.

Yesterday a rebil Soldier with all his equipments was found in a closet up stairs. I do not imagine his is the only one that might be found if they had searched houses.

Henry wrote to Chauncey Smith around the same time, thanking him for a package and giving a short recap of their recent march:

The bundle sent did not arrive before we left but I was so fortunate as to get it at Williamsport. It came just in time. The next day we left there and have been on the march ever since & been out of reach of nearly all mails & express. After leaving Williamsport we went direct to the Potomac. Crossed at Berlin. From there to Lovetzville then to Snickers Gap. Next to Union. Crossed the mountain by way of Middleburg down to White Plains. From there to Thoroughfare Gap. Stoped & got rations. Then went to New Baltimore. Stoped there three or four days & got some clothing & a new stock of provisions & started on. We left New Baltimore at six A.M. & arrived at Catletts Station or Weaverstown a distance of about sixteen miles. ... The next morning we left for Aqui Creek. We were expecting to go to Fredricksburg. If we had I should have tried to have found Major Lyndes daughter. Do you know what her husbands name is? It would not be surprising if we should go there before many days. Heavy firing was heard in that direction day before yesterday. The cause or result I have not learnt as we have not received but little news of late. Your papers were welcomed by Charles & myself. I received a daily from home containing Senator Foots speech. It was very interesting & spoke my views exactly. I hope this will be a very short campaign as we shall suffer dreadfully with our present accommodations. We have nothing but the small shelter tents & a blanket & overcoat &c for comfort. It is very cold nights. Fortunately there is plenty of woodland in the vicinity of Richmond. ... What do the people think of McClellan being superceded. It was hard to believe here but I suppose the President was compelled to do it & if stories are true he ought to have been a long time ago. I hope Burnside will push the enemy so that they will cry for peace. Today it is reported that the enemy are in strong force at New Baltimore. I should like to know why they are there.

Please excuse my not paying the postage but we are destitute of postage stamps & cannot do any better. Please excuse this letter as it was written in haste & a very few spare moments to do it in. I have been in command of the company the most of the time since I left Washington. The Capt is acting Maj of the Regt. The first Liut is on Gen. Brooks staff.

The health of the army was never better. The Williamstown boys are all well. Charles is much stronger than at any time before. Please answer at your earliest convenience & tell all the news. Also give my respects to Hattie & Nellie.

Despite being busy with his added duties and the army's rapid movement, Henry managed to make several entries during the next week, beginning November 21, in a letter to his parents. It appears that the talk among the soldiers was turning more strongly against McClellan and that the unfolding of Burnside's plan was providing renewed optimism:

Have you seen the French Princes account of his experience under McClellan? It is a good report & he thought the cause of our failure in that campaign was our slowness. One thing is certain. He never followed up a retreating army as he should. At Antietam if he had pressed on the next day he might have captured nearly all their artilary & baggage. This is not an isolated case. A number of opportunities have presented themselves but not improved. ... Today the news is very encourageing. The report is that Jackson is left in our rear with seventy five thousand men. That we have efectualy out wited him by feigning an attack on Gordensville so drawing his attentions there while we sliped by him to Fredricksburg & we are six days march of Richmond while he is twelve. I should be rejoiced to hear of his unconditional surender. His name seems to be a teror to some of our Generals. ...The rainy season I fear is upon us. The clouds have been very dark for the past four or five days & occasionally a little rain. What little has fallen has made the roads very bad. The soil is peculiar. Two thirds red clay & not very productive except of white pines. What few inhabitants there are own the entire lands & are very rich. Also own a large number of slaves. These people are awful liars. When

*asked if they have anything to sell they answer they have nothing anyway.
Upon that the soldiers satisfy themselves by a search & always find any quantity of potatoes, turnips, apples &c, &c so they help themselves. ...*

On Tuesday, November 25, Henry presented more of his thoughts on slavery
and southern society:

*Today it is clear comfortable & the mud is fast drying up. Yesterday we went
on picket & stayed twenty four hours. Then I saw some thing that may interest you. You have read of hermits living in caves &c. As I was posting my
pickets I saw a little log hut eight by ten & no larger located near the mouth
source of Aquia Crick on a bluff very baren & a mile from any neighbors &
off from the road. The hut contained two old maid sisters very strong secesh
& very aristocratic & would tell some large stories. They pretended to be very
poor & destitute but on a thorough inspection of some of our soldiers they
discovered the garet filled with hens & turkies. Also three cows back in the
woods. They say that they are of royal blood and are very proud of it. They
curse the slaves & think them the cursed race & consequently fit for nothing
but slaves. They considered the yankies a barbarous set of men lower if anything than the negroes. But I find it is the curse of the south. They are beastly
ignorant & old fashioned in the extreme. I have almost decided that this war
is for the civiliseation of the south. To see people so ignorant & old fashioned
only twelve miles from a city of eleven thousand inhabitants is attributable
to some bad management some where. The evident cause is slavery but it is
almost an imposibility for them to recognise [that] the abolition of slavery
[would benefit] the lazy land proprietors. ...They hardly know how to do the
first thing. Their destitution is a mark of being destitute of all delacacies &
living on corn & hogs rather poor stuff for northern people.*

Later the same day, Henry continued in a somewhat lighter tone:

I hope you will not be wearied in reading my very long letter. If so just say so.
  *Tonight the news is that Gen. Sumner on arriving at Fredricksburg sent
in a flag of truce giving the enemy so many hours to surrender the city & if
they decided to hold it to give them so many hours to clear out the women
& children. At the close of the time he opened with shell but they had made
ready & answered us with forty cannon - some thirty two pounders. I expect
an awful battle here soon. But I pray it may never take place.*
  *The removal of McClellan causes a great deal of talk. Some think him
a traitor. I think it time to try some one else. There is some one to command*

this army & that succesfuly to. That one can never be found except on trial. If Burnside can't, try Sumner or Franklin. You know how it was in the Crimean War. Lord Raglan was not the man nor his successor but the next one found himself equal to the task. I think if Burnside ever gets them turned he will not let them go unmolested but do his utmost to haras & capture their rear. The enemy say that McClellan let him leave Antietam unmolested & held in check vastly superior force & lost but few men. So says one of their papers. They say when we could go into Richmond we did not. The like remark on the retreat. The clearing of Cold Harbor.

I am glad to learn that you have sold your butter so well. If it could have been sent here it would have sold readily at forty cents per pound. Cheese sold for the same the other day. Your beans will be wanted in the army as we have them about twice a week. I should suppose pork & beef would sell high. Also horses. The army needs a new supply through out. Evry thing is worn out by exposure & hard labor.

The greatest luxery I have had lately is dried rasberries. The last of some Mother sent in the fall were cooked tonight. I wish I had more.

Lord Raglan was a British commander who, despite achieving much success during the Crimean War, also received criticism for his role in the chain of seemingly ambiguous orders leading to the high casualties in the Charge of the Light Brigade in 1854. He also was criticized, somewhat unfairly, for providing inadequate provisions for his men prior to his death in 1855. The reason why Henry now had time to muse on historical battles and agricultural prices in Vermont was that Burnside's plan was beginning to unravel. Union forces had arrived across the Rappahannock from Fredericksburg well before Lee's army; however, due to bureaucratic blunders, the pontoon bridges had not yet arrived. Burnside, greatly concerned for maintaining the secrecy of this operation, had shared it with so few people that moving the pontoons to Fredericksburg became a low priority for the War Department. Arriving first with his Grand Division, Sumner requested permission to lead his forces across a ford in the river and drive out the small Confederate force of about 500 men defending the city. Sumner planned to then occupy the heights outside the city, where the Army of the Potomac could await an eventual Confederate attack. Had this occurred, perhaps Henry would have been part of a Union defense of the heights against a Confederate charge in the Battle of Fredericksburg. Burnside, however, rejected this plan, fearing that if the river rose due to recent rains and the pontoons did not arrive soon, Sumner's division would be cut off from the rest of the army and surrounded by Lee's approaching forces. The Army of the Potomac therefore came to a standstill and positioned itself across the river from Fredericksburg, on Stafford Heights, giving Lee and Jackson time to move into place and occupy the heights around the town themselves.

Henry continued his letter on Wednesday, November 26:

> *Today nothing of importance has transpired to my knowledge only the war one day nearer its termination. Very cold northwest winds prevail. Tomorrow is Thanksgiving in Vermont but here it is the same old story. No Sunday, no public days observed. But the one old thing marching or drilling or attending some intolerable review. All our noted achievements were at some review for we have done hardly any thing else. It is remarked that Napolean had battles while we reviews. I am sorry to [say] it is too near the truth.*
>
> *In reading a paper sent to the Captain I read the dying words of General Mitchell which may interest you. "Death is swallowed up in victory." Also he pointed his finger heavenward & said that he had endeavored to live a Christian life & finished his course with joy. His last words to his children were Serve God sincerely & each other fondly are the last words of your dying Father. A better death than Generals generally die.*

Henry concluded his letter on Friday the 28th, apparently unaware of the entire problem of the missing pontoon bridges:

> *Yesterday we moved our camp for winter quarters & are today busy fixing our quarters as comfortable as possible. I do not imagine we shall stay long. I suppose one great battle is to be fought at Fredricksburg. I hope soon. The enemy are concentrating a strong force there & we have got to ford the Rappahanoc to get at them. It is awful to fight in water where if wounded you must be drowned certain. So death is inevitable. If not shot dead to be strangled in deep waters.*

One can only imagine Betsey's reaction to her son's imagery, but Henry concluded with a casual request:

> *If we do go in to winter quarters I shall want you to send me some butter & some dried fruit &c. The dried rasberries were excellent & the last was cooked this week. ... My love to all.*

Besides the "Williamstown boys" of the Vermont Brigade, another of the boys, as mentioned earlier, had enlisted in the regular army. Henry's cousin, George W. Smith, was a cadet at Norwich University when the war began. Norwich, the oldest private military college in the United States, is located in Northfield, eight miles west of Williamstown. Norwich graduates provided considerable leadership for the Federal forces during the war, including one head of a corps, seven division commanders, 21 brigade commanders, and 38 more leading regiments. Four Norwich graduates earned the Medal of Honor. George Smith left school early to enlist, and at this point he was a second lieutenant in the U.S. Seventeenth Infantry. George was six feet tall with dark black hair, according to his enlistment papers, and in his letters he presents a more fun-loving and adventurous side than his more reserved cousins. When Henry saw that the Seventeenth Infantry was positioned near his own camp, he sent a letter to George, who responded on December 4 from "Camp Near Potomac Creek ten miles from Aquia Cr":

> *Yours of 29th Nov. is befor me this eve rec'd and as you were so prompt to answer or to write, I will do the same. It seems that we have been near each other all the time since H. Landing. Altho one may be near yet not be able to get nearer. At Warrenton you were not over one mile off. I tried to get a pass to call on you which I could not do without trouble as I had command of the company at that time. I was at Bull Run and had our first fight there. We engaged the enemy on the left. We were ordered in on the left by McDowell. After lying under fire all day amongest the flying shells we lost quite a number of men that day. We were in camp near Chain Bridge a week. Also at Rockville. At the last place I had a fine time. Thru luck I met a young <u>Secesh maiden</u> and Henry she was not so course. I was doing Prov Gd duty at her establishment to keep the boys out of his peach orchard. I can't vouch for the orchard, but you can bet I kept them away from the <u>house</u> & <u>the gal.</u> I can't forget all my old tricks if I am a soldier. Before going farther allow me to congratulate you on your promotion. Hope you will not stop progressing but keep advancing. My prospects are good. I am at the head of the list of 2nds <u>anxiously</u> awaiting for some one to resign and make me a 1st Lt. You got the start on me on the 2nd. Hope you will on the 1st. I rank from 12th October. Hope you will write more next time. Tell me more about your affairs. Do you get any thing to eat these times. We can not except company stores. I wish you would come and see me. We are at Gen Hookers Hd. Qts. in Sykes Div., Butterfields Corp. The Red Leggs are in our Div. What is your Corps? I suppose Franklins. We were at Antietum & remained at Sharpsburg for six weeks. How are all the boys? Write me soon and a long letter and I will do the same. Give my respects to the boys.*

Chauncey also wrote to Henry during this first week of December:

I had the pleasure of receiving your late letter from Aquia Creek and found it unusually interesting. I had not heard from any of the boys since you left Hagerstown, consequently your letter was all the more acceptable. So full was it in particulars relative to your marchings, deprivations, hardships and health, that I thought it was to good to keep the whole to myself, so I inclosed it to Mr. Ainsworth at Williamstown for the benifit of those having boys in the army from that town - and from him to your parents. It was a very excellent letter, and therefore I felt justified in sending it on for the joy it will afford them all.

I congratulate you and all the boys on the preservation of life and the good health that has thus far attended you, and trust the same will be continued till the end of the war. You ask me for all the news, but I confess to a scarcity in our city, and indeed from Vermont. Time has passed very monotonously with us since you left, but we have all been well, and so among our friends so far as I know. I have myself been very busy on our new book, and also furnishing some portion of the Postmaster General's report, but we are getting through with those extra jobs, and erelong will have more time to myself to write letters &c.

For an "item" however, I can say that congress has convened, and the Vt. members and Senators are all here at their post. Mr. Walton is in rather poor health, and was sick during the fall, but I think will improve under this climate. I send you the last "Watchman" which contains the last days of Vt. Legislature, and also the President's message. For another "item" I can inform you that Nathan is now making me a visit and I find him in better health than I expected from his letters. He is not rugged, however, having weak bowels, but I trust he will pick up and yet become strong. I think he will remain all of this month and perhaps all winter, and will not go back into the army unless he is stronger.

Our fair friends are well, and when I see them will give them your kind regards. I heard the other day that Hattie is soon to be married to a cousin of hers, but know not the day, nor the "lucky one" for I consider Hattie a model young lady. I almost know they would send you their best wishes did they know I was writing.

You enquire for Maj. Lynde and I presume he is with his daughter (Mrs Fitzhugh) who lives about eight or ten miles up the Rappahannock from Fredricksburg, near the junction of the Rapid Ann, on the north side of the river. I hope you will be able to find them, but they may be too far off. I have a letter for the Major, but have had no way of getting it to him, but through you I may ere long do so. Mr. Fitzhugh is a farmer and was pressed into the rebel service a year or more since.

Our weather is variable but generally warm for the season. Yesterday it snowed all day, but mostly melted as fast as it came. I thought of the poor soldiers without proper tents to shelter them, but hope we will have a long pleasant spell to make up.

The "Nathan" named in this letter was Chauncey's son, who had attended Norwich University in the early 1850s and began the war as a first lieutenant in the Wisconsin Infantry. As Chauncey hoped, Nathan did later regain his health and reentered the military. Chauncey's hopes for pleasant weather, however, did not materialize as the Union forces prepared for the upcoming battle. On December 9, Henry sent an update to his brother from "Camp Near Potomac Crick Virginia":

Yours of November 27th came to hand some days since. I have not been able to acknowledge the receit of it untill the present time. We have been on the moove all the time. I have been with seventy men guarding the telegraph wire. Was out five days. Nothing was left of our Corps but the picket & my guard. My men were forgoten & were two days without rations but we did not starve. Providentialy we found some hard bread so did not suffer much for food. Finaly I started for camp to see what the occasion was of our not being relieved. After traveling all day I got on their track & about eight I found Gen. Howes' quarters, reported to the Adjutant General & found we were forgoten but they had not the authority to with draw us so they ordered a mounted orderly & an extra horse & I started for Gen. Franklin. Arrived there about nine & reported to Major [?] & he immediately ordered us in & sent a calvelry man to order them in. They arrived the next day about eleven P.M. The snow was two inches deep & you can imagine how comfortable we were there without tents & a few blankets. While the Regt. was marching three men died in the ambulances & frose &c. It was a dreadful time. Many of our mules perished in the mud & many were stuck fast in mud.

Yesterday the paymaster commenced paying off the Brigade. I shall receive mine today but shall not risk it in the mail but eventualy send it to Washington - from there home. Tomorrow morning we expect to cross the Rappahannoc. How much fighting we shall have I do not know. I fear a general fight will insue & a bloody one. If so it will be a trying time. My humble desire is that I may not flinch from my task & if it be the will of the Lord, I may pass through unharmed. It is my prayer. I trust yours is the same. I can only submit myself into the hands of the Almighty & await the result. The saying that old soldiers fear danger less than new ones is not true. The old are more cool & fight more desperately but always concious of the danger.

The delay in getting the pontoon bridges gave Lee time to move both of his corps, totaling 78,000 men, into strong defensive positions around the town. Although Burnside's plan could no longer be implemented as originally devised, with the January 1 deadline quickly approaching he felt there was no turning back at this point. Unable to locate any other viable undefended areas for a river crossing, he ordered his men to attack directly into the entrenched Confederate defenses in the hills behind Fredericksburg. With Lee's defenses spread out over a wide area, Burnside hoped that his considerable numerical advantage (he had an army of 120,000 on hand) would enable his men to break through the defenses on these heights. Under this plan, Hooker's Grand Division would be held partly in reserve and in support of the other two Grand Divisions. Franklin's Grand Division was to cross the Rappahannock on a pontoon bridge several miles downriver from the center of town, and then to attack and drive Jackson's corps from Prospect Hill. At the same time, Sumner's Grand Division would engage Longstreet's corps on Marye's Heights. Without support from Jackson, Burnside hoped, Longstreet's overmatched corps would eventually be unable to withstand the attack. Lee's army would then be in such disarray that an unencumbered road to Richmond, and the end of the war, would stand before them.

On December 10 Henry wrote to his father from "Camp Near Potomac Crick Landing Va." He was unaware that this plan called for him to move out early the next morning, cross the river on a bridge about to be constructed, and attack into Stonewall Jackson's defenses. Henry had his mind on other more mundane matters:

> *Last Monday we were paid off but on account of a new order concerning promoted officers which was that they were to be mustered out of the service & sworn in again so I did not get my pay untill last night. Then I settled up my clothing account. My noncommission pay payed my three percent tax which is assessed on all salaries over five hundred dollars. The final deduction &c being settled my pay amounted to three hundred & seventy dollars & twenty five cents. Quite a contrast what I used to receive. Still I cannot save as much according to amount of pay as when a Sargent. My expenses are much larger. Myself to board & clothe in the field as we are, it is almost impossible to get any thing. Poor boots seven dollars - butter one dollar per pound - cheese are fifty cents.*
>
> *What a newsance these sutlers are. Newspapers are sold for ten cents. We want the news so have to pay their abominable prices. I think many times this army is nothing more than a great speculating machine. The Doctors will not discharge a man untill his hope of recovery is hopeless. But time will develop these frauds & abuses. ... Enclosed you will find a draft of two hundred dollars. I wish to have some by me all the time so at present I will not send more.*

When at Washington I borrowed forty five dollars of Mr. Smith & shall pay him now or wait untill next payday. If not I shall send the remander home in state orders. The boys will want them cashed soon & so I will send it in that form soon. If you would like you might send me a small box. If you do fill it with dried fruit &c, a few pounds of butter & make your calculations. It will be a long time on the road. Possibly never get it. As for shirts Mother need not provide a long ways ahead for I do not ware them out very fast. They last longer than cotton. As for stockings I prefer army socks. ... Tell Mother I often think of home & would be glad to make a call but I do not see as anything but sickness or wound will permit me to go. I prefer staying than run the risk of the two alternatives.

Today our Major Foster received his commission as Lieut. Colonel. Also Lieut. Col. Stoughton a commission as Colonel. He is not twenty two yet. There will be a strife for the Majorship. I saw Gen. Burnside the other day. He looks more like a Gen. than McClellen.

Henry was about to learn that looking the part does not necessarily transfer into being a great military strategist. Early on Thursday morning, December 11, Franklin's Grand Division started moving several miles downriver to where it would cross for the attack. The soldiers had little difficulty constructing the pontoon bridge as they effectively used their artillery to ward off the limited sniper fire from across the river. Sumner's Grand Division had a much harder time as Mississippi sharpshooters in buildings from across the river fired at the engineers. Even with the support of federal artillery from Stafford Heights, the assembly remained extremely slow and dangerous. In response, Burnside eventually permitted boats to be sent across the river with sufficient troops to drive out the Confederate sharpshooters. Henry described the events of that day in a letter written shortly after the battle:

[Thusday] last we received orders to march at 5 am. It was expected by all where we were to go so they started with a strong determination to do their duty. Just before the break of day we heard the booming of cannon at Fredricksburg not of one battery but of more than a hundred guns. At the appointed time we marched forward. The canonaiding grew more distinct and finally we arrived at the banks of the Rappahannoc then halted & assisted in laying the pontoons. It took all day. At night it was completed and part of our div crossed & took possession of the opposite bank. Then Brookses Div. crossed & held the position all night while we retired & encamped in the woods in our rear for the night.

On Friday morning, the rest of Franklin's Grand Division crossed the river. Sumner's bridges were completed as well and Federal troops crossed into the town. Those troops spent much of Friday looting those homes and shops that had not been destroyed by the bombardment. Sumner's Grand Division spent the day preparing for the upcoming battle.

Next morning we crossed the river halted on its banks until the whole army crossed. Then Gen Burnside crossed & commenced forming his lines. Column after column moved to our left. We were left on the left of the center. A few of the columns mooved up to the front & established a line & drove the enemy into their fortifications. They retired as we advanced. That night we were ordered on picket. We could hear & see the enemy making great preparation to receive us.

The battle for the heights started with an attack by Franklin into Jackson's defenses on Saturday morning, December 13. Two days later Henry sent a short note to his parents from "Camp Across the Rappahannock" letting them know that he had survived but indicating that this Union strategy had not succeeded as planned.

Saturday we had a hard fight and lost fifty six men. Co. B lost nineteen. I lost eight, one shot dead and another lived a few hours. The six are doing well in Co. B. Both Clarks, Mayette, Clark Wilson were badly wounded. It was an awful fight. Thousands were slain but we did not carry the day. We held a strong skirmish line in an open field & was so exposed to the sharpshooters that we lost heavily. I will write more when I get time. I passed through unhurt. I expect the fight will be renewed soon.

The fight was not immediately renewed as Henry had anticipated. As a result, he had time to write a much longer letter a week later, describing all that the army had endured in the battle. Although Franklin had 60,000 men under his command, he had very cautiously interpreted Burnside's ambiguous instructions and held back much of his fighting force rather than unleashing an all-out attack on Prospect Hill. General Meade, with support from the other two First Corps divisions of Doubleday and Gibbon, spearheaded the attack with just 4,500 men as artillery was deployed against Jackson's position. Meade's Pennsylvanians, after facing an intense artillery attack from the Confederates, managed to find a gap in Jackson's defenses and break through temporarily. But as overwhelming numbers of Confederate reserves were deployed into the gap, Meade's division was driven back. Howe's Second Division of the Sixth Corps was positioned along Bowling

Green Road, just to the left of Deep Run, with Brooks' division on the other side of the creek. The Vermont Brigade, within range of Confederate artillery, was primarily kept in reserve, although regiments were at times sent out as skirmishers. From this vantage point on the open field, Henry was able to clearly observe much of the fighting. He was particularly close to Gibbon's charge into a gap between three North Carolina regiments. Like Meade, Gibbon was not given additional support and the breach could not be exploited. Henry described the day's events from early in the morning, as he had been positioned as a picket during the night:

Soon the gray beam of light appeared & disclosed a formidable line of cannon & about eight a line of skirmishers advanced on them to draw their fire. They went within about five rods of their cannon before they opened their [cannons] the contents of two batteries into them. Still they stood their ground. Soon one of our batteries opened but could not silence the enemies but all of a suden six twelve pound brass cannon were let off at once. They had accurate range & you can imagine the result. Their fire was soon stopped and they retired them. The skirmishers kept up a brisk fire. About eleven the infantry advanced five Brigades one in rear of the other. As soon as they entered the woods voley after voley of musketry was heard. Whole lines were cut down still on they went & finally drove them from the hill but for some reason they did not hold it. Such a roar of musketry & artillery I never heard before. Whole Regiments cut to pieces but not hardly a man could be seen to run. Such beautiful lines I never saw before. They moved steadily forward regardless of the danger. I could see holes cut in their ranks but they closed on the colors and kept a perfect line. The enemy could be seen running into our lines by hundreds. In one instance our men ran around four hundred of them & drove them in to our lines. They took eight brass cannon.

The eight cannon were actually not taken, but disappeared from Henry's sight because the Confederates moved them back. Henry, from his nearby vantage point on slightly elevated ground, had never before witnessed such a battle without being a participant.

This is the first fight I ever saw. It was as plain to be seen as a battle fought on our meadow. I could compare the grounds to the same place. Our men across the Rappahannoc on the east side of the branch, the enemy the other side along the top of the ledge right to Mr. Poor's pasture. Also [imagine] the hemlock noll & the Blackberry side hill covered with forts and masked cannon. Our lines were formed in their sight in range of their cannon which spoke to us occasionally. They did not care much about us, only wanted us to come on. We did it and did it well but did not whip them. I never saw such daring before. Our men & batteries would go right forward as though there was no danger ahead & every time the enemy opened our men would with a few shots silence their batteries. Our cannoneers are superior to the enemy but our soldiers are but little.

Later in the battle, as part of an assault by General Early's division, North Carolina troops tried to advance and outflank the Federal lines along the Deep Run ravine. The Fourth Vermont was one of the regiments called out to help in repulsing their charge.

I will now tell you about the position of the Fourth Regiment. As I said on the other sheet we were sent on picket the night before the fight & remained on until eight a.m. About seven a.m. we were ordered forward when the regiments on our left advanced. There was no charge made on our front but it was done on our left. I will send you a picture of the position and fight sketched by one of the soldiers in Co. F.

You can imagine the position of our lines on the left & the position of my regt. supported only by batteries when the brigades were ordered to charge. Our line of pickets were ordered forward with them & advanced within ten rods of the enemy. We were in an open field without the least bit of shelter so were exposed to the deadly aim of the sharpshooters & lines of Rebil infantry. Evry

few moments some one of our Regt. would fall. I was in command of my Co. The Capt. being detached as Maj. & 1st Liunt. det. on Gen. Brookes staff, so I was the only one left. As I advanced my men kept under cover of a little bluff but soon I was ordered forward. Just as we went over the hill we were fired into by a line of infantry. There one man fell shot dead by a miney through the forehead. Soon another one through the bowels. He lived a few hours. The shot flew like hail arround us & we had to lye and take it. Soon two Regiments came out & charged on us. I did not let my men retreat untill they were within about ten rods of us. I found it useless to try to stop them any longer, as the shots from only one company did not stop their progress at all only killing a number. Just at that moment they let a whole voley into us. I ordered a retreat of a few rods, halted & commenced firing. Still they came & gave another voley, wounding six men, none mortaly. I ordered another retreat & halted on the brow of the hill all the time giving them a deadly fire. Just then I saw the third Regt coming to my assistance. Also our batteries opened. The third stagered them. They turned & run & I after them. We retook our old position & nine prisoners. They lost I should judge one hundred men. The ground was strewed with dead all the way back to their old position after which they ceased firing. They came on us so close before we retreated that two of my men were taken prisoners but they were so fortunate as to escape while they were retreating. The Commander of the Regt never went back. Also a Capt & Lieut. One of my men went out among the dead and wounded. One Capt. asked a favor & it was granted. He was so thankful that he wished to know his name, place of residence & said if he ever recovered he would be remembered & the next day one of our wounded was sent into our lines & my infrence is he was the cause of it. I was not hit but had many loud calls. I lost eight men two killed & six wounded. The rest of the Regt suffered dreadfuly. Co. D lost Capt. Quimby shot through the neck, Co B lost nineteen men, fourteen at one charge of cannister. Lewis Clark is mortaly wounded. Clark Wilson lost his foot. Chester Clark not dangerous. Mayette not dangerous. Durkee son of Brookfield lost leg. Curier of Randolph fear mortal & a number of other fine men will recover. Sy Cleveland & three others shot dead. It was an awful time & a wonder how any of us ever escaped unhurt. Only think of a Regt of skirmishers loosing fifty six men for skirmishing. It is a extremely great loss. You will see our account of it in the papers. Our flag was torn into threads, the eagle shot off & the flag ridled by bulets. The Colnel intends sending it home to the Govner.

Eli Mayette had been shot in the shoulder at Dam No. 1 and sent to a hospital. Now back with his regiment in this battle, he had a shell fragment force his rifle into his groin, resulting in a hernia. The war was over for him, and also for Clark Wilson, whose left leg was amputated, with complications leading to his death in early January. Chester Clark was shot cleanly through the left calf, with the ball then entering his right leg. Although he was unable to walk very far or stand up for long periods for the rest of his life, he was able to retain both his damaged legs. His older brother, Lewis Clark, was more severely wounded and transferred to a hospital in Washington, D.C. When their father heard of their injuries, he immediately left Williamstown to join them, but Lewis died shortly after his father arrived.

General Burnside refused to abandon his plan despite Franklin's failed attempt to dislodge Jackson. Starting at 11 a.m., wave after wave of Union brigades were sent to attack Longstreet's defenses on Marye's Heights. Those who made it through the intense artillery fire of the open field eventually faced the concentrated fire of lines of Confederate infantry entrenched behind a sunken road and a stone wall. Sixteen ill-fated charges were attempted before nightfall finally brought an end to this day of carnage. The next day Burnside requested a truce to attend to the wounded and Lee consented. Federal casualties numbered over 12,000, more than double the Confederate casualties. What was left of the Army of the Potomac then retreated back across the Rappahannock and the Battle of Fredericksburg was over.

> *Thus ended the fight & what we have accomplished I do not see. I hope something. Our whole loss is reported 18,000. Sunday there was a flag of truce & the wounded brought off. They are very friendly when a flag of truce is up. The lines immediately join each other & exchange coffee for tobacco. I crossed the lines Sunday & saw some of their dead & wounded where our regiment fought. The enemy were very eager to have the war closed & wished that the leaders of their rebellion could be drawn up & let both sides fire at them. They must suffer a great deal. They have plenty of cotton clothing but no woolen. Cotton is not the stuff for a soldier to wear. ...*
>
> *Monday we were relieved & went back to the rear. That night the whole army was ordered across the river & have remained there ever since. I have been in battles before but not in one equal to this last one. How I ever escaped I do not imagine, exposed to solid shot grape & cannister & rifle balls by the voley. It seems as though I must have been shielded by some unseen power. I was the object of the sharp shooters being so I could not get much cover so I could do nothing but stand up & see them fire at me. ... I had the privalidge of seeing all that was going on & see a rebil Regt advance on us. Also to see a battle in open field. I have seen enough & hope never to see the like again. If I ever felt greatful it was when darkness covered the field.*

Chapter 7

WINTER
IN VIRGINIA

Following the Fredericksburg debacle, the Army of the Potomac settled in across from the city on Stafford Heights. On December 26, Henry was not in a particularly charitable mood. In his letter to Francis he did not even mention Christmas. He was concerned for the future and feeling a sense of unfairness in how the war was being conducted of late.

> I am in hopes we shall go into winter quarters. Still I do not see how they can & meet the demands of the country. In about four months the two years mens time will expire. Over twenty New York Regiments are two years men. How many more I do not know. Next the nine months men. So you see that those men cannot be of any service to the country unless they are kept at work. But I do not know but it would be as well to have them discharged on the whole for they are seldom brought to the front. There were but few engaged in the last fight. The new Regt. in our Brigade was not called into the fight at all, but left in the rear. Look at the 2nd Vt Brigade back at Fairfax. Their time will soon expire & return home not seeing any of the hardships of the old soldiers. I think they should be brought to the front & take the brunt of this service. We had to learn. Why not they? One lot of troops have maintained the front during the whole war. Taken the same place in all the battles. You can imagine the result of being the first to receive the prepared reserved fire for the first advance. You recolect do you not what a man said about the first lines. When troops met in the Mexican war, a shower of brains. It is the case here. The front line as they entered the woods on our left was nearly anihalated.

The promotion of officers was another area where Henry saw a pattern of unfairness.

> At the present time there is considerable excitement in the Regiment. The Colonel has returned & in filling the vacancies has neglected some of the

oldest Captains & worthy men. They have appointed Capt. Pingree Major. He is one of the youngest Captains in the Regt. & not considered by only a few fit for the place. Our older Captains are much more capable of filling the place, have done double the duty & been in evry fight while Pingree has been in only one. This does not look right. The same partiality is shown in the minor appointments. It will proove great damage to the Regiment. Three Officers have resigned already & three of the Captains are going to follow suit. I am sorry to see such things take place as it will deduct largely the efficiently of the Regiment. It

Stephen Pingree
Courtesy of Vermont Historical Society

will give a chance for others to go up. That is not what we want. It is experienced Officers. Last night the Colonel was so drunk as to be unfit for any duty. Could not walk straight. It is not the first time. How can we expect to conquer our enemies when we are so wicked ourselves. I am told it is not the case with the rebils. Have we not lost men enough to make our people begin to have serious thoughts?

Having witnessed the loss of so many at Fredericksburg, Henry had very vivid memories of the excruciating suffering:

This war is a wholesale business. This old Potomac Army is fast being converted into limbless men. Hopson in Co. B had his leg struck by a solid shot & severed from the body except a few ligaments & thrown back onto his side. This is one instance. Four out of Co. B lost legs. One received eight bullets & is still alive. A man in Co. G had one side of his face split open &c. Co. D lost their Captain hit in the neck severing the jugular vein. He lived a few moments only. In Co. A our first Sergt. was hit in the hip. Our fourth in the leg. Our Corporal in the arm. The Doctors were on the point of amputating it & went so far as to taking off his clothes & shoes preparartory to lying him on the table but another doctor came along & said it was not broken & so saved his arm. By this you can see what kind of surgeons we have to take care of us. Another Corporal was hit in the groin & lived only a couple of hours. It lodged in his bowels. It was painful to see him. He was struck with death. The instant it struck him such a change I never saw the like before. Another Corporal was lost I suppose taken prisnor. One Private was hit as near the center of the forehead as possible. He fell forward & died instantly without a struggle. Two others were hit but very slightly. On the whole, we escaped very lucky. We were showered with musket balls & cannon shot.

I suppose you have read the testimony of our Generals given to that committee. I agree with Gen. Franklin that if the enemy had opened their cannon we could hardly have stayed. Their chance was so good to drop them in our midst. We got back all right leaving nothing behind. The report is that Burnside has commenced planting two hundred heavy seige guns on the Stafford Heights. I hope we shall never be ordered across there again. I should not expect better success than before. I have just read the President's thanks to the army of the Potomac. It is well enough to thank the army but they will never like fighting any better. The more a man fights the less he wants to. Those so craving are not used to danger, cannot imagine the horrors. They are like little children not knowing the result of touching a hot stove puts their hand on unconciously. It was the case with our recruits. They would expose themselves not knowing the result. But an old soldier dreads a battle before hand but once engaged are not easily driven back. Our frightened old soldiers will not last always. ...What will we do for men after the army commences discharging? Our Chaplin Mr. Robberts says they think in Washington that it will be settled before spring. He saw Mr. Morrill & he thought the same. Mr. Roberts has prooved himself just the man for his position. He did so much for the wounded that it was the remark of all that saw him he will never be forgotten by our unfortunate boys. He accompanied them to Washington. Probably a number would have died had it not been for his care of them. There was no provision made for them anywhere & as it was they suffered unaccountably riding in cars without a bed or bit of straw with amputated limbs &c. He was a father to them.

Henry was also not pleased to hear the outcome of his own letter that Chauncey Smith had forwarded to George Ainsworth back in Williamstown. One townsperson who read the letter felt that Henry's harsh criticisms of the army would be bad for morale.

The reason of my letter being sent to Mr. Ainsworth was Mr. Smith was so interested in it that he thought Mr. Ainsworth would like to see it so he wrote. I am sorry if I said anything to set Mr. Ware to talking. True, we are tired [and] worn down by four campaigns. Have suffered for want of food & clothing. Also lack of propper care for the sick & wounded &c &c. & various other trials which I occasionaly mention, not wishing to complain nor the most distant thought of deserting the cause. A number of chances have presented themselves. The last battle we could have evry one of the Company been taken & hardly been blamed. The enemy had us almost in their grasp. Two were taken but escaped. Still we were fighting for Country. I think the head of the government intends well & does all they can to make all right. Tell Mr. Ware I hope he will be careful what he says. I hope you will reprove him.

Chauncey Smith wrote on December 27 that he had visited with five wounded soldiers from the Fourth Vermont in the Patent Hospital.

The young Mr. Clark, you allude to, has the most dangerous wound, but he appeared better this morning than any previous day. His father has come on, so that his two boys, and the others, will be well taken care of. We shall give them all the attention possible. I am glad Mr. Clark has arrived, as it is a source of joy to all the boys, and I presume he will stay till they are out of danger. ... Besides the Williamstown boys, there are others from different parts of the state in this hospital and I believe all are doing as well as could be expected.

Henry may have been less than overjoyed to read Chauncey's closing statement that another letter critical of army strategy was on its way to Vermont.

I let Nathan read your letter (about the Fredericksburg defeat), and we both thought it so good that it ought to go on to Williamstown, so I inclosed it with a note of my own to Mr. Ainsworth for the general information of all in town, like as I did the other. I am sure they will be pleased to get it.

On the 28th, Henry did paperwork and ruminated on the recent setbacks. Later in the day, he shared his thoughts and concerns with Francis:

As I was looking over my old roll call which I used while 1st Sergeant in Company B, I was astonished to see what great change there was taken place since we left Vermont. We numbered ninety-eight enlisted men aggregate. Commissioned & enlisted & one hundred & one, 3 commissioned officers. The change in com. officers is Lueit Chamberlain resigned. There are but very few of the old Soldiers left & are daily decreasing in numbers. Nearly twenty have died since we recrossed the Rappahanic. I was detailed to superintend the burial of one yesterday. Today another died. The hospital is full of worn out skeletons of men so poor you would not call then human beings. It would frighten you to see them. War speeks for itself. What are not killed by bullets will be by disease & hard marching. Many are deserting. One fellon from the 5th was caught Courtmartialed, drumed out of camp & sent to the Rip Raps the remainder of his three years. Nineteen have deserted from Company E 2nd Regt. but that is not an average number for the Brigade. The only way to stop it is to shoot every one they catch. War is stern business here caried out. No one can truly see the necesity of it untill they have served awhile. The longer he serves the more rigid he becomes. The three years men are under as strict discipline as are the regular service. This is but little fairness taken with the nine months men. So little regard have they for their superiors I do not imagine how they keep them under. A man for speaking a wrong word can be court marshaled and have his pay taken away. Such observations comes hard on our recruits.

Colonel Reides of the 3rd Regt is being courtmartialed for cowardice at Fredericksburg. I hope he shall be dismissed from the service.

On the outside of the envelope he continued his record of changes in the regiment, listing several who had been wounded or killed:

By looking this list over you will perceive the great change there has taken place in a few months. I have not got the names of the recruits down. They have been thinned out more than the old soldiers. Some of the sick will return, only a few. Most will be discharged. I could hardly believe the change to be so great.

Still feeling disillusioned from the recent defeat, Henry began writing a letter home to his parents on December 29:

The past has added interesting events for pages of History but nothing decisive as far as I can see in queling this rebellion. One year of the war is ended clothing the country in mourning. I hope that the sheding of blood is done. Yesterday I could hear distant Cannonading. The same today. It is almost revery in such a desolate spot as we are in now. The report is that we are to moove in a few days. Many have built comfortable winter quarters to leave again. There is but little enjoyment in trying to build anything for comfort. Today we have been making out our muster rolls for ten months pay. I understand Congress has decided to pay the Soldiers before the government clerks. I think they are deserving of their pay when due.

Henry continued the next day:

11 A.M. we have just received orders for three days rations in haversacks & two in the teems & evry man to carry sixty rounds of cartridges. It looks rather suspitious especialy the sixty rounds of ammunition. Some predict back to Washington. I am sure we cannot go forward. I understand we are to cover the retreat. I hope the enemy will let us alone but I fear they will not. They threaten to destroy our army before they arrive. Perhaps they will. I expect another Bull Run fight. Many of our men are barefoot & destitute of clothing. It is almost impossible to keep an army well Clothed when on the run.

Colnel Reides Court Marshal is not finished yet. I know a little about the affair. The Lieut. Colnel commanded. I could not see any thing of the Colnel. One of my men saw him in a ditch a fine place for a Commander of a Regt when a whole Brigade of Rebils was expected in this engagement. He has never been in a fight yet. I was a little amused on a remark I herd from one near report from Washington. Mr. Walton saw Colnel Reid come into the hotel. He immediately remarked theres to be a fight soon. Why? Because Colnel Reid is here. He is a Colnel but never fights.

While Henry was writing this letter and a similar one to Francis on December 30, Chauncey visited some of the wounded in Washington, D.C. and sent the following account to Henry:

Although I wrote you a short letter lately, I drop a few lines today to fulfil a request on the part of Sergeant Martin of your company who is in the Patent Office hospital wounded in the knee. In my visits to the Vt boys I found him, and during our conversation, which was quite interesting, he wished me to send you his kindest regards and good wishes, and also to ask you to send him his "descriptive list." I think this is the term he used, and I suppose it to be the description of his person at the time of enlisting, so that he can make himself identified here. He said you would know what he wanted and you inclose it to me, and I will deliver it to him. He is a very intelligent young man, and his wound appears to be doing well, though of course painful, but we will take good care of him.

Young Clark is also doing well, considering his wound is in his groin. His father came on, and is now with his boys, which is a source of joy to them. The other brother is getting along finely. Young Wilson has suffered much, but is of good heart. The nurse told me that the amputation was not done skillfully, but this morning the wound run largely, which we think is highly favorable and the worst part is over. There are some ten Vt boys in this hospital and we believe all will recover in due time. Mr. Clark left Williamstown on Wednesday last and all were then well about town. We shall keep him here till his son is out of all danger.

Nathan made the boys a visit this morning, and finds them comfortable. The box will be sent tomorrow. We were delayed about getting it at the

Express Office, and we take out such things as belong to the boys here, and then send the box along. Visitors are admitted to the hospitals from 12 to 6 p. m. and so far I have dropped in every afternoon to see them, and shall continue so to do.

Henry had commented that it looked "rather suspicious" that the men were ordered to prepare to march with three days' rations and sixty rounds of ammunition. He feared that another attack on Fredericksburg was intended, and indeed that was just what Burnside had in mind. Burnside planned to surprise Lee by having most of the army cross the river south of Fredericksburg while the cavalry attacked north of the city, disrupting Lee's supply lines. But when some of his officers reported what they viewed as an ill-conceived plan to Lincoln, the President rejected it. The Vermont Brigade settled back into its old camp at White Oak Church.

Henry's first letter of 1863 was written to Frank on January 5:

We have been musterd for two months more pay & commenced a new year & pleanty of fighting ahead. Perhaps it will be our turn again soon even before the close of this week. Some thing is on foot. The rumor is we are to cross the river which I fear is true. Some of the pontoons have gone down to the banks of the river for something. It does not seem possible that we are again to cross & offer our whole army to a dreadful slaughter & perhaps defeat. I hope for the best. It is surmised that the enemy are evacuating & this force left is very small. I hope so. They have been making a great display of late & some very foolish demonstrations. A long line of them came down to the banks of the river & seated them selves & commenced eating their rations &c. but our guns did not disturb them in the least. They might have done so if they chose.

I am now in camp summoned there for to testify what I know concerning the Colnel of the 3rd Regiment & I fear it will go hard with him. It is a grave charge. One if prooved against him will destroy his worldly prospects as well as transmiting a disgrace which his children cannot out live. The Lieut Colnel of the 11th Vermont is here doing all he can for him. His regt is doing garison duty. It is strange how lucky all the Vermont Regiments are in regard to fighting but the old Brigade. We are expecting to take part in another before many days & as near as we can learn we are to cross in the same place we did before. What will be the result. A little we can imagine a warm reception when we start. I hope all will go on successfuly unless they evacuate. It will surpass any battle fought yet. Burnside is desperate & if permitted would sacrifice evry man rather than be beat. If men ever dreaded any thng it is crossing that river again. It will be harder than it was before. But soldiers are not dictators but only to obey orders [and] go where they are told. A soldier is nothing more than a very small cog in a large wheel & is little mised when swept aways.

Last Wednesday I saw George Smith. It had been five months sinse we had met. He was well. Has alterd conciderable in his looks. His experience in war is not as agreeable as he anticipated. Still he has not seen the worst of war yet. He was a little exposed at Fredricksburg. The Regiment lost a few men. Tell Uncle Ira [George's father] George is doing well never looked more healthy. He said Jane [his sister] was at New York & would soon join her husband at New Orleans soon. I do not think she will enjoy living south – espetialy at this time. It would be bad enough in time of peace. The climate is delightful but outside of its Cities it is worse than in Vermont seventy five years ago. I received a letter from Mr Chauncy Smith stateing that Mr Clark had arrived & was doing all he could for his sons & that they were geting along as well as could be expected. He had found some belonging to my Company [and is] taking an interest in all Vermonters. I can testify to his attending to a sick person. I was not aware of Mr Benedict being at Washington none of his sons being sick. Please write the particulars. I would like to see him. One of our recruits died last Friday. He was confind but five days. Two brothers joined the Company at Georgetown. One died there. ....

An anecdote has just occurred about Gen Sumner. A forageing train was sent out by him & was taken by gruillas. He immediately sent out eight or ten wagons more & loaded them with soldiers. They were atacked by the same party but they all prooved to be like the old horse filled with men spoke of in history and they took the party consisting of 40 men & horses & retook all previously captured, &c. A little strategy on our part.

The following day, January 6, Henry wrote to his parents:

Tonight the loss of our celebrated Moniter was anounced. It is a great loss & will cause great rejoiceing in rebildom. Still we have more. She has payed for her self.

The rebils are going through strange menovers. Last night not a campfire was to be seen & they are paradeing their troops in our sight. Batalion drills, reviews of infantry & artilary take place quite often on the flat we occupied on the 13th December. Some times they double their pickets. Yesterday they were with drawn. To me this is blind strategy. Also all those new tents have disappeared &c. The 6th New Hampshire crossed in boats into Fredricksburg & stayed there all day, were not disturbed in the least.

Gen Brooks was placed under arrest & orderd to Washington for saying no one but a fool would have ever crossed the river when Burnside did. He has since been released. Colnel Hides Court Marshal is not finished yet.

Four companys of our Regt have been detached. Building barns & quarters for Gens Smith & Franklin. They have been there about five weeks. The 2nd are detached with Quartermaster Stone at the landing, a good job for them. I will tell you what ranks compose Colnel Hides Court Marshal 1 General, 5 Colnels, 2 Lieut Colnels, 3 Captains. Quite a respectable board.

Today we have been cashing up the amount of Company savings since April amounting to $24.28 cts. Quite a respectable fund. Another of our men received his discharge. It made him a new man. [Another man's] limbs are so badly swolen that he can hardly ware his clothes. I fear he will die.

Henry Smith made the prayer at the grave of the man we buried last satirday. People were astonishid at his remarkably good prayer. I will tell how he was buried. It was impossible to get any boards, so his uniform was put on him, a blanket wraped around him & his grave was dug about two & ½ feet deep. The botom strewed with bowes. His remains were lowerd into the grave, three volies fired, then a few bows were scaterd over the corpse & the dirt on top of them. It was the best we could do for him. It seems as though we might be furnished with boards for cofins when we are lying still. It does not seem as bad to us as to you. We have become some what hardened to such seens. The prediction of Gen Magruder is prooving true. He said evry farm in Virginia would become a burying ground. Many a fine soldier is buried under some shady oak or pine.

Chauncey wrote to Henry on January 9.

Your kind favor inclosing a letter and descriptive list for sergeant Martin and also a letter to Mr. Kranz came to hand yesterday, and I made no delay in going over to the hospital and delivering it to him. He was overjoyed to receive it, and expressed a thousand thanks, and specially requested me to tell you how much pleased he was, and to assure you that he should write you as soon as he could. He is getting along very well, but still has a painful knee, but the joint is not stiff, and the wound gradually improving. Doty is near to him, and has so far recovered as to use crutches some; so also, Chapman, Chester Clark, and Whitcomb, and I believe all others except Lewis Clark. Lewis we think cannot recover; still, he lives, and bears up heroically, but he has no appetite to support him. Could he eat hearty I should think there was some hope. His father came on, and is with him. Wilson died on

Wednesday morning about 4 o'clock, very unexpectedly to his comrads. I was with him the evening before, and really thought him improving. He rested very well, and at this hour requested to be turned over, which was carefully done, but he breathed but a few times after. Probably some internal afection, as his leg appeared to be doing well, though we think diseased all the way up. His whole system was not healthy nor did he have any appetite, and suffered more or less pain every day. I have been in every day, and do what I can towards cheering the boys up, and think all will recover except Lewis. Doty, Chapman, and Cooper are set down to go to Vt. And I suppose they will soon be off. Wheeler, Kranz, Rand and others have been transferred to the Stanton hospital, and all doing well, and in due time all will go to Vermont. Well, out of this dozen or more of men that at first came to the Patent Office Hospital, it is pleasant to think that all will recover except two, and yet some hope for Clark. Still more pleasant if all could live. I told the boys last night that I should write you, and all with one accord sent their love and good wishes to you and Charlie and all others. I take it that you hold pretty rugged, and I trust so with all in the army. ... The western army appears to be doing well, and Genl. Rosencrans has whipped the rebels at Murfreesboro, Ten. handsomely. All well in Vt.

With the army still in camp on January 11, Henry started a letter home.

I was glad to learn you had received the money for your willows. ... Also glad to learn that you keep the old oxen. A yoke of oxen as highly educated as they are ought not to be sold for beef. Only at an advanced age. ... Our Chaplain returned from Washington day before yesterday bringing sad news. Clark Wilson died a day or two after his arrival. His limb was not skillfully amputated. Consequently trifling as his injury was comparatively speaking only loosing a lower part of the leg below the knee. Mr Smith said he was not doing as well as he would like to see him but that day the limb had macerated & run freely so he had more hopes of him. Lewis Clarks case is hopeless. Unfortunate for him his catching a severe cold. His wound was doing as well as could be expected & they entertained hopes of his recovery but when one complaint is all he can bare two might prove fatal. His cold is so bad that for want of streangth to cough he nearly chokes to death.

The Chaplain is sick. I fear it will go hard with him. I hope not. Lieutenant Colnel Joice of the 2nd Vermont Infantry has resigned & gone home on account of ill health (occasioned by hard drinking). He is from Northfield a Lawier by profesion at home.

(Charles Joyce regained his health and later served three terms in the U.S. House of Representatives.)

Col Lord of the 6th has resigned. Ill health. It is a loss to the Brigade. Colnel Whiting now in command of the Brigade is the only truly temperate man high in command in the Brigade. It makes him unpopular.

I am thankful to hear that success is once more attending our army. The Western troops have never had as strong army to contend with as the Virginia troops. They are well drilled, & I suppose as good soldiers as our own. We have never been able to fairly whip their army yet one side may be driven a little & that is all thus far. We were not whipped at Fredricksburg but handsomely repulsed.

Making such a profound distinction between being whipped and handsomely repulsed may have been enough work for one night, so Henry continued the next day:

This morning I received a letter from Francis & one from Mr. Smith. The later letter contained the news of the death of C. Wilson. He died Wednesday morning 7 a.m. very unexpectedly & in Lewis Clark's condition I am glad his Father is with him. All that can be mooved are to be sent to Vermont. It will do them more good than medisin would.

Vicksburg is not ours. General Sherman is superceded by Gen McClenard. I fear it is to late to take it. I think Braggs whole force will go there as soon as possible.

Another flying report is in circulation that we are to be transfered to heavy artilary. I hope it will proove true. I mearly mention it not expecting it to be true. The four companies detached at Gen Franklins HdQuarters are still there at work.

We are all well. The wether fine. I have not worn an overcoat twelve times this winter.

Neither the start of a new year nor the passage of time could erase Henry's awful memories of Fredericksburg. On January 18, Henry began a long letter to his brother:

Your welcome letter barring date January 8th was received a few days since & this evening I commence to answer it. A few thoughts have occurd to me which may be interesting to you concerning the late battle of Fredricksburg which I have not thought to mention before.

About 7 p.m. Dec 13 after dark everything was quiet along the lines. Soon that quiet was broken. My attention was attracted by heavy canonaiding on our right. I turned around & could see fire belching forth from the enemies cannon & whole lines of fire the entire leangth of their brestworks. Also the fire of our men. It was our men once more trying to carry their earth works. The cheering of our men could almost be heard. It was in vain they tried & were obliged to retire because of their lines of fire being on a side hill. Their entrenchments like a pair of stairs so one could fire over the heads of the ones below doing no harm &c but the point I wish to speak of was the splendid sight. It was beyond description. The distinct fire of evry musket seemingly could be seen. It turned darkness into daylight. To imagine the result of such a fire was chiling to my blood. Still it surpassed all the fireworks I have yet seen. On our left four bataries opened simultaineously on some of ours on the flat only a short distance from them. I can compare it to a thunderstorm, the roar similar & the fire to lightnening. It is a very good ilustration. My experrience learns me that I have seen & heard true illustrations. In the heavens the thunder & lightning are complete.

The gloomy picture you speak of is a true one that you can see for yourself. I mearly mentioned it so you might see how we truly stand. I suppose it is nothing more than has occurred in other wars. It cannot be otherwise. Camplife agrees with but comparatively few men. It very soon undermines the constitution of most men. I hope that report about the French Minister will proove true. I truly think humanity demands it but I fear it will not be regarded as we are still having disasters. Very unsuccessful at the west. It is a severe trial to be held back & still meet with such terrible slaughter. It seems as though if the army of the Potomac was there there would never have been such a skedadleing as there was then. It has never been the case yet with us.

The article in the Chronicle about the convertion of a soldier speeks truly of the drunkenness of the army. For two or three nights past two thirds of the Regimint have been dead drunk. A true patern of their leaders. I don't wish you to make this very public as coming from me. I don't imagine this is the case in the entire army. It seems as though this war was continued to rid the country of such a base set of men.

It is supposed Marden has deserted. I think if you would go to Westfield you might arrange maters so as to draw Thurbers pay or see if he had any property so you might attach it. I think I would consult a Lawier that day. Are not Fathers western taxes very heavy now? I have sent in my last letter to Father two orders one of $6.00 & one of $10.00 on Uncle Bass. The first John Green second Dek Jones. They were out of money & I accomodated them.

Dek has been promoted to Corporal recently. He is a smart looking soldier. Capt Brown has resigned & the Quartermaster but I do not think Browns will be accepted as it is nearly as hard to resign as for an enlisted man to get a discharge. Burnside has passed an order forbidding the accepting of resignations except on Surgeons Certificate of disability.

I was a little gratified to read the account of a remark made by Gen Brooks to his aid about the Vt Brigade. He was reviewing his Division. One of his Jersey Brigades had just received new uniforms & looked very well. Lieut Parsons remarked that such a Brigade looked finely, better than the Vermont Brigade. You are mistaken Sir. I wish you to understand Sir. I concider the Vt troops ny to regulars & it was spoken in his rough style, & the aid wished he had held his tongue. It was saying a great deal for him. He would never acknowledge it when we were under him, but called us cornstalk Militia &c.

I have just noticed an account of the Pennsylvania reserve corps. It originally embraced 15,760 men. After passing through the Penninsular, Virginia & Maryland campaign they musterd about 4000 men. After the battle of Fredricksburg they musterd 2600 men. There are Regimints commanded by 1st Leutinents. Capt Pratt saw one of the Reg numbered less than one hundred men. This is a true condition of the old Regts. War is wholesale business. Regts that have passed through ten or twelve battles cannot be otherwise than very small. Evry thing indicates a forward movement soon perhaps another battle of Fredericksburg.

Perhaps fearing what might result from that upcoming campaign, Henry next proceeded to chronicle all the engagements in which the Vermont Brigade had been involved up to this point of the war. Henry did not include the dates, which are added parenthetically.

THE NUMBER OF BATTLES in which I have taken a part and a little history of them.

1st Youngs Mills [April 4, 1862]
Youngs Mills are about one days march from Newport News. There we heard the first rebil shot fired. Our lines were formed in the woods. On advancing into the opening we saw a long line of brestworks built so as to command the opening & cannon arranged as to take affect from three sides. You can imagine our feelings. There was considerable excitement. Gen Brooks dashed forward & his men after him. But luck was in our favor. The fortifications were guarded by a few Cavelry who retired as we approached

them in forming their men of our approach. We shout for joy. Took possession of the works. Stoped over night & went forward in the morning.

2nd Lees Mills [Dam No. 1 - April 16, 1862]

Rain was pouring down in torents when we arrived in a piece of woods about a mile from where we had a bloody fight. That night we were sent on picket with the aid of Colnel Joice & his compass in acceptional darkness & rain & in a Virginia swamp we were posted. The next day were relieved. We remained there a few days. One night we received orders to be ready to march at 3 a.m. light. [Under] orders we advanced about a mile. Then were deployed as skirmishers. Cautiously we went forward. Soon we came in view of their brestworks. We crept up to the waters edge undiscovered. The negroes were at work in the trenches also some soldiers. In rear they were having a guard movement we could see them distinctly. The Colnel took one of our guns & told the men to fire when he did. He fired & such a yelling & ske-dadling was very amusing. The battle was opened in earnest. They rushed to arms & commenced returning our fire. The first rebil cannon we ever heard was fired there. Our bataries opened soon. One of our shots dismounted their cannon. Finaly our guns silenced all their guns. Our skirmishers picked off numbers of the enemy. They could see them fall. About 4 pm four companies of the 4th, four 3rd, four 6th were ordered to charge the works. With a cheer they rushed forward. Some threw water boiling with led hail up to their waists. Our cannon four bataries six guns each advanced within 300 yards of the enemy & fired as fast as possible. Also the remainder of the regiments advanced to where they could fire without endangering the charging force. The rebils tried to repel the attack but as they showed their men they proved food for our bateries & muskets. Our men drove the enemy from their rifle pits but darkness ended the scene & what was left of the three little bands returned leaving between two & three hundred dead & wounded. There was never a more galant charge made than by those twelve Companies. At night we were ordered out to build earth works. The dawn of day revealed strong earth works protecting cannon that demanded silence in their works & it was kept.

3rd Williamsburg [May 5, 1862]

One Sunday morning it was discovered the enemy had evacuated. We pressed on & late at night arrived at Williamsburg where there was a strong line of fortifications. We were ordered to take them that night. We formed &

advanced into a clearing in their front but [there was] some mistake. One regt mistook another for enemy & fired into each other deranging the plans so we lay down on our arms all night & awoke within a short distance of the enemy. As they stood on the parapets we thought them to be our men but soon they threw a shot that told which side they belonged. It was Monday morning. It commenced raining about light & continued all day. About 8 am Hooker made a charge on Fort Magruder which proved unsuccessful. Soon another. They drove them but could not hold their position. About three pm one was made by our division on the enemies extreme left. At the same time one more by Hooker. Our division turned their left flank & slaughtered the enemy by hundreds with our cannon. It was dark so we could not persue them. If the sun could have stood still we would have taken their rear guard & part of their teems.

4th Garnets Farm [June 27, 1862]
This was our farewell to Richmond. The day before the Mechanicsville fight took place we drove the enemy a mile but next day Jackson came down on our right flank & compelled them to retreat in haste. We could see the enemy as they drove our men back. Soon they had passed into our rear. A hundred pieces of cannon came to our assistance. I had the pleasure of seeing the enemy advance within range of our guns & take such a shelling as they could not withstand. I saw one thirty-two pound shell plough into the flank of one regt & burst causing them to run in every direction probably killing a great many. I saw a man & a horse killed. It was very gratefying to see them run so. Soon we were ordered to the picket line about dusk. A line of the enemy was seen advancing. We opened fire & drove them back killing & wounding nearly one hundred men so we learned from a prisoner next day. A few of our men were hit none killed. They did not try to advance again. I suppose we might claim a little hand in Fair Oaks fight. We went to the river &c. were shell[ed] but did not cross [with] the water rising so fast. Those of the Sixth who crossed had to swim some of the way to get back.

5th Savage Station [June 29, 1862]
After the Garnet Farm fight we stayed in our old camp that night & next morning commenced to cook beens & carry on business as though all was right. About eleven we were ordered to pack up & be ready to start. We formed a line in front of the Colnels. We had hardly formed when a messinger was sent to tell us to get out of the way. It did no harm but made

the dirt fly well. Soon another & another & another. The Gen ordered us to get out of range if possible. Before we got any cover we learned what it was to run the gauntlet. After Countermarching a spell we spent the night in the woods back of camp. In the fournoon the enemy advanced to feel out our position but when they arrived at such a point a few masked bataries & muskets sent them back. Many were killed & wounded. The next morning the whole line retired & the enemy after them. We went back to Savage Station halted about dark. They pitched on to our rear. The 4th Regt was ordered to the left to prevent a flank movement. The remainder of the Brigade went to the Station & had a bloody fight loosing hundreds & had to quit the field & march all night leaving all our dead & wounded in their hands. The march was aweful. I never knew what it was to be thirsty before. We halted at White Oak.

6th Malivern Hill [July 1, 1862]

Malivern Hill is to the left of White Oak Swamp. We had taken our position on a hill just across the stream running through the swamp. There we were at our ease some asleep, some gambling & some cooking their coffee. I was a sleep at the time. I think it was about 2 P.M. when the dead silence was broken by the discharge of forty pieces of Cannon & the bursting of shells all around us. There was a little excitement there. We were ordered to the woods & form to repel an attack. I was not long waking. My things were scattered in two or three places. I collected them to gather & started with the rest. The shells were bursting all around me. One came so near my head that it knocked me partly down & turned me nearly around. It was so warm I could hardly breathe or run so I took a moderate pace. The Regt formed in the woods & waited an attack but they could not cross. Our bataries began to reply & in less than thirty minutes we had silenced them. Then the fight commenced at Malvern Hill. The incessant roar of musketry was heard. Soon we expected to take part but we were only lookers on. The enemy were fighting to secure their prise but we were too much for them. Our cannon ploughed their ranks slaughtering by thousands. At night we were ordered out to meet them once more but we halted them. We started for Harrison's Landing about eleven P.M. & marched until broad day light. I can not describe my feelings or looks. I saw Gen McClellan come riding past. He looked as though he had not seen sleep for a fortnight. I was glad to see him. I felt it ment something. ... We were safe under cover of the gun boats at Harrisons Landing.

7th Cramptons Pass [Sept 14, 1862]

We had left Virginia & gone to Maryland. Had tried a number of times to engage the enemy but they retired. Finaly they made a stand in the mountains. In the morning Gen Burnside commanding the right opened the fight. We kept marching to our left & just about four P.M. we arrived in rear of Burketsville. The enemy had made a stand. Slocums division was to charge on our right & as soon as they were turned to charge with Smiths Division. The enemy had cannon planted on top of the mountain so high that we could not reach them at all. So as we advanced they gave us a thorough shelling. We arrived in the vilage expecting they would not fire into the town. None of the inhabitants had left because they promised not to but they disregarded their promise. Some shots passed through the houses but fortunately none were hurt. Arriving within a few hundred yards of the woods the shot began to fly. Immediately skirmishers were thrown out & commenced to pick their sharpshooters. Finally the propper time approached for us to charge. Never did men form better for drill. The shot & shell were flying all arround them but on they went expecting every moment the entire stone walls would become one sheet of flame. But luck was on our side. We had appeard where they least expected us & could no better than run or surrender. To run prooved to be impossible & one hundred & fifteen Officers & all surrendered & were paroled. We took the last of the 16th Va. We have fought her before. We lost a number of men killed & wounded. The sides of that mountain looked like impassible barrier to our further progress.

8th Anteitam [Sept. 16, 1862]

We remained one day at South Mountain. The next morning we marched for what proved to be Anteitam. The cannonaiding commenced at light in the morning. As the sounds grew more & more distinctive we were reminded that we should be there soon & perhaps take an active part in the engagement. On arriving at the stream we forded it up to our knees & there were in full view of the battlefield. We could see Hookers men charge see the enemy run & just as we arrived on the right Gen Sumner & Smith & Franklin met. Sumner felt relieved. He had hardly been able to maintain his position but as we were there, he was all right. The 3rd Brigade of our Division led by Gen Smith double quicked into & through the woods, met the enemy, charged & broke their lines completely. Then the grape & canister was poured on the field [in] their rear mowing them like grass. Just then we received orders to about face & march to the left. We could see two rebil *bataries firing at us. We expected to be badly cut to pieces. They did their best to hit our ranks but did not &c. But when we came very near they were affraid of their batary so retired. But as we were forming in the cornfield the ground that had been taken & retaken twice before we occupied the ground was strewn with the dead & wounded. There I received a bayonet wound in my instep & before we were formed the enemy got range of us & poured in a shower of grape shell &c. We deployed as skirmishers advanced within full view of the enemy halted & watched their movements. We had full view of their cannon & also saw the 7th Maine charge.*

9th Fredricksburg [December 12, 1862]
    As I look back [and] think of the dangers I have passed through without being harmed, it seems miraculous & I hope that the God that has preserved my life through so many battles will still guide and protect me through as many campaigns as take place during my term of enlistment.

General Burnside was also no doubt fixated on the Fredericksburg defeat and desperate to make up for that humiliation with a winter victory. After having been rebuffed by Lincoln in his earlier attempt, Burnside took more time to prepare his next plan. As Henry had mentioned in his earlier letter, the weather had been so unusually warm that he seldom even needed an overcoat. It had also been dry and so, with the roads in unusually good condition, a winter attack could be prepared. Burnside altered his earlier plan so that the main invading force would cross the Rappahannock about six miles north of the city at Banks Ford. Hooker and Franklin were to start moving their divisions towards Banks Ford on January 20. The pontoon bridges were to be quickly put into place on the morning of January 21, and the invasion would begin. Sumner was to wait until Hooker and Franklin were across the river and then send his division across at Falmouth.

On the morning of January 20, Hooker and Franklin moved their divisions out along with wagons full of supplies, artillery, and the pontoon bridges. Unlike George Washington, who had once escaped a British army during a winter campaign by reading the weather signs and realizing that an approaching frost would make a marshy area passable, Burnside could not divine the changing weather patterns. A light rain began to fall in mid-afternoon; as the day went on, the rain became heavier and it continued relentlessly for the next several days. Roads turned into quagmires, and soldiers found themselves sinking to their knees in the mud. Rebel soldiers from across the river watched in amusement as the Union soldiers were stagnated in what became known as "Burnside's Mud March."

The day before this debacle began, Henry had written to Frank and was apparently unaware of any of the upcoming plans.

I am just in from three days picket. The picket line has been shortened and we have details for three days only and none for only one day. The weather was unusually favorable so that I did not suffer much from exposure. It is pleasanter for me to remain in camp than to go out on picket but I never do either picket or guard duty without learning many new things and forming new acquaintances or what is about the same seeing men from the different Companies in thier inercourse with each other. In camp one seldom makes acquaintances out of his own Company. I almost invariably find men possessed of good abilities often of with minds more or less cultivated and usualy of extensive acquaintance with human nature and a degree of self independence & command which I think is not often acquired in any other school than the Army de camp, on campaign and on the battle field. I meet with some quite old men and these are usualy <u>ripe soldiers</u> with hardly an exception. So far as my observation has gone-fine looking-fine appearing, intelligent men. Some trained in schools & others supplying the lack of Education or book knowledge edge by native shrewdness, observation & that experience & knowledge of the world which the disposition which at last called them into the army in previous life gave opportunity for development & exercise. Still they rank with inn Keepers & horse jockeys and while ones respect for thier natural abilities and acquirements is increased by contact his confidence in them as men is diminished by thier lack of moral virtue and the degrading objects for which thier talents are exercised. True moral worth carries with it a power better calculated to awe as to inspire confidence than intellectual power whether manifested in wit or wisdom or both combined.

There is probably more of whiskey drinking in the army than at any former period as it is obtained with less difficulty than formerly. I am convinced that the <u>social</u> glass should never be indulged in. For a vast majority, of those who thus indulge or live in communities where the prejudice against its use does not exist to exert on them its restraining power go too far and the duty of those who possess better judgements or self command is to set thier face against its use for examples sake if nothing more. While I was out George Ainsworth called to see me. I expect he will be round again in a week or so. I have just been informed that he has been assigned to the 2nd Division of the 2nd Corps Genl Ewells head quarters. I suppose that the letter in the Vt Watchman of Jan 15th from Brandy Station signed Observer was written by him.

I would like to have Mother make you another woolen shirt so that I can keep the one you left with me.

A week later, on January 25, Henry explained to his brother the ordeal they had just endured.

Last Tuesday Ten AM we started for a ford three miles above Falmoth & twelve miles from White Oak Church. The morning was clear & no prospect of rain but before we arrived the clouds indicated rain & before we had our tents pitched it began to rain & continued all night next day & part of Thursday &c. The rain caused the roads to become impassable for the pontoons & artilery. So Wednesday the Brigade in the rain & cold mud was orderd out to draw the pontoons to the river. The mud was knee deep, the horses fast in mud & so cold & wet that they would not draw. So with a will our men with shoes waided into the mud & helped draw them out. We worked till dark & were not able to get them all out of that. Three men were run over & ones rist smashed to pieces, two over the legs not braking them & one across the bowels. They got fast in the mud & could not get out of the way. After dark we returned wet & very cold to camp in some thick pine woods & slept till morning on the wet ground. That night we had whiskey rations finaly. We remained till friday morning when we started for our old camp the mud very hard & deep so that it was almost impossible to get along. When we arrived in camp we could not get any wood to make us comfortable. … It looks as though the Lord was against us. The people at the north must let our Generals alone. It is impossible to moove in the dead of winter. … Today we are fixing up our old shanties. Also have received orders to draw all clothing wanted for February. It appears we are to stop a while. I hope so.

Henry continued with a litany of complaints about army life, no doubt accentuated by the events of the previous week:

We have never sufferd so much before & the army was never in so low spirits as now. They uterly detest soldiers life. I think it is badly managed. If I had been hurt up there I could not have had anything done for me. If I had been able to live I should but I could not had any care. There is no encouragement for a man to go into danger. If he is killed, he is out of misery & a hole dug, his remains wraped in a blanket if he has one & buried. Some times a head board is put up but seldom. Such is what this army is coming to. It seems as though we cannot stand long. A certain few have served faithfuly & when friends, wives or children are taken sick they ask a short leave but cannot get *them. This is not right. A number of like instances have occurd. Such things I do not like. Many say they will go let the consequences be what they will. A number have gone. <u>I do not blame them</u>. A number of men fell out because they could not keep up & are now under going severe punishment. This is not right. Many are not well but they cannot get excused, but after undergoing what we have for the last few days & being so completely exhausted that they cannot keep up & to be punished is not making men like to try and do much for their country. If they are to be used in this way I cannot blame them for deserting. Again we were the first to have crossed the river. Why is it that we are to be always in danger? I think we had better not raise any more men for they do no fighting. I must close. I am well, but extremely tired. Dek Jones got badly hurt that day, perhaps will do no more service.*

Burnside now presented President Lincoln with an ultimatum to either relieve him from command or dismiss much of the leadership of the Army of the Potomac, whom Burnside believed were disloyal to his command. Considering the events of the last month, Lincoln probably had little difficulty deciding to accept Burnside's resignation and replace him with General Hooker on January 26. The next day, in a letter to his parents, Henry described further the aborted attempt to invade across the river under Burnside:

I wrote a hasty letter to Francis just after our arrival to our old Camp which we left about one week before. We did not expect to come as soon if at all but providence did interfere in a pointed manner. No one could dispute that the weather had been remarkably fine ever since we arrived at White Oak Church but just as we were ready to try our streangth once more we were withheld by the roads becoming impassable. So severe was the storm on the horses that twenty died out of one batary. Only think of the general loss. It did not stop with the horses only but the soldiers were many of taken down with Typhoid feaver. The Hospitals are full. Burnside has lost his command. Is our government going crazy? He did his best & no one could have done better as far as he went. I think they ought to have tried him in one more battle. Certain the first was only a breaking in experiment which all will have to go through before they can understand themselves but you know I do not want to be the tool in their hands. It cost too many lives. Hooker will not spare us at all. Also Sumner & Franklin are removed. Are we to loose all our best Generals? I dont know but it is all right but it does not agree with my opinion. As I remarked in my letter to Uncle Bass after Napoleon parted with his wife, success left him. So it has been in our case since McClellans removal. I did not know but it was all right when it was done. Now I do not think as then. He is slow but never was whiped. True he did not accomplish all we might desire to have done. Still he is far ahead of any thing we have had over us. Some men can command a division others a corps but to command an army is another thing. I am opposed to his political sentiment but I want a General to lead us successfuly laying party feeling asside.

Yesterday morning I saw Bliss Davis from Danville. He is visiting a sick son in the 2nd Brigade & being so near the 1st he came down to see us. To day he has gone to Falmoth to get a flag of truce to cross the river & visit a son there. He is a surgeon. We saw him at Antietam. He is a rank secessh.

Henry concluded the letter on January 28 in an even more dejected mood:

Yesterday we had one of the severest storms we have ever experienced since we joined the service. With nothing but shelter tents the men could hardly keep from freezing. The snow fell six inches deep. Soldiering in the winter is not very pleasant & never should be alowed. Our fires would not burn but smoke us out of our pretended shelters. I thought yesterday we had better give up & go home. I can hardly see the point we are to gain. To subdue the enemy is to anihalate them. How long will it take? I have fought under a certain set of leaders about as long as I wish to. Mr Davis says he cannot see how we are to get along. After next june to draft is not to be done for all have volunteerd that ought to. He thinks there will be a general separation north from south east from west. Strong [as] an anti slavery republican as he is he thinks the sooner we let the south go the better & not sacrifice any more men. We can never whip the south so they will stay whiped. Their army is composed of a share of northern men & ours a share of southern & they can fight as well as we can. They care better for their men than we. They have large & comfortable tents while we none & no stoves. This is more than we know how to be without. We shall loose more men in this storm than at Fredricksburg. ... A light infantry brigade is geting up & one regt from each brigade is to be taken. I hope we shall not be chosen. We are light enough now.

The thought just occurd to me, how you have been prosperd during this time of great trouble to be able to onse more to see yourself out of det. I can imagine how relieved you must feel. I hope I may be spared to return & see how it seems myself – some times I have wished myself at home but if I return it will have prooved a good lesson. I shall not regret that I enlisted at the commencement of the war. For all the pomp & show the reality is more than anyone imagines at home.

Such hardships must have been all the more difficult to accept when the soldiers did not even receive their promised pay. In early February, Henry sent a fellow soldier to find Chauncey Smith and present him with the following message:

I have the pleasure of introducing to you Corp. John G. Green, Co. B. 4th Vt. He is on his way to Vermont & like many others out of money as it has been a long time since he was paid &c. If you will help him to fifteen or twenty dollars I will see that you are paid.

Although the pay did not arrive, letters from home, dearly valued by the soldiers, continued to be delivered. Henry's uncle Ebenezer Bass, who lived across the road from the Martins and who had two daughters (Lorette and Eunice) close in age to Henry and Francis, sent a letter on February 1:

Although a long time has passed and you have gone through many dangers seen and unseen since I wrote you last, be assured that you nor any one else of my townsmen in arms have been forgotten by me. While you with others of my fellow townsmen are bearing your breasts to traitors steel and your warm blood is weting traitors soil, think not that I am unmindful of the sacrifise you have made for the common defense of the best government on earth, which I hold to be most dear. Stay, I say to you, although you may feel that I am among others at home do not realise the awful horrors of war, and have not, as often as we might, cheered you on in the glorious cause in which you are engaged by writing you oftener. The only apology I have to make is the press of business. How it may be with others I know not, but presume they will claim a reasonable excuse. ... Since you wrote from Fredericksburg I have been overtaxed with business. In addition to my own ordinary business I have much of other peoples to attend to. Since my girls left home early in September, they claim that I must write them evry week and I have done so. Beside I have many business letters to write and care for many widows and orphans also collect the taxes as when you were here, and I have been honored with a low seat upon the Judges bench for the present year which has taken over two weeks of my time the past month. So you see I have made out a pretty good excuse for my seeming neglect. The girls are still at 125 Benefit Street, Providence, R.I. Eunice is gradually going down to her grave with Consumption. They would be glad to hear from you. ...

Lewis Clark's remains were carried to Worcester and laid beside his Mother week before last. Clark Wilson's remains have arrived at Montpelier to be brought here to be buried with Father and Mother and loved ones. Chester

Clark is improving and reports to Burlington tomorrow bodily. He seems in good spirits, is able to hobble about some on crutches, says he might have taken a discharge before coming home but would not, so you see if he lives you may again see him at his post. Chester Clark says Henry Smith wants to know Truman E Blodgetts address, or another Soldiers with whom he has business and who is with Blodgett. I had a letter from Blodgett dated Dec 19, 1862, United States, General Hospital, Lexington Avenue, corner 51st Street, N.Y. I send his address for the benefit of Smith and that any one may know where he is that may take any interest in him. He says he has not heard from the boys since he left them. I have not much doubt but he is still there. We are having a fine warm winter for Vermont. Have had but little snow and so warm that fresh meat wont keep without stinking. There is no news worth writing, beside I suppose your brother Francis keeps you posted in Williamstown matters. ...

Since I have been writing this letter, Clark Wilsons remains have passed by in the hearse and gone up to Abram Goodrich and I am requested to go up there to make arrangements for his funeral. Although I am over sixty years of age and have made up my mind not to do such business any longer and have refused of late when called on yet I shall go in this instance for the love I bear to the man, and the glorious cause in which he like a martyr fell. If our townsmen must fall I will be first and foremost to pay the last tribute of respect to their lifeless remains and that is all that can be done on earth. Poor fellows, their career on earth is at an end, but their friends may well say they died in a good cause. And now let me say to you and your townsmen comrads, prove true to the good old flag though evry high officer in command be cashiered, and you are left without a commander, another may rise up greater than them all, then patiently bear the burden of the day, and be of good cheer, trusting that all will come out right in due time and our country once again be at peace.

Around the same time, Henry also received a letter from Chauncey.

Your late letter found me laid up with a severe cold and some fever, but by timely medicine and care I am able to be at my duties again. I think I can procure all the articles you write for, at reasonable prices at our stores, and will devote this evening to the purpose, and send them as soon as maybe. ... I will carefully inquire among the stores, and get good articles, at the lowest prices, and take a bill of each one, and inclose to you by mail that you can see the exact amount the whole amounts to, and so write you again tomorrow or next day.

For the past week we have had stormy weather, snow and rain, and of course we are litterally covered up in mud; but this morning it is a little cooler, and the mud is drying up. I presume you have faired as badly as we have, and have not been able to get about much, or out of your tents as little as possible.

Had a letter from Mr. Ainsworth last week, relative to taking up and forwarding the body of young Wilson, and our friends were then all well. We sent the body on last Wednesday, at an expense of $53, including taking up, boxing, and Express. Mr Ainsworth wrote that Mr. Clark and Chester arrived safely with the body of Lewis. Most of the wounded boys have been sent on to Vt, or fast as they were well enough to go–all doing well.

John Clough, a 42-year-old farmer in Williamstown, also wrote to Henry during the first week of February:

My healths very good and hope when this few ill composed lines reach you that they will find thee in perfect health. I dont know how you like the last change in the Army of the Potomac but I am almost discouraged to think of the affairs that is going on in that army. I hope they will choose soon and get the right commander of the Army of the Potomac.

Under General Hooker's leadership, changes occurred in the army that caused the Union soldiers to sense that this time they did indeed have the right commander. Henry optimistically described some of the initial changes in a February 6 letter to Francis:

Your kind favor bearing date January 28th is received. I had just returned from picket. We had been out three days but the weather was good so it was rather pleasant staying there. There was pleanty of wood to burn, so we could keep comfortable. The most disagreeable part was having nothing to do. Reading was scarce so we were left to our own thoughts. The next day after we returned the weather changed. It has stormed ever since. The mud is so deep that it is almost impossible to get rations from the landing. This morning a number of bataries have passed supposeing to be bound for Washington. It is reported here that portions of the army are on the moove. That only enough are to be left to guard our present line. I hope we shall be left. Gen. Hooker is changeing this army. Gen. Smith is removed & takes command of a corps on the peninsula. Hooker is going to consolidate the army have full Regiments & dismiss all dissatisfied field officers such as are complaining of the Presidents proclamation &c. He don't want them & will not have them. So far very good. Also he has orderd no leaveing of camp without leave. Guards have been orderd around the Regiments. That is hard this wet weather. Also he wants no Major or Brigadier Generals who cannot lead their men in battle. He says it is their place & if they are not wiling to take it he will dismiss them. One thing is certain he will have to record the loss of many Generals. But if we are lead by such Generals I pity the rebels for men will do more lead by their Lieutenant than by the Colonel. Hookers place is in the thickest of the fight. He asks no man to go where he can't lead. One of his men speaking of him says just before a fight he is rather nervous, his saddle is not right & his collar chafes him &c. But when the fight is to commence they know it for down comes that standing when out with his swoard waves it over his head & says come on folow me.

Colonel Stoughton is under arrest for bad conduct. I hope he will get his deserts & be cashered. He is to be court marshaled. He has been very unwise, & Col. Whiting now in command of the Brigade has resigned. Col. Heide has done the same. He was very lucky ought to have been dismissed from the service. Furlows are granted for fifteen days. One man to a hundred & two commissund officers to a Regiment. John Green is going home for one.

What does Chester Clark say about army affairs. He has got to go to Burlington or Brattleboro. It is thought that better care can be taken of them by the experienced army surgeons. It must make the people feel bad to see two of their townsmen brought home dead. Did they have a soldiers burial? They ought to. I received a letter from Mr. Smith. He said he had forwarded Wilson's body. I am sorry for any man who has the Chronic deirehea. I have seen lots of men die with it. It is awful. They looked so bad.

I have concluded to send for a small beef. The butter was very acceptable & the only good we have had for a long time. I would like fifteen or tweanty <u>lbs</u>, a <u>little</u> only dried apple. A pair of calfskin slippers Sise 6. A pair of good styled shoes calfskin thick bottoms no. 6. I want them to do some servise. They cost much here. Two lbs. green tea & its price, a couple wash towels. 1/2 dosen iron spoons. Chunk of coarse soap & cake of fine. A decent pocket knife, a pair of twesers. I don't think of anything more. I dare not get much on my hands for I can't carry it. The Captain was greatly pleased with the butter & dried apple & wanted to know if you made it to sell. Supposeing you would not want to furnish him. I did not [give] him any encouragement. He is very rich & cares nothing about money.

The next day, Henry sent a short letter home from "Camp Near White Oak Church."

I received a letter from Uncle Bass. He spoke of the arrival of Clark Wilson's body &c. ... John Green received one from Lorette. ...The weather's fine today. The sun is very warm. The mud deep enough. ... I have just read of more reverses at Charleston. It is discouraging to see our men all asleep. It seems as though they would begin to see what weakness there is in great armies & navies. People at home will begin to hold their troops & stop urging forward faster than the generals can plan. If they want to fight so bad come out & try it. The Fabian is the policy for me & I think it the time now for us to pursue.

The Fabian strategy for which Henry advocated dates back to the Roman general Fabius Maximus, who faced Hannibal in the Second Punic War. Fabius avoided a decisive battle while wearing the enemy down through a drawn-out war of attrition. Washington received the nickname "American Fabius" for using similar tactics during the Revolutionary War. Henry apparently believed that the North's advantages in resources and manpower could be used to wear down the Confederacy, much as Winfield Scott had advocated with his Anaconda Plan at the start of the war.

While Chauncey was purchasing supplies for Henry, there was a concern that items might be stolen en route to the camp. Fortunately, Mary Farnham was in Washington and heading back to the army camp. Mrs. Farnham, from the Orange County town of Bradford, was staying with her husband, Lieutenant Colonel Roswell Farnham of the Twelfth Vermont. According to Chauncey's letter on February 7, Mary offered to personally handle the box's delivery. Mary may have offered to help Henry because Roswell's cousin, Nelson Farnham, serving with him in the Twelfth Vermont, was a friend of Henry's from Williamstown.

As good fortune would have it, Mrs Farnham has come up from the army and is willing to take charge of the box. We have procured all the articles you wrote for, and to facilitate the convenience and safety of their transmission, she proposes to put all the things which she may get with yours and then all into one box that she may keep an eye upon it after arriving at Belle Plain. By her and other accounts we hear that there is great "plundering" at Bell Plain and so we mean to obviate it if we can.

Mary had only recently arrived at the camp and moved in with her husband on January 19. It was gracious of her to volunteer to deliver packages after (according to a letter that she wrote to her sister-in-law) she had just endured a difficult trip back to Washington, D.C. She was traveling with her husband and George Benedict, an editor of the *Burlington Free Press* who was acting as a war correspondent. The three rode in an ambulance because both of Farnham's horses were ill.

Mary and Roswell Farnham on horseback at the Twelfth Vermont Camp
Courtesy of Bradford Historical Society

It was snowing hard when we started and the mud up to the axletree half the way and the driver would stop and take a drink out of every canteen he met. ... I should judge they contained whiskey by the way he took us over logs and everything that lay in his path. I was obliged to keep hold on to a strap or rail of the Ambulance to keep myself on the seat. But at last I was tired of holding on and thought I would sit up independent. I had hardly got my independence established before I was thrown up a foot and landed at the bottom of the carriage at Mr. Benedict's feet!! I could not help myself for some time, Mr. B and Ros tugging with all their might to raise me. I never was so mad when Ros said, Well, you cut a PRETTY figure! I was VERY WELL AWARE OF IT. I told them I hoped they would both find themselves in the same situation. ... I think Ros did get just a little taste of the floor once but it was when he was looking the other way and he hurried himself up. I never saw anything like it.

George Benedict later wrote a history of Vermont's role in the Civil War. Roswell Farnham was elected Governor of Vermont in 1880 by the largest margin in state history.

Henry's cousin George Smith sent a letter on February 13 from "Camp Sykes Division 5th Army corps Near Potomac Creek, Va."

You no doubt consider me indebted to you for a letter which I confess in the strict sense of the word I am. At the same time I consider one visit iquivilant to two letters and that on the whole you are indebted to me instead of me to you.

I have been expecting to see you constantly since I was at your camp but have been disappointed. I must say I think you are quite <u>reserved</u> in your <u>military career</u>. But enough. I trust I have said enough to stir you up. I am just getting a little better of the Dypatheria. I did not have it the hardest that could be but I assure you it was hard enough. I am in hopes to be well in a few days. I heard by way of father that it had been very sickly with you sinse the "stick in the mud" so has it with us. Our Batt has had but one die this winter of sickness however & he from my company.

Can you not get a leave of absence to go home the last of this month. I am in hopes to get one of fifteen days (which by the way is the extent given now) & should like yur company. I am thinking of going to Williamstown. I should have had a leave before if there had been another officer with the company. All the officers in this corps are getting leaves. I wish you would come up and see me and we will make some arrangement to go home together. If you cannot come possibly then write me at onse. I hear Clark Wilson & Clark have died from wounds rec'd at Fredericksburgh. That 14th day of Dec will be a memorable day for many. I do not wish to trouble my memory with more of the kind.

I have no news. Jane [George's sister] has gone to Florida [to join her husband, who was stationed there]. I have never rec'd so good a letter from father (at least for a long time) as I did a few days ago. I hope he will continue in well doing.

They are talking of consolidating the Reg army making full companies & having 1 Capt 3 Lt's. I cannot tell what effect it will have upon us yet.

On February 15, Henry shared revealing details about the army's spiritual environment in a letter home to his parents:

On a visit to George Smith I learned a little news which will not be inappropriate to write on the sabath. One of Gen Howards Aids came to see George (an old acquaintance of his at Norwich). He had just received an appointment & been out a couple of weeks. The first morning he was called into the Generals tent & to his surprise it was to attend morning prayer. He said it was the first time in his life that he was on his knees. He did not have much of an opinion of it &c, &c. Gen Howard is a Vermonter & a fit man for a General. A braver man cannot be found in the field. He lost an arm at Fair Oaks. He commands a Division. He compells all immediately under him to attend prayers. I suppose he is not the only praying General. Gen. Phelps is another. I learn we have a number of prominent Generals in this army. From Ernest,

Hawkins, Hitchcock, Brooks, Smith, Stoughton, &c, but this is away from my subject for Sunday. It rained today, we had no religious services. Finally, no one to preach. Such has been our luck ever since we came out.

Fred Lynde is coming to make us a visit soon. Good testimony on the sabbath in the army & navy. At a meeting held in Washington Maj. Gen Casey gave utterance to sentiments worthy to be proclaimed in the ears of the army & the nation. "I have been thirty-six years in the military service," said he "& I know that the army needs a sabbath. I was five years in the Florida war. In long marches better time will be made, & the men will go through in better condition, by resting on the Sabbath than by continuous marching. No prudent Gen will plan for a battle on Sunday. I would appeal to the American people to save our American Sabbath. If our wealth is lost in this terrible war it may be recovered. If our young men are killed off others will grow up. But if our Sabbath is lost it can never be restored & all is lost." The audience were affected to tears by these words from the gray headed warrior. Rear Admiral Foote followed in behalf of the Navy & illustrated the value of the Sabbath to the discipline & efficiency of this branch of the service from his own experience at sea & on the western Flotilla. He said he had always taken the Chaplains place when there was no such Officer present as he thought evry commander should & he advocated the same courage & decision in the discharge of Christian duty as in the performance of military or naval duties.

I thought the above remarks would be interesting so I copied them. In looking over our Generals I find many more Christian professors than I expected. Gen Burnside is another & a truer man cannot be found in the United States army.

As I was reading a book from the Soldiers Library titled Farmer & his Family I noticed a striking fact. The subject of the chapter [was] marriage of several of his children. It says marriage is honorable in all &c but many persons have not made wise choices. Some marry for the purpose of allying themselves to families of distinction, acquiring or repairing fortune &c &c. These persons do not intentionally marry either husbands or wives. They marry distinctions, fortunes, titles, villas, luxury & grandeur, but the farmers children studied the gospel rule. "Marry only in the Lord." I thought the farmers childrens choice very good.

While on Brigade review a Major General rode past with only one orderly. He was a splendid looking man. He attracted evryones eye. Splendidly dressed sitting very erect in his saddle, &c. it prooved to be Gen Hooker. I thought it might be him but other Generals have four or five hundred *cavilry & their aids. He is taking the right course to command the respect of both Officers & men.*

Our Chaplain is very sick. His legs are swollen & they are as large as his body, such is the effect Southern Climate has on him. It is feared one of our men have broken out with the small pox. I hope not. The most of us have been vaxinated since we entered the war. Today this Regiment is being vaxinated fearing that the case may proove to be smallpox so then only a few may have it. I hope it will be checked if it should commence to rage in the ranks. I think we should be taken better care of here than at home for they would not be so afraid of it. Many prefer it to typhoid feaver. It is universally fatal.

Capt Platt has finaly obtained an enviable position. He stays in Washington & when a lot of deserters are on hand he sends them to their Regiments. His pay is increased fifty eight dollars his Capt Pay 130.00 + 58= 188.00. Majors pay. His wife is there with him. Excellent chance. Col Howard is at Washington trying to get his Regt into our Brigade. He would be the ranking Colnel & probably our General.

PS Has John Green arrived at Williamstown yet. What does he have to say about the war? Did he come by way of Rhode Island to see Lorette & Eunice? John has had an easy time since he left the Co. He has been Co Clerk a position I got him before I left. It is very easy considerable writing but no company duty except fights &c &c. Please if this arrives before he leaves tell him to get me a small dictionary. Also a good morocco covered memorandum or account book costing from a half dollar to seventy five cents as near like my old one which he has seen. ... Do not forget to send some Postage stamps. I am all out.

Despite having written such a long letter Sunday evening, Henry had time to write further the next day:

I will now tell what I saw on my visit to George. I got a pass signed by the Major & obtained the loan of my Captains horse & left camp about nine A.M. I directed my course to Falmouth to see what the enemy were doing. The roads were almost impassable even on horseback but I made out to get along & arrived opposite the old battleground about eleven A.M. The view was splendid from the banks of the river, it was like climing our cow pasture hill & looking down on the meadow. It is a complete illustration. Seemingly standing on the bank we must be friends so near are the Pickets, only across the river, which is five or six rods across. Standing on the bank I could see evry house & street in the city. Our side is about forty feet higher than the rebil side so you can imagine what an observatory we must have. I could see the enemy hard at work throwing up rifle pits all over the city but just back is the iresistable barrirs forts crowning the top of evry hill & all around could be seen miles of rifle pits. Such a formidable sight I never saw before. It surpasses Yorktown & evry thing is such plain sight. They are working more brisk than ever before. They have sent word to the people of Falmoth to leave the place as they are to cross the river & shell the place. A part of our supplies are brought within shelling distance of the rebils probably seeing the trains come in three or four times a day in plain sight. Gen Hooker hopes they will come over. He says he shall not fight them behind their works but in the open field. It will take great stratagem to draw them out. They think our army is weakened, most of it sent South. I guess there is enough left to attend to them. From Falmouth I went to the 17th Regulers, found George sick with diptheria. He has seen the worst of it & is now about [but] not on duty. I saw a number of the Officers. They looked very well. Nothing extra but dreadfuly conceited. They drill some better than our troops as they have less to do. They are in rear of the army have but little to do but drill. I dined with George & about five I started for home. Darkness came on me before I got on the right road. The country here so changed by clearing up the woods & the woods so cut up that I could not tell where I was right. I enquired & wandered around a long time. Finaly I let the horse have his head & he brought me safe into camp.

Today is very pleasant and comfortable. We are all well. We are in hopes the smallpox will not spread among us. It is not decided whether he has it or not. My health continues good.

The next day, Henry started a letter to Francis, to which he added throughout the next week:

Siting by my fire this cold stormy evening I thought I would busy myself by writing a few lines. When I awoke this morning I was surprised to find it snowing very fast for the day previous it was as pleasant as summer. It has continued all day & fallen to the depth of four inches - a very heavy snow for this part of the country. It effects the negroes very much. They can hardly stir. The Capt has a boy which is very smart. His features do not resemble the African at all. He is rather handsome & remarkably capable. Can do anything any one can. I wish he was my boy for I could make a smart man of him. He ought to be sent to Colage. Seldom find white boys as smart.

Another of our men have been discharged, leaving sixty nine men & 30 present for duty. Also Lieut Burten has resigned & gone home. We have very good accomodations for cooking. The Capt found a Conant stove outside the picket line & got the loan of it while we stoped here. It was to be a present to their daughter when maried but she was accidentaly shot just after we arrived by her brother. A stove here is as rare as they used to be sixty years ago at home. All work is done by fireplaces. ...

February 18th

Today it rains. It makes it hard procuring wood. I wish you could see how they clear land. After the trees are all cut & burned, the men commenced on the stumps. Hundreds of acres have been cleared. Houses that were in the wilderness are now in plain sight.

The soldiers that have been so long hanging around the Hospitals are now being sent forward in great numbers & most of them Court marshaled for desertion. ...

February 19th

Still the rain continues to fall. Our chimnies do not draw so we are driven out of doors. Another man discharged today. Eight AM we go on picket for three days. Fortunate for us the storm is just over. I received a letter from George. His throat was getting better. The Report says that four hundred thousand men are to be called for to have all men examined & ready to come whether they wish to or not. Very good. Also have commenced drafting negroes, they will make good soldiers.

I am expecting if I may so term it every day when we may be called north to fight the rebils in your midst for such they are & ought to go & join the south. So be in their proper places.

February 23

Yours of Feby 16 was received while on picket. I hope you will not be obliged to come into the army. Still I should not shrink from coming if your health would permit. I do not think it good enough to hold out long. ... I have not time to write more in this letter & have it go out today. Snow fell twelve inches yesterday. We were on picket & had a rough time.

A day later, Henry began a letter to his parents, expressing concern about his older brother joining him in the Vermont Brigade and describing life in the winter camp "Near White Oak Church, Va."

I suppose Francis has either got a certificate or been enrolled as one of the reserved soldiers. For his comfort I hope he may be left at home. He will surely be sick on first arrival here. The water & change of climate creates feavers, Diarreha, & most evry thing you can think of. All the humers come out &c some are three months in getting aclimated. Stout men generaly die. Slim men become as fat as hogs. The open air agrees with them.

Last Friday we went on picket. The sun shone bright & the sky was clear. Thus it continued untill Saturday night when the clouds indicated rain which before morning proved to be snow. I told my men to prepare for a storm. Some did some did not think me a true weather prophet so they did not put up their tents but spread their blankets as usual occupying the spacious bedroom which is the common heritage of all of the children of Adam. They were very soon fast asleep About one AM the storm commenced. They closed all of the holes in their blankets & went to sleep again. Morning found twelve inches of snow on top of them. It would seem rather rough to sleep out such a night. One man almost froze to death (last night three men did while on post) but like wise men they do not stop for rough weather but make the best of it. We returned Monday twelve A.M. ...

The Co. subscribed $100.00 to purchase their Captain a sword belt & Pistol. It will be very nice sword. A number have been presents in the regiment to the Captains. ...

Thursday, 26

Yesterday we had a great time. The 26th N.J. Regiment chalanged the 3rd [and] 4th Regiments to snow ball with them. The 26th was larger than both of our Regiments. Still we were not going to let such a chalange go unnoticed so the Colnels called out their respective Regiments, drew them up in battle array. We were formed by division. Just out of sight, the 3rd on our left a part of the 4th & 3rd sent out to attack them in front & a reserve of 5th Company were held as flankers. At the word they attacked. Such a sight. The air was full of snowballs. Our men charged & took their Colnel prisoner. Just at that critical moment we rushed forward & cut them off from their camp. At that moment there was desperate fighting & finally we took them all prisoners & took their camp & then such cheering you seldom hear. We took all their horses & officers & hauled them off their horses such was the determined purpose of the men that that nothing could with stand them. Quite a number of eyes are black this morning. It was a regular battle. The plans were laid accordingly. The Enemy took a position on a hill & got pleanty of ammunition on hand & we had to drive them from their works. You can imagine how we were received by eight hundred men. It was a hot place in front. There was no fighting but some washing of faces. ...

The absent men have not returned yet. Being two days over their time I am sorry for it will stop any more going home.

Three men were froze to death the night after we were relieved on Picket. Another of our men are to be discharged. John Green returned this PM. He enjoyed his visit very much. [There are] 2000 men left in the Vt. Brigade. When we came out we had 5200 men. It is reported that Capt Ayers is to be our Brigadier. He is a brave man & at Antietam during the battle Gen McClellan asked Captain Ayers - Can your bataries cross Antietam Crick? My bataries , Sir, can go where they are needed replied the Captain.

With referance to my leaving the service &c under this conscription act the old Regiments will be filled up instead of consolidating them but I do not stand much of a sight at being again put into the ranks. Being an officer they cant put me there again in this army but I feel that my services are needed as long as my health holds out so good as it is. Men are wanted & having become accustomed to life in the army I wish to remain during my term of enlistment. I hope & pray that my life & health may be spared to return alive & whole. I hope I may get a leave of absence by next April or May.

My Captain started for Vermont this morning so I am left to make out the pay rolls & muster the company no small job I will assure you. Fred Lynde came to the Regiment today. He looks finely. His father is at Fredricksburg yet his mother has been north & wanted to return but Gen Hooker told her she had not better cross for there was to be troublous times there soon. So she has not returned. ...

Whereas Henry wrote in a very straightforward and matter-of-fact style, his older brother Francis had a much more literate, yet often wordy, writing style. In a March letter to their cousin Henry Smith, who was also from Williamstown and in the Fourth Vermont, Francis exhibited this flowery prose as well as some reflection on not yet having joined the war effort:

I have had the pleasure of reading a letter from you to Uncle Bass bearing date March 2nd in which you express much gratitude for the interest he has manifested to you and others. This with the account you give of your perils and hardships–of the oppression to which you are subjected and of the despondency of the soldiers resulting from defeats and fruitless victories–and above all the spirit of earnest devotion to our country's cause has so enlisted my sympathies that I wish to give them expression in a few words of heartfelt kindness which would certainly be cheering to me were I placed in your situation–and I hope will not be unacceptable to you.

How this war will result I can judge no better than you - but we can derive encouragement from the belief that "God's providence over states and kingdoms as times and seasons, is all for the best; that the revolutions of state, and changes of empire, the rise and fall of monarchies, persecutions, wars, famines, and plagues, are all permitted and conducted by God's providence, to the general good of man in this state of trial." And if we are God's children and faithfully perform our duty we shall in due time receive our reward. As I have said before–this letter is merely the expression of the feelings of my heart. To you as a soldier I cannot give such sympathy as you might receive from one of tried courage and patriotism–my experience in the service of our country is that of the old men–the infirm, the women and the children–but I can appreciate–in some degree & admire and aspire after your brave and heroic Spirit & assure you that you have our confidence and prayers for your welfair. Believe me we all feel that with officers fit to lead such men–our brave boys would have crushed the rebellion ere this. As a brother in Christ saved from the same corruption, delivered from the grasp of the same foe by the same Redeemer–partaker of the same conflict with remaining sin and fellow heir to the same glory–I would say to you, have faith in God–believe that "all things work together for good to them that love God, to them who are the called according to his purpose" and soon you will come off "more than conquerors through him that loves us." I do not expect that this letter will be of much interest to you–but I hope it will be received in the same spirit with which it is written.

Henry wrote a short letter home on March 2:

Sunday it was very pleasant but windy. The day before it rained very hard but the strong southwind has dried up the mud wonderfuly. I have had a very busy time of late. The Captain leaving just as he did left all the mustering &c for me to do alone. Four muster rolls have to be made out containing the names, date of enlistment, when enlisted by whom where mustered into the service, by whom last paid by whom, to what time & state whether absent sick detached or present &c no small job of work. ... Col Grant of the 5th Vermont is in command of the Brigade. He is generally liked. ... All of the men absent on furlough have returned but one. He has deserted & ought to be shot. One in the 5th went back there. He was safe across the Canada line.

Colonel Lewis A. Grant replaced Henry Whiting as commander of the Vermont Brigade. A few days later, on March 5, a letter arrived from Chauncey:

Was glad to hear from you, and found your letter so pleasant that I sent it on to Mr Ainsworth as heretofor for the benefit of Williamstown people.

Truly, poor soldiers have a hard time of it amid snows and storms, but thank God they continue. ... Congress adjourned yesterday, and our city will be thinned out considerably, but so long as the war lasts there will be a great many strangers with us. All our friends are well, and it is reported that Hattie Coyle, on whom we called, is soon to be married to a distant cousin of hers. I told her she must invite us to the wedding.

The next day, Henry wrote to Francis from "Camp Near Bell Plain, Va."

On account of the Captains absence, I have not written as I should if I had had pleanty of time. He left at a very busy time two days before muster so I had the rolls to make out alone &c &c. They consist of four distinct rolls each containing the name rank date of enlistment, where enlisted, &c date of muster into the service name of Officer who mustered–when last paid & by whom, whether present if not where they are, &c &c. On the whole you see it is a weary job. Also I had a monthly return to make out & other writing. Last Monday we had a Brigade inspection in the afternoon were reviewed by Gen Howe & ever since we have had Brigade drills[so] it has been a very busy week. We hear all sorts of news. Its now reported that two Regiments are to be sent to Vermont to enforce the Conscription act. I hope we will be one. We are the smallest in the Brigade by fifty men. Have you seen Charles Lynde yet? Fred returned with him to Washington. I have not received the box yet. Transportation for this landing is very scarce.

The weather is very pleasant but windy. The furloughs are to be leangthened to thirty days. That will be very satisfactory. Fifteen is too short. I received the dictionary & acct book sent by mail last week. I was glad to receive them.

Henry then waited several days, until March 11, to write his next letter home:

Your favor bearing date March 2nd was received the morning of the eighth of March. I had been looking a long time for it as you have not written for some weeks. I take these few moments to write you an answer.

You spoke of the orders etc. You have now acknowledged their receipt. I keep an account of what I send home so if any is lost I can get new orders & finaly obtain the money. I received pay as Sergeant at Harrison's Landing to the 30th of June. You say you have drawn up to April 30th so that two months more allotted pay is due me from the State Treasurer. I received the box you sent Jany 20 yesterday March 10. It contained just the articles I kneed. Every[thing] in it was fresh & nice. ... Mr. A's reference to Mayett's

Acct. I do not think it would be of any use to try to get the amount as he spends all he gets &C. He being so ignorant would not be likely to remember it so would think I was trying to cheat him &C. He has borrowed money of me & paid for the use of it more than the amount of the account. If it were mine I would let it drop.

Emily Pride I fear will want for money sometime unless she is less extravagant. She does nothing more than waste what her husband earns.

I am glad to learn that Dr Bailey is liable to do military duty. It would not hurt him to come any way. He is just the man I would like to see here. I should think James Abbott would be ashamed to stay at home if I may so term it. He ought to be here as well as some others. I understood his mother was afraid he would hafto come &C. She is not the right kind of a mother. She ought to say <u>go</u> & cary the burden which your friends have taken. He will never know what has been done for him unless he takes a part in this struggle. The Soldiers that have been home say you do not begin to feel as you should. Your business is prospering & no noticiable change except the scarcity of young men. You cannot conceive the desolation by an army passing through a country. It is like a famine & a little more. All the wood fences are destroyed. Also most of the dwellings. How it would rouse you to have an enemy come into Vermont.

Does the taxes increase much on that western land? I am glad you have found Marden. I think he will pay if he ever gets money. He is very anxious to get an education. I received the account book & Dictionary.

John Green thinks Alden Whitney must make an officer alike many others, smart, but a complete drunkard. If he were in this Regiment he would be very popular. Henry Davis was dismissed [from] the service for cruelty to his men. In one or two instances he tied up men by the thumbs <u>a common occurance here.</u> Some have been stood on stumps nearly a whole day. Others caried a heavy log every two hours for twenty four hours. They are as strict in this Brigade as in the regular service & it is necesary. Men are made to respect & fear their officers, to know their places & rank &C. Nothing will make a good soldier but discipline. It seems hard sometimes & it is. Still an army can not be kept together except under a despotic rule so experience teaches me.

Lieutenant Henry W. Davis,
Twelfth Vermont
Courtesy of Vermont Historical Society

I am sorry for Jane. She can not enjoy herself in Florida. I supose she must have been seasick. I pity her if she was. I know something what it is. There was a storm when we left Fortress Monroe & could not get out of Cheasepeake Bay untill next day. The vesel rocked and tiped & my stomach was dreadfully agitated & no relief.

I have received one paper from Montpelier. It affords news of considerable interest to me. I see they mean to show up McClellan's true character. I can testify much against him. I think he has played the part of Arnold in [not] going to the assistance of Pope as soon as he might. Day after day did we lay still when Pope was fighting desperately and bravely. ... I have seen a long report of his fighting there, his orders, &C &C the direct disobedience McClellan offers.

General Stoughton was taken prisoner last sunday. He was taken by some thirty men. There was a guard there of nearly fifty men but they played the part of the coward & instead of taking them prisoners they all ran & not even fired a gun. It seems as though none of this Brigade would have permited the like to be done. The 2nd Brigade can not say much more.

(Edwin Stoughton had earlier been in command of the Fourth Vermont, but he had taken a leave of absence from the military and his brother, Charles Stoughton, took the post. When Edwin Stoughton returned, he was promoted to Brigadier General commanding the Twelfth Vermont and became, at just age 25, the youngest general in the Union Army. On March 8, while sleeping in his bed, he was captured in a surprise raid near Fairfax, Virginia by John S. Mosby.

Stoughton had chosen to stay in more comfortable surroundings several miles from the main body of his men. He was held prisoner for several months in Richmond. After being released in a prisoner exchange, he retired from military service. Henry never had good things to say about Stoughton, and Abraham Lincoln seems to have eventually come to agree with Henry's estimation. Fifty-nine horses had also been taken in Mosby's raid, and Lincoln sarcastically commented that he could make a much better brigadier general in five minutes, but horses cost $125 apiece.)

Brigadier General Edwin Stoughton
Courtesy of vermontcivilwar.org

We are now under marching orders. Everything is being got in readyness for a moove.

One year ago yesterday 10 March we left Camp Griffin. The typhoid is present to some extent in the Brigade. The doctors are very particular to have all vacinated. What are we not exposed to in the army & how little does a soldier mind a rageing disease until it takes him. We are now the smallest Regiment in the Brigade. We have a fraction over two hundred men for duty–last week 219. We kneed a lot of conscripts immediately. My Captain returns Friday. I have had a busy time since he left.

John Green said he saw you drive past a very smart prompt horse. Was it the colt? I imagine he makes one of the best horses you ever had. If so why not keep him? Is he trained to work &C&C? You ought to have a flock of sheep if you want to make money. A man needs to change stock for the times so in time of war as well as peace be geting honorably what can be got.

I received a letter from Lorrette yesterday. She said Eunice was not much better &C. She was strong McClellan &C.

Henry, on the other hand, had clearly turned against his former commander and could only hope that President Lincoln had discovered, in "Fighting Joe" Hooker, the one who would finally lead the North to victory.

Chapter 8

ANOTHER ATTEMPT
AT FREDERICKSBURG

Still camped "near Bell Plain" on March 16, and sensing that the lull in the
fighting could not last much longer, Henry wrote to Francis:

*Having a few spare moments I thought I would write a few lines. We are
still in our winter quarters but how long it is uncertain as it appears now the
enemy are on the point of taking the ofensive. Saturday heavy skirmishing
took place on our right in the vacinity of Stafford Court House & the baloon
discovers a heavy body of troops mooving in that direction estimated at fifty
thousand. I guess that Gen Hooker would be glad to welcome them on this
side of the Rappahannoc. The enemies pickets say they are coming over &
drive us back to Washington but we are in readiness to give them a good reception. The picket lines are more strict than ever before. Not a man is allowed to
take off his belt &c. Roads are cut so the pickets can raly in case of an attack.
An excelent arrangement. Evry man has to have fifty rounds cartridges & all
the bataries have fixed ammunition so in case of a surprise evrything will be
ready for use. I am glad to see matters caried out so strict & regular. The troops
are being drilled & put in fighting order. We expect settled weather soon. We
had a thunder storm Sunday. The secesh say the winter is broken up. The
weather continues very cold. Last night we had a hailstorm. In the morning
the ground was white, so we shall have another foot of mud. ...*

*Another of our men has been discharged. Sy Cole [Charles G. Cole] who
was wounded at Fredricksburg in the hip. Three [others] all got Certificates
of disability from the Surgeon. Has the conscript law been put in force much
yet? It ought to be immediately. We need the men <u>today</u>. Gov Holbrooks son
was out to visit the Regiments last week. Col Stanard has got Col Stoughton's staff away from him. It must be rather humiliating when he learns it.
Gen Brooks said if his men could live in tents he could <u>& did</u>. Had Gen*

Stoughton folowed his example he would not have been taken prisoner. Supporting fancy style when in active service seems to be risky now a days. Such is the path of flashy men. In reading so much of General Rosecrans in diferint papers I have been interested in his course. It agrees with my views exactly. He gives all rebil sympathisers ten days to go south of his lines. Also prohibits certain papers which are damageing his men. The N. Y. Herald ought to be served in the same way. I can see evil efects resulting in this circulation. It makes some men strong secesh. Also a little more news that <u>*Hannibal was a full blood African.*</u> *They are certainly a quick wited race of people & most of them true friends to the yankeys. It would amuse you to see them. I have seen a great deal of slavery since I left home. I think it worth fighting to release such men from such wicked hands as they are in. I have seen them whiped &c. It is awful.*

On Sunday, March 22, Henry began a letter home, which he completed two days later:

We are having strange weather now. Yesterday it snowed. Today sap would run a stream. The sun is quite warm so we do not want fires in our tents. The robins & other birds are singing. Their was no services today. Our chaplain has been sick since the battle of Fredricksburg. Friday I saw Mr Stone of Northfield. He made himself acquainted with all he met. He would make an excellent Chaplain. He has a number of sons in this army & Brigade. Two or three in the 2nd Vt. one a Lt Colnel some in the QM Dept. & one or two in a Pensylvania Regt. Col Stannard has got General Stoughton's star. How the papers do rake him, but I fear they all tell the truth. I could testafy to a great deal. No one can blame the people for not wanting fops & perhaps rebels for their Generals. They are Breckenridges men & voted for him last.

March 24

 This afternoon I was detailed to act as <u>*Quartermaster*</u> *of the Regiment while [Henry] Cushman was absent in Vermont. The weather has moderated, & is quite warm. The frogs sing us to bed nights & robins & black birds waken us in the morning. Spring is fast approaching & businiss in the army has commenced in earnest. Evry Regimint is out on drill & evry batary. All the teams and ambulances are inspected to see that they are properly used & cared for. There is a great revolution in the whole army. All are in favor of Hooker. Evry soldier can see what a wonderful change is being brought about.*

Tonight it rains. Tomorrow we were to have been reviewed by General Hooker but I fear the rain will prevent. Charles Lynde returned last week. His absence has improoved him very much, not only in appearance but health. The health of the Brigade was never better. The camps are kept clean & the men are aclimated & healthy, black as Indians. Did George Smith go to Williamstown. I heard he was in Vermont a short time since he has attractions this side of Wmstown, &c &c. There was brisk picket firing heard this afternoon, I have not lernt the cause.

On the same day when Henry finished this letter, P. F. Barnard, a Williamstown minister, was penning words of encouragement to Henry:

I need hardly say to you that we are deeply interested in the affairs of the country and tho by no means unmindful of reverses & the sad scenes of war. Yet I think the best of the people are hopeful. Our cause is just & I do believe that notwithstanding the efforts of the enemy, the frauds & corruptions of pretended friends, we shall, by God's blessing, prevail. My hope is in God. It may seem perhaps sometimes when you see the great wickedness of all around you, that God must forsake us & leave us to perish but there are good men & true, doing their work faithfully & honestly. We would hope that God may remember those in the army that cry unto him & those at home that pray & save the country by their hands & for their sakes. Be of good courage then, keep the flame of piety & patriotism burning in the heart. In looking over the whole field I think from present appearances there is reason to be hopeful. Fraud, heartless selfishness, suffering, wickedness, I know there is. But God has blessed & prospered us. See what has been done. Our army has been collected & fitted for the field & from the first it has been steadily advancing not always successful to be sure, but the general direction has been onward. We hold what has been taken. We are crowding upon the enemy, enlarging our possessions, limiting his – and now we are as prosperous, as well fed throughout our borders, even [better] perhaps. But it is not so with the enemy. Taking such a view, I think we may go forward. I think the feeling should be, this rebellion must be put down. While I deeply sympathise with our soldiers in the field, while I appreciate their sacrifices & shed tears over the graves of those who have fallen, I think also of the object hard in view, the salvation of the country, the preservation & perpetuity of free institutions. Generations yet to come will rejoice at our success, or mourn over our defeat. Courage then & the Lord make the right to triumph. ... May God preserve you & give success in fighting the battles of your country & make you a good soldier of Jesus Christ. Remember me, if you please, to the Wmstown boys.

On March 30, Henry confided to Francis that he was considering leaving the Fourth Vermont Regiment:

I have been thinking of trying to get a Captaincy in one of the conscript Regiments. On some accounts I would like to get away from the Regiment because of the drunkenness of its officers & men &c. As a 2nd Lt I have had to do Captains duty two thirds of the time when on drill. If the Captain commands Co A. I have to command some of the others & unless there is some epidemic or most of the officers get killed I cannot get a like position for a long time. If I have got to do Capt duty I want the rank & pay. So on the whole, all things concidered, I have concluded to try my luck. There is nothing rong about it certain & by that I can get home a few days. Leaves are stoped for the present &c. I shall get Uncle Bass to recommend me to the Governor. John Lynde is acquainted with him & is going to try for Charles. I shall send him a recommend. I do not want much said about it as it may not work. Many will try for positions. I shall not be disappointed if nothing is done. It would be a little better for me so far as pay is concerned. $13.00 dollars, month.

I received the articles sent by John Green. George Ainsworth has not been seen yet. We expect to be on the move soon & expect harder times than ever known before. We hope Hooker may proove another second iron-sides & his army as invinsible. I saw him last week. He is a New England man in looks & actions. The most splendid looking officer I ever saw. I saw half a dosen of the Major Generals. They are fine looking men. If they were as good principled men as they look what blessings would they be to the country. I believe the rebels fear Hooker more than any other General in the army. He is well known.

I have not seen George Smith since he returned but saw a soldier from this Regt who saw him & requested him to call on me &c &c. His camp is about nine miles from ours. We are very near the extreme left. Last spring we were near the extreme right, about June were near the centre so we are changed about. The centre is the safest place the flanks the hotest in fights.

We expect to be paid in a week or two. Five months have passed & not been paid. This is not right. I suppose the money was given the pay master & why he keeps it I do not know. I rather like Quartermasters berth. I have a horse to ride when I pleasse &c. Two more of our men are discharged, leaving us a total of 60 men. ... Last night it commenced snowing & this morning it is two inchs deep. We are having strange weather for Virginia. We are expecting the enemy will evacuate Richmond this summer & we shall have to follow them. The 9th Corps that left us after the battle of Fredericksburg have gone to reinforce Rosencrans.

Henry received a letter in early April from another cousin: Jane Davis, Uncle Ira Smith's daughter and the younger sister of George Smith. Jane attended Kimball Union Academy in the mid-1850s, graduating between Francis Martin and her older brother. Her younger brother, Willie, was 15 years old at this time. Jane had married Mahlon Davis in 1860, and he was now serving with the Seventh New Hampshire. The regiment was positioned in St. Augustine, Florida, and Jane had decided to join them. She sent this account to Henry:

... [Southern] women dont have to work as our New England women do. They let everything go as it choses. They live easy & take comfort as they go I suppose. No white people work here. They all seem to look so surprised to see us women even in the kitchen. I do not presume I ought to judge the Southerners generally by what is here but they with very few exceptions are rather limp & languid. The Regt have their meettings in the Episcapal Church. Not more than half a dozen others go, that is of the inhabitants. Mostly Catholics and the Episcopalians all attend there now. They are the nearest alike you know.

We have a choir here. There are two Union ladies here that sing. Nice old maids they are too and there are two lady teachers here that sing & teaching negroes. Capt House plays the organ. We have two regimental singing schools a week. The surgeon is the teacher. The other day while the Lebanonese [Lebanon, N.H.] company were out on picket, they were fired upon by a Co. of rebels prowling round here. No one was injured but narrowly escaped. They think the rebels are feeling round & will attack us here but I do not believe it & feer no such thing. The most that worries me is that they will be ordered away. I am here & some Reg. has got to stay & they might as well stay as any other. I never enjoyed myself better. Now dont worry yourself about me for I shall be cared for. The Regt. have some very fine prayer meetings. I enjoy them. I had a letter from Geo. yesterday. He is well & talking about going to N.H. soon if he had not already. He wants Willie to go to some good school, says if he lives & is not disabled he will do all for him he can. Will pay all his expenses. I want you to speak to uncle Bass about it. His time is out 1st of May & it worries me thinking what will become of him. If he could go somewhere where some one would look after him & keep him straight I would be glad. He does not know anything at all that a boy his age should. It would do no harm to try him & see what he would do. If he was as far along in his books as he should be I would prepare to have him go to work. If he don't go to school now, in a year he will be ashamed to go. You talk about it with Uncle Bass. When his time is out if his bills are paid he can come home himself &

save any ours going after him. I protest against his staying there longer than his year out. If the Regt moves I may be home by that time. On his account I would like to be. I should if he went to school, go to the same place & live or board so as to look out for him. I hope he will be disposed of some way where he will do well. Give much love to all the friends & let Aunt Lucy read this letter & it will do as well as tho' I wrote her. Tell Uncle B. & Aunt Lucy to write to me. I believe they owe me a letter. I want to have them write & tell me the news & how they all do and about Eunice. I feel anxious to hear from her. You must not expect to hear from me very often. Give much love to all and write soon and direct to M. E. Davis 7th N.H. Vols. St. Augustine, Fla.

After the war, George Smith remained in the army and was stationed near Houston, Texas. Mahlon Davis, Jane, and her father also moved to Houston, where Mahlon served as a town marshal.

On April 4, Henry wrote to Chauncey Smith, further expressing the new confidence that the soldiers were feeling under General Hooker's seemingly able leadership:

Your favor of the 5th March was received in due time & would have been answered sooner if I could have found spare time & any news to write but little of interest has transpired since I wrote you last. There has been a pleanty of drilling & reviews when the weather would permit. Yesterday we had a grand one. The Division was reviewed by General Hooker. It was much more interesting than any we have had before. The soldiers have forgotten their proved traitorous pet McC & now put great confidence in old fighting Joe. He has proved himself such an able General in evry battle in which he has been engaged that they all look up to him as their true loyal & successful leader. But time will decide. Such a change as has been brought about under his short administration is almost misterious. The Quartermasters have been compelled to furnish the men better than they ever did before and the result is one of the healthiest armies ever known (if I may so term it.) There is hardly a man in the hospitals. Such a remarkable change is noticeable to evry soldier.

Have you ever seen Gen. Hooker? He is one of the best looking Generals in the army. He resembles the New England men. The review was attended by nearly all the Generals in the army. Gens. Casy & Wardsworth were present &C. The Division did credit to its self in appearance & marching.

On the 10th April there is to be a muster & the number of men required to fill the companies to the number required by army regulations are agregats of 101 men. I wish we had them here today. There begins to be talk of a moove soon. The strong south winds are drying up the mud remarkably fast & the dust is beginning to fly. The wood has been cut away so extensively on both sides that the enemy are distinctly seem drilling &C. They show a good front. They can see us very distinctly. Evry thing remains quiet.

All the Wmtown boys are well. George Ainsworth arrived yesterday. We were all very glad to see him & hope he may be assigned to this Corps. We have had a remarkably severe spring so far. I was hoping when April came in it would be more pleasant but it is not. The winds blow so hard that a person can hardly stand on his feet.

The next day he added:

It snowed all night. The wind blew unaccountably hard. The snow fell about four inches. The drying wind has carried the most of it away. We were not on picket this time but go tomorrow.

On that same day, George Smith, in his regular army camp nine miles away, wrote to Henry:

I beg your pardon for not writing to you before and all that I can say in way of apology is that I have been home on leave & since I returned to camp have been quite busy on picket, fetigue, drill &c. I have been thinking seriously of coming down to see you & mean to soon. I do not know however as you are there. I expect you will be getting your leave and for what I know are away now. I had a splendid time when on my leave. I did not go to Wmst. but had father meet me at Montpelier. I did not have time to go to Wmst. Father was well as were also all of our friends. You doubtless know of Duncan of Lebanon & Em Pools marriage and a fine couple will they make. I saw Charlie Lynde's name on the [Hotel] book when at Montpelier.

I spent about a week on the road home at Wash - N Y - Boston. Stopped at Manchester to see Willie. His time is out there 1st May when he is going to Exeter, N Y to school. He is quite a lad. All of our friends at Leb are well. Harrison Buck has lost his little girl this winter which causes them a deal of sorrow. I did not know before that I had so many good friends in Leb as I found come to make them a visit. I could have spent as many weeks as I did days among them and had no time to waste. I have several "carte de visites" of my friends which I will show you when I see you and I have one a group of nice young ladies from <u>Mrs. Sherman's nunnery</u> at <u>Hanover</u> which is framed & to see that you must come over to our camp. I keep it hung up over my head in my tent <u>to keep off the blues.</u>

Henry, what do you think is to be done with the army of the Potomac this summer? Are we to remain here or go west. We have for seven companies twenty nine officers and more coming into the field every week. So Hooker says he is going to make promotions in the Rg. Army probably this season. It does not look much like it now. Henry, do not wait for me to come down to see you for I have no horse & you have & can afford to come up oftener than you do. Write me on receipt of this so that I may know where you are.

As mentioned earlier, by "the nunnery" George referred to the boarding school at Hanover that Caroline Martin had attended and that Dartmouth students called by that name. George had spent most of his childhood in New Hampshire, so it is not overly surprising that he had used his time to visit friends and acquaintances there and meet his father at Montpelier rather than return to Williamstown.

Also on April 5, Henry's eighteen-year-old cousin, Lucy Lynde, wrote to Henry. Lucy was attending Barre Academy as Henry had done just a few years earlier.

You may imagine me somewhat surprised a few evenings since on receiving your letter, but it gave me the assurance that home and acquaintances were still remembered in the hustle and toil of a <u>camp life</u> . I have often wondered if the cares of a soldier would cause him to forget former days, but the testimony of all is that "Time will not obliterate the remembrances of 'Home sweet home'".

It was pleasant to learn of the health and prosperity of "our Williamstown boys"- they have (so it seems when we compare with the neighboring towns) been remarkably preserved from harm, still some have fallen in defense of our beloved land, and the unknown future alone can reveal what is yet in store for us.

I agree perfectly with you in saying that Charlie [Lucy's older brother by two years] could have remained in his Vermont home without being discontented for an indefinite length of time. It is so lonely without him that if it were not for our studies to claim our attention, we would be tempted to take a trip to Virginia. I pity him for it must necessarily seem more dismal than before.

As an opportunity has appeared I will <u>sincerely</u> <u>thank</u> <u>you</u> for the kindness you showed my brother in that awful campaign on the Peninsula last summer. He often wrote of it and spoke about it when at home - and attributes his present good health if not life itself to your excusing him from duty at a risk of your own.

You inquired after the disposition and good nature of the respected "Uncle Jake" [Jacob Spaulding, the founder and principal of Barre Academy] - as age increases he grows "worse and worser". I will relate a little trouble that occured this term. The people of Williamstown held an exhibition similar to those they held before. We asked permission to go, but an accident prevented our going, so went on the following evening. When he learned of it he threatened to expell us unless we wrote confessions stating "That we were sorry we went, and ask his forgiveness". Of course we said "I wont" but told him if he chose to accept us as scholars again, we would say we were sorry for the disturbance it caused in school but nothing more. At first he refused but after some thought he concluded to do it. We did not choose to write confessions for one evening is as good as another - so we claimed.

Yesterday Mr. S. informed me that a Essay would be expected from your humble servant at the close of school. I think now I shall resign - or procure a substitute. Charlie sent me a Photograph a few days since of yours. If it is a correct picture you are very much changed. I will preserve it very carefully for him in an album that he presented while at home. I know of nothing new transpiring at home but presume they are traveling on in the same beaten track. With the kindest wishes for your health - will close.

A few days later, on April 8, Henry had a new concern: his most recent pay had not been received back home and, according to the army records, it had been collected in camp. This would be the start of a long bureaucratic struggle. Henry tried to clear up the matter with the following message to Army headquarters:

There must be a mistake concerning my allotted pay. I have never drawn any in camp since I entered the service. I made Chester Martin my attorney immediately after allotting my pay. If it has been drawn in camp it was by an unauthorized person.

On the same day, Captain Platt also sent a message to the Sixth Army headquarters concerning Henry:

I take pleasure in testifying to the good conduct & ability of Lieut. W. H. Martin of the 4th Vt. Vols. He was a member of my company for one year as 1st Sergeant & always proved himself a brave & thorough Soldier. He has well & honestly earned promotion & should have it.

Henry wrote to Francis as well on April 8, addressing the pay confusion as well as other recent events in camp:

Your favors of April 2nd & 3rd are received. I answer them sooner on account of the 30.00 dollar business. There must have been some mistake about the matter. I have never drawn one cent of my alloted pay. If it has been drawn it must have been a forgery or they must have made a mistake & charged to my name what ought to have been charged to some one else. I hope you will be able to get the money for it was hard earnt while in the ranks. If a soldier ever ought to be paid for anything it should be his service in the ranks.

George Ainsworth arrived in camp Saturday. He was very fortunate in being assigned to this Division. He looks strong & healthy. He is a little disappointed with the looks of the army. Their quarters are much more insignificant than he could imagine while at home. He thinks the men have changed very much in their looks & they have. Henry Wilson left for home yesterday. The Williamstown boys are certainly proud. He was promoted a corporal the day before. He is an excellent soldier.

(Henry Wilson continued in the army until the war was over, mustering out in 1865. Unfortunately, within two years he died from tuberculosis.)

Wilson Hopkins has just been promoted a captain in the 16th N.Y. I saw him yesterday. I saw George Smith the other day. He is looking better than when I met him last. He never intends to visit Williamstown again so he says. He feels he has more friends at Lebanon, N.H.

April 6th I attended a grand review of all the Cavilry & flying artillery of the army of the Potomac. It was a festive & interesting affair. The President, his daughter [probably his son Tad, who had turned ten two days earlier] & one of his secrataries were present. Also a number of Government officials were present. All the Generals & a portion of the subordinate officers were there. It took place on the plain in rear of Falmoth & in plain sight & cannon shot range of the enemy. On this occasion I found that acting Q^r Master was quite a privalage as it gives me a horse to ride when & where I please. I got an excellent view of the President & all the Generals. General Hooker is the man to attract the attention of all. Such a fine majestic looking man (& his well earned reputation) has done more to gain a victory with his little Division of Corps than old M^c has with his whole army &c. I saw a man who just came from Washington. He said that evryone had perfect confidence in old fighting Joe. He was astonished. He could not have believed it had he not heard with his own ears.

The President looks as though he was completely worn out with care & the man that says he is not a second Washington, a true patriot, an honest

*man, having nothing but the true interest of his country at hart must be a
rebil & a traitor. Any one can read the President at first sight. I heard many
a man [speak] of his true honest countenance. His looks compare well with
what he is doing for his country &c &c. General Stoneman commands all
the cavilry. Twenty thousand were on review. It was a grand sight. You can
little imagine how they looked. I never expect to see the like again. Things are
carried on on a big scale in this army. The best looking cavilry was as usual
the New England. The men all look smart, intelligent & handsome. (The
southerners say they can tell a Vermonter as far as they can see him. Why?
Because they are so handsome.) You can hardly imagine the difference. Pensylvania & NY troops are not half as good looking as a Vt., Me, or Mass.&c.*

*There is to be a muster on the 10th of this month to see how many men
it will require to fill the companies up to 101 men & then we are to be filled
with conscripts. Snow fell two inches deep Monday & not all has left us yet. It
is a remarkable cold spring. Lastly I shall try & get a leave to come home the
first [of] May. I suppose it will be dry & nice then.*

The Army of the Potomac was indeed being reorganized under Hooker "on
a big scale." The "worn out" President, desperate for a victory over Lee, supplied
General Hooker with an army of 130,000 men. Lee's army was down to just
60,000, and Longstreet's corps was laying siege to Suffolk, Virginia, too far away
to respond to a rapid advance by Hooker. It was now time for Hooker to show
that he truly was the answer to General Lee. Based on relatively accurate intelligence reports on the size and position of the Confederate forces, Hooker prepared
his plan. Rather than order an all-out charge into the center of the Confederate
defenses at Fredericksburg as Burnside had done, Hooker intended to deploy his
massive army to find openings in the Confederate flanks while feigning another
attack into the center. He planned to simultaneously attack both flanks of Lee's
army and then respond quickly to stop a Confederate counterattack, or to exploit
an opening in the southern flanks if Lee attempted to retreat toward Richmond.
Under Hooker's reorganization of the army, John Sedgwick had replaced "Baldy"
Smith in commanding the Sixth Corps. The plan called for Sedgwick's Sixth Corps
and the First Corps, commanded by John F. Reynolds, to form the left wing of the
attack. The Sixth Corps was to cross the river at Franklin's Crossing, about two
miles below Fredericksburg. The First Corps would cross two miles further down
the river, and then together they would engage the rebel forces defending Marye's
Heights. The Second Corps would attract the attention of additional Confederate
forces in the center by feigning a crossing at Banks Ford, and it could also be called

in later as circumstances dictated. The Fifth, Eleventh, and Twelfth Corps would simultaneously surprise the Confederates by crossing on the Union right at Kelly's Ford and attacking toward Chancellorsville.

As Hooker's army began preparing to move out of camp, Henry dashed off a quick letter to his father on April 14:

> *Once more we are on the point of a moove. The orders are to carry eight days rations & sixty rounds of cartridges. Where we are going no one can conjecture. Twenty eight Regts. cavilry left for somewhere yesterday. We are to be paid today & be ready to start tomorrow morning. It looks as though we are going to Richmond. No teems are to accompany us. Pack mules only. I hope success will attend our efforts. Pray for us. We expect to see hard times. We are all well & as ready as we ever shall be. I hope for the best and go forward. You will without doubt hear from us in the papers before you receive this.*

As it turned out, the newspapers had little to report in the days which followed. Two days later, still in camp, Henry sent another letter home:

> *We did not moove as we expected on account of a heavy rain which commenced that night. Providence did not seem to think best for us to leave at present. I suppose it must be for the best. It is very fortunate that we did not start the day I wrote you. We hear but little news from what is taking place at Charleston. We heard General Foster has been taken prisoner.*
>
> *We were payed night before last. I received 547.00 Dollars. There is a tax of .03 percent on all salaries over five hundred dollars, so I paid quite a little tax. Also my allotment continues just the same as though I were in the ranks. Have you drawn it right along? Enclosed you will find 120.00. I should have sent more, but I wish to pay a note held by Mr. Smith of about 60.00 dollars which I borrowed of him last fall. I could have paid it long before but I thought the money would be more benifit to you at that time so I let it lay. Mr. Smith said he did not wish me to pay until I found a convenient time. Perhaps I may get a leave & it will be the best chance I can have to settle with him.*
>
> *I saw twenty-five thousand dollars in twenty dollar bills that the soldiers had given him to send home. Probably much more will be sent.*

Back in Washington, in the more comfortable confines of the Avenue Hotel, Chauncey Smith was also composing a letter on April 16:

> *I have of late received your choice letter, inclosing a quarter, and embrace my earliest moment to let you hear from us, though as you will say, we have*

nothing very interesting to communicate in return. I had the pleasure of receiving a nice letter from Mrs. Lynde a few days since, by which I learn that all of our friends there are in usual health, and winter wound up with a cold snowy March, full equal to ours in this region. April does a little better, but yesterday and today are both cold and rainy, which we suppose will house up the army for a time longer. Never mind. We shall yet have some warm dry weather. Of late, to, Charlie and Oscar have both been up to Vt. and thus through them we have all the detail of family visits, which you know is far better than letters. They appear to have enjoyed themselves among the homes they visited, and of course they would among the young ladies they met with. Oscar is really quite lucky, and I judge he strives to merit his honors, and will prove a faithful officer. I hope you will also come up in rank in due time. Have faith, hope, and patience, and all will come out well. Oscar made only a single nights visit on his way or return, and Charlie about the same, but I was glad for even these. Fred Lynde is yet with his mother in this city, and I hardly know whether he contemplates remaining here or not, but I presume he will for a time.

Our city presents nothing new, or novel. There has been a large number of visitors during the winter, hotels crowded and boardinghouses full, nor do I perceive much diminution since congress adjourned. The Departments are busy, and we have our hands full of work from morning till night. So busy have I been that I have not made a "call" this winter, and therefore am sorry I cannot tell you something about the young ladies you know here, but I hear sad news of them, sad I say, for I learn that two of them are engaged to be married and so they are gone! Never mind. Vermont affords many better. I get out to church on Sunday's, generally to Dr. Sunderland's, and whenever I get an evening to myself I drop into the Masonic lodges, which I enjoy better than in early life. This makes up my usual enjoyments.

I did not remember how you were indebted to me, and still think you are not, but I will keep it till I see you. I took the same liberty with your last letter as with the others, and sent it on to Mr. Ainsworth for the good of the whole people. You write such a good letter that they may safely be read by all, and all news from the boys is interesting to parents and families.

Nathan has returned to Wisconsin, and will resume the law. He came very near going down to see you for a visit, but weather and other things prevented at the time he could go. Wished me to remember him to you when I wrote. George Ainsworth I suppose is with you, and of course you were all glad to see him. He made me a short call and hope for a longer one when he returns. This fills up my sheet, and so I wind up. Please write us as often as you can find time. Make my kind regards to all the boys, and whenever you are in want of any thing, let us know, and we will lend a helping hand.

The inclement weather continued to delay Hooker's plans. On April 27, Henry was still in camp when he wrote to Francis:

I have been looking for a number of days for an answer to my last letter sent from Camp April 16, 1863 which contained 120 dollars. When I wrote last I expected to moove but a rain set in which prevented. Tonight we are expecting to moove in the morning perhaps to take part in a great battle or a reconoite or reconisance in force. The pontoons are laid (or reported) but it looks like rain tomorrow. I saw George Ainsworth today. He is deeply interested in his work & can do a great amount of good if he only tries. He has very full meetings & very interesting.

Henry's weather forecast was correct. The next day it rained, but Hooker decided it was time to put his plan into effect regardless of the conditions. The three corps attacking to the right had already started moving toward their positions the day before. As part of General Albion P. Howe's Second Division, the Vermont Brigade broke camp on the morning of April 28, moving closer to the Rappahannock but remaining out of sight through the night. The next morning, Brooks' First Division surprised the rebels by sending soldiers across the river in boats to drive off the pickets. They then quickly assembled their pontoon bridges at Franklin's Crossing. The remainder of Brooks' division crossed the river, but Howe's Second Division was retained in reserve. Meanwhile, the three corps of the Army of the Potomac to the right were moving rapidly around Lee's outnumbered army. Upon reaching Chancellorsville, Hooker established headquarters with an army of about 70,000 men. Sedgwick was ordered to march his soldiers into positions to give the impression that the offensive was centered on his Sixth Corps attacking Fredericksburg. The ploy did not fool General Lee, however, and only Jubal Early's division was left to defend Fredericksburg. In a move that most military strategists of the time would have considered extremely dangerous, if not foolhardy, Lee divided his small army. Rather than be concerned with the Union cavalry, deployed to block his lines of communication with Richmond, Lee had Jeb Stuart's cavalry seal off the roads around Chancellorsville. Confusion and misgivings began to flow from the beleaguered Hooker as he felt hemmed in by Lee, and he set up defensive positions rather than moving closer to Fredericksburg as planned. Late on Saturday, May 2, Stonewall Jackson succeeded in Lee's risky gambit of secretly moving his Second Corps into place for a devastating attack against the unsuspecting Eleventh Corps.

While all this was transpiring, on the other side of the Rappahannock, Henry composed a short letter home from "Camp in Front of all the Fortifications of Fredericksburg, Virginia." Hooker had just ordered Reynolds's First Corps to Chancellorsville, leaving the Sixth Corps alone on the left flank.

> *Thinking you might wish to hear from me as often as possible I improve this opportunity. We are stationed in exactly the same position we were in when last here but have not made an attack. All the army but our 6th Corps has gone to the right & a fearful fight is taking place. Hooker is in their rear. We can see the smoke of our guns immediately in its rear. There has been fighting since Tuesday. A dreadful fight took place yesterday. We have not heard the result.*
>
> *At light the cannonading commenced. A corps was mooved from our left to the right so if the enemy should attack us we should have a hot time but we are determined as long as we have any men left to oppose. The enemy are trying to shell us away. Thirty two pound shot are bursting around our men. General Brooks is across the river. Heavy cannonading is taking place. All expect to hit their right & such a shelling we will give them.*

Later that night, the Vermont Brigade and the rest of the Second Division crossed the Rappahannock to support Brooks' division. Hooker was desperate to take the pressure off his forces at Chancellorsville and therefore ordered Sedgwick to attack the Confederate forces at Fredericksburg and then move toward Chancellorsville. Although Sedgwick's men outnumbered Early's rebel forces by about 27,000 to 12,000, the attack meant once again trying to scale Marye's Heights.

Sedgwick quickly devised a plan to attack the defenses simultaneously from different directions. While a frontal attack was launched against the famed stone wall as in the earlier battle, forces were to attack from the left and then swing behind the Confederate defenders. The Second Division was to charge across the open field to the left and drive the Confederate defenders off Lee's Hill and Howison Hill, then move back towards Marye's Heights. The Second Division began its charge, and the Confederates opened up on them as they ran through the artillery fire. The advance required working their way across a drainage ditch, then driving back Confederate infantry from their positions along a railroad bed, and finally attacking the rebel breastworks at the top of the hill. As the Federal forces quickly scaled the hill, the Confederates began abandoning their positions. The Fourth Vermont was deployed to the far left of the division and joined in taking Howison Hill. Other regiments from the division successfully secured Lee's Hill. On Marye's Heights, with one-eighth the number of soldiers from the previous battle, Confederate defenders withstood two charges. Finally, facing a bayonet charge in their front and the approach of the Vermont Brigade from their right, the overwhelmed rebels abandoned the heights. The Vermont Brigade joined in a pursuit of Early's forces down Telegraph Road. Sedgwick's orders, however, called for him to move toward Chancellorsville. Therefore, the pursuit was abandoned and Sedgwick cautiously began moving his corps down the Plank Road.

The Vermont Brigade must have felt as if they were taking part in a great victory, but the Second Battle of Fredericksburg was far from over. Henry, like many Union soldiers, had placed too much confidence in General Hooker. Jackson's surprise attack at Chancellorsville had thrown many of the Federal forces into disarray. Confederate forces now moved back toward the recently gained Federal positions on the unprotected heights outside Fredericksburg as Lee began to concentrate on defeating Sedgwick's Sixth Corps. When Confederate forces were reported at Salem Church, about four miles out of town, Brooks' division was sent forward alone to try to break through the Confederate lines blocking the road to Chancellorsville. The battle at Salem Church, on the evening of May 3, was a Confederate victory and Brooks' division was pushed back.

Sedgwick then established a defensive position, deploying his forces in a U-shape near the river to the west of Fredericksburg. The Vermont Brigade was in a concealed position along a ravine on the eastern side of the formation, acting as a last line of defense. An attack against the Federal positions came on May 4. The Federal defensive lines were hit repeatedly by Confederate charges, and they gradually began to fall back further in what is known as the Battle of Banks Ford. While others were retreating, the Vermont Brigade stubbornly held its position and even launched a successful countercharge into two of Early's brigades. The rebel advance had been temporarily stopped as nightfall arrived. Sedgwick's lines had been pushed back but were not broken. Nevertheless, having lost Marye's Heights, cut off from Hooker's main force, and facing an approaching Confederate army of undetermined strength, Sedgwick concluded that the Federal position was untenable. He ordered the Sixth Corps to retreat back across the river at Scott's Ford, just downstream from Banks Ford—much to the chagrin of the Vermont Brigade, whose reward for having fought so valiantly was to be placed in the dangerous rearguard position of protecting the rest of the corps from an attack as it retreated to safety across the Rappahannock. Only one small Confederate attack came during the night. When the Vermont Brigade finally made it to the bridge, which had been damaged by Confederate artillery, the men found that its cables had already been cut to allow it to drift to the northern shore. Now they faced the prospect of being trapped between the river and a large army that could suddenly appear at any moment. But before that happened, the Vermont Brigade escaped in pontoon boats sent across the river. Hearing of Sedgwick's retreat, General Hooker also dejectedly made the decision to disengage. Having sustained 17,000 casualties, the disappointed Army of the Potomac retreated back to safety on the northern side of the Rappahannock.

On May 5, from "4th Vermont Camp Near Banks Ford Virginia," Henry began a letter to his brother in which he seemed somewhat unsure whether to express pride or discouragement at what had just transpired:

> Since I wrote you last there has been great changes in our position &c. Sunday we carried the heights of Fredricksburg. We had a severe engagement. We charged where the Irish Brigade & another Division were repulsed all day. When last over we charged about twelve P.M. We received showers of bulets, cannon shot &c but we were determined to cary them & did. The whole hill was one flame of smoke and fire. We took twelve pieces of cannon. The 2nd took the brunt & lost about one hundred men. We only one. We advanced from there & they made a desperate stand. Brooks Division could not start them. Soon they (Rebs) came out five lines deep on a charge. Our men could [not] hold them & gave way. We planted our cannon & when they were within a few rods we opened with grape & canister & such a destruction of men was never equalled. Hardly a man escaped. Then Weatons Division charged & occupied the field. The next day we were quiet untill about five P.M. when the rebils tried to capture us. They charged four lines deep. Our men took a position under the crest of a bluff & let them come on. Some of the Division broke but when they came to the Vermonters they were met & driven in every direction. We took between two & three hundred prisoners but the enemy were so strong that we could not hold our position & fell back to Banks Ford & crossed. The enemy were said to be fifty thousand strong while ours was twenty, only one Corps but we were very fortunate in holding our position & geting away. We lost about three hundred men, about 40 of the 4th. It was the hotest engagement I ever experienced.

Henry stopped writing at this time, for good reason, but continued the next day:

> The enemy sent a shell into our camp so I could not finish my letter yesterday. It struck in a tent of the 6th Vt & about ten feet from me. We mooved camp so I will finish this morning. Stewarts Cavilry are across the river to make a raid. We have not seen them. The enemy are shelling very briskly for some purpose. We have not heard from Hooker. Till yesterday he was strongly intrenched. We need reinforcements very much with us. If we could have had

sooner we could have held the heights of Fredricksburg. We have heard that Vicksburg was ours, is it so? Then we have a great many more men to oppose us. The night we evacuated, they received 25000 men. We have the honor of saving the 6th Corps, for evry line but the Vt Brigade was broken. Men were runing in evry direction. The rebils came cheering. The 6th, 2nd, 4th, 3rd, 5th waited untill they could almost reach us with their bayonetts, then we fired & charged. You can imagine how they ran. The ground was coverd with dead & wounded & to see them give themselves up was gratifying. My Company was deployed as skirmishers & took about 50 men. One Major showed fight & was shot dead by one of the men. Yesterday our guard took three hundred men to the station. Some of the prisoners taken by the Brigade also three Colnels, two Lt. Cols, 3 Majors, 1 Brigadier. The day before a Major General was taken in the City. As we were not able to hold our position I can term it one of the greatest & most successful raids ever accomplished. The Corps must have lost about four thousand men but the enemys was greater. Brooks was strongly resisted & lost many men. Finaly they gave way & the enemy charged five lines deep. Our cannon were thrible shoted with grape & cannister. They let them come a certain distance & then opened & hardly a man returned but the worst of all is we had to leave all our dead & wounded. Fred Doyel was killed. Captain Ainsworth 6th Vt, Adj't Clark from Brookfield 2nd Vt & a number more I do not recollect their names.

(Fred Doyle had been very concerned about his mother. She had divorced her husband, based on intolerable cruelty, and was having a difficult time caring for the family. As a result, Fred was having almost all of his monthly pay sent directly to her. He was shot and killed when the Vermont Brigade made its unexpected countercharge at Banks Ford. Captain Luther Ainsworth of the Sixth Vermont was a cousin of George and Laura Ainsworth and had grown up about twenty miles from Williamstown in Waitsfield. Luther was shot in the abdomen at Banks Ford and died later that day.)

Our Regt lost no officers. I was hit by a spent ball in the calf of the leg. I was never in so hot a place before & how a man escaped it is a miracle. There is nothing like standing our ground - less are lost. The 2nd & 6th have sufferd the largest loss. My Company lost three. I commanded the skirmishers & came near being taken prisoner. I advanced farther than those on my left & when the regiment withdrew I was not informed of their movements & was left. The enemy passed my left & fired into my men but I withdrew so they did not get me. I was shelled from our guns once. They not knowing any of our men were there but I seemed to be Providentially protected. The way we mowed the rebs was like grass. The ground was coverd. It was one of the most horrifying sights I ever beheld. None of the Williamstown boys in the 4th was hurt. The enemy keep up a heavy cannonading all the time.

A few days later, on May 8, from "Camp Near Aquia Crick," Henry began a letter to his father in which he tried to explain what had gone wrong in this recent battle:

I thought you would like to learn about my movements. At the present time we have mooved from Banks Ford to the vacinity of the Potomac. We conjecture it is to go to Washington or further south. It is not thought the army of the Potomac is to be relied on. To tell the truth we have got some cowards & the only way to make them men is to shoot all that run. It may look rough but such is our business & our officers & men must suffer as much for running from our own shot as the enemies. The reason of our not loosing ten times as many men as we did was our standing our ground. The 26 New Jersey at the battle of Banks Ford when they saw the enemy coming on them immediately broke & ran in evry direction so the enemy came on the more furiously but we waited, not a man wishing to run untill they were within reach of our bayonets, then rose, fired & charged & took General Fitzhugh Lee son of the Commanding General, 4 Colnels & 300 hundred prisoners. The enemy charged our Brigade with a whole Division. They thought they had us all prisoner & they thought nearly right. We were out flanked & says General Howe, had it not been for our bravery & coolness would have been cut off from our bridges which would have resulted in our surrender. One Regiment was mutinous & laid down their arms & started to give themselves up to the enemy. Our bataries seeing it opened on them & mowed them like sheep. Also one Regt opened on them. I hope evry man was shot. In our Brigade we lost 580 men, took twelve pieces cannon, the celebrated Washington artilary. We have done some thing briliant once but seeing by no means the end of the rebelion.

The next day he continued:

Very pleasant this morning. Have rested quite well during this night. It will take a long time to get well rested. I received Franks letter. I am sorry to learn Joe has left for some reasons but on the whole I imagine you have rid yourself of a disagreeable man. His laboring qualities are very good when he has a good direction. As you estimated you can do your spring work with but little help.

Your haying will take good help which I trust you may be able to obtain. I suppose two or three hundred thousand conscripts will be called out immediately. They ought to have been here before we tried to cross the Rappahannoc when we were over on the Fredricksburg heights. More men would have held them. Hooker would have been able to have held out & joined us resulting in the defeat of Mr Rebil. I conjecture the enemy will be over after us before many days. Cannonading is occasionally heard this P.M.

Wilson Hopkins Regiment is to be musterd out of the service next Monday. They were two year men. They lost nearly half of their men across the river. It seems hard when they were so near geting home alive to be called into battle & half killed.

On May 9 Henry wrote another letter to his father. By this time, apparently after hearing more opinions and rumors in camp, he was feeling quite satisfied with the results of the fighting and the leadership of General Hooker:

Tonight we have heard some cheering news about our last moove which for some providential decree was not successful as we might have desired but much more so than I even anticipated. I have concluded the enemy were nearer being whiped than ever before. What we wanted was a few more men. No General ever fought the whole army like Hooker. I saw an aid or one who witnessed the fighting. He said he never suposed Hooker to be such a fighting man before. He was always in front & in the hotest of the fight. If any of the men falterd he was among them ralying them. When his old Division was advancing he was in front leading them & nothing could stop their progress. They say who would not fight for such a man. He asks his men to folow him & sharing their dangers make all faint hearts strong. He drew evry man from Richmond & evry surplus man in the whole South. We fought troops from Longstreets command. Troops that were doing patroll duty in Richmond. I will describe our moovements. We left camp on the 28 April & went to the same place where we crossed Dec. 15. The 29th we went to the river. Brooks crossed. All this time we could hear Hookers cannon in their rear. The next day we saw them taking away their heavy cannon & moving their men to the right. This was taking place on the 30-1st & 2nd. The night of the 2nd Brooks advanced to the woods & found but little opposition. Then we all crossed & laid on our arms all night. Just at break of day we advanced to a road near the City & in front of their most formidable works our cannon came up & commenced shelling the enemy with deadly precision. About 12 PM a charge was orderd & the Vt Brigade went over the heights in face of an almost overwhelming fire of musket, solid shot & the most destructive of all grape & canister. So determined & unflinchingly did they advance that the enemy could not hold them & we took their cannon & a number of prisoners. Our Division halted. Brooks passed in pursuit up the plank road. His orders were to push forward on the road regardless of his right, left or rear but cut his way through & join him. He advanced within sight of Hookers shells but the enemy massed their force & he was repulsed. Our Corps had the most desperate fighting of the whole army. I never saw the like before. Just before dark the enemy tried to take our cannon. They were allowed to come a certain distance but they found their advance was only so far. We opened with grape & canister with such deadly effect that hardly a man got back whole. Finally night stoped the awful work. We lay on our arms all night. The 4th opened very pleasant & still about ... [Here a rectangular section of the letter has been deliberately cut out to remove the signature on the other side of the page.] ... have our rear but we soon... quiet (expecting some ... of prisoners &c) untill 5 P.M. when line after line of rebils came out of the woods & attacked us. Men on our right & left gave way. The enemy were sure we were theirs. One Captain of a batary rode back & said to the 6th you are my only salvation if you can not check them or stand by us, our batary is gone. The 6th said they would do their best &c. As a whole Division was advancing on our Brigade Commanded by Gen Anderson under Jackson we all laid low. Evry gun was silent. The enemy came on untill seemingly within reach of our bayonets then the order was given to rise, fire & charge. The lead & cold steel was more than they could stand so evry man turned & did his best to get back but they found diferent commanders who told them to lay down their arms & follow them which they did trembling & cheerfuly. Our coolness saved many a mans life & thousands of men from being taken prisoners. Says General Howe the Vt Brigade saved the whole 6th Corps from being captured. The enemy got in our rear but we turned & faced them there & drove them back. The other Brigades would not stand & they lost many men. Our Corps has lost the heavyest of any in the army. ... Our Brigade 580, very small considering where we were. That night we went up to Banks Ford & crossed the river. This is a description of where & what we did across the river (not at all minute). I wish the Washington Artilary we took could be sent to Vt. Large brass 12 pd. cannon. Very nice. Our Cavilry has done miracles of late & left Stewart in the shade. Give us brave & true men & we will have a victory sometime. I have been where I hardly dreamed of being & got back safe *not ingloriously. We must have struck terror to many of the hearts of the enemy. The prisoners could hardly believe we had ever occupied Fredricksburg heights. The women are intolerable rank sesech.*

Several days later, on May 14, Henry wrote to Francis:

Ere this you must have heard full particulars concerning our last moove & safe return to our old position north of the Rapahonnoc. It seems hard to look back, see our selves once masters of the long coveted heights & today reoccupied by rebil soldiers but such is the decision of over ruling providence & we must content our selves & be in readyness to try the enemy again & never be dishartened. Let our service be ever so great. When we were surrounded by overwhelming numbers we were not aware of our desparate condition but like true men we obeyed orders & repulsed four rebils to one union soldier. After dark we withdrew unmolested except by a batary that tried to destroy our bridge but did not the least harm to man or bridges.

Today we are encamped within sight of Potomac River as pleasant camp as we ever had in the army. I saw George Ainsworth yesterday. He is at Potomac crick Hospital helping the wounded. He finds enough to do & much that is not done. There is great suffering & neglect among the wounded. War does not seem to him as it did in Vermont. There are two sides. One the glory of the fight, the other the dreadful suffering of the wounded & the careless treatment of the dead &c. George received news of Franks [George's brother, Frank Ainsworth] sickness & said he should return today if he was not better.

Yesterday I sent in my leave of absence for fifteen days & hope it may be approoved soon. If so, I shall be at home some time next week. The Captain wishes me to go by the way of Bennington to see his wife. If I should I should take the hudson main road to Troy from Bennington to Burlington &c. I have not decided to go there yet. It would take me three days instead of two to get home. I do not wish you to make your selves any trouble for I may not come for some time. We may moove so it would not go through. I will come as soon as I can. I shall want Mr Riker to make me some clothing, &c.

Henry's request for leave must have been lost because he sent another short, succinct message on May 15, addressed to "M. T. McMahon, Lt. Colnel & A.A. Gen 6th Corps":

Sir, I have the honor to request leave of abscence for fifteen days for the purpose of visiting friends in Vermont.

Henry was also still trying to straighten out the misunderstanding involving his pay. Medal of Honor recipient John Wesley Clark sent a message on May 15 to an officer of the Second Brigade, stating:

This may certify that Lt. W. H. Martin, Co A 4th Vermont Regt. is not indebted to this Department.

Three days later Henry received an answer to his leave request from McMahon in the form of Special Orders #125:

Leave of absence is granted to ... Lieut Wm. H. Martin 4th Vermont Vols. for 15 days, By Command of Major General Sedgwick.

It was time to take a break from the war and escape to the peacefulness and tranquility of Williamstown.

Chapter 9

GETTYSBURG: A SACRIFICE OF THOUSANDS

After his hiatus from the war, Henry returned to camp in early June 1863. On Friday morning, June 5, he dashed off a quick letter home from "Camp near Belle Plain, Va."

I am once more in camp the same one I left. I arrived yesterday about three P.M. I saw Lorett & Eunice at Lebanon. I was fearing they would not be there but I had determined to call & see how the people were. I arrived about Twelve & took the six o clock train next day. I was very glad I stoped. Eunice & Lorett arrived just after I did. ... I did not see Darwin Green in New York. I was sorry for I wished to see him.

(Darwin Greene was the older brother of John Greene of the Fourth Vermont and was working as a mechanical engineer in New York City. At the close of the war, John married Henry's cousin, Ann Martin. Henry, John, and Ann had all been classmates at Barre Academy just a few years earlier.)

I arrived in Washington about six o clock Wednesday morning & left for the army of the Potomac Thursday. I have arrived just in time to take part in a moove of some sort. Some say to Culpeper, some across the river. Cartridges & rations are being issued. I had a pleasant journey & will when I get more time, write you all about it.

Henry had no time to settle back into camp life, for he arrived back just as the Sixth Corps was moving out. On the Confederate side, despite victories at Fredericksburg and Chancellorsville, General Lee was not overly optimistic about the war's direction. Although he had forced Hooker's army back across the river again, Lee had lost over 12,000 men at Chancellorsville. He could not withstand many more "victories" with losses of that magnitude. Furthermore, those casualties had included Stonewall Jackson, who had figured so prominently in many of Lee's successes. Given the North's industrial and manpower advantages, Lee might not be able to keep thwarting invasions by means of a defensive strategy. Moreover, the rebel cause was not faring well in the west. Vicksburg was besieged by Grant, and its fall would give the Union complete control of the Mississippi River. On the other hand, believing that the Army of the Potomac must be demoralized after its recent defeats, Lee surmised that an invasion of the North was the best hope of victory. Defeating the Army of the Potomac on its own soil and bringing the ravages of war onto Union lands could sway popular opinion in the North toward demanding an end to the hostilities. Furthermore, drawing the Federal forces north would help to reduce the pressure on the beleaguered farmers of the Shenandoah Valley. Invading the North was certainly a gamble, but one worth taking. Lee began moving troops north on June 3 as Henry was traveling south.

Now without Jackson, Lee reorganized his army into three smaller corps. Confederate commanders Longstreet and Ewell each moved out while the final corps, under General A. P. Hill, remained at Fredericksburg. When Hooker began receiving reports of Confederate troop movements, he deployed the Sixth Corps to once again cross the Rappahannock and determine how much of Lee's army remained at Fredericksburg. Shortly after Henry had finished his morning letter on June 5, the Sixth Corps moved toward Deep Run to make its third crossing. Confederate sharpshooters from across the river made placement of the pontoons most difficult, so Sedgwick responded with artillery fire against the Confederate pickets. This action failed to dislodge them, so two regiments of the Vermont Brigade were sent across the river in pontoon boats to drive off the Confederate defenders, after which the Fourth Vermont was in the next wave of boats to cross. Most of the Confederate pickets soon surrendered, and construction of the pontoon bridge could continue. During the night and into the morning of June 6, the Vermont Brigade was alone on the southern side of the river and fought sporadic battles against small numbers of Confederates. Not knowing the Confederate strategy, the brigade must have been concerned that it might be confronted by Lee's entire army at any moment. Instead, the engagement, known as the Battle of Franklin's Crossing was much smaller in scale. On June 7, while positioned on the Confederate side of the Rappahannock at "Camp Near Banards House, Va.," Henry wrote to Francis:

> We are once more across the river in front of the same place we were when last across. I returned just in time. Stoped in camp one night only. Friday ten A.M. we received orders to march. About one P.M. we started & marched to the same old place where we have met with familiar success. It was about

three when we arrived at the bank of the river. The enemy saw us & prepared to resist our crossing. They manned their rifle pits & fired at evry man they could see. Soon twenty pieces of cannon opened on the rifle pits which made the enemy lay as low as possible. Next our Brigade was ordered to cross the river in boats & charge the enemy. When we came to the banks of the river they fired on us but did not check our progress in the least. We put the boats into the river, were rowed across & charged the enemy & took 45 prisoners besides killing & wounding a number of the enemy. Some cut their belts flung down their guns & escaped. There we advanced driving the enemy back. When we had gained their most important points we halted & formed a picket line which has been held. The enemy tried to drive us back but were not able. The 6th Vermont lost 18 wounded & 4 killed. The 4th Vt. did not loose a man. We were under the fire of protected sharpshooters our selves unprotected. The enemy at dark threatened an attack by Cavilry but could not advance. There is something misterious about this moove. Only our Brigade was across untill last night when the 3rd Brigade of our Division crossed, the 1st Division & 30 pieces of cannon. Today it is quiet along the lines. It seems much like a Sunday at home. A company of the 4th took 32 deserters & 2 Lieuts. They report the enemy reinforced. They show a formidable front. It does not seem as though we could cary the heights as easily as we did on the 4th of May. We shall learn the lay of the ground after we have crossed a few times more.

The army is all on the moove. A great deal of manouvering is taking place. Florida & Mississippi Regiments are in our front. Something will take place before many days. Cannonading was heard far on our right & left. It is rumourd here that eighty thousand are advancing on Richmond by way of the Peninsula. Hope it is true. If any thing of interest transpires I shall write again.

Eventually, more of the corps arrived, and they started to move towards the heights. When they began facing strong resistance the next day, Sedgwick determined that the defenses were too strong for an attack and ordered his corps to return to their own side of the river. Hooker therefore remained uncertain of Lee's troop movements and consequently sent out his cavalry to investigate, leading to the Battle of Brandy Station against Jeb Stuart's cavalry on June 9.

During his home visit, Henry had apparently caught the attention of some of the eligible young women in Williamstown. Martha and Maria Benedict were twin sisters whose mother had died in 1859 when they were sixteen years old. They were now living at different locations. Martha sent Henry the following letter on June 14:

As Maria and I have been down to your Father's pealing willows we have thought of you many, many times and wished that you could be with us but it is ordered otherwise as we did not see you to ask you to write to us. We thought that we would write you first as we wished to make you one of our correspondance. Perhaps you may think me very unlady-like in so doing if so—please tell me. I have been to church all day. I think you were there two and three weeks ago today and would like to been today would not you.

Did you have a pleasant journey back south as you did coming home? Henry I think that you was rather partial to Maria to go and see her and not call on me but I must think that I live on the hill not in the city. I would [have] been very happy to received a call from you and Maria that night that I spoke of but didn't. I know that you didn't stay at home but a short time and that your folks wanted to see you more than any one else.

It is four years today since my dear mother was taken from me and that is a long time to do without a mothers care aint it! At times when I think that I have no mother I do not wish to live any longer and then I think who took my mother from me. We must think that God will not afflict us willingly. He will not send any affliction upon us that we cannot bear. You don't know how many times Maria and Martha have wished that you could be at home a few weeks perhaps you wouldn't like to be would you? When did you go away the first time? Don't you wish that you was one of the nine months men [so that] you could come home pretty soon?

That girl that went into Mrs Staples's with us didn't think much of Maria and me. She wanted an introduction to you and I hope that you both will forgive us this time won't you? Charlie Davis is very sick with a fever. If you can read this you will do well. Excuse all mistakes and accept these few lines from your ever true friend. Henry if you think this worthy of an answer I hope you will answer it as soon as you get it. I suppose you are enjoying yourself. I don't see how you can take one night of comfort. I know that I couldn't. I hope that you will come home again is the prayer of your friend. May God bless you and keep you and may angels guard my dear—soldier friend. Write soon. So good night.

Charles Davis had volunteered immediately in response to the initial ninety-day call for the First Vermont Regiment. After the confusion and disappointment at Big Bethel, he returned to Williamstown and remained out of the army for the duration of the war. Henry's response to this letter was probably not very encouraging for Martha. As we will see in the next chapter, Henry had indeed fallen in love with a girl from Williamstown, but it was neither Martha nor her sister. Martha next turned her interests towards Henry's former classmate at Barre Academy, Nelson Farnham, a member of the Twelfth Vermont. As such, he was one of the nine-month soldiers of the Second Vermont Brigade to whom she referred. After fighting in one battle, the Battle of Gettysburg, they returned home. Farnham and Martha were married almost exactly one year after this letter to Henry.

Meanwhile, General Hooker concluded from the information obtained by his newly enhanced cavalry that the bulk of Lee's army was indeed on the move. Hooker's army began a fast pursuit, and the Sixth Corps moved out late on Saturday night, June 13. Contrary to Martha Benedict's expectations, Henry was not particularly enjoying the endeavor. On Wednesday morning, June 14, in the midst of a long and difficult march, he wrote a rushed letter home from "Camp Near Occoquan Crick":

> We are now on our way to Maryland in all possible haste. We left the Rappahannoc Saturday night & marched to Brooks Station. Stoped till ten Sunday & commenced to march till Tuesday night not stoping to rest once. Two nights without rest. We arrived at Dumfries three P.M. Monday night. Next morning we started at three A.M. & marched twenty miles in the hot sun & arrived where the 2nd Vt. Brig. are on duty. We stoped with the 14 two hours. Have seen some of the whole Brigade but we are a long way from the Wmtwn boys & have not seen any of them yet. They seem very glad to visit us. All that can getaway are here but they are not allowd to leave for some reason. We expect to march for some where at twelve P.M. We are expecting one of the roughest campaygns we ever had. It is reported that 40 men have died on the road most on account of heat. Many are sun struck. We never saw such hard marching before. Hardly a man drops out except he can go no further. We coverd the rear of the Potomac Army & have got the trains all safe within our lines. I will write more if I can get time at some future date. We hear that all the Charleston & New Bern Army are with Lee. If the thing is properly managed we will anhilate the Lee army. We are dreadfuly worn down. Pray for us. Thousands are to be sacrificed within the next few weeks.

Henry's closing line was indeed prophetic, as the Battle of Gettysburg was less than three weeks ahead. At this point, however, the army did not know where it was headed—only that it was moving fast, marching 20 miles a day in the intense summer heat. On Sunday evening, June 21, Henry wrote to his father again, from "Camp Near Bristow Station Virginia":

Having a chance to send you a few lines this evening I thought best to improove this chance for another may not present itself. Mrs. George wrote me to help her to get a certificate so she might [receive] a pension, which I have done & wrote her today. I thought I would enclose a line to you.

We are all well but dreadful tired. We have been on the moove ever since I arrived in camp. Yesterday we marched twenty miles & arrived at Bristow station. We crossed the Bull Run battle field & took a very responsible position protecting the left flank of the army. We may have a desperate fight any hour. We are ten miles from the rest of the Corps. Our Division composes our force & 6 Bataries. The 2nd Corps under Handcock had a desperate fight today at Thoroughfare Gap. This advance was not anticipated by the enemy & they lost posession of it. Handcock worked all night fortifying. At light the enemy tried to dislodge him but were three times repulsed with slaughter. I hope we may be able to keep them away from the old battle ground. They must guard their rear else we will be there. It is reported that 14,000 rebils are at Dumfries & the 12th Vt has been sent to reinforce the 14th Vt at Wolf Run Sholes. I have seen the Williamstown boys in Vt 2nd Brigade. They fear they will take part in the coming fight. They ought to see a little service before they return. The Vt. Cavilry are looking fine. A splendid looking Regiment & efective troops when properly led. I saw Holden. He was not entirely well from the sabre cut on his head. They have been scouting of late. Night before last they left for Maryland. We are holding ground formerly held by the 16th Vt. They [have] gone to the rear. If Handcock is driven we shall see one of the most desperate engagements since we joined the service. The railroads are coverd with ruins of train after train of cars. Great destruction is caused by war. 40 men droped dead out of the 6th Corps while marching from the Rappahannoc. The heat was intense. I hope this will be a decisive battle. If properly managed Lee will not return with a good army.

My health is good. So is all the Wmtn boys. Remember me to Lorett & Eunice, Mother & all. Write soon.

William Holden was in the Second Brigade and was another of Henry's former classmates. Reuben George was significantly older than either of them, having enlisted at age 37. He had died of disease in November 1862, and Lydia George was having difficulty convincing the government that she was eligible for a pension. Although her husband had been in Company K of the Fourth Vermont, she apparently believed that Henry was in the best position to solve the problem for her. Unfortunately, what Henry sent to Mrs. George was not sufficient for the pension officials in Vermont. On June 25, she wrote back to Henry:

I am informed that my aplication for a pension is incorect and I send the letter which came to me from the pension office and if I can get you to see Mr Georges Captain or first lieutenant or second and get him to say that the statemant which I send in this letter is true and sign his name to it that will make all things rite. If it should not agree with his statement please state to him what you know about the case. You probably know whare his disease was contracted and verry near how it was. I think the riting that I send you must be correct. If you will see to this business for me I will be verry much obliged to you and you must know some one must help me or it will take a great while to bring the pension round. I must say to you that your father and Mother are both well and my oldest boy Henry is to work for your father peeling willows. Your brother has a nice time puting them through the mashean. Mr Bass and his family are well as usual.

Lydia George did eventually receive her pension, backdated to the day her husband died. That would come later, however, because Henry was neither receiving nor sending mail as the march continued. On that same June 25 he began a letter to Francis which he carried with him for many days. The first section was written from "Camp Near Broad Run Virginia":

Since we left Fairfax the mails have not been permited to come to or leave the Regiment. So I have not heard from home for nearly a week. We are in a very exposed position so much so that we have to keep half of the Division on picket. The people are very kind where we are now. They give us food & use us like men. They pretend to be union but we doubt their being very true. There are no young men & the girls are out doing mens work hoeing, planting, ploughing &c. They are dressed very plain. Many go bare footed for it is impossible to get shoes because sesesh money is not worth half its full value. Prices are as extravagant as reported in the papers. The girls are greatly pleased with the attention of the soldiers. They are invited to dine & take tea if around at such times. We are where Pope was so unfortunate & lost so many teams & 125 cars & 6 engines. The road is strewn with the cars & their contents. Many were loaded with clothing. We passed a plantation owned by a Mr. Wm Nari. He owned one hundred slaves. His chief book keeper was a Negro. His overseers Negroes. How he must feel their loss.

The country has not been over run so much by the two armies as some sections. The land was sold before the [war] broke out for one dollar per acre. One man bought a farm at that rate & pays in ten years. Good land is almost valueless in slave territory. A number of northerner men have settled in this vasinity & such a difference in looks is remarkable. Business is conducted on a diferent scale, houses much more convenient &c. The people are very destitute. They depend on our army for food when we are near. They say the army are well fed but their families are in a destitute condition. The hard fight last Sunday prooved to be Pleasantons Cavilry instead of Hancock. It must have been a fierce one, I should judge from what we heard. A company of the Vt Cavilry went to the Rappahanoc & found but few rebils. They had a brush & took a cannon & lost but few men. One had a slice six inches long taken out of his head but was still on duty. We expect to be on the march for Maryland soon perhaps tomorrow. We have heard that the enemy were fortifying. A very wise course on their part. We are having Division, Brigade & Batalion drills. It does not seem quite right. We have not got half rested from our march from the Rappahannoc & this last one & Bristow Station was peculiarly hard. The mens feet are sore &c still they have to drill. It dishartens the men very much. It has commenced to rain. It has been threatening for a number of days past. Today we learned that E.H. Stoughton was to take command of this Brigade & would arrive tomorrow. Perhaps it is time. It matters but little with us who all are from the same place. I have but little choice in the army. Our Stoughton will drill the Brigade finely &c. We moove at 6 P.M. for some where. This letter will not be able to get under way for some days. I write as often as I can. How do the willows peal? Tell all the news &c. Has Eunice recruited any yet? George Ainsworth what is he about. I supose the draft will take efect next month. Did you receive a letter by Mrs. George. I sent her a certificate for a pension & a letter to be handed to father. I supose it is about time to begin to prepare for haying to get all old trash out of the way.

George Ainsworth
Courtesy of Williamstown Historical Society

Henry's question about George Ainsworth was answered by Ainsworth himself in a June 30 letter:

When I bade you "good morning" after our ride when you were here, I little thought "things" would be in just the condition they are at present; you "boys" so far North, yes, & the Rebs too; and I going about as a sort of "lecturer." Let me tell you how it comes about that I am doing what I am while I ask you to tell me, how it comes about that you are doing what you all are. After Frank was sufficiently recovered so he could go back to the store to work, I felt a strong desire to be again in the service of the "Christian Commission"—a work which I love beyond telling. I enlisted in the service not knowing where it would be thought best I should go to work. It was decided that I remain in Vt awhile & acquaint our people with what the Christian Commission is doing for our soldiers and enlist all the sympathy and effort in behalf of it that I should be able to. And so Henry, I am at work in Vt. I go about from place to place & tell the people what our "boys" are enduring & suffering for us and stirring them up to pray for you all a great deal more, write to you all a great deal more, and do & think more for you.

U.S. Christian Commission serving the soldiers
Courtesy of Library of Congress

I believe Henry I am doing some good at least. People know but little, after all, of what you are going thro'. I also solicit hospital stores, money &c for the C.C. and I also ask for delegates. I have as yet only lectured in Brookfield, N. Randolph & So. Royalton. In Brookfield, one young man talks of going as a Del. & in So. R. Mr. Haynes, whom you know, said he should ask his people to let him go six weeks as a Del. I hope he will for he would make a grand good one. I shall try & have him go to you boys, to be with you, if it is possible. Tomorrow I go to Norwich, next day to Bradford. I want to speak 3 to 6 times a week hereafter. I am just getting under "headway". It is very exhausting to speak in public, even if you don't say much that amounts to anything. But I get perfectly enthusiastic talking of the soldiers & the C.C. but Henry while I feel I am doing more good than I could in the Army perhaps, I think I must go back after a while. I want to be there and do myself for the men. My happiest days were at "White Oak Church" & "Potomac Creek." I often think of you boys and pray for you that your lives may be spared & that you may all be true men, ready for life, ready for death, ready for anything that may befal you.

How hard your march from the Raph'k must have been. I judge from what one of the 1st Jersey Brig. Boys wrote me that it must have been terrible.

How do Henry Smith & Charley Snyder do? Wish I was near them to look after their bodies if they are yet sick. And how is Dec Jones & Sancry & in fact all the fellows? Give them all my love and tell them I am trying to work for them all here in Vt. We are having warm weather. There is little news. Walter Bass I hear came last night. Ellen (his wife) is secesh.

(Henry Smith survived his wounds from Chancellorsville, but died of wounds suffered during the siege of Petersburg. Walter Bass, age 34, was a nephew of Ebenezer Bass. Walter's wife, Ellen Lynde Bass, had been a classmate of Henry at Barre Academy and was a niece of Isaac Lynde. Walter and Ellen were both older cousins to Henry and were now living in Illinois. After the war, they settled down on a farm in Ottawa, Kansas.)

We had a convention in Montpelier the other day that seems to me to smell of "Copper" a bit. You boys are needed to give "tone" to our corrupt "Copper" Communities. I reckon you would "tone" them, give you the chance, don't you? ... Oh! I must ask how you like your new commander & how you liked the idea of Hooker's removal? Perhaps you are so accustomed to those things you don't mind them much. [Hooker had been replaced with General Meade on June 28 and already it was known in Williamstown.]

Well Henry, I have a lot to do to-day. Among other things I am trying to make arrangements for every family in town who will, to give one bottle, at least, of preserved fruit for the C. C. to give to the sick and wounded. I feel sure it will go better thro' the C.C. than in any other way. Henry if you will you may let the others read this letter. Tis not worth showing but I cannot write to all now as I would like to. So they may feel this is for them, as well as you. God bless you all my good friends!!

Almost a week passed before Henry could continue the letter he had started on June 25. He resumed writing on Wednesday, July 1, unaware that one of history's epochal battles was commencing that very morning. A few days earlier, Lee, who had moved north to Chambersburg, Pennsylvania, received information that the Union Army had crossed the Potomac. Abandoning his plans of crossing Pennsylvania and threatening Philadelphia, he began to concentrate his forces near Cashtown, just eight miles from Gettysburg.

On July 1, A. P. Hill, on his own initiative, ordered two of General Henry Heth's divisions to advance on Gettysburg, where Union cavalry activity had been spotted the prior day. At about 8:00 a.m. these forces met John Buford's cavalry northwest of the town. Buford, realizing the importance of high ground after the Fredericksburg fiasco, was determined to hold his position. Although outnumbered, his men dismounted and, using the repeating rifles favored by cavalrymen, they held off a stronger opponent. Jubal Early, returning from the York area toward Cashtown, received orders to head for Gettysburg and reinforce the Confederates already engaged there. Early arrived from the north on the Harrisburg Road. Now the Union position became untenable, and they retreated through the town to the south until they reached the more defensible ground at Cemetery Hill. The Federal forces had been pushed back but they had not been routed, and they remained in a strong defensive position on high ground.

All during this time, General Lee was trying to formulate a strategy while missing vital information. He was out of touch with Jeb Stuart, the eyes of his army, and had no idea where Stuart was now located. Lee had to fight blindly as Stuart was making a wide swing around the sprawling Army of the Potomac. Unlike Lee, Henry knew exactly where Stuart's cavalry was, as shown by what he wrote from "Camp near West Minister Mary Land" on Wednesday morning, July 1:

> We have arrived within six miles of the Pensylvania line. We have seen some of the hardest marching since we joined the service. We have marched twenty miles per day since we left Bristow Station. On May 28 we marched twenty six miles. There seems to be nothing but the 6th Corps on this road. We had a triumphant entry in to Westminister yesterday. Fifteen thousand of Stewarts cavilry were there & we drove them away. The soldiers think Stewart will not be able to hold out much longer for his horses must be worn out. We have worn out all the field officers horses &c. It does not seem as though we were used right. I saw two men drop while marching who were taken crazy & died in a short time. This must not have been the only instance &c twenty miles a day is more than human nature can endure. There is not a man who has not blistered feet. It seems hard to be forced along in this style but I supose it is absolutely necesary. We conjecture we are to go to Harrisburg but we are as likely to retrace our steps or go to Hagarstown.

The Sixth Corps was ordered later that night to begin the thirty-mile march to Gettysburg in the blistering summer heat. It arrived in the late afternoon on July 2, as the day's fighting was concluding.

July 2 saw a continuation of the hostilities as Lee chose to go on the offensive against an enemy who he believed would be in some disarray after having been pushed back the first day and who was adjusting once again to new leadership, as

General George Meade had just replaced Hooker as commander of the Army of the Potomac. During the night, both sides had rushed forces forward to gain the advantage for the next phase of the battle. Besides being on higher ground, Meade had amassed about 90,000 of his men from his spread-out forces to face Lee's army of 75,000. The Union line formed into a very strong position often referred to as a "fish hook" after the shape of the ridges they occupied, which created internal supply lines that made Meade's defensive lines even stronger.

The fighting on July 2 was centered primarily on Cemetery Hill and Culp's Hill on the right end of the Union line, and on the left end where Little Round Top anchored the Federal line. On Cemetery Ridge, General Sickles, without orders and searching for a more secure position on higher ground, moved his Third Corps forward to the Peach Orchard, dangerously exposing the left flank of the line. If the rebels had broken through there, or at the right end, they could have swept in behind the Union defenses and decisively won the battle.

During a rest stop in the midst of their long march, Henry sat down to conclude his letter, seemingly unaware that such a monumental battle was taking place so very near to him. (He started the letter at 4:00 p.m., wrote the entire letter, then continued marching and arrived at the battle at about 5:00.) Henry started the letter just as General Longstreet was beginning his attack on the Union's left flank.

July 2 Thursday, 4 P.M. We left Bristow Station marched til three A.M. about at Centerville, slept till five then resumed the march & kept it up till three P.M. when we rested for the night. Struck tents at four A.M. & arrived at Edwards Ferry at three P.M. crossed the river & encamped for the night. Left at 4 A.M. Arrived at Poolsville 9 A.M. Passed to the right of Sugarloaf Mountain through Hyattstown to Damsville. Halted for the night. Started at four A.M. arrived at Westminster at ten A.M. We expected a severe engagement. The 3rd & 4th Regt. led the advance of the whole Corps. The 3rd skirmished all the way but our Cavilry succeeded in driving 6 thousand of Stewarts Cavilry under Lee & Stewart. The rebils were well received by most of the men & women. When we arrived we were used equaly as well. The ladies waved their handkerchiefs &c gave the soldiers milk, bread & water. We were not expected as it was not known that an infantry man was near. They were taken by surprise but I must close. We are to start for somewhere immediately.

I am well. The Captain is sick & has to be carried in an ambulance. I [have not] received a letter from you a few days since we do not have any mail of late nor any papers. This part of Maryland is a perfect garden. Evry man has a very nice house & barn. Their crops are heavy. Wheat is ripe. Hay very good. Their fences are very nice & durable made of oak & red cedar. They have very good horses for service, large but not handsome. Their cows are the best. Bags as large as bushel baskets. Hogs are kept in fields of clover but with cherries as grow beside the roads. The black cherries are as large as our towns & so sweet. Evry man keeps barels of whiskey & cider. It looks very odd to temperance people. Most evry family has slaves, some white as you but curly hair. I supose there is great excitement at the north. The army is the place where news of the enemies invasion gives but little concern. We are ready for any imergency. How this will terminate no one can tell. The enemy are very strong & get some recruits in this state. It is conjectured that some of the bloodiest battles of the war is to come off very soon but I must close. The Wmtn boys are well but very foot sore. ... It has rained nearly evry day since we commenced to march. Hoping to hear from you soon.

Union troops, including Chamberlin's soon-to-be-famous 20th Maine, finally moved into position on Little Round Top just before the rebel attack. Shortly after the Union's successful defense of this strategic position, the Vermont Brigade arrived. The Fourth Vermont was placed in reserve behind Little Round Top to help secure the left flank during the final hours of the day's fighting. As the Fourth Vermont settled into place, George Smith was not far away and was facing some of the most difficult fighting in the battle. His 17th U.S. Infantry was ordered into what is now simply known as the Wheatfield. This part of the battlefield became important once Sickles advanced his lines, creating an opportunity for rebel forces to break through. The Wheatfield, located next to the Peach Orchard, had already changed hands several times as the 17th approached past Devil's Den, where it faced heavy fire, and then into the intense and chaotic struggle in the Wheatfield itself. The mission of the 17th was to delay the Confederate advance as the reserve units of the Sixth Corps set up their defensive positions at Little Round Top.

In the midst of this fighting in the Wheatfield, George was hit in the chest by a Minié ball. Distance and wind velocity combined caused it to arrive with enough force to knock him to the ground but not enough to penetrate and cause the usual lethal damage. As a result, although George was nearly killed, his name does not appear among the more than 51,000 casualties at Gettysburg. He returned to his feet and continued in the fight for control of this portion of the battlefield. The Wheatfield changed hands six times during the day and control of it remained in question by nightfall, but more importantly, Little Round Top was under firm Union control. The 17th U.S. lost a staggering 58% of their men in the horrific struggle for the Wheatfield. George Smith survived and was brevetted captain for "gallant and meritorious service" for his efforts in this battle.

General Lee initially planned to attack both flanks again on July 3. Had his plan been implemented, the Fourth Vermont would have found itself in the path of Longstreet's offensive. Delays among the Confederate commanders, along with an early-morning Union offensive to secure Culp's Hill on the right flank, caused Lee to dramatically alter his plan. Believing that Meade must have reinforced his flanks by weakening the center of his line, Lee ordered a major offensive by the Confederates into the Union center on this final, decisive day of fighting. Although General Longstreet argued strongly against this strategy, his forces, under General Pickett, were ordered to lead the assault. Vermont's inexperienced Second Brigade, despite the fears that some members had confided in Henry prior to the battle, performed admirably in its one military engagement. The brigade was later praised by General Meade for leaving its defensive position and moving forward to outflank the rebels, thereby helping to stop the Confederate charge at Cemetery Ridge. The Union army held off the massive attack and the Confederates were forced to retreat after having come so close to a potentially decisive victory at Gettysburg. Now Lee's concern was how to get what remained of his army back to safety in the South.

While the Second Vermont Brigade suffered 342 casualties on July 3, the Old Vermont Brigade was held in reserve, exposed to shells landing around them but suffering no casualties. The next day, Independence Day, the Vermont Brigade's commander, Lewis A. Grant, sent the Fourth Vermont out on picket to determine the position of nearby Confederate forces. It advanced about a mile and a half and fought a small skirmish with a group of Confederate pickets. One unfortunate soldier was shot in the arm and knee. John Marshall thus became the only casualty of the entire Vermont Brigade at Gettysburg and one of the last casualties of the battle. He died from his wounds about a month later.

The Sixth Corps was sent in pursuit of Lee's army on July 5. On July 8, writing from "Near Middletown Maryland," Henry finally had time to tell his parents what had transpired:

> One of the greatest battles of the war has just passed & one of the greatest victories of the war. The 6th Corps was not engaged but little. We were the grand reserve of the Army of the Potomac. Twice we came very near being put into the hotest part. July 2 we marched over thirty miles. We left West Minster at two A.M. & arrived at Gettiesburg about four P.M. When we came in sight all of our cannon opened on the enemy. The infantry charged &c. & finaly drove the enemy at evry point. Lee massed his forces & tried to

brake our center. We were mooved within infantry distance but our front lines refused them with great loss. Then our left was tried. Four lines of battle made the attack. Our first could not hold them. Then the fifth Corps was flung in the enemies front. The regulars were ordered to make a charge. We were double quicked & formed a line in their rear. The regulars repulsed the enemy but with great slaughter on our part. Out of eight hundred regulars five were killed or wounded. In Georges Regt fourteen officers were wounded. George was hit in the left brest & knocked down but providentialy it was a spent ball & did him no harm. He wished me to say that he was well & to mention to Uncle Bass that a suit of clothes for Willie was paid for by him when at home.

The morning of the 3rd of July was opened by heavy firing. Lee had made an attack. Eighty pieces of cannon was the opening of the great battle & for five hours the most terrific war of artilery & musketry was kept up without cessation. Six times did Lee charge our lines with three lines of battle three quarters of a mile in length & evry time repulsed. The slaughter was immense surpassing all former battles. I visited diferent parts of the battlefield where charges are made. The men lay in almost perfect lines & so many of them. The rebils had buried all they could but half had not been done. Hundreds of horses are strewn over the field. Our Brigade was on the extreme left flank of the army. Our Vt Cavilry had a terrible fight in our front. Flying artilery was used in magnificent style. They would go into the rear of the enemy & often on this if they showed a week spot the Cavilry would charge & take a lot of prisoners. So it continued all day. Our cavilry charged through two lines of battle passing through the center of the rebil army. Many were killed but many more returned than was expected. When they came to our picket line the Sgt. of Co. B thought them rebils & steped out & halted them. At that the Co. drew their pistols & prepared to charge. The Sgt halted him. The officer said we never halt & was on the point of dashing through when the Sgt recognized one of the men & let them in.

(Henry would have had a very good view of the First Vermont Cavalry in its desperate actions on July 3. General Judson Kilpatrick had validated his nickname of "Kill Cavalry" by ordering an ill-conceived charge into a heavily fortified Confederate position beneath the Round Tops. The Vermont Cavalry was the one unit to actually break through the Confederate lines at least temporarily. After it returned, it was ordered to charge again. Little was accomplished by these maneuvers in terms of the outcome of the battle, and the 400 men of the First Vermont Cavalry suffered 65 casualties.)

We have marched night & day of late which has prooved the secret of our success. The enemy expected to find green troops but were dreadfuly deceived. We were on the ground one day sooner than expected & prooved the secret of Napoleons great success. We are now nearly between the enemy & the Potomac & shall have a desperate battle soon. The 1st Corps has just left for Williamsport. Cannonading is heard in that direction. We are hopeing to whip the enemy before they return to Virginia. We have taken lots of prisoners. Meade has shown himself a General. He sent a circular to the army complimenting them for good conduct &c & ending by saying what great obligations we are under to the ruler of battles & prayed for his guidance in future. [The circular was] the best of any heard since the war. One said it could be compared to Washingtons. We are hoping this will be our last battle & some of the most desperate fighting is expected. We have had our share since we enterd Maryland. I will, when I have time, write more minutely. We are as wet as we can be. It has rained a little evry day prooving very favorable on our part not to the enemy. Many of our men are bare footed. Still they march, the stones sometimes cuting to the bone. Our order has been to look for any citizens shoes even from their feet so urgent is the need of men & the dificulty of getting enough to wear. We are all the time on the move, ragged & dirty. Mud from head to foot. Some have been two days without food. We were one & a half days but we marched all one night & part of a day. We think it rather of an active campaign but few fall out. I must close. I am well &c. P.S. The Wmstn boys are all well.

On July 10, the Sixth Corps caught up to the rebel rear guard at Funkstown and went into action. The Battle of Funkstown was primarily a cavalry battle between the forces of Jeb Stuart and John Buford; however, the Vermont Brigade arrived and entered the battle as well, facing a Confederate brigade under George T. Anderson. The 479 casualties at Funkstown pale in comparison to the 51,000 a week earlier at Gettysburg, but for the Martin family back in Williamstown, Funkstown was the source of greater anguish, for Henry was among the wounded. Both Henry and Colonel Charles Stoughton were hit by shell fragments, Henry in the neck and shoulder and Stoughton in the head.

The injured were taken to the Chaney House, which served as a hospital, and then to a hospital in Baltimore. Four days after the battle, Henry sent an "Application for leave of absense at Baltimore, MD July 14, 1863 because of being wounded in the battle of Funkstown." He wrote:

I have the honor to report that Colnel C B Stoughton & myself of the 4th Vermont infantry were wounded near Funkstown on the afternoon of the

10th. That we were sent here and in compliance with orders from the war department report ourselves we are unable to report in person. We desire to go to New York this evening if possible. Will you do us the kindness to state what steps we shall take that we may do so.

Charles Stoughton, a Norwich University graduate, lost his sight in one eye and never returned to military service. Instead, he began practicing law with his father in Bellow Falls, Vermont. After the war, his brother, General Edwin H. Stoughton, joined their practice as well. (The famous pediatrician and anti-war activist of a century later, Benjamin Spock, was Charles Stoughton's grandson.) As for Henry, just one week after being injured he was back home in Williamstown. On July 17 he wrote "To Adjutant General Washington D.C.":

I have the honor to report in compliance with General Orders No. 188 that I was wounded in the battle of Funkstown wd. in neck & shoulder by a shell, was sent to Baltimore. Obtained surgeons certificate of disability for twenty days from the 13th July 1863. Should I not be able to return at the expiration of my leave of abscence will you do me the kindness to write what steps I shall take to have my leave extended.

The required steps were soon taken. Dr. Edward E. Phelps, previously a surgeon with the 4th Vermont and now in charge of Brattleboro Hospital, sent the following report on Henry:

Having made application for a certificate on which to ground an application for extension of his furlough (dated July 13th, 1863) for twenty days I do hereby certify that I have carefully examined this officer and find that he is unfit for duty in consequence of a shell wound of left shoulder received at the battle of Funkstown, Maryland in pursuit of Lee's army, July 10, 1863: & that, in consequence thereof, he is, in my opinion, unfit for duty. I further declare my belief that he will not be able to resume his duties in a less period than twenty days. Dated at Brattleboro this 30th day of July, 1863.

When they had encountered Lee's rear guard, Sedgwick requested further instruction from General Meade and was ordered to alter his route rather than initiate another large battle. Sedgwick continued shadowing the Confederate army for the next week, but Meade chose not to attack, and Lee's army crossed the Potomac and secured a safe position on July 13. The Sixth Corps crossed the river and continued to follow, but now at a much more leisurely pace, establishing a camp at Warrenton on July 25. The Army of Northern Virginia had been defeated, but it now had time to regroup and prepare to fight another day. Henry would do likewise.

Chapter 10

A RIOTOUS ENGAGEMENT
IN NEW YORK

August arrived and Henry was still convalescing in Vermont. He wrote on August 1 to the Army Adjutant General:

Sir, I have the honor to report in compliance with Spetial Orders no. 188 that I am not able to return at the expiration of my leave of abscence. My wound is not as well so I can not ride that distance. Enclosed please find a surgeons certificate.

From the camp near Warrenton, Virginia, Captain Pratt sent Henry a letter on August 10.

Your letter of the 30th was received last evening. I was very glad to hear from you but am sorry to hear that your wound is not doing any better. You must have received some internal injury. You must not try to get back to the regt till you get well. We are here in camp doing nothing and you can just as well stay in Vermont for some weeks as to be here and I think your wound will do very much better there. The weather is extremely warm here. The men of the company inquire about you very often. They are all enjoying excellent health. I wish you would go to Bennington & make my wife & family a visit. It would please her so very much. I hope you will be sure and do so if possible. Capt. Brown has gone to Washington for a few weeks and I am acting Inspector of the Brigade. I understand that there is no doubt but Col Stoughton has lost his right eye. I hardly think he will ever return to the Regiment. (I hope not) Please to write quite often and believe me as ever your friend.

While home, Henry tried once more to solve the problem of his missing payments. In a somewhat testy letter to the state treasurer, he explained:

There being a misunderstanding about my allotted pay. I write to inform you that I have not received (or my assignee, Chester Martin) anything for

the months of May and June 1862. A number of letters have been writen
when asked to produce the number of orders to include the two months wrote
they could not. I have not drawn it in camp nor has it been by my assignee.
There must be a mistake on your part & wish you would rectify it at once.

By August 17, Henry's forty-day furlough was over and it was time to return
to duty. He chose, however, to combine family business with his return trip. Henry
stopped in Boston to meet with two book publishers, both located on Milk Street.
He carried with him a letter of introduction from George Ainsworth for Samuel I.
H. Smith. Smith's occupation was described in a Boston business directory as "pocket
book manufactory book/paper/printing trades." Henry also met with Charles Asp,
who was listed as a "book seller and publisher." In all likelihood, the venture involved
selling willows to the book publishers, for either paper making or bookbinding. On
August 18, Henry wrote home from the Marlboro Hotel in Boston:

I did not arrive in Boston at as early an hour as I expected. The train was a
slow one, did not arrive until past seven PM. It was too late to do my business
so I stoped at the above named hotel. Early in the morning I started on my
errand but could not see the man I wished to til business hours [at] ten A.M. I
had no trouble in finding his place of business but the man was not in. I went
to his residence. On finding it he had gone to 89 Milk Street so back I went. I
was not able to find him til eight oclock at night. Finaly succeeded in finding
him and told him my business. He said it was all right & if I would wait til
next day 12 PM he would meet my wishes. I shall wait but what will be my
fate for not being in Washington on time I do not know. I hope to get all but it
is at some extra expences stoping him. I have spent the day pleasantly visiting
the City. Have not got lost once. Boston is a beautiful City.

I met a number of the men & officers that came home after conscripts.
They say that they will not be able to get over two hundred men to a regiment.
We ought to have more. Every thing is quiet here. A number of Regts have just
arrived (nine mustered men). The conscripts desert when they can. Yesterday
when a squad was being taken to Long Island, two jumped out of the cars
when under the speed of thirty miles an hour & were instantedly killed.

With his business concluded the next day, Henry resumed his journey back to
camp. But the impact of his two-day delay turned out to be far different from what
he had anticipated. As Henry was traveling from Boston through New York City
to Washington, D.C., the Fourth Vermont was being transported from Washington to New York City, having had departed on the evening of August 19. Henry
arrived the next morning. He explained the situation in a letter home:

I am in Washington. My Regt is in New York. They left last night by boat from Alexandria. Arrived probably this P.M. I would like to have known they were to have been ordered there so I would have met them there but I did not so I am here & shall return tomorrow. I have just seen Mr. Smith & stopped with him. He is well & as kind as usual. I have not got all the pay of Mr. Asp. He said he would have the full amount collected & send it on to me at Washington next Saturday. I thought best to have him send it there at that time for certain reasons since I have changed my mind and ordered it by express to you. He paid me 39.00 dollars & I think he will pay the rest. He had writen Frank about the affair but Frank had not received the letter. He had not sold the books on account of Appleton's [a Boston bookbinder] disliking his purchasing of anyone but him. He has arranged it now. Mr. Asp is called an honest man & I should judge the same. He is doing a large business. Is a Sweed by birth. I hope he will pay prompt. I was to 8.00 dollars extra expense the amt you will receive 108.00 dollars. I shall visit the city tomorrow. At 6 PM start for New York. The weather is very warm. I will write at some future day all about my stay in Boston. Had an excellent chance to visit the city.

The reason for moving troops to New York was that draft riots had recently broken out in the city. With historical hindsight, it is apparent that the Union victories at Gettysburg and Vicksburg marked a turning point in the war, but the shift in momentum toward the North was much less evident at the time. Congress had passed a Conscription Act in March 1863, and the drafting of soldiers in New York City began one week after Gettysburg. The resulting riots arose in part from opposition to the war effort, but also partly from social-class resentment, since those with sufficient financial resources could hire a substitute if drafted or pay a $300 fee. There was also racial resentment against the northern blacks, whom many Irish immigrants viewed suspiciously as competition for urban employment as well as being in some sense the cause of the war itself. Mobs attacked the building where the draft was being held, draft officials, and law enforcement figures. They then turned their rage toward black residents of the city, destroying homes, lynching individuals, and even burning a black orphanage. Federal troops from nearby forts were sent in on July 14 to start restoring order, and when they found that they could not restrain the violence, regiments from the nearby Army of the Potomac began arriving a day later. Casualty estimates vary greatly, but it seems likely that the number killed was measured in the hundreds with injuries in the thousands. When the Vermont Brigade arrived on August 24, its camp was placed in the park at Washington Square, a wealthy residential section of the city. It was deployed in part as a buffer between local townspeople and troops who might have been tempted to loot or otherwise exact revenge against a city with which they had been in conflict for the last month. Henry wrote his first letter home from Washington Square on August 27:

> *Today I have the pleasure of writing you from New York. I arrived one week ago today & found the Regiment encamped in one of the pleasantest parks in the City of New York & among the most aristocratic people of the place. Generals Fremont & McClellan live on the avenue below the 5th. It is much different living here than in Virginia. The people are all anxious to see all soldiers from the Army of the Potomac. Many are very kind, some dreadfuly coroded with copper. They wish to know what we are here for, want to know what we are going to do if they keep in their houses & shoot who ever tries to molest them or how we are to make them do duty &c, &c. It is supposed there are thirty thousand troops from the Army of the Potomac. We tell them in answer to their questions that we are here for some purpose & if ordered to quell riots intend to do it at all hazards. They wish to know what we could do if they posted themselves on the house tops & pelted with bricks & stones & we answered that we had all our artilary with us & we imagined that we could make the bricks fly the fastest. All the bataries that accompanied us when in the Army of the Potomac are with us in New York. There is considerable talk about why such a great force of vetran troops are detached from the Army of the Potomac. Some think we are bound for some expedition some where, some say to Mexico some to Canada & some to Texas. This is all talk. It seems to me that we are not here for the purpose of enforcing the draft alone. I was gladly surprised to learn the fact that the whole of the Vermont Brigade was ordered to New York. It is quite a treat as well as a great honor to be selected as the choicest troops of the Corps. We are now with the regulars & compose a division under General Ayers, formerly Chief of Artilary in our old division. I saw George Wednesday & this evening. We are quartered with the Third & 4th VT. Infantry commanded by Major Dent, son in law of Isaac Lynde. We have had great kindness shown us since we arrived. We seem to be a curiosity to all. When there is a parade there is always a great crowd to witness it. I have visited the City conciderable. Have met numbers of friends who have taken great pains to show me about. I visited Central Park one of the finest in America. Saw the dears, bares, eagles &c running wild in a large enclosure. Also the swans which you must have heard so much about. Had a ride on*

some of the artifitial ponds, went up to high bridge which was built for the purpose of convaying the water across East River for the use of the city. The water had run the distance of forty miles on reaching the bridge. It is built of granite & some hundred & twenty feet high & the longest of any in New York.

Have you heard from Mr. Asp yet? I wish you would write me all about it. How about Frank. I have not heard from him since I left. You may direct my letters to Washington Park, N.Y. They will come direct to me. I am about the same as when I left. We meet a great many Vermonters who have come to visit their friends. Now is their best chance & all ought to improve it. I am enjoying my self very much but it costs as it never has before since I joined the army.

Henry was concerned about Francis because of his brother's determination to join the army. Although five years older than Henry, Francis had not enlisted earlier and Henry had never encouraged him to do so. Henry believed that all able-bodied northerners should be doing their wartime duty, but Francis appears to have had a rather weak constitution and was often sick. There are some indications that he may also have suffered from depression. On August 31, Henry composed a letter to his soon-to-be comrade in arms:

Your favor of the 28th arrived on the morning of the 29th coming very direct. I was glad to hear from you & this evening write an answer because of some news contained in your epistle. I was not disapointed as to the result of your medical examination. I thought it would be as you thought. No external show of disability so you are one notch nearer being drawn into the army. Did you get a furlough to go home after examination. You must be sure that there is a proper understanding about your being absent. Did you expose yourself to take the bad cold you mentioned in your last. How long did you remain in Windsor before they came around to you. Is there any to be discharged? But there is no use in even thinking of that for then you might be disappointed. It really seems as though providence meant you should go. I hope your health will improve very fast & be able to do whatever duty demands. I was hoping on some accounts you would not pass still I felt you would. I feel sure your health will improve. The open air works miraculous cures but I will not say you are to [have] a very easy time before you. If we go to Texas or Mexico we shall see rough times but not harder than we have before experienced. I should not wish to change my mind now and buy off for most would think your heart failed you when the testing time came. Still I do not wish to advise for being in the army. I may not be the right one to advise others. I suppose you might have been exempted on the ground that the parent has a right to one when he has others in the service. It is an excelent thing to understand the law. Has any of the other men concluded to go?

I visited Doranns Saturday. Found him agreeable & gentlemanly. He had not sold any yet the market was good & would sell before long. He has had trouble with Colby. He thinks Howden [?] a scoundral Colby a little better. Was there any two years growth among our lot? They do not sell as well as the first growth. He thinks they will sell as well as ever. He has had them on hand about a month. I am lucky you gave me his adress. I had no trouble finding him. The directories found in every place of business helps to find many that would go unfound were they not in use.

Perhaps Mr. Asp has sent the money to Mr. Smith in Washington. I shall hear from him soon. He is to write if he does. If you do please do the same for the bill must be collected if possible. I judge him to be an honest man doing a respectable business amongst respectable men who would not be connected with none but honest men. His friends & neighbors speek well of him. When I met him he ... told a straight story & did his best to get what he could while I stayed there. ...

New York is a busy city. Everything to kill time and get the money is invented. Central Park is one beautiful plot of ground. One small bridge to the miniature lake costs one million of dollars. Not a very small sum of money. On that lake is Cleopatra's barge & a very good imitation it is. The population seems to be mostly foreign decent, hardly anyone can talk without a broge. I have been astonished to see what a difference there is between the rich & poor. The rich live like kings, the height of splendor. The poor intolerably debased so filthy that you could hardly bare to walk through their streets. They are crowded into the houses nearly as thick as a swarm of bees in a hive. The children are numberless. None look healthy & strong & but few can read or write so they tell me. I visited Greenwood Semitary & saw a magnificent graveyard. There are over one hundred thousand graves in the semitary. It is of long standing. Is ornamented in the greatest style that money will make nice. Monuments of the greatest designs. Cost could not have been consulted. There are toombs as splended as need be seemingly too good. A waste of money. The Firemens monument is one that attracts much attention. It was erected by the Firemen of New York. Is very large. On top is a statue of a Firemen rescueing from the flames an infant. It is truly very nice. The Sailors is another. On top is a statue of a man who seems to be standing at the helm in a storm & etc. There is so much magnificense that you cannot *appreciate half the reality. I visited Henry Ward Beechers church. It is very plain without a steeple, resembles the Universalist Church at Barre South village. Brick, no outward show. It is very large & said to be very nice inside. The churches are very nice, built mostly of sandstone. Hope this letter will find you well or convalescent. I am about the same as when I left.*

The Fourth Vermont remained in New York City through the first week of September. On the sixth, Henry wrote home to announce its departure:

I write at this late hour to inform you that we start for Alexandria tomorrow. We were much surprised to receive marching orders for we had anticipated a much longer stay. The 2nd, 3rd, 5th & 6th left yesterday at four Oclock. We are remaining behind to get our pay. The 4th Regiment was not payed at Alexandria. The rest were. Col Foster says he will not move his men until they are payed. Today has been very busy with us for a sunday in N.Y. I attended a meeting this evening. It prooved to be Episcopal. The service consisted mostly in reading the scripture, singing and playing the organ. The latter was very fine. I never heard better singing. I tried to attend Dr. Chevers Church but he was away so I did not. One day last week I visited Trinity. It is one of the most magnificent Churches in the City. Grace Church is a building not to be but in the United States. It cost eleven hundred thousand dollars. Stewart's Store is very fine, so is Wall Street. John Smith does business only a few rods from there. His sisters arrived Friday night. I have not seem them. I met George last night. He is well. Henry Smith has found a lot of Waller connections here. I received Franks letter & answer it in this. I suppose he is at Brattleboro now. Has he fully recovered? We have heard that the 2nd has been sent to Powcepsie [Poughkeepsie], the 3rd to Newark, N.J. the 5th to Harlem N.Y. the 6th to Kingston & are to remain at Alexandria to guard the conscripts & take them to their Regts. We have heard since that they have all been ordered to Alexandria. The people fear to have us leave. They think there will surely be an outbreak before long. They threaten it but dare not as long as we remain.

I have had a very pleasant time since I arrived in N. Y. but expect a hard trip to Alexandria. We go by water, shall be between three & four days on the water. I dont expect to be sea sick as I have been before this. I have been told that a person is sea sick only once. We shall have a very interesting trip as it is so pleasant weather. The scenery is very good on the Potomac. We anticipate that an attack is expected or we to make one. If they could have got along as well without us we would as soon remain a while. Mr. Lynde has been expected all the week. He is a little too late now. Many have hurried to visit their friends.

All should. A soldier is a moovable planet & the only time to catch him is as soon as you hear of him[to] start to meet him at once. I met Sally Staples today. [Eighteen year old sister of Charles Staples.] She is well &c &c. ...

September 7, 1863.

We have just been signing the pay rolls. Shall be paid early this P.M. There will be an allotment of 60 dollars. I have thought it would be better to put it in Chelsea Bank than have it remain that long time in the treasury without being on interest. You can do as you think best. I will send you 250 dollars. Perhaps I may send for it if I can arrange matters with Mr Smith. ... I have got a new way to send money. It is the only way from New York. It is a certificate of deposit payable to your orders. I think you will have no trouble in drawing it at Montpelier.

We expect to go by boat to night, perhaps not untill tomorrow morning. John Smith called to see me last night. No news from him. I am to visit him if we do not leave tonight. George Smith is detached on recruiting service, a good job [and is] at Ft. Preble, Me. I am to send home by express a bundle of stuff that I do not want. The bundle will be composed of all sorts of articles, some not very clean. ...The 3rd Regt have had some trouble in Newark, have killed a number of men. ...There was the drunkenest lot of men last night I ever saw since I entered the service. We are all well. Love to all.

Henry had also written to Chauncey Smith on September 5, and Chauncey responded on September 8:

Glad to hear that you are all so comfortably quartered, and withall attract so much attention. Of course, some few young ladies don't mind going a little out of their way to take a peek at you; albeit, you may not have the chance to talk with them but their good looks is something. ...

Have not received any money from Boston or heard from there. I have most forgotten what you told me about it, but believe I was not requested to write. I will therefore leave the subject with you, but will cheerfully do what you request me.

We are still having pleasant weather, without any rain for two months, except three showers. About the same state of things "outdoors" and "indoors" as when you were here. Many are off on visits to the mountains, watering places, &c, but there are some of the pretty girls left, just enough to make things <u>lively</u>. Make my kind regards to Charlie, Oscar, and all the boys, while I remain very truly yours.

The idea that a person gets seasick only once had been a nice thought, but by the time they arrived at Philadelphia the men of the Fourth Vermont had learned that there was no truth to it. Henry wrote about the experience on September 13:

We left New York Friday morning for Alexandria. We sailed all that day. At night the sea was rough & the engine gave way & came very [close to] leaving us to the mercy of the waves. So the Captain decided his freight to precious to risk out of sight of land so he put in to Delaware Bay finaly arriving at our present destination. I wish you could have been with us to have seen what a commotion was created in all our stomachs. The sea was rough. Were out of sight of land. The boat rolled, pitched & etc. each lurch causing us to wish we had never seen a boat. It was amusing to see how quiet it was. Every man took his bunk & kept it until driven up to get relief in emptying our stomachs into the sea. Eating was out of the question & the next morning found us in better turn as sickness seldom lasts over twenty four hours. So we came on deck & enjoyed the beautiful scenery of Delaware Bay & the river leading to Phila-delphia. We passed Fort Delaware where 7000 rebil prisoners are confined. It is a beautiful Fort, is on an Island commanding the mouth of the river lead-ing to Philadelphia. It is built of stone not a modern Fort. Would not stand long before iron clads. The whole river is fortified so a wooden fleet would not have a very fine time passing. All our seaports are lively with men building fortifications. Down Long Island are some very formidable forts being built. Some of the heaviest guns being mounted. They are expecting to use them before many months (so they say). I presume they will. General Stanard is in command of the forts of N.Y. Harbor, quite an important command & honor to a Lt. Colnel of the 2nd Vermont. He has been a very successful man & deserving. Had Stoughton been contented to remain with the Vermont militia last fall he would have been in command of the Brigade today, perhaps the Division. It may be lucky he did not.

We are today beginning in the harbor of Philadelphia just below the navy yard. Are having a still time. None can go ashore. So the time seems long. The men prefer land to water, especially they did the first day of our trip. There are a number of gun boats lying in the harbor, undergoing repairs. One left last night. Its remarkably quiet for so large a place, no business is being done in the city or harbor. It is not allowed. In New York it is not so. ...There is a great activity in all the navy yards. Most are engaged in building gun boats. We expect to leave here tonight either by rail or steam boat. If by boat we shall go down the river a little way then cross by a canall into the Chesapeake

Bay. From there into the Potomac, then to Alexandria. I will close & send this letter by a small boat come from the City. We are all over our seasickness & never want to be so again.

While they were delayed near Philadelphia, Henry traveled around the area. Three days later, after they finally reached Alexandria, he wrote home with his observations:

We have just arrived at the place we started for six days ago. We were delayed one day at Philadelphia from which place I mailed a letter to you. Sunday morning we left for Chester, Pa. Arrived about ten A.M. anchord & waited untill six o clock monday night when a screw propeller came & took us on board & carried us to Alexandria. We passed through the Chesapeake & Delaware Bay Canall into Chesapeake Bay. From there into the Potomac. The cause of our delay was a failure in the engine of the vesel. I think I mentioned it in my last. On arriving at Chester the officers were allowed to go ashore. It was remarkably quiet there, they all observing the Sabbath. I visited the United States Hospital one of the largest in the country & the best arranged I ever visited. There were eight hundred rebil wounded there. They were as well used as our own men. Their quarters were lit by gas, had bathing houses with cold or warm baths as the person prefered. It seemed almost too good fair for men who have been the destruction of so many of us. There were thirty officers in one room. They do not look as well as ours do. The southern Soldiers far behind ours. It was astonishing to see how extensively the work to be done was & how perfectly it was executed. Evry thing seemed to be done in the most perfect manner and order. Then we returned to the boat. Slept quietly all night in a tight state room on a straw bed & straw pillow. Next morning we were rowed ashore with the Captain of the vessel. (It was named Cambria an English iron clad vessel captured while attempting to run the blockade at Galveston, contained a cargo worth five hundred thousand dollars &c &c.) We visited one of the best ship yards in the country. All our best moniters were built there. There were being built one almost finished. There is a contract for twelve Moniters & sixteen iron clads to be built as soon as possible. There are two thousand hands employed. In evry harbor are being built some of the most formidable iron clads invented. This must mean something. From the iron clads, we visited different parts of the town. The people were very kind. We purchased quantities of fruit &c. The peaches were excellent & cheap. I never improoved a chance to get fruit better than I did there. I felt that fruit would not be as pleanty as when we arrived at Culpepper.

Once they did finally arrive at their destination, rumors began to immediately circulate concerning their next assignment:

It is amusing to hear camp stories. First was that a riot had broken out in N.Y. & we were ordered back at six tomorrow morning. 2nd was that the new troops were to be sent to the front & we to remain in the defences of the City. Third that we were to guard a train of five hundred waggons to the front. I guess the last is true. We are drawing clothing for two weeks march. The whole Brigade arrived to day. Probably day after tomorrow we start. Mr. Lynde arrived here yesterday. Has gone with Charles to Washington.

It is very busy here. Train after train of cars are leaving for Culpepper. The track was completed to there to day. The army is pushing hard for Lee. A large number of prisoners came in today. Heavy cannonading was reported to be heard at Culpepper by the engineers on the trains. Captain Pratt has gone to Vermont leaving me all alone.

Where is Frank, is he well? Will you have Enos Walker make me a pair of boots made of good calf skin or some leather not too thick, rather thin bottoms, not near as thick as the boots sent to John, & sewing with irons on the toes & heels & round headed nails on the bottom. The legs to be large so as not to trouble in fitting pants inside. My measure for shoes was a little small. Espetialy across the toes. I wish him to be very careful & not cut the leather when pairing the soles. My shoes were cut & are giving way. Square toed. Not to cost over five or six dollars, not to be sent before you hear from me again. To be made soon as possible. I need them now. Did you receive the bundle? How is Eunice, have you heard from Asp?

PS Please hand this measure to Walker. It is the size I wish the legs. I wish them made tastey not heavy. I want an excelent pair of boots. Two leather straps to strap my blankets onto my valise to be an inch in width, five in leangth with buckles & loops &c. The next letter you receive from me will be directed to Frank. I have the envelop super scribed & a stamp on. I do not wish to waste the stamp so you will know what is ment by receiving a letter directed to him. I some times super scribe a number of envelops for many times in the field I do not have a good chance to write as well as I wish to.

September 17, 1863

Not mailing my letter last night I thought I would add a few words more. Those bullets I wish you to preserve. They were three that droped by my side at Funkstown. I picked them up when they were flying like hail-stones. I intend to get all the relicks I can & wish you to keep them. You will find two Photographs of Genls. Mead & Sedgwick. I have a number more which I shall send at different times. I thought you would like to see them. They are taken from the original & rather natural. You can see a little of the features. Have you received the check I sent to you at New York?

There is a sight of work down on the Orange & Alexandria Rail Road. Now trains are running night & day. Some loaded with mules, some forage, some troop &c.

All seems to be quiet here. We lye just under the forts covering Washington. The Potomac is being fortified as fast as possible. Many new forts have been built since I passed up the river. The fortifications around N.Y. are being made very formidable. The weather is very warm, has not rained for a long time. The ground is very dry. Alexandria is a deserted city. All the secesh have been driven away. Their property has been confiscated. The houses are for government use as hospitals & storage. The streets are barricaded to prevent a surprise. Just heard that a car load of wounded from the 6th corps came in last night. Shelter tents seem rather hard to live in.

It appears that Henry had an additional reason besides his wound for extending his stay in Williamstown. Henry and Laura Ainsworth became romantically involved during his time at home. Shortly before his return to the army, while on a picnic, Henry and Laura informed several of their friends that they were engaged to be married. They then swore the others to secrecy because they did not intend to make their plans known for another year. We do not know why they decided on a secret engagement, because their letters to each other no longer exist, but one extant document suggests a possible explanation. Henry, the consummate record keeper, had a small notebook in which he recorded the dates of every letter that he sent and received while serving in the army. The notebook reveals that prior to his forty-day leave, Henry and Laura had never corresponded. Growing up in a small town with common friends, they no doubt knew each other, but apparently they did not feel close enough to correspond when Henry left for the war. That relationship now changed and they began to regularly exchange letters. Perhaps they felt that their parents might not look favorably on an engagement after such a short courtship. Although they had decided to marry after the war was over, as a matter of propriety they chose not to make a public announcement for another year. At the picnic, however, they were probably excited and wanted to share their news with someone, so they confided in their friends. Interestingly, Francis, who was less gregarious and more proper than his brother, was neither invited on the picnic nor informed of the secret.

Seventeen-year-old Lucy White was one of those at the picnic when the engagement was announced, and apparently they then gave a name to the nearby waterfall based on what had just occurred next to it. She subsequently returned to school in Burlington and sent Henry a letter on September 18:

> *It was only last Wednesday that I received your letter it having lain in the P.O. nearly a week. I forgot to mention to you to direct it in the care of Dr. Carpenter. I left Williamstown a week after you went. We did not have any very wonderful times after you left. Only a Mr. Pond a friend of George was there a few days. I think he had seen you in Virginia. He was with George in the Christian Commission. We all went down to call on Lorette. We had a very pleasant call, something after the style of the picnic. George professed to be very anxious to know what we named the falls when we were on the hill but he still remains in blissful ignorance and we are going to demonstrate the fact that three women can keep a secret for a year.*

> *I went from Williamstown to Northfield where I staid until the day before school began when I came up here where I shall stay until next winter when I hope to be released for a while from school. Gen. Sickles and staff have been*

> *stopping in town a few days. I hope he is not a fair sample of the Generals for I must confess I was not very agreeably impressed with his looks.*

(Daniel Sickles remains a most interesting figure in American history. In 1859 he shot and killed Francis Scott Key's son in response to his having had an affair with his wife. Sickles then became the first person to successfully win a court case based on temporary insanity. As a politically appointed general, his controversial decision to move his corps at Gettysburg could have

An elderly George Ainsworth at what later became known as Ainsworth Falls
Courtesy of Williamstown Historical Society

brought on a Union defeat according to many analysts. A decade later, he is credited with devising the Republican strategy by which Rutherford B. Hayes gained the presidency in the disputed, perhaps stolen, election of 1876.)

General Daniel Sickles
Courtesy of Library of Congress

For a few days the weather has seemed more like summer than autumn. Yesterday we had a regular old fashioned equinoctial storm and it has cleared off cold and we begin to think that fall is upon us in good earnest. Yesterday I thought of you and wondered if you were provided with tents. I am disgusted with the people of New York City for treating the Vermont troops so shabbily. I have always owed them a grudge ever since Ethan Allen had so much trouble with the Yorkers. I for one feel proud of the Vermont soldiers and think they deserve all the praise given to them. Accept my thanks for your vignette which I think is very good. Have you recovered the use of your arm yet? If you are able to do duty I hope that it can do its part. All is quiet here as well as on the Potomac. I see by the papers that your Brigade is together again and that there is some movement in front but I presume it is nothing more than a rumour. If we could go ahead and finish up this war before another hot summer it would be a blessing to the soldiers as well to the country. It is to be devoutly hoped that England and France will mind their own business and let us alone. I will close by wishing you health and a safe return home.

Twenty-six year old Laura Ainsworth, who would late in her life return to Williamstown as an enormously wealthy widow, no doubt shared these concerns for her fiancée's safe return home as his unit settled back into the dangerous terrain of northern Virginia.

Chapter 11

BROTHERS IN ARMS

Back in Williamstown, Chester Martin received a letter, written on September 18, 1863, from "Camp Vt., Long Island, Boston Harbor." It was the first letter sent home by Private Francis S. Martin, a new recruit of the Vermont Infantry. After passing a physical exam, Frank had finally become eligible to be drafted even though nearly thirty years old. Rather than wait for the draft call in Williamstown, he enlisted in the town of Randolph as a substitute for George Chandler. He probably made this decision for financial reasons, as he could combine the bounty that Randolph was paying with the $300 substitute payment from Chandler. Standing five feet, five and three-fourths inches, with brown hair and gray eyes, Francis Martin joined the Old Vermont Brigade. His letter home stated:

Francis Martin
Courtesy of Special Collections,
University of Vermont Libraries

Yours of the 16ᵗʰ was receid this afternoon and afforded me much pleasure. I cannot tell how I shall endure nor how I shall like army life. I seem to be on the gain but as yet have seen none of the hardships of Camp life. I sleep warmer in my tent than in my bed at home. The rations and fresh air agree with me but I could not stand the fatigues of a long campaign yet. I wrote to Henry a few days since but he probably will not receive my letter. I have been obliged to make some purchases since I have been here & although I expect to receive pay when I leave the Island, I think you had better send me $10.00 by return mail which I can refund when I am paid off. I may yet prove unfit for duty & be discharged in which case I shall need the money. ... Let me know how you get along on the farm and how you are enjoying yourselves alone.

While Francis and the other new recruits were receiving a hurried training program, for Henry and the veterans of the Fourth Vermont it was time to return to the front lines. After Gettysburg, the Army of the Potomac had followed the Confederate army down into northern Virginia. Meade and Lee stood facing each other, neither wanting to take a major initiative until having a clearer sense of their opponent's strength and intentions. On September 19, Henry began a letter home from Centerville Heights, Virginia, which he continued over four successive days as they marched along a now-familiar route.

> *This evening we are twenty miles from Alexandria. Yesterday we marched to Fairfax. It commensed raining early in the morning & continued untill we arrived when we encamped. I was never much weter than when we halted. I never saw it rain harder. We made the best of it and found ourselves quite comfortable this morning. We started on our journey at eight A.M. Had an easy march of twelve miles & halted on the heights of Centerville. It is more quiet now than it was a year ago this month. ... We are escorting a train of one hundred & fifty waggons & eight hundred cattle. The gerrilas are anxious to get the train. The cavilry had a skirmish yesterday. It is quite cold tonight. Yesterday I applied for a Captaincy in the vetran regiment. I do not know what will be my luck.*

> *September 20*
>
> *Arrived at Catlets station at five P.M. Marched eighteen miles. Quite a days work for the sabbath day. I suppose it was necisary as all the troops are wanted at the front. Twenty eight trains of cars run over the road daily. The track is strongly guarded by the Eleventh Corps. The Division that ran so at Chancellorsville has been sent to Charleston. Twenty five hundred rebil cavilry were at Warrenton this P.M.*

Henry added a few more lines on September 21 from "Rappahannoc Station":

> *Left Catlets at eight A.M. passed Warenton Junction. The country is beautiful, so level & so little disturbed by hostile armies. One can see miles on the railroad track. There was hardly a curve for ten miles, trains run like the wind. Arrived at the above named station at four P.M. It is a strongly fortified place. Our forts command the whole line of the river. We crossed the Rappahannoc very quietly for the first time & encamped for the night. Tomorrow morning Eight OClock we start for Culpepper Court House, a distance of twelve or fourteen miles. The rebil army is retreating. We have taken a number of prisoners. It is reported that Richmond is being evacuated. I hope it is. I hope to receive some letters when I arrive at Culpepper. We have marched fifty two miles in the last four days, are traveling on sore blisters & very cold nights so we get but little rest.*

As the now-renowned Vermont Brigade approached Culpepper, it was surprised by the welcome it received from soldiers, some even from other corps, who lined the roads and cheered as it marched through. Henry finally concluded the letter on September 22:

Marched from Rappahannoc Station at eight o clock. Passed Brandy Station where the famos cavilry fight took place last spring. There were a number of dried horses & pieces of shells &c. The country was level & well adapted for cavilry fighting. Arrived at Culpepper twelve P.M., ate dinner & started on past Meades Hd quarters. Marched through the town in good order. Soon we passed the Third Corps. Halted half an hour by the camp of the tenth Vt. I saw all the Wmtown boys. Denton &c. all were looking well. They were very glad to see us. Fay is in a waggon train. Our Vt cavilry charged through Culpepper. Took three pieces of cannon. When we were near camp we heard music. On arrival we found the third Brigade of our Division came out to receive us. They seemed as glad to meet us as though we were brothers. All the troops are glad to welcome us back. The road was lined for two miles to see us pass.

The army is crossing the Rapidan today. We expect to start tomorrow with eight days rations with the men & fifteen in the waggons & in case of an immergency to last thirty days. This looks to us like a long march. We expect as far as Richmond & hope to take it. News is that Rosencranz is whiped. ...

We expect a fight soon & all are well but very tired. I wish you would forward the boots &c in a box with our extras in care of Chauncey Smith. Then it will be forwarded to me by him. Also half dollars with postage stamps.

Henry's cousin, Lorette Bass, also sent him a letter around this time. She had been at the picnic when Henry and Laura Ainsworth had announced their engagement, and she obviously had enjoyed Henry's visit. Lorette's main focus at this time, however, was caring for her sister, Eunice, who was suffering from tuberculosis.

I suppose you have left N.Y. and that all your bright hopes of rest, and a short comfort are disappointed. I am sorry. You must all be feeling rather sober by your necessitated return to Dixie, and a letter now will be as welcome as ever. We are having very warm weather. I hope it is not much warmer where you are, if so, the change will not be pleasent or beneficial. It does not agree with Eunice very well. She coughs a great deal today.

Immediately after you left home George Ainsworth had a friend come to spend a few days with him, a young clergyman, and as lively as one as Mr. Mathews. One evening they, with Emma, Laura and Lucy White came down to our house. They were all feeling pretty well, and we had as lively a time as we did at the Falls. I thought of you and wished you here too.

With that exception our life has passed along in its old, even current. The Monday you left Mrs. Hendrick took dinner with us. ... She said Mr. Mathews wanted to write to you. Do you know Henry? It was you that he was looking at that Sunday P. M. Mrs. Hendrick said that you were in his mind all day, and he thought of you in the selection of his sermon that there was much in it to comfort one situated as you were. That he felt very sad to think of your returning to the Army. It was very kind of him I am sure. He told me on Monday that he had enjoyed his visit here very much, and had gained all the while. That he had not laughed so much in a half day since his college days that he felt sick when he started from home that day, but he got over it and felt stronger when he went home than when he started. I am sure I am very glad if he enjoyed it. I did. I do not think it would have required much persuasion to have induced them to have staid longer. He threatened coming back with Sarah when she went to carry them to Montpelier.

And Lucy White enjoyed her vacation here very much. She said she meant to have her father come here to live, but I fancy she would find it a pleasenter place to visit than to live "all the year round." She is a sweet affectionate girl, I love her very much. That night before she went away she was down here and after I had kissed her "good bye" she came back for another kiss. Her mother says she shall not marry as young as she did. Perhaps she thinks if she had waited longer she might have made a wiser choice. She was either 18 or 20, Lucy now is 17, I think. I do not believe in being in too great haste, but in waiting till one is perfectly satisfied that one will be happier married than otherwise and has found the one to make one so. Does she write good letters? Can she write letters as entertaining as her conversation? If I had asked her I presume she would have written me, but I could not take another correspondent while I had so many.

Ellen and Esther Smith have gone back to N.Y. perhaps you saw them there. Sarah Bass has gone back to Mass. Ellen Lynde Bass and Lucy, gone west, and almost all the young people, away to school, so that it is very quiet, more so than when you were here. I expect great things of Lucy Lynde's going west. I think it was just what she needed to bring out the best part of her to make the frivalous girl into a noble woman. I think there is a great deal of good in her but her life, thus far, had not developed it. She will be differently situated now. She goes to Racine to spend a year with her aunt, Mrs. Smith, and attend school. If you have seen Mr. Lynde (and I presume you have for he followed you on to Washington) you will learn that Jack has been at home. I presume he would be as indignant as he used to be at being called Jack but you will know better who I mean, and I should spare his feelings if I were talking to him. He has improved since you saw him, has grown a little taller, and wears full beard which is an improvement to him as well as any other men, makes him look more manly, less boyish. Very few people knew him. He took them so entirely by surprise. Even his own mother treated him like a stranger and talked with him some time. At last he told her he was from the Army stationed at Corinth. Then she asked him if he knew her son John Lynde. He told her he did but the corners of his mouth began to draw and his eyes to dance and when he laughed she knew he was her son himself. After we had seen him a little he looked natural. He only staid a week.

John Lynde, Jr.
Courtesy of Williamstown Historical Society

Dolly Smith Lynde
Courtesy of Williamstown Historical Society

(At the age of 21, John Lynde, Jr., one of Henry's former classmates at Barre Academy and the son of Judge John Lynde, had moved to Illinois to teach school and study law. He then began his law career in Iowa. When the war began, he joined the Second Iowa Regiment, eventually rising to second lieutenant. With his appearance so changed, it is therefore not so surprising that Dolly Lynde did not initially recognize the second of her twelve children when he made this surprise visit. After the war, John Lynde married and returned to Iowa, taking a high-level position with the post office as his uncle, Chauncey Smith, had done. His younger brother, Charles, was in the Fourth Vermont with Henry. Their younger sister, Lucy, was part of Henry's close circle of friends even though she was six years younger than he. When Dolly Lynde died in 1881, after sixty years of marriage, Judge Lynde then married Laura Davis. Laura was the same age as and a former classmate of his daughter Lucy.)

Judge John Lynde
Courtesy of Williamstown Historical Society

Laura Davis
Courtesy of Williamstown Historical Society

Sept. 22

Henry I wrote the above several days ago but have been writing not knowing where to direct. Last night, Laura A. told me she had directed to Washington and so I will venture to do likewise. Old Mr. Elisha Flint is dead and burried. It is quite sickly in town around us . .... Mrs. David Gale has an easy run of Typhoid Fever and Willard Smith is very sick indeed with the same. They do not think he can live. I do not think of any other sickness more than usual.

Eunice is not as well as when you were here. Is very much as she was immediately after our return from Providence only she has not the strength to bear it now that she had then. She does not weigh 100 lbs. and is very weak. There is a look of suffering about her face now that you never saw her wear. It seems to extend down into her neck. Is even noticable in her hands in the appearance of the cords and veins and often tightly clenched fingers. O Henry! I used to think I should prefer death by Consumption to any others but I have changed my mind. It seems to me now anything else is preferable but Dropsy and Cancer. But we can not choose the way, the time nor place but we know however, whenever or wherever if we are God's children He sees fit. That is best for us and for our friends. That is our only sure place of rest and that never faileth. God grant that when he takes my poor sister it may be to his own blest home free from suffering, sorrow and sin! And may he bring us there too.

We are having very cold weather. The 20th it snowed up in the Seaver neighborhood and a few flakes flew here this morning. It does not seem much like Providence last year. Your folks heard from Frank and you both last night. He was at Long Island, said he thought he was a little better than when he left home. ... Eunice sends much love. Also Aunt Lucy and you have that and many good wishes from your cousin.

From the training camp at "Long Island, Boston Harbor," Francis sent his brother a letter on September 21, not knowing that the Vermont Brigade had moved towards Lee's army:

You have probably learned ere this from father that I am now in the army. I wrote you a long letter which you probably have not received as it was directed to New York. A series of strange providences have placed me here. How long I shall remain I can not tell as I may prove unfit for a Soldier when I come to meet the actual hardships of war. Camp life agrees with me better than any other – in good and healthy quarters – in comfortable weather. The constant desire and need of sleep goes further to unfit me for military duty than anything else. I do not have a very high opinion of the moral character of one Soldier whom I have observed at all, & of course do not seek nor find sympathy in those things which I value most highly. About Seven hundred left the Island the other day – the Vt soldiers are for the 4th Regt. ... If I remain in the army I ought to be in the same Co & if possible to tent with you.

Living with a veteran officer, especially one's brother, would no doubt have been a comforting dream for a new recruit, but it was not to be. After completing his initial training, Francis was assigned to the Second Vermont Infantry. On September 29 he was still at the camp and wrote home:

We were paid off to day. That is we reced the first installment of our bounty money, and shall probably leave the Island soon – perhaps tomorrow – for Alexandria. There was a rumor about camp that we were to return to Brattleboro to fill up two companies which remain in the State to do guard duty. I should have been pleased with such an arrangement as the service would not have been hard and the danger of no account at all. I received a letter from Henry this morning. He was sorry that I was not among those who were sent out to his regiment. It would be much more pleasant for me to be in the same company with him, especially if we could tent together. I find but little society in the army suited to a person of my temperment & character. There is much in which I take an interest and but little in which I can take a part. Moral principle seems to have no existanse here, but the shrewdness, intelligence and capacity in all its grades is surprising to me. I do not know how I shall stand the actual hardships of Army life, but here my health is better than at home.

The work is comparatively nothing and the fresh air and the army rations agree with me better than home fare. I have done guard duty several times – twice during cold rainy nights, but to my surprise I experienced no injurious effects. I cannot tell how I am going to like it. I could get along with what I have been through well enough. My tent mates are better than most that are here but when we join the Regt it may be different. This morning five men belonging to the Massachusetts Regt. stationed here to do guard duty were wounded by the accidental discharge and bursting of a gun which a Soldier was cleaning. One is mortally wounded and will probably die to day. A few days after my arrival here four men deserted. They passed the guard and attempted to reach the main land in two small boats. One boat was upset and the bodies of its two occupants were washed ashore where they were found the next morning. The other two were arrested on the other side and sent back & are now in confinement. One or two have been shot while attempting to run the guard during the night.

Perhaps a short description of this Island may interest you. It comprises an area of about two hundred acres. It rises perhaps two hundred feet from the water, is tolerably level & smooth on the top and slopes gently in some parts, & abruptly at others down to the seaside. There a number of conscripts, guards &c arrives at different times from 1000 to 2000, as they are constantly coming & going. In each camp the tents are arranged in paralell rows and surrounded by a walk or beat which the guards pace. Outside near the sea the pickets are stationed. They carry loaded pieces & none can cross their beat without a pass. As my sheet is full, I will now close by sending love to all.

One can only imagine Betsy's reaction upon hearing that her son preferred army rations to her home cooking! Also, while Francis was hoping to be assigned to the Fourth Vermont, Henry had contacted Judge John Lynde back in Williamstown, hoping that Lynde could use his influence to get Henry a promotion into a new infantry unit. Lynde wrote back on September 29:

Today I went to Montpelier and saw Col Randall and enqured of him if he thought there would be a chance to obtain a Captain's Commission for you and a Lieuts. for Charles in one of the Vetran Regiments now raising in this State. He replied that he had numerous applications of this kind but that he had made no pledges to assist any one. Should not but advise me to apply to the Governor and he said if you could get recommendations from your officers he thought you would stand a fair chance for an appointment as he thinks the Commissions are not nearly all disposed of. I think you had better send such recommendations as you can obtain soon as the sooner the application is made the more likely you will be to succeed. Col Randall says the new Governor will probably have the appointment of the officers and I shall want to make the application soon after the Legislature commences session as I can make it in person then as the Governor will be at Montpelier. The people here are generally well. Dana Simons died very suddenly last Wednesday of Appoplexy. Willard Smith is dangerously sick of Typhoid fever. Your friends are in usual health as far as I know. The last accounts from Meads Army which I have seen say that they are moving towards Richmond so I suppose you will have warm work soon. May God soon open a way for the suppressing of this unholy rebellion and for the safe return of our young men to their homes.

Neither Lee nor Meade was prepared to plunge into this "warm work" without a clear strategic advantage. When Lee learned that the Eleventh and Twelfth Corps had been transferred to the West, he tried to slip around the Army of the Potomac and position himself between it and Washington, D.C. This would force Meade to fight in a place of Lee's choosing. When Lee began moving, however, Meade refused to fall into this trap and started moving back. Eventually, the early October troop movements became a race to secure Centreville Heights, the best strategic position in the area. Henry began a letter home on October 1 from "Camp near Culpepper Ct. House" after some new recruits, but not Francis, had arrived:

We are still on the same old ground we first encamped on and no prospect of a moove at present. There is but little transferring of interest. The enemy are very quiet. We are very busy drilling the conscripts. They are a much better lot of men than they were represented to be. Older than any we have yet received larger, stronger men. They try to learn and do, but there are exceptions. We have learned some of the southern prices of a lady inside our lines. I copied them thinking they might be of interest to you. Bacon $2.50 / lb. Calico /4.50 yard, butter 3.00 /lb. few, when to be had 6.00 /lb salt /1.00 bag, coffee 1.00 /lb thread /1.00 spool, candles 4.00, cows 600.00. I would like to sell a flock at that price in green backs, one dollar green back is worth the Rebil scrip.

Early the next morning the Fourth Vermont moved out, so Henry could not continue writing until October 4:

The 2nd of Oct. was a wet day. The night before we had orders to be in readiness to moove at day break next morning. Previous to that all were to have gone back to Catlets Station to guard the railroad but we had been marching so much of late that the order was countermanded and the third Division of the 6 Corps sent in our stead. They started their night with orders to march nights, lay still days. We were glad to be relieved except morning came, we were ordered out early. The clouds threatened rain. About six it commenced. We were open to all that fell. It was useless to try to keep dry. We marched about two miles, halted & encamped. Had we not been used to such fare we should have found more fault than we did but all went to work pitched their tents in the mud and made ourselves as comfortable as circumstances would admit. Night came finding us wet to the skin. No fires to dry us so to bed we went covered ourselves up. It was not long before I was reminded of the Packs I used to take when sick with typhoid feaver. The blankets steemed nicely next morning, but surprising as it may sound I was all right, had not taken cold nor laid a foundation for a sickness. At nine oclock I was detailed to command the picket sent from my Regiment. Am now on post writing this letter. Perhaps it might be more interesting on that account. We are on the extreme right wing of the army and in front of the enemy. I am in command of the line on Gordons Mills Road. Am in plain view of Ceder mountain where Banks fought so desperately. Also lying under the range of Blue Ridge. It is remarkably well defended by nature. General Lee would have his match to drive us away from our present position. The rebils have learned that the 11 & 12 corps have left this army.

The people are very destitute here, have hardly anything to live on, what little they had has been taken away by the soldiers. It would amuse you to see how antiquated they are. It would remind mother of her old school days going to school. I saw yesterday a man and wife on one horse. I was very much interested to see them today. A lady passed through our lines with her family. She was on one horse her negro servant & children on another. It showed for itself the true southern life. It seems to grow worse the nearer Richmond we get. They make their own cloth something our people would [be] ashamed to do. It is a fair sample of Tom Flints boys.

(Tom Flint's sons, Benjamin and Jacob, were in their early to late forties respectively, unmarried, and living on their father's farm during the war. In 1863 Benjamin was drafted for military service. Although he had listed a personal estate of only $500 in the 1860 Census, he willingly paid $300 to hire Henry's thirty-four-year-old cousin, Henry Martin, as his substitute.)

A few days since thirty Guirrillas were captured on the post I occupy. It was a well managed little affair. The Citizens told the General of the proposed plan.

So the line of Pickets were withdrawn from the road and two Regiments of Infantry secreted in the woods on either side. Night came and the expected party appeared, movved cautiously into our trap which was sprung in due time, capturing the whole party, horses & all. It was a great surprise to the enemy, a lucky one for us. We are rather pleasantly cituated, but not quite so pleasant for the inhabitants for their horses and barns suffer for the want of covering. I am sure I would not like to have them arround my premises. When we first encamped in this vacinity the fences were excelant, today hardly a rail is to be found. Then there are quantities of Chestnuts here, which are very good. Also the corn has not lost its sweetness. So the fires are well occupied with roasting corn. Also a herd of cows do not suffer for not being milked. Some of the Officers have caught them & will take them along with them. They will come very handy this winter. We expect to remain here some time. The Generals have appropriated about a hundred thousand feet of prime lumber for floors in their tents and stables which looks like a stoop. The Cavilry are in front of us. They live on the country, find plenty of forage &c. They had a skirmish & finaly traped three hundred & brought them in. They are very anxious to get horses. They sell well [and] are worth from five to twelve hundred dollars. Since the skirmish the enemy have been quiet, converse freely &C.

I received your letter day before yesterday also one from Frank. He expected to be in this camp before it arrived. He is to go into the 2nd Vt. I shall do my best to have him transferred to my Company. I do not expect any success. He should have come with the last squad then he would have been assigned to this Regt. but an order has been issued prohibiting transfers from one Regt to another. I am sorry, but it will be of no use. I shall try and get him a detail, for business men are very scarce nowadays. The 2nd Vt. is a good Regt. Rather rough like all the rest. Concerning the box I wish to have it sent by Adams Express so I shall know where to send when it arrives in Washington. Before this arrives you will receive a paper containing a number of articles which I wish you to keep. The report of the 2nd Fredericksburg Battle will be read with interest by you as it is a very truthful one. I have just seen Elijah Williams. He is on Picket with me. He looks well. Is a good soldier. All the men are well.

(Elijah Williams, a forty-one-year-old widower and a new recruit from Williamstown, would be killed seven months later in the Battle of the Wilderness.)

The recruits are stronger men than we have ever had before. The Regmints are to be filled to their maximum number. The organization to be continued as long as the war lasts so that as the mens three years expire they will be mustered out as in the Regular army. Captain Pratt has got a detail on General Sedgwicks Staff. Is in charge of the Ambulance trains of the Corps, a very good position to hold. He got it through the influence of Captain Platt. So I am for the present left alone. I have been in command since the 10th of September. There is a little too much work for one officer.

A camp rumor has just started that we are to moove in the morning for the rear or the extreme south. We hope not south. Sedgwick wanted to send south when the other Corps was sent but General Meade was opposed to it and so we remained. There is to be some desperate fighting south very soon. If we go we will have a chance to win new laurels or something else. It would be more interesting to go to a new department. Chaplain Robberts has been reappointed & reported for duty. Have you heard from Mr. Asp?

If we do not move I want to have you get a box made to carry company books. ... I have met a number of the 10th Vt. of late. They are looking friendly but feel some what sober about the service it being a little different than they anticipated when they left home. Being where no shelter from rain is to be had marching so far in a day regardless of sleep & rations &c. all taken together, show them a little of the reality of war. The Corp starts for the Rappidan tomorrow morning to relieve the 2nd Corps. It is conjectured they are to be sent south. It is twelve miles from here near the extreme left of the army. We dread the march for we are fixed so comfortable in camp.

Oct. 5

Raccoon Ford is our destination. Start at six AM.

When his mail arrived, along with the box, Henry also received a letter from eighteen-year-old Lucy Lynde. Like many Vermonters, Judge Lynde and Dolly had traveled to New York City after the riots in an attempt to see their son, Charles, while he was stationed there. Unfortunately, they were unable to locate him before the Fourth Vermont moved out. Lucy's older sister, Ellen, had married Walter Burnham Bass, Ebenezer's nephew, and moved to Illinois. Lucy had just joined them there.

So long a time has passed since our correspondence was interrupted I hardly know who is in fault for this remissness in writing. However, as I have entirely changed my place of residence since last I saw you I deem it a part belonging to me to inform you of it. Yes I have changed and after a stay of three or four weeks on the Prairie I begin to realise it is not precisely like teaching school in the old brick house where I "taught young ideas how to shoot" for the space of three and one half months last summer. Time alone will tell which will best suit me.

Perhaps you may have learned from Charlie or my father of our journey to New York and of our disappointment in not seeing my brother and friends. It seemed to me "too bad" as it will probily be a long time ere I will see them again – so long, in fact that all will forget me in their own cares, and each one's time be devoted to the "little farm well tilled, the little wife well willed" and nary a thought of Lucy Lynde – spinster!

Some days to prevent home sickness I try to imagine what place each will fill in the space of two (or nearly that) years. I can find the right one for only a few – and this perhaps will fall short – for "there's many a slip, twixt the cup and the lip" in more ways than one. There was a great disarragement of things too, as we were to see the sights, do much shopping, have photographs taken &c. and in the <u>wonderful</u> city of N. Y. all would have been done to perfection.

I have no news to record but the marriage of Myron Bass to Bessie Kelly – a young lady of this place with brown hair, blue eyes. Once judging from her looks she wont make him "toe the mark" a <u>bit</u> – I should presume, tho it would'ent make any difference if she did try to. I shall for the present remain with my sister, so please to direct in care of W. B. Bass. Excuse this hastly written note – wishing you a pleasant good night.

Lucy did not end up a spinster. She married Eldon Tilden back in Williamstown about two and a half years later. Tilden, one of Henry's former classmates at

Eldon Tilden
Courtesy of Williamstown
Historical Society

Barre Academy, had enlisted in the Second Vermont at the start of the war and remained in it through the war's conclusion, eventually becoming a second lieutenant. Nine years after her marriage, Lucy died at age 31 from what was then termed Bright's disease, a kidney disorder that was incurable at the time. Tilden remarried and became a Boston merchant. He lived only ten years after Lucy's death.

On October 5, in the midst of all the troop movements, Francis and a new group of recruits arrived to join the Second Vermont. Like his brother, Francis had closely observed all that he had witnessed while being transported to Virginia. He wrote home on October 8 from "Slaughter Mountain, Va.":

You have probably received my last written from Long Island ere this also a remittance of $15.00 by Express. Did you receive $25.00 from me which I sent home before I left Woodstock? You have not mentioned it if you have reced it. Has Mr. Asp of Boston sent you any money yet? And last of all while I am on this subject – Have your willows been sold yet? The above questions might with more propriety have been reserved for the latter part of my letter but as I found it necessary to commence my letter with allusions to remittances I thought I would write all I had to say on subjects of kindred character at once.

We left Long Island on Thursday the 1st were on the water four days and nights. Had a rather rough passage. Enough so as to make most of the men more or less sea sick though it was nothing that could be called a severe storm. We passed Fortress Monroe and landed the New Hampshire Conscripts at Portsmouth near Norfolk. A beautiful place with many fine residences surrounded by an abundance of handsome shade trees. From Portsmouth we returned – repassed Fort Monroe and steamed up the Potomac to Alexandria. The banks of the river are high and perpendicular in many places of yellow or reddish color. The color of Virginia mud – and covered for the most part with secondary growth trees. Through the openings plantations could be seen. Many of the houses and fields having the appearance of the same in New England. From Alexandria the marble dome of the Capitol in Washington is visible. We received our guns & tents at Alexandria where we passed the night & took the cars the next morning for Culpeper. We arrived at that place about 60 miles from Alexandria at one o clock P.M. & were at once marched a distance of 10 miles to the 2nd regiment of the Vt brigade which we reached about eight o clock P.M. & attended roll call & were assigned to different companies. I was assigned to Co. F. There I met Tom McClury who was so kind as to make a cup of coffee for me – a luxury which the rest of our boys were not so fortunate as to obtain. By the way I have found it necessary to drink coffee since I have been in the service & care more for it than for my food. Thos. McClury is our Sergt – an excellent soldier – very kind and attentive to my wants. I feel myself under greater obligations to him for favors & attention than to any other person I have met with since I left home – and am happy to received his instructions when on drill & to obey him as an officer. If you ever have opportunity to make any return for his kindness either by substantial assistance or by favorable commendations to Mr. Lynde or others – do so.

(Thomas McCauley had enlisted at a young age at the start of the war and was promoted to sergeant just a month before this letter was written. He was later wounded at Cedar Creek, returned home to Montpelier, and died in 1867 at age twenty-three.)

I did not consider myself fit for a soldier when I was drafted. Should not have gone as it was had I thought I could have remained at home honorably. And now consider myself unfitted by health, temprement, character, and education for any such enjoyment of a soldiers life as some seem to have. And am prepared to appreciate the attentions which those who have had long experience can render.

I have seen Henry twice and am glad he is so near. About our position I can give you little information. I write respecting what I also see & understand but many others are better informed & see more than I. Yesterday Henry tells me the enemy thought of making an assault on our position. My health is better than when at home. I have nothing of the dyspepsia – but suffer some from billiousness & dullness at times. The open air and light work which as yet has been assigned me has been beneficial rather than otherwise. What kind of a soldier I shall make time alone can determine. Please write soon. Send me all the papers you can spare. Inclose some powdered camphor gum – which is said to be a sure preventative of lice when rubbed on the clothes. Send a few postage stamps. Give love to all my friends. Shall be happy to hear from any of them. We may be attacked by the enemy any day, so those who are posted say.

Two days later, at 4:00 p.m. on October 10, as the Sixth Corps raced Lee towards Centreville Heights, Henry began a letter:

Today we are in readiness to advance at any moment. We were up all night preparing to go. Evry man had eight days rations issued at two A.M. Also clothing which made the chance for rest very slim. I do not feel any brighter for the night's labor. At light our order came to have tents struck & be ready to moove at the word but we did not moove & have not yet. This is a general moove. Some where heavy firing was heard nearly all the afternoon. [It is] supposed to be our Cavilry at Chester gap. The enemy in our front have disappeared and the 1st Corp is across the Rappidan. Evry horse has been saddled, evry batary harnessed so as not to be delay'd if attacked, waggons loaded, &c,&c. It has been a rather interesting day. Nothing done but in complete interest to do at the word. The new men are a little anxious. It is noticeable in their countenances. The old men perfectly unconcerned. We expect the enemy to do their best to fight us at Bull Run. Our pickets exchange papers daily.

The secesh inhabitants are very inquisitive to learn what is taking place. Our picket line encloses a house belonging to a rebil General killed at Gettiesburg. The family are the biterist of secesh. They signal to the enemy at night by lights &c (have done so). It has been stoped. Stationary is very scarce at the present time so I cliped a part of a leaf from my Descriptive book.

Perhaps we shall leave tonight. The weather is cool just right for mooving about, if wounded much less dangerous. Our army is being filled rapidly by the released Parolled prisoners. Fifteen or twenty thousand have been released on account of the breach of paroll by Davis at Chatanoga. The government seems to have been very decided in the matter which is truly gratifying to us. A number of the men taken prisoners at the battle of Banks Ford from this Regiment have returned. I had two but they are sick. I guess they are not very anxious to return but they are not so much to blame as the Doctors who permit them to remain. There has been an over hauling in that department in the past year. There was a time when a soldier could remain away from his regiment as long as he chose & in hundreds of cases got discharged by paying five or ten dollars but such a course of proceedings could not last forever. It has been looked into and their schemes disclosed so that the convolescent camps are not filled as they were one year ago. All of our recruiting officers returned yesterday, three Captains, ten Non commissioned Officers. We are glad to have them return because we are very short for officers. Before they returned we had seven detached. Cannonading has just commenced again, quite brisk but not very near us. Some think they are retreating. We all pray for another Gettiesburg & in Meade we look for it. There was never a man at the head of the army in whom more confidence was placed. Still he may never be so successful again. One thing is evident. Lee is affraid of him.

Henry concluded the letter the next day:

We left Robison run at seven oclock P.M. and marched until three A.M. of the 11th. Just before day the rebil cavilry intended making a charge on us but we scarid them out of it. We had a hard march of it. At half past four we started on again. It was so cold that we could hardly keep warm marching. We are now at Rappahanoc Ford in the fortification built just before we advanced. The cavilry had a hard fight, the enemy geting the better of our Cavilry. To day they are fighting. The enemy intended turning our right flank but they are too late now. Meade was too shrewed for Lee. Hope he will continue the same. Everything was conducted in perfect order and in such a manner that the rebils could not make anything by attacking. Now will come the race who will occupy Bull Run first. We can get there in one night and one day. The men feel very sober after the incesant march of last night & today. Miles of cannon & baggage trains are passing. We expect to moove on tonight or in the morning.

Despite the hard marching, Henry started another letter home the next day, October 12, from "Camp Near Culpepper Virginia":

We have again crossed the Rappahannoc. The enemy seem to be in force in our rear. Kill Patrick & Bufords cavilry are passing to feel their strength. The 5th & 6th Corps are supporting. At three the Cavilry & 6th Corps advanced. The Vt. Brigade in advance. We all appeard on a perfectly leavel plain simulteniously. The Cavilry dashed forward and being so strongly supported that evrything gave way in all possible haste. We captured some prisoners & part of a train & drove the enemy past Culpepper & shelled their trains & we remained until our next moving. It resulted in drawing back part of Lees forces. He finds we are too much for his rear guard so lost a distance of fourteen miles. We encamped in line of battle.

The next day they continued their march:

We crossed the Rappahannock for the last time for the present. As we were crossing the bridge they were preparing to blow it up. At light we started from Rappahannoc station. The bridge had just commenced to blow up. It was a good sight. All the trains were on the double quick. We marched to Warenton, arrived at noon. Also all the trains, more than the town of Williamstown could hold. The enemy were on our flank pressing for Bull Run. It seemed to be a race to see who would occupy the ground first so with out rest we were started off & arrived at Bristow Station at 9 P.M. The trains were all night moving, did not get there [until] just at light.

The entry for the next day was headed "Bristow Station October 14, 1863":

We left the station at eight A.M. Were the rear guard. The enemy pitched on at six A.M. The 5th & 2nd Corps were sent ahead to take a position at Bull Run which they did (commenced to rain). We passed them at two P.M. Went to Centerville, formed lines to protect our rear. About three the enemy attacked. The artilary was massed to receive them. On they came & finaly they were repulsed with great loss. The 2nd Corp took a batary & the Regiment that was supporting them. Also, Kill Patrick charged. A batary rushed to the regt supporting them. The enemy turned the gun on both our & the enemy but we took the batary. The day closed with our taking three thousand prisoners. At dusk we were sent to Chatilla to protect the right flank of the army. We lay in line of battle all night &c, &c.

The next day's entry was from "Chantilla, Va Oct. 15, 1863":

At 9 A.M. we were mooved a little to the right. At 12 P.M. sent further to the front. At 3 P.M. the enemy opened again. Just now the enemy made a charge. The battle is rageing fiercely. The result I do not know. One thing is certain, the loss of life must be great. It seems to be an Infantry fight on the Rebils part. Our Cannon jar the ground where I am writing and hope to be enough for both Lee & Bragg. I imagine there is great excitement north. A few Rebil Cavilry ought to go to Vt & pay their compliments to the men who have payed three hundred Dollars. If they had answered to the call, the rebils would not have been here today. They think our army small by the loss of the 11th & 12th Corps. We are not as strong as we should be to meet so powerful a foe, but there is trust to be put in what remains. We have had hardly any sleep since we left Cedar Mountain. Have marched three nights & greater part of the day. We do not know what is the order of the day. Some expect to go to the defences of Washington. If they are too much for us, we can retreat in one night. Our teems are all safe there awaiting safe keeping which I trust they will have inside the fortifications of the City. The roar of musketry is terrific. We expect the enemy will give us a try before dark. We have every good position & evry man ready to receive them if they come. It does not seem natural to be within hearing & not be engaged. On some accounts we are glad we are not there.

Frank is well, stands the march remarkably well, almost better than I. His feet are not sore (mine are). The old knapsack is trouble. Our eight days rations are about exhausted. The train four days ahead. We anticipate rather lank times. I must close. Write and answer the questions I have asked in some of my previous letters. I have not received a letter since 30 September.

A short entry concluded the letter the following day:

There was a terrible fight yesterday. It is reported that we worsted them, turned their right wing. We were not attacked but strongly threatened. We expect our turn will come today. It is rainy. A hard time for wounded men.

On the same day of that short entry by Henry, October 16, Francis wrote a full letter home from "Chantilli, Va" in his more formal and structured style:

For nearly a week I have had no opportunity to write even if I had felt so disposed. We have been marching & counter marching regulating our movements by those of the enemy. Our rests have not been long enough & I have been too tired to write. To give you a clear idea of our movements since last Saturday I should need a more thorough aquaintance with the geography of the Country & of military matters. Henry will give you a better account of what we have done & of the times & distances of our marches. As it is I will endeavor to state as clearly & briefly as possible what I know respecting our last move. We were ordered to strike our tents, pack knapsacks & be ready to move at any moment. At 9 o clock PM we left our encampment and retreated towards Culpepper. The night was very dark. For the first few miles our march was through woods & fields across ditches & small streams. Then the march was easier over traveled roads & smoother fields until we reached Culpepper. Marched through the city & some distance beyond when we recd orders to halt, face about & move in another direction, probably because we had lost our way. After moving about four miles through the fields we spread our blankets on the ground at 1 o clock A.M. & slept until 4. I never slept sounder, was warm until I stirred & then began to shiver. We were at once ordered to move & marched until broad daylight when we stopped & cooked our meat & coffee. We then pushed on, recrossed the Rappahanock & encamped in the woods at Rappahanock Station before dark. The next morning we heard the enemies cannon who were engaged with our cavalry who covered our retreat. Presently we recd orders to march, recrossed the Rappahanock again, marched a few miles went into the woods, loaded our pieces then advanced & formed in the rear of a breast work where we remained a short time. Then were ordered forward to another trench & breast work where we remained until sometime in the afternoon. In the mean time long lines of soldiers, supply waggons, ambulances &c could be seen moving in the direction of Culpepper. Canonading was at times heard in our front. We were soon ordered to advance again to a piece of woods where we formed in line of battle & rested until we recd further orders. Here Henry came over to our Regt for a few moments. From the woods we advanced in line of battle, the cannonading growing louder & more incessant, expecting to meet the rebels. But just before dark we recd orders to encamp & build small fires. At 12 AM. we were ordered to march again, recrossed the Rappahanock & soon heard our men blowing up the bridges. We then marched until dark, making about 25 miles. The next day we advanced a little beyond Centerville. Yesterday we made several short moves & to day are encamped at Chantilli. I suppose that we shall ultimately reach Alexandria. We hear some heavy canonading every day. Yesterday I hear that the rebels in our rear were repulsed. Some nine or ten hundred were taken prisoners besides the capture of some pieces of artillery. Our loss was light. I am tired but not so much so as I should expect. There are many things about army life which are very unpleasant but there is no condition of life devoid of enjoyment if rightly improved. I could write much more but wish to rest. I wish that I had a small pocket testament. This you could send me by mail. Whenever you send a paper or letter you can put in something. I should like a skein of black linen thread and a drawing of good black or green tea would be very acceptable at any time. If I crave anything now it is fruit. I would like some dried berries or pickles. The last can be obtained at sutlers when we are not on the move. I wish to have Mother knit me two pair of socks & make me two wollen shirts with pockets inside which can be sent to me at some future time.

By moving so quickly, the Army of the Potomac gained control of the lands around Centreville. Lee recognized that he could not plan a major offensive at this time. Meade's army began to establish winter camps, with the Vermont Brigade camped at Warrenton. Francis wrote home from the Warrenton camp on October 24:

I can not tell you all I would like to respecting our movements though I could easily fill this sheet. It is one thing to travel over the country at your leisure when every man is at your service if he can thus obtain your money & another to march through the woods & fields burdened with the accouterments of a Soldier. The man who can go through all this with ease will be able to observe much that will of necessity be overlooked by one whose attention is absorbed by his own wants and who finds it necessary to improve every opportunity to obtain that rest without which he finds himself unable to perform well his duties. In addition to this the want of geographical & military knowledge as well as inexperience unfit me for giving any such account of what transpires as to afford satisfaction to myself or to be relied on implicitly by others. While such knowledge is an important skill & an acquaintance with the affairs of every day life such as is obtained by working on a farm or in providing for ones daily wants is indispensible. Since we last wrote we have been on the move much of the time & are now encamped on the summit of a hill overlooking the city of Warrenton. I have been very tired. Have suffered some from diarehea & billiousness but am better now. Today it is rainy, muddy & unpleasant. Our Co. expects to go out on picket this afternoon. I am in need of some articles. Would like to have a pair of thick boots made for me as soon as possible. One woolen shirt (now) two pair socks, 1 Pair yarn gloves, 1 Pint of Castor Oil, 1 lb Green

tea, 2 lbs crush sugar, dried berries &c. Direct to Henry when you send the box.
I shall probably write again before you will get it ready & may think of some-
thing else which I need. If you could buy one of those deep 3 Qt pails, a two qt
pail will answer, & send it full of good butter it will be acceptable.

Give my love to Eunice and Lorette. Say to Lorette that I shall be pleased
to hear from her. She has more leisure than I (all my letters are written in
haste) & she ought to open the correspondence. Give yourself no uneasiness
about what I write her. I have had no opportunity to see Henry for some
time. Remember me to Uncle Ira, Aunt & Uncle Pride & all friends. Please
furbish up (& color if possible) Henries old military cap and send it in the
box as it is better than the one I wear.

The next day was Sunday, and it occurred to Francis that the children at his
home church might be interested in hearing firsthand what army life was like. He
wrote a letter to Mr. Lynde, asking him to read it to them.

Dear Children,

Would you like to hear from an old schoolmate? While I write you are prob-
ably engaged in the exercises of the Sabbath school, a place where I can truly say
I have passed many of the happiest hours of my life, and my mind very naturally
turns back to you and in fancy again unites with you in those exercises in which
it may never again be my lot to participate. Would you like to know where I
am now? It is the pleasantest Sabbath I have enjoyed since I came to Virginia.
The air is clear and bracing. The sun shines brightly on a landscape not unlike
my New England home. Our tents are pitched on the summit of a hill near a
forest of oak, walnut and chestnut trees. On a hillside on the left lies the city of
Warrenton with a few church spires and some handsome residences peeping out
from among the shade trees which abound in all Southern towns. On the right
front and rear presents the same unvarying prospect of hills and plains and
woods and open fields with here and there a farm house or the white tents of
an encampment of soldiers. The whole bounded by ranges of mountains, blue
in the distance. It is a pleasant scene but how different from a home Sabbath.
Shall I tell you how my Sabbaths have been spent since I came to Virginia? On
the first Sabbath we were ordered out before light, marched a few miles and
formed in line of battle with loaded pieces in the rear of a breastwork where
we remained several hours listening to the distant cannonading of the enemy
who were engaged with our cavalry and watching the long lines of soldiers,
artillery, supply waggons and ambulances to carry the wounded as they filed
past. By and by we formed in line of battle again and were ordered forward.

The cannonading all the while growing more distinct and as we passed over fields which had just before been occupied by skirmishers now and then finding a shell in our path or seeing a dead horse by the roadside and as we neared the enemy's lines and could see clouds of dust raised by bursting shells while regiment after regiment in line of battle were hastening to take part in the conflict. We began to realize something of the danger to which we were likely soon to be exposed. In view of this children how do you think I felt? But few soldiers look at these things seriously. They have no inclination to live a religious life, a serious consideration of things as they are is not only unpleasant but unfits the Soldier for the performance of his duties. So he gives no attention to the future but makes all he can of the present and meets danger recklessly or hoping that the chances of war may allow him to escape unharmed. In my own case, I found that I could shut my eyes to the danger to which I was exposed or pain myself with its realization. No man who believes the truths in which you are to day being instructed can look with indifference on the prospect of being instantly called into the presence of his God, then to give an account of his past life & to receive that sentence from which there is no appeal, either forgiveness of past transgressions for Christ's sake & admission to everlasting happiness or eternal condemnation. I felt the need of the protecting care of my Maker and that I could not even hope to claim this without I was willing to obey his commands. I knew that I was dealing with a being who could not be deceived and could not feel at rest until I had resolved to perform my duties more faithfully. Then with the assurance of divine support I could go forward. What passed through the minds of others to how many the Holy Spirit made this the occasion of another appeal I cannot tell but to me it was made the means of quickening the Spirit of religion in my soul. After all, the enemy were too wary for us and declined giving us battle in ground where the Union forces would probably have been triumphant. The next Sabbath was spent in changing our encampment twice and laying in the intermediate time near our stacks of guns in line of battle. Today is a fair sample of every Sabbath in the army when no important movement is on foot and no danger apprehended, so I will endeavor to describe it. At day break we are called up by the beating of a drum, called the revilie. Next comes roll call. Then preparations for our breakfast. This morning some of us brought wood three fourths of a mile. Then our guns and accoutrements must be oiled and furbished up ready for inspection. My entire forenoon was occupied with duties like the above.

[The remainder of the letter is missing.]

Henry was busy at this time attending to other duties. For example, he was asked to resolve the following situation by a resident of Swanton, Vermont named William Blake:

> You have in your Company one Richard McCrea. McCrea went from here as a Substitute for me. He was a Minor and in order to get him to pass the board I was obliged to have a guardian appointed and at his request I was appointed. I have Two hundred & forty dollars of his money. I received a letter from him about a week since saying that he was in trouble and wished [me] to send him his money as it would take it all to clear him. Now the question is Capt is he in trouble and does he need this $240. If he does I should be happy to send it to him. If not it is best to leave the money where it is. Please answer as soon as convenient & oblige.

Henry's decision is not known, but we do know that Richard McCrea deserted less than six months later.

The Fourth Vermont was also encamped at Warrenton. On October 25, Henry sent home a letter recapping the events of the last two weeks:

> Your letter of Oct 11th has been received. I have not had a chance to answer it until this evening, the first we have had in camp since we left the Rappidan. We have been mooving about evry day since I wrote my last. Before we left Chantilla we were attacked by Cavilry trying to gain our rear. The next day they left for Dixie & our army after them. We chased them across Bull Run finally the Rappahannoc where they will stay for a while. Lee was never so completely fooled before. He had a force of Infantry numbering forty thousand & all his Cavilry. He was just as sure of gaining our rear as he lived. He thought he had two days to start before Meade dreamed of his advance. It was not the case. Evry moove seems to have been anticipated & nobly met & repulsed. An officer at Meades Hd Quarters told me today the circumstances &c. The enemy were orderd to occupy the forts of Bull Run with fourteen pieces of cannon & one Corps of Infantry with the Cavilry. Our moovements were made under cover. Our trains were in plain view a tempting bate. The enemy saw them & planned their capture expecting to meet with but feeble resistance. Their lines were mooved forward supported by cannon. Our men were secreted behind the railroad also a batary masked to open on their flank. The enemy were allowed to come within pistol shot. Then our lines rose & fired. Also the cannon unexpectedly opened in an unexpected place. The slaughter was terrible. Some escaped. Our men advanced, took their batary & four

hundred prisoners. At another point the same trap was set & sprung resulting in the capture of fourteen pieces (in all). The Cavilry have been fighting evry day. At one time Buford was surrounded by Cavilry & Infantry. The General did not seem to be at all disturbed. He orderd his band to play Yankee Doodle then asked his men if they would fight. All answered yes. He gave his orders then started for Camp where he arrived by free use of the sabre & carbine. He cut his way through their combined force with but small loss of men. It was pure generalship that got him out.

We expect to advance soon. It is reported that Burnside is near Linchburg with a large force (and) has destroyed the railroads, cut the communication between Lee and the southern armies. It is almost too good news to believe. Also one more Corps is to be sent south.

I will tell you one sight I saw at Bull Run in crossing the old battlefield. I saw the bones of many our unburied men some so poorly covered that the dirt had washed from their bones, skulls, toes, and bones of the different parts of the body lying about uncovered. The Rebels are reprehensible for such brutal treatment of the dead. I had heard of the like before but could hardly believe it to be true until I saw it with my own eyes. Also, as we advanced driving the enemy before us on the twentieth a number of our cavalry were killed. Their bodies were stripped and left in that condition for us to see as we passed. It makes our men feel revengeful & who can blame them. At New Baltimore the 6th VT were sent out to a piece of wood to watch the rebel cavilry which were driving ours back as they supposed but they soon found out what was up. When our men had passed the whole regiment discharged a full voley into their midst causing great confusion and hasty retreat minus a number of horses and men. The number I have not learnt. It is much more pleasant to have a chance to fool them than to be fooled with as we have been in times past. The people at Warrenton think their cause ruined but hate to give up yet. Fifty of the prisoners last taken took the oath of allegiance & have gone north. Others would but for their pride.

The weather is very unpleasant cold & rainy. Last night we were on picket. Yesterday morning we mooved camp to the south side of Warenton. It being our turn to go on Picket we did not stop to arrange camp but went direct to the front, established a picket line two miles from the Rappahannoc. We had hardly completed the line before the 3rd Division of our Corps came out & pitched camp so then the right of my company was between two Regiments. I reported the fact to the officer of the Picket about two PM. He said he would change the line. We waited patiently until it was dark expecting to *be relieved or drawn in but we were not until ten P.M. All were disgusted at such negligent work. It was twelve before we arrived in Camp &c, &c.*

I have not heard from Mr Asp of late. I directed him to send the money to you. I will write him once more. Expect to march all night Oct. 25th to Centerville. The enemy is on our left in force.

Francis, meanwhile, was thinking of more things from home that could make his life more tolerable in these new conditions. He sent a short note on October 27:

I neglected in my last to send for all the articles I wanted. When you send the box put in a pocket testament. Tell Mother to make bags to put the sugar and tea in. I would like to have you spread a plaster with hemlock gum, which I can use. The deep three qt pail I would like to have you procure & fill with butter. I would also like a half yd of bed ticking, and two or three skeins of thread. My boots are giving out. The nights are cold & my feet are often wet. The box while we are shifting from place to place will not come very soon by Express. If you think best you may send the boots & gloves & a little Castor oil by mail prepaying the postage & the box at another time. Many do so as they come right through though the expense is much greater. At another time I hope to write more that will interest you.

Although Lee was not launching a major offensive, skirmishing continued all through the area in the Battles of the Bristoe Campaign. One problem in particular for the Union army was that the Confederates had destroyed much of the railroad line running north to Bristoe Station. As a result, all the supplies for the army had to be brought in by wagons, which meant facing raids by the guerrilla forces of John Singleton Mosby. One particularly successful Mosby tactic was to have his men approach the wagon trains dressed as Union soldiers. Henry continued recording the events of the Bristoe Campaign in his next letter, commencing on October 28:

We have again been threatened on our left. The enemy crossed last night in very strong force & drove our Cavilry back to Bealton's Station. They were strongly supported by Infantry & their men dress in our uniform which came near surprising our men. Our Cavilry had all they wished to do to prepare for them. The bataries were all hitched up ready for any emergency at light. Also the Infantry formed line of battle. At daybreak the enemy retired at light to their old place across the Rappahannoc. Our Cavilry crossed the day before, drove the enemy back to Culpepper. The enemy have some object in view in reconoirtering in so strong a force. We hardly think they intend an advance but intend to know what we do & how we are progressing with the railroad. We are anxious to have it in good running order soon for we were never so short of eatables before. Nothing but Hd Bread, Pork & sugar & coffee. It is very difficult to get hay enough for horses & mules. The latter have been without for eight days. The teams have today been drawing bushes for them to eat which is nearly as good for a mule as hay. They will eat coats, rubber blankets limbs an inch in diameter &c. General Meade has mooved his Hd Quarters today. They were beside our Brigade, has gone nearer Warenton Junction.

The weather is very cold making camp life not so very pleasant. Frank was over to see me this morning. He holds out remarkably well almost as tough as the old soldiers. He showed me a letter from you. I have written Mr. Asp. Have not received the box yet. When you send Franks I wish you would have a box made to cary my Company books & papers in. I will get the measure & send it in this letter. A busy time is before me for a few days. Saturday we are mustered for two more months pay.

Since he was busy preparing for winter camp, Henry had time for only a short entry the next day:

Had a Division Drill this afternoon. Have been fixing up my tent, building a nice stone fire place. It smokes some but it is a great improovement on a fire at my tent door. Friday a man in the 4th New York is to be shot. All the Division is to be present. The rebils are quiet today. Prospect of a storm before many days.

He added another short entry the next day, October 29:

All quiet today. Had a Brigade drill at two P.M. News from Corps Hd Quarters are that preparations are making for an onward march soon. Could see shells bursting in the vicinity of Sulpher Springs. Probably our Cavilry are scouting in that vacinity. A fine sight in the night, certainly to new men.

I had the unpleasant job of making two non Commissioned officers. Unpleasant because all are wanting some thing &c, &c. Worked until about twelve P.M on my muster rolls. It takes a great deal of writing. One mistake spoils a muster roll (rather close work).

On October 30, Henry had a bit more to discuss:

The clouds indicate a storm & am officer of the Day. Have five prisoners in the guard house. Two charged with desertion are dressed in Citizens clothes. That alone is enough to convict them. Captain Beattie of the 3rd Vt is being

court marshaled for shooting an officer of his Regt. They were gambling &
at last there was some misunderstanding arose (they were well soaked with
Comisary Whiskey) between them & words were not enough when one drew
his revolver & shot the other twice wounding slightly. Both will immediately
be cashiered [out of] the service. Ought to be sent to the ripraps. Cashiering is
not severe enough. ...

A Brigade review this afternoon. We muster tomorrow ten A.M. The
man sentenced to be shot today has had his time extended one week. Prob-
ably will not be shot but pardoned by the President. The whole Division was
to be present. It is customary to have all present to see the execution & take
warning, &c., &c. News tonight is that Colnel Stoughton has been ordered
to report to General Canby of New York for light duty. Also that General
Stoughton has been confirmed, waiting orders from Secretary of War for a
command &c.

The next day's entry found Henry still unhappy with the circumstances in
camp:

It has commenced to rain very early this morning. It will not add much to
the muster & review which was to be had after the muster. We that go on
foot undoubtedly do not feel that degree of disappointment that the mounted
officers do while setting on their horses. They do not realize what it is to march
&c. After some delay we were mustered. The Colnel had just commenced mus-
tering my company when it commenced to rain but he completed mustering
my Co. The remainder of the Regt. was sent in. The rain continued about two
hours & cleared away very pleasant. After the Regt. was mustered we were
ordered on picket to remain twenty four hours. ...

At a sesech house the proprietor two days before had left supposed for the
purpose of capturing some of our trains &c but his premise [was that he] had
to have a guard to protect the hogs & cows [from Union soldiers] which is
very wrong. The men are thoroughly disgusted at such conduct & regardless
of guards they took a fine pig creating some disturbance. The officers tried to
learn who stole the pig but all were very ignorant implicating no one. Also
[we are] not to burn any rails but that order was not much respected as the
night was so cold that we had all we could do to keep warm by hot fires. It
was a sleepless night for all.

Henry's discontentment continued on November 1. After all the hard marching and fighting, the soldiers were getting little respite.

As it prooved we were fortunate in being detailed for picket. We had no sunday morning inspection to attend nor the Division review which was ordered. The like never occured before, a review on sunday. It prooved a broken affair. Both the Brigadier Generals were unhorsed & one aid. The men hollared out so as to be heard. So much for drilling us sundays. We were relieved by the 77th New York at four P.M. They are a different set of men. Hardly had they got their guns stacked before they commenced to kill hogs hens & destroy everything generaly. It did me good to see it done. Our men were not allowed to do any thing of the kind. If a man was found with his belt off the officer in command was to be sent into Division Hd.Qu under arrest. We called the order strict. Excellent news from General Hooker. Is doing as well as when commanding a Corps in the Army of the Potomac.

Henry added a short entry on November 2:

Had a Division Drill this A.M. Am very busy completing my muster rolls. Have got Frank to assist me. I must close. All are well here. Have not rec'd his box. Little hope he will get it.

The letter ended with a short, but unpleasant, event on November 3:

Yesterday a man from Company E was run over by the cars & completely smashed to pieces.

Henry started a new letter on November 5, still compiling his complaints about camp life:

Having a few spare moments to write I commence a letter & finish when I can. Not much of interest is transpiring certainly to our knowledge. Drills are frequent. Yesterday we were reviewed by General Sedgwick. The men were not uncomonly well pleased with it for before we returned to camp we had a drill. There is the normal reports circulating. One that we are to be sent on to the Peninsula & Tenasee &c, &c. Artilary was mooving toward Bull Run all day. The weather is uncomonly pleasant. Tonight a Lieut was returned to the ranks in the 2nd Vermont for Absence without leave. We begin to think that Uncle Sam is not doing all for the best for it is breaking down the army to use Officers in that way. They should be punished but not make it too coarse an affair.

Significant events were transpiring of which Henry was unaware. General Lee had established a bridgehead on both sides of the Rappahannock, connected by a pontoon bridge at the town of Rappahannock Station. General Meade decided to attack rather than allow the army to remain in winter camp. On November 6, the day after Henry had started his letter, the Vermont Brigade was issued six days' rations, meaning that they would not remain in winter camp. They marched out very early in the morning on Saturday, November 7. Under Meade's plan, Sedgwick's Sixth Corps was to cross at Rappahannock Station while the Third Corps crossed five miles downstream at Kelly's Ford. Once both were across the river, they were to unite and proceed to Brandy Station. The Sixth Corps met strong resistance from Jubal Early's forces at Rappahannock Station, slowing down the advance. For several hours Sedgwick relied on artillery fire, and the Confederates answered with their own guns. Sedgwick then suddenly unleashed an infantry attack at dusk, spearheaded by the Sixth Maine, which seemed to take the rebels by surprise. Union soldiers drove into the Confederate defensive positions and engaged in hand-to-hand combat. Most of the overwhelmed Confederate defenders, unable to quickly cross the bridge, were killed or surrendered. The few who escaped across the river burned the pontoon bridge to stop the federal advance. Nevertheless, it was a clear Union victory and, as a result, Lee was forced to cancel his plans to attack the Third Corps, as he might have done if Sedgwick had been stopped. Instead, he ordered a hasty retreat of the Confederate army to a position south of the Rapidan. Henry recounted the events when he continued his letter on November 10 from "Camp Near Beverly Ford, Va.":

> The morning of the 6th I was ordered on picket to remain two days. Before night it was rumored that a moove was to take place on the morow. Six days rations were issued & fresh beef evry night. Orders were to moove at early break of day. All was quiet on the line during the day. The men are unusually destructive of Rebil property &c.
>
> The 7th is to be another memorable day in the campaign of 1863. At early dawn of day our picket line was drawn in joined our Regt on the road toards the Rappahannoc. It was a new one, certainly we had never traveled it before. All conjectured something was up. Soon we passed the cavelry out posts who informed us that we should not advance many miles before coming in contact with the Johnies (a name we give them since England has taken so active a part in our affair) that they ascertained their position the day before. Said they were fortifying their side of the river (North). We arrived about noon at a large plantation, went through some manuevers, finaly formed two lines of battle, deployed skirmishers in front, sent the 5th Vt to Beverlies Ford to prevent any flank moovements. Then all rested for nearly an hour,

made coffee, ate dinner &c all done in plain view of the enemy. When we halted I noticed some mounted pickets on a hill about three quarters of a mile in our front on a hill, seemingly agitated about our presence. Some said they were our men, others the enemy [and we were] being placed in an open field at their mercy if they chose to open on us with their cannon. Caused much speculation as to what party they belonged. I was sure of their being rebils, because our lines were so regularly formed &c. About one P.M. the bugle sounded to fall in. Then to moove forward. More perfect lines never advanced. The enemy silently watched us until we were within easy musket range when they opened on us but their balls were not sent with precision enough to stop our line. On gaining the sumit of the hill the forts were in plain view. Mounting eleven guns from which they threw shell & shot with a vengence at our lines of battle. Some shots took effect. One instance killing four men in the 3rd Brigade & one in the 4th Vt. On the crest of the hill we halted but the skirmish line advanced and met a whole line of battle behind rifle pits & strange to relate the skirmishers were invisible. Lines of battle were vanish[ed] before them & they did, carried the rifle pits, took a number of prisoners, sent them to the rear. The enemy rallied and drove the skirmish line back out of the pits but not to stay. Again they rallied retook the rifle pits & held them in face of cannon & Infantry. A rebil prisoner asked the reason of sending a skirmish line to drive a line of battle. They felt insulted. He was answered it was some of the 6th Corps to which the rebil replied he no longer felt particularly disgraced if it was that Corps was coming. We had met the same men three times at Fredricksburg. On gaining certain positions our bataries were brought to the front & commenced to fire on the enemy who payed their compliments in particular to them but most of their shot went a little too high & lodged just in our rear. Some came rather close. One struck under a mans feet giving a warning for him to jump & he did very handsomely (I suposed that to be the order &c).

Soon the 1st & 3rd Divisions came up, took position on our left & rear. The enemy threw their shells among them very carelessly wounding a number, but all was perfect order not a sight of confusion. Took their position & advanced. A charge was made before dark but it was only to delude the enemy. They were orderd back at dark. Two lines were sent to charge the front works of the enemy. At the same time two Regiments were sent to the extreme left with orders to creap up unseen to the fort, break the line & take posession of the Pontoon bridge, hold it &c. The Regt in front appeared first & drew the enemies attention on them. The 6th Maine crept up within ten feet of the works (the Colnel orderd evry cap to be taken from the guns for fear some one would accidentaly fire). With a cheer they rose and mounted the rifle pits filled with rebils, broke the line, rushed for the bridge & gained it before the enemy could stop them. Finaly, the whole force were taken prisoners with seven pieces of cannon & 17000 men, their Brigade, staff & all. Over a hundred officers & 7 stands of colors. It was one of the ...[this section of the page has been cut out to remove the signature on the other side]engagements we were ever engaged in. The cleanest ... to capture all ... our loss was not heavy considering the work done. The 6th Maine were the principal loosers. Out of twenty two line officers nineteen were killed & wounded. Their Colnel killed dead. There was never a closer action. Some of the rebils had three bayonet wounds, others their skulls smashed so that no face was to be seen. One of the Maine boys was speaking of the part he took when he leaped into the rifle pit. The enemy were on evry side of him. He demanded a surrender but the first of his recollection were that he had his head terribly mangled. The rebil instead of surrendering knocked him down with the but of his gun. Many of the enemy tried to cross the bridge when our men were crossing but few of them reached the opposite side. They were sent headlong into the Rappahannoc. One General escaped by swimming the river. One thing that pleased us was when the Rebils found themselves taken they began to cheer & many said they were glad it had happened so luckily on our side & for them.

Very soon after we commenced our battle, cannonading was heard still farther to our left. It prooved to be at Kellies Ford. The 3rd Corps had made an unexpected offensive there & commenced to cross. It is a very strongly fortified position besides what nature did for it but the enemy were not able to check their advance across the river. They waded, the water nearly to their necks & captured seven hundred men. The next day joined us at Brandy Station. Then most of the eighth was spent in caring for the wounded & burying the dead. There were forty killed of the 6th Me. They bore the brunt of the fight. Most of the wounded were hit in the body mostly mortal. The slaughter among the enemy was heavy. Some had large knives which are of no use to anyone. Some were very poorly clad. Some of the Cavilry taken had no shoes on their feet but stocking & old rags. About two P.M. on the eighth we all crossed the river. Gary's Cavilry Division was sent to Beverly Ford. Our advance & his was simultaneous. The rebils fell back in great haste. The Cavilry not regarding infantry or cannon, rushed on, broke their lines, took many prisoners & one whole batary. We advanced to Brandy Station, halted for the night. The Cavilry chased the few across the Rappidan.

The next day all the Cavilry withdrew in plain sight, halted in our front, took dinner, then started for Fredricksburg heights. At four P.M. we started for our right & halted about seven, took up quarters in shanties that the rebils had just built for winter quarters. They did not dream of our advancing this fall. The quarters are excellent, good fireplaces, &c. Had not stayed in them one night. We are to remain right here until the railroad is repaired which will not be many days. Not less than a week. Then perhaps cross the Rappidan. It is supposed the enemy were mostly away south. If we cross the Rappidan, the loss cannot be any thing but heavy on our side. At Brandy Station there were a number of officers wives were left behind so great was the haste to get out of the way of our Cavilry. In one house the ladies came to the door & waved their handkerchiefs. It was the plantation owned by Mr. Cobb, a noted southern gentleman who was sent to Richmond last month when we retreated for not telling which way our army went when we fell back. They profess to be union sympathizers.

The weather is remarkably cold. You can imagine our suffering especialy nights. One can sleep two or three hours then wake up with numb feet &c. My box has not arrived yet. It is at Washington. Mr Smith called to get it but they would not let him have it. The Division Commander has to order it, then it will be sent along, not until then. I am glad to learn that it is on the way as far as Washington. I expect to get it some time. They would be acceptable this stormy season. Soon the mud will be deep enough. Yesterday it snowed right smart. There was a heap of snow to be seen on the mountain tops.

We expect stirring times soon if at all this winter. Now is the only time. The season is remarkably favorable so far & if Meade is as successful in out Generaling them as in times past, we shall make a mark before we go into Winter quarters. He has the confidence of all his men. His removal would be as deeply felt perhaps more so than McCellans was. (By the way, I had an introduction to his brother at Corps Hd quarters. He is a pretty little man, is a Captain on Sedgwicks Staff.) All are well. Hope your patience will not ware out before you read this long letter. Kind regards to all especialy Eunice.

Henry viewed the battle through the eyes of an experienced, battle-tested veteran, but for Francis this was his first real taste of actual combat. He too described the experience to his parents in a letter from "Camp Near Brandy Station, Va" on November 10:

When I last wrote, I think it was from Warrenton. Remained there two weeks. Many of the boys loged up the sides of their tents and built fire places inside although none of them expected to remain there any length of time. A tent can be made very comfortable in this way and it pays for the labor even if not occupied more than a week. I did not fix up my tent partly because I was inexperienced in such work and chiefly because I had no axe or hatchet of my own and must look to others for tools who want of course [to] use them first and when I was ready to commence I was prevented by being assigned to other work. All this seemed almost providential to prevent useless labor for last Sunday we were ordered to pack up & march at day break. We advanced in a Southernly direction about eight miles when we were formed in line of battle and moved on again. Soon we heard cannonading in front and occasionaly saw a cloud of smoke in the air occasioned by the bursting of a shell. We were halted in a sort of hollow & presently a shot passed over our heads causing many of the men to bow to the ground. Our Lieut did not like this & told them to stand on their feet. Shell after shell passed over our heads quickly following the reports of the guns, a few bursting in the air. The Colonel told us to lie down, so they came quite low. One struck under the feet of a man about two rods in my rear not exploding however or doing him any injury. One man, in the 4th VT which lay to our left lost a leg but I have heard of no other casualities. The cannonading was soon succeeded by musketry which was kept up until dark. We then advanced a short distance receiving orders from the Colonel to lie down for the night but to be in readiness to move on a moments notice as the enemy might any time commence shelling us. Whether they would or not he could not tell. This was the first time that I was in danger from the guns of the enemy. Every man showed that he had some realization of his situation. I felt less discomposed than I often would when going into a room full of company. The question which was uppermost in my mind was am I prepared for eternity. I could not feel that my past religious life would compare with that of others or that I had lived as I should. I felt too that no opportunity for preparation was there allowed me. Still I hoped that my sins were pardoned and felt that I had an interest in Christ and could not be otherwise than calm although it gave me no assurance that I might not be killed or mutilated. Sometimes I think that I shall not survive a battle or at most the war and at other times it seems that there is work which I can do as yet unaccomplished. God can protect me, keep me alive or take me to himself in such manner as he chooses.

Our forces were victorious driving the enemy from their fortifications & capturing 1200 prisoners & 6 pieces of artillery. On Sunday we (Co. F) were sent scouting and then marched across the Rappahannock & on to Brandy

Station where we lay yesterday until five O'clock and then marched two miles & encamped in the woods near the quarters just occupied by the rebels where we are now. It was very cold last night and I suffered more than I have any night since I have been in the service. There is some thing peculiary penetrating about the air in Virginia when it is cold. Our winter clothing has not got along. Yet with a little less hardship I should enjoy better health in the Army than at home. There is much exposure calculated to undermine one's constitution and develope disease but I have nothing of the dyspepsia here. My apetite is good and I enjoy my food better than when at home. We have excellent coffee here which I have learned to prepare so that it will bear comparison with home coffee. I usually toast or else fry my hard tack in pork fat which with a good apetite makes them very palatable. If we were in winter quarters we could make ourselves comfortable and should have better returns in quality, variety and quantity. When on the march it is nothing but hard tack, pork & coffee but now & then rations of fresh beef killed from the cattle which accompany us.

If we were in winter quarter I should like a tub of butter, a cheese &c. I could easily dispose of what I did not want. If you have not sent the box I should want you to procure for me a hatchet to weigh at least one and half lbs, one table spoon & one case knife and a pocket knife worth 75 cents or $1.00. I do not know when I shall get the box but it will come some time. If I were to order another pair of boots I should be particular to direct not to have the upper leather too heavy as one needs to have lightness, comfort & duribility combined in a soldiers boot. I wish to have you procure for me a comb which opens & shuts, one side coarse & the other fine. Also a paper of pins and 1/4 yd of Elastic Ribbon. The last three articles can be sent in newspaper to me & I do not care how soon. I suppose that you must be very lonely at home and hope that Henry's letters & my own are some relief to that loneliness. Henry hardly knows how much he can help me here if I do well. An officer has so much influence. I should like to know how you get along. Does your work prosper? Does Joe do well? Is it hard for you? Are the willows cut? Remember me to all. Write as often as you can.

The Battles of the Bristoe Campaign, depicted by a member of Lee's staff as "the saddest chapter in the history of the [Confederate] army," had come to an end. Feeling content that it had established a strong position for a spring offensive that could conclude the war, the Army of the Potomac settled into its anticipated winter quarters near Brandy Station.

Chapter 12

THE VERMONT
WATCHMAN

Williamstown was too small to support its own newspaper. Instead, residents purchased newspapers from other towns such as the *Vermont Chronicle* or the *Vermont Watchman and State Journal*, published in Montpelier. These newspapers employed local correspondents to provide news on events in the surrounding towns. Francis seems to have had a great passion for the written word and had served as a Williamstown correspondent for different newspapers. After deciding to enter the service, he made arrangements to become a war correspondent for the *Vermont Watchman and State Journal*. Francis chose the pseudonym "Conscript" for his articles, although this was technically a misnomer since he had actually enlisted as a substitute after learning that he was soon to be drafted. He was perhaps misrepresenting himself to make it harder for readers to identify him. His first entry, from Chantilly, was written shortly after he arrived in Virginia and was published back home on November 6, 1863:

Mr. Editor:—I purpose to give the readers of your journal, from time to time such account of my experience as a soldier as I am able. I do not pretend to possess the capacity, knowledge or experience of other correspondents of your paper, but hope that a plain statement of the facts which I understand will not prove uninteresting.

On the 3d of August I was drafted into the service,

The Watchman Building
Courtesy of Washington County
Historical Society

234

was duly notified, and went to Woodstock, where I passed medical examination, was mustered into the service on the 8th of September, and left for Brattleboro with other conscripts and substitutes on the 9th. There we were confined under a close guard in a prison-like building, less comfortable than a good Vermont barn, for two days and three nights. On the morning of the 12th, with that feeling of satisfaction which attends the removal from a place to which no "sunny memories" are attached, we left for our place of rendezvous on Long Island, Boston Harbor, where we remained nearly three weeks. Here the invigorating sea breezes, and the novelties of camp life, into which we were just being initiated, enabled us to pass our time pleasantly rather than otherwise. The number of soldiers on the island, including guards and conscripts, varied, as they came and went, from one thousand to two thousand. All classes of men were there congregated together, and almost every shade of character exhibited. Our time was occupied in drill, guard duty, going about the different camps, listening to stories around the campfire, often from men who, from cultivated minds, or extensive experience in life, could draw forth treasures of information, or make such displays of mother wit as it is seldom our lot to hear at home; eating, sleeping, and all that goes to make up a soldier's life in camp.

Leaving the Island on the evening of Oct. 1st, about one thousand of us embarked on board the steamer Forest City, and after a rather rough passage, which occasioned much seasickness, we came in sight of Fortress Monroe on the morning of the 5th, passed on to Portsmouth, a beautiful city, containing many fine residences, surrounded with an abundance of shade trees clothed in the rich green of the sunny South, where we landed the New Hampshire detachment. Then returning towards Fortress Monroe, we steamed up the Potomac, and arrived at Alexandria in the afternoon. Here, for the first time, many of us saw the white dome of the Capitol in Washington. We were landed at Alexandria just before dark, furnished with guns and shelter tents, and then marched through the streets to one of the soldier's retreats, where we passed the night. We left on the cars the next morning for Culpepper, from which place we marched a distance of ten miles to the encampment of the Second Regiment of the Vermont Brigade, on Cedar Mountain; arrived there at 8 o'clock P.M., attended roll-call, and were assigned to the different companies. My lot fell to company F, where I was so fortunate as to find an old townsman, Sergt. Thos. McClury, who was so kind as to prepare a cup of coffee for me, and render me such assistance in pitching my tent, and in making preparations for the night's rest, as was particularly acceptable to one so tired *and inexperienced in soldier's life as I. For these, and subsequent attentions, I feel myself under great obligations, and give this testimony as a tribute of regard to his kindness, to say nothing of his abilities as an officer, which position he fills with honor. We remained at Cedar Mountain four days.*

On Saturday morning, the 16th, we received orders to strike our tents and be ready to march at a moment's notice – with that pleasure which a soldier always feels when anything occurs to relieve the restlessness which the monotony of camp-life always, sooner or later, occasions. The order to fall in and march did not come till 9 o'clock P.M. We then pushed on through woods and fields, across ditches and small streams, at times losing our footing and floundering under the weight of our equipments, until we again obtained our equilibrium – until we reached Culpepper, beyond which place we were marched a few miles to a hill side, where we spread our blankets in the open air, at 1 o'clock A.M., and slept soundly until 4 o'clock A.M., when the order came to fall in and advance. Soon after day light, we were halted to cook our meat and coffee, and then pushed on, crossed the Rappahannock, and encamped in the wood, at the Station, at 2 o'clock P.M. Before light, on the morning of the 12th, we recrossed the Rappahannock, marched a few miles in the direction of Culpepper, then were ordered into the woods where we loaded our pieces, and were marched out and formed in line of battle in the rear of a breastwork. Soon we were ordered to change our position and formed again back of another trench and breast work, where we remained till afternoon. The road to Culpepper in the meantime was filled with troops, artillery, supply-trains, ambulances, &c; cannonading in the front, where the enemy were engaged with the cavalry, who covered our retreat, was heard from time to time. A little after noon we were moved forward again, formed in line of battle and then marched towards the front. The cannonading grew more distinct and incessant. At times we saw ambulances returning with the wounded, and passed dead or disabled horses. At Brandy Station we were nearest the enemy's lines, and could see clouds of dust raised by the explosion of their shells. Our officers wished them to give us battle there, but they declined and at dark we received orders to build small fires and encamp for the night. At 12 o'clock M, we received orders to move again, retraced our steps, crossed the Rappahannock on the railroad bridge, which was blown up by our rear at 9 o'clock A.M. — encamped in the woods at the Station, kindled fires and slept until nearly daylight, when the order to fall in came again, and we pushed on, the most of us tired and hungry, having neglected to cook our meat and coffee, under the supposition that we were to remain in our encampment through the day; marched a few miles, halted for breakfast, and drew rations of sugar and then advanced until 12 o'clock, when we halted, two hours, perhaps, for dinner and rest, and drew rations of coffee, pork and hard tack. Resuming our march, we went on until sometime after dark, and encamped near Bristow's Station, having made about twenty-five miles; a hard march for us conscripts – though the old soldiers seemed to make little of it. Since then, our marches have been easier and our rests longer. We have passed through Centreville, and since yesterday have been encamped at Chantilly, tired, foot sore, and glad of any opportunity to recruit ourselves. We have heard some pretty heavy cannonading, and it is reported that we have gained a decided advantage over the enemy. When the battle was fought or how great the victory on our side, we have not been informed. Hoping that the above account of our late movements will prove acceptable to your readers, I subscribe myself, CONSCRIPT.

Two weeks later, the *Vermont Watchman* published another article:

FROM THE SECOND REGIMENT

Camp Near Brandy Station, Va., November 12, 1863

The readers of the Journal who took the trouble to peruse my last, will recollect that it was written at Chantilly. I now purpose to give such an account as I am able of our subsequent movements and of my further experience as a soldier; again pleading their charity for such failings as I may be betrayed into by my ignorance and inexperience– for I only claim to be a soldier – often obeying commands whose import I do not understand, going I know not where, "taking no thought for the morrow," what I shall eat or drink or wherewithal I shall be clothed, and (though often reminded by pressing and unsupplied wants that they are neither infallible nor omnipotent) relying for support and protection on those whom I serve. We stopped at Chantilly two days, obtaining the rest we so much needed, and on Sunday, Oct. 18th received orders to pack up and march again. Moved about one and one half miles from our encampment to the summit of a hill where we stacked arms and lay in line of battle during the day. Most of us expecting to remain over night, pitched our tents – just before sundown – and pulled weeds or cut grass with our knives on which to spread our blankets. This was hardly done, before the order came again to pack up and fall in, and we were marched in another direction about three fourth of a mile, but our discomforts did not end here, for we had hardly pitched our tents again before our company were ordered out on picket and guard duty. During the intervening hours between our reliefs, we spread our blankets and slept soundly, but just before day break we were exposed to a shower of rain which drenched our blankets thoroughly, and had no opportunity to dry them before our fires before we received marching orders. We then proceeded in the direction of Warrenton. The march was unusually tiresome, as we were not yet thoroughly recruited from the fatigue of our late moves and were burdened with the extra weight of wet blankets, while our route lay over steep hills and through fields crossed with ditches and creeks and overgrown with weeds and briar vines. At length we were halted to rest, and as we stopped longer than usual some of our boys began to kindle fires to cook their coffee, and I, with the advice of an old soldier, took out and spread my blanket in the sun to dry. This was hardly done before we received orders to sling knapsacks and fall in, giving me no time to refold my blanket which I was obliged to wear on my shoulders, over my other accoutrements, like a shawl, for miles under a hot sun, until I began to entertain serious thoughts of throwing it away but was prevented by an old soldier, to whom I applied for counsel, who said that I "would rue the day that I parted with my blanket."

The next morning at 4 o'clock, we resumed our march, which we continued until afternoon and then stopped until sundown, near New Baltimore. At dusk we were ordered forward again, and after making a rapid march of about six miles, we encamped on a hill top about one half of a mile west of Warrenton. About ten o'clock on the morning of the 22d, we packed up again and marched through the city of Warrenton – a beautiful place, but, I think, in its best days lacking that appearance of thrift and elegance which characterizes our most flourishing New England villages. Moving forward in an easterly direction, we soon reached the summit of a hill overlooking the city and surrounding country where we encamped and remained two weeks; occupying our time in military exercises, and fitting up our tents so as to make them comfortable for winter, or any kind of weather.

On Friday evening, Nov. 6th, we received orders to be ready to pack up at a moment's notice. During the night that increased animation which is always observable when an army expects to change its quarters, prevented the most of us from retiring to rest at all or until a late hour. At three in the morning I cooked my breakfast, which I had hardly finished before I, with three others, was called upon to carry rations to the pickets, about two miles from camp. A box containing about six hundred hard crackers was handed to me, but my shoulders unaccustomed to such a load, required to be relieved oftener than those of my companions, who seemed to make but little of it. At day break we were in camp again, just in time to sling knapsacks and join our regiment. We then advanced about eight miles in the direction of Rappahannock station. As we neared the station, we marched in line of battle hearing heavy cannonading in front, and soon seeing shells bursting in the air. At five P.M., we were halted in a hollow. Soon a shell passed over our heads, causing many of the men to stoop to the ground. Our Lieutenant did not like this, and told them to keep on their feet, for shell never hurt any one.

Shell followed shell, coming so low that the Colonel soon ordered the men to lie down on the ground. A few exploded in the air, but the most of them fell into the woods in our rear, doing no harm. One, a percussion shell, buried itself without exploding, under the feet of one of our men, giving him some alarm, but doing no injury. The only casualty which I have heard of, occurred in the Fourth Regiment which lay on our left, where a conscript lost a leg. The cannonading was succeeded by musketry which continued until dark, when we moved forward again for a short distance, then halted, stacked arms, and received orders from the Colonel to build no fires, but to lie down in readiness to move at a moment's notice, as the enemy might or might not commence shelling us again during the night. The next morning our company was sent out to a hill overlooking the surrounding country, on a scouting expedition. Returning we cooked our dinner, and then followed the rest of our brigade, passed yesterday's battle ground, which we learned was the scene of a Union victory, resulting in the capture of 1200 prisoners, six pieces of artillery, and the enemy's fortifications – crossed the Rappahannock on a pontoon bridge, and joined our regiment at Brandy station, where we remained until the next day at five o'clock P.M., long enough to make preparations for a longer stay, when we were marched about two miles to the north west. On our march we passed the quarters just vacated by the rebels who had built comfortable log houses, with the grounds well policed in front for the coming winter. We are now encamped in the woods, but to furnish the requisite supply of timber for fuel and our dwellings it is fast making the ground a clearing. How long we shall remain here we can only conjecture – long enough, we presume, to make such preparations for winter as our health and comfort require, which even if not enjoyed, furnish exercise for the skill of our soldiers.

Hoping that the foregoing will meet with such acceptance as to encourage me to continue my descriptions of army life, I subscribe myself, CONSCRIPT

Just a week later, on November 27, the third installment was published:

Our Army Correspondence

For the Watchman

A Conscript's Letter—No. 3

Camp near Beverly Ford, Va.,

Nov. 20, 1863

Mr. Editor – Since writing my last (which might with more propriety have been dated at the above named place which is nearer to us than Brandy Station), we have not changed our encampment, although at about half-past three o'clock, A.M. on Sunday the 15th we received orders to pack up all but our tents and be in readiness to move at any moment, and a short but heavy cannonading at daybreak in the direction of Brandy Station left us in no doubt as to the reason. There had been cannonading previous to this, but we did not distinguish the reports of the guns from the thunder accompanying a heavy shower of rain with which we were at that time visited. The engagement resulted – if the camp rumor is to be credited – in the repulse of the attacking party and capture of two rebel brigades. Our success rendering a change of position unnecessary, we again unpacked our knapsacks, rearranged the few articles which comprise our household utensils and furniture, and affairs in camp again took their accustomed course.

The camp is the soldier's home, where the greater portion of his life is passed, maintaining peace and order by his presence, and making those preparations which are necessary to fit him for those extreme hardships which he must at times endure, as well as for those short but thrilling scenes where the fate of nations is sometimes decided and his own career often terminates. Accounts of camp life, as its different features are presented to him in his progress through that process by which the peaceful citizen is thoroughly transformed into the soldier, must constitute the principal part of the letters of your correspondent. While your readers may think the subject already exhausted by others more able than myself, yet as the picture is drawn by a different artist, and some new feature may be presented, it is my hope that they will be entertained if not instructed.

The newly arrived conscript or recruit is first sensible of the vast difference between civil and military life, which others from familiarity do not perceive, but acknowledge its truthfulness when it is again presented to their minds.

The recruit may be aglow with patriotism, but he has no experience, and old habits working against those efforts which the little military knowledge he may possess enables him to make, betray him into continual blunders in spite of his best attempts. In his ignorance, carelessness, or over carefulness, he often innocently or pardonably subjects himself to penalties which may fail to reform the guilty, but as the result of his own mistakes serve as way marks to keep him in the path of duty and to stimulate him to a more careful observance of those regulations which military discipline requires. He knows no difference between the different calls, reveille, roll, orderlies or drum call, and after their imports have been explained, it is often forgotten at the only time when such knowledge is of value. Your correspondent can testify that the fatigue duty done by him at the commencement of the late march described in my last, was inflicted as a punishment for being absent from roll call, for wood or water, which is allowed, but the orderly was not informed when he called the names, he of course only discharged his duty. On drill, his very desire to excel is often the cause of many blunders, mortifying, because it is the failure of well-meant endeavors, exposing the green recruit to the ridicule of the more experienced soldiers, and doubly irritating because that charity is withheld which should have been shown.

To illustrate this disposition to blunder and its cause, I will give my own experience. At our general inspections every soldier is required to appear with knapsack, musket, haversack, canteen, &c., with the brasses on his belt and cartridge box polished, gun well cleaned, and above all, with clean face and hands. He may or may not be required to unsling and open his knapsack, but each soldier must present his arms for inspection as the officer passes in front. The soldier is instructed "to raise smartly his piece with his right hand, then to raise it with the left between the lower band and guide, sight the lock to the front, the left hand at the height of the chin, the piece opposite to the left eye; the inspecting officer then takes it with the right hand at the handle, and after inspecting it returns it to the recruit, who receives it back with the right hand, and replaces it in the position of ordered arms."

At one of our general inspections I became suddenly perplexed to know between which of the hands to seize my piece, but did the best I could without acting in accordance with any prescribed rule, bringing up and presenting my piece with the lock inside. The officer smiled and asked me to do it again; supposing that my failure was in grasping my piece wrong I endeavored to correct my mistake and presented the piece as before – lock inside. Our Lieut. then told me to present the piece with the lock to the front and by that time my lesson was well learned. In the various military maneuvers the recruit has ample opportunity to prove the truth of the observation of General Scott, that "it takes three years for a man to learn to know his left hand from his right."

The desire to excel and to win the favor of others as well as the irritation experienced from the injustice to which the recruit is sometimes subject soon gives place to the desire to do what is right for its own sake, things vexatious in themselves considered are expected and taken good naturedly, and with that composure of mind which is necessary in order to make improvement from instruction of any kind. The wants of the soldier soon call into exercise his observation and skill in the production and use of such articles of comfort and luxury as can be improvised from the scanty materials at hand. He remains in camp but a short time before his tent becomes the roof of a shanty logged up or stockaded at the sides, with a good fire place inside and bedstead of poles, two resting upon crotched stakes, across which the others are arranged lengthwise and covered with boughs, over which blankets are spread, making a bed as healthy if not as luxurious as the one he was accustomed to enjoy at home. Hard tack is perhaps the most tasteless form in which flour can be used, but the soldier finds exercise for his skill in the culinary department, in various contrivances, to render it more palatable. It is often fried in pork fat, toasted on the coals of his fire; soaked in beef broth; pounded fine and made into hasty pudding, and sometimes when the soldier is disposed to be unusually luxurious, soaked soft in cold water – any amount of boiling only serves to make it tough and soggy – then salted, sweetened and cooked in a frying pan. For sauce a little pork fat is melted in vinegar and sugar mixed in equal quantities, which with a good appetite makes a dish which will bear comparison with the puddings eaten at home. Steak broiled on coals is superior to that cooked by the ordinary methods, as it is more tender, and all the juices are retained in the meat. The coffee issued to the soldiers is usually of good quality, but to obtain all its strength it requires roasting a second time. This is easily done in a frying pan, care being taken to keep it from charring, and to remove it when it is thoroughly cooked, that is when it shows signs of the presence of its volatile oils by sticking to the spoon with which it is stirred. Coffee prepared as it should be, sweetened and mixed with condensed milk, is superior to that furnished at the majority of our hotels. Among the articles most highly prized by the soldier on the march, and in remote camps, are the axe or hatchet and frying pan. But few of these can be found in any company, and the man is considered fortunate who obtains one. These, like other articles of value tempt the cupidity of the unprincipled and they are often stolen. I was first taught the value of a frying pan by my own wants, being obliged to fry my meat in my tin plate, or borrow a spider after the owner had cooked his own meat. Then for a few days I rejoiced in the possession of one for which I paid 50 cents, but was soon called to pass through one of those trials which tend to improve or destroy one's disposition, for last Sunday morning after breakfast it was left for a short time outside of the tent, and temptation proved too strong for some passer-by who pilfered it, and every effort of my own, and others, has as yet failed to bring the thief to justice.

With many thanks to those who have been so patient as to peruse this letter to its close, I subscribe myself – CONSCRIPT.

Besides his newspaper correspondence, Francis also continued sending very descriptive letters home to his parents. On November 17 he wrote from "Camp Near Beverly Ford, Va":

It is now 1 o'clock P.M. I am on my post as police guard & remain until three. The police guard are the sentries in front of the Col's head quarters, Commisaries tent &c. There are five posts, each occupied by one man. 15 men in all are detailed from the Regiment. These are divided into three bodies called reliefs, 5 men in each relief. Each relief is on post eight hours out of the 24. Two hours at once. The guard is called out & mounted – as it is called – at 9 A.M. I am on the 3rd relief today & of course am on my post first from 1 until 3, then from 7 until 9, next from 1 till 3 again & last from 7 tomorrow morning until 9. Then my guard duty is done for a week or so. We have brigade guard, differing from police guard in that it is at the brigade head quarters instead of the regimental, also picket duty, at the outposts. Our camp is now in the woods & quite pleasant in pleasant weather. Today it is mild & pleasant. The cold weather here is more raw & penetrating than in Vt. The spot where I stand commands quite an extensive prospect & look where I will I see the tents of our various regiments which surround us.

Except on the march, although I find it a very busy life, I do not have so hard a time as when at home. I do not always feel well. Seldom as well as I could wish but I pass for a strong man I suppose. And my acquaintances tell me that I look better than when I came out. I read my letter first in a paper which I rece'd from Henry but have since rece'd a paper from Mr. Walter with the request to write often. I think I shall also write for the Chronicle if Mr. Bishop will publish my communications. Henry's regiment lies but a short distance from the 2nd. I see him as often as I wish. He is all to me that I could wish of a brother in his position. He is certainly a fine officer & it is not only credit to him to have obtained such a situation but still more to fill it so creditably. But few in this army have sustained such a moral character. The temptations which have led many others astray seem to have had but little influence upon him.

Henry may have avoided some of the pleasures offered in camp, but he continued to covet packages from home. A letter from Chauncey arrived and Henry found out why it was taking so long to get the box for which he had been waiting:

[I]called at the "Express Office," and found the box had arrived, and was assured that it would be forwarded very soon. Yesterday Mrs. Farnham came down from the Army and I called again, but singular to say, the office is waiting for an order from the corps or division commander in order to forward all at once, which arrangement, they told me, had been adopted by the office. I begged hard to put yours on the cars without waiting for the order from the Commander, but they did not seem willing to depart from the rule which at present governs them. Under these circumstances, all that is required is for the Commander to order up the boxes and packages, and I presume you, with others, will apply to your general and have it done. Seems to me the commander ought to make such an order weekly, or at least once in two weeks, and not have the soldiers and officers delayed so long for their necessary presents from home.

On November 20, Henry wrote home, still at "Camp Near Beverly Ford, Va.":

All remains quiet at present. Drills are frequent & some picket duty. The celebrated U.S. Congressman John Minor Botts lives just below us. He is a strong firm union man. The same when the rebil army is encamped around him. He is occasionly sent to Richmond (Libby Prison) but they do not dare to keep him long. His great estate has been destroyed by the enemy. Still he will not be driven from his home. I saw him day before yesterday. He is a fair looking man. Was out to see our Division Drill. The same day two deserters were branded. The Division was drawn up in line. The deserters brought to the center with a guard on each side. Then the adjutant General of How's staff read the sentences, charges, specifications & dicision of the court marshall which was to forfeit all pay due him at the time of his desertion & all pay becoming due during the remainder of his term of service which is to continue the term he enlisted for & the time he has lost to the service by desertion to be added (so Uncle Sam intends his men to make up lost time, you see) also one to have a letter D branded on the right hip with a red hot iron. The other letter D on the right shoulder. After it was done were marched to their former quarters to do what duty might be found for them to do by the Commanding

General (the branding was done in the presence of the whole Division, rather humiliating.) One of my men who deserted at New York has been caught & returned, is now in the Division Guard house under charges of Desertion. A man belonging to the 7th Maine deserted, was tried before General Court Marshall & sentenced to be shot with musketry on the 27th Nov. at 2 P.M. Probably will have some thing else done.

We are expecting to advance on Richmond once more this Fall. To start certainly the fore part of next week. The sick are to be sent away to Washington today (a sure sign). The Quarter Masters to draw eight days rations. The ambulances are all repaired & are being reviewed today.We expected to be payed before this but have not been. The rest of the army has been. The railroad is completed to Culpepper. Our Cavilry is at Slaughter Mountain where we were when Lee started for Washington. If we get to Gordensville Lees raids are up for we can occupy such a position that he can not gain our rear. We are protecting any flank moovement of Sulpher Springs. Our camp is just in rear of Meades Hd Quarters. We have the charge of all the reserve artilary consisting of one hundred guns of heavy caliber, one batery of 32, one 24, one 18 &c &c, 6 guns to a batery. We are well pleased to see them along with us. When one of the shots drop it takes effect. We have been very destitute of vegetables & most evry thing else. This morning I managed to get a peck of potatoes. Have not had but two apples since we left Warrenton & only one dozen there.

Frank was over to my tent last night. He is looking well & is so. I always thought it would agree with him here. The weather is fair, warm days & some cold nights. A remarkably pleasant fall.

I supose Lorett is very busy. I have not heard from her or Uncle Bass for a long time. I wrote him the 24th Sept but have received no answer. Please remember me to Eunice. I wish she was here to take a Virginia horse back ride. Its the only style here.

How does recruiting prosper? How it would be better for some of the young men to show their true warrior blood & join the Army of the Potomac. It is an honor to be connected with such a brave reliable army of men, so well led.

I supose the willows are all cut now. I should sell them green. It would be too much of an undertaking to peal them. I expect to remain in the army some time. The Brigade is to be kept & all officers promoted have been bound three years from date of promotion so you see how the case stands. (Ink is very scarce, red is all I have, excuse it)

Although Henry displayed a very high opinion of John Minor Botts, the Congressman probably did not reciprocate with such a favorable impression of the

The Botts family in 1863
Courtesy of Library of Congress

soldiers. Paul Zeller relates that as a result of the Vermont Brigade camping on his plantation, by the time spring arrived all 600 miles of Bott's fencing was gone, no trees remained on his lands, and one of his daughters was pregnant.

Henry and Francis also had to deal with some difficult news from home during this time. Eunice Bass, who was the same age as Francis, succumbed to consumption on November 14. Her sister, Lorette, two years younger, had been caring for Eunice during her extended illness. Besides being cousins, the Martins and Basses had grown up across the road from each other, and Lorette had attended boarding school with Francis at Kimball Union Academy. Henry received a letter from Lorette shortly after her sister had died:

Yes Henry, she is gone! Gone home to her Savior to enjoy the home in the "house of many mansions" which he went to prepare for her. I wish you could have seen her once more! Her last days were perfect peace, all dread of death was taken away and she was able to give up her own life, her friends, and every thing she loved here, into her Heavenly Father's hands. She maintained to the very last the same uncomplaining unselfish spirit that you saw when with her. In all our memories of her there is not one complaining, fretful or impatient look or action. Every memory of her is a precious legacy that will last as long as life. She did not suffer any more at the very last than she had for days before, not so much as at some times but fell asleep gently, returning even till we buried her. The same expression of inward peace and happiness. Every one who saw her said how happy she looks! And thus we believe her to be.

O Henry! I can not tell you how the conviction of her blessedness takes away from the bitterness of our sorrow. We would not call her back here to suffer for another day or hour if we could. She does not seem to us as dead. And yet we know we shall never see her here again. There is a dessolation in our house and in our hearts, but we "mourn not as those without hope."

I hope you are well, and unharmed, and to hear from you soon, and I hope not many months will pass before we welcome you, and the other 4th Regt. Boys back to our homes, but if it is not so, I hope as our dear Eunice told you when you parted for the last time, "that we shall meet in a better world." Give a great deal of love to John, and tell him I shall write him again soon if he is not going to answer my last. I shall also write Frank at my earliest opportunity.

Somewhat lighter and happier correspondence arrived from Lucy Lynde, still living with her sister and brother-in-law in Illinois.

Lorette Bass
Courtesy of Williamstown
Historical Society

In the papers sent from home I see you have made recently a "masterly advance on Washington" as some army correspondent has termed it. I had hoped that the brave army of the Potomac might ever here- after meet with that success in all undertakings that this courage and noble deeds deserve. ...

After a stay of more than two months in the West I can give you but little idea of the country or how I am pleased with it. I had drawn many pictures in my own imagination as to the place and people but zero of them I find are "true to nature." Instead of the flat muddy country I expected I find the surface so undulating or rolling and the "timber" in the distance so much like home that I forget it is a wonderful Prairie that so puzzled my heart to describe in the days of <u>Primary Geography</u>. With the people it is different though so many are from "Yankeedom" they are but little like them there. As they leave their homes for the far West all romantic and refining elements are forgotten and only those sterner qualities that best fit men for a new country are remembered or practiced but one thing is equalled even in Williamstown if it were possible, 'tis gossiping. It is amusing to me to hear the War cur- rent news & discussed by the maids and maidens as they gather at a "social tea drinking". Still they are so kind and free hearted I like them and respect many of their qualities and customs.

As for the news at home I repeat it only "second-handed" so will not search for the truth, and your correspondents there are no doubt better able to inform you. It seems the young ladies are fast-leaving, Silkie Martin at Burlington, Sarah Bass and Em Beckett for the Factory. Esther Smith at N.Y. What will the brave patriotic young men at home do now? I fear they will be obliged to descend the scale of age, and go to flirting with the <u>rising generation</u>!

In your next please to inform me in regard to those <u>stories</u> you mentioned. My curiosity is somewhat excited. I know what they might be - <u>don't forget</u>.

My design in coming West was to go to Racine Wis. to spend some time in going to school and taking music lessons. I find the commencement of next term is in the Spring so will spend the winter here. My father was somewhat opposed to my coming West. But as I intend to make a finished "school marm" concluded to do so.

Although we generally assume that most nineteenth-century Americans spent virtually their whole lives close to their home, many of the Martins' relatives travelled extensively. One of Henry's older cousins, Emily Pride, had married James Tileston and moved to Hopkinton, Massachusetts. Henry received one of her letters, forwarded through his mother, while in winter camp. She had just returned from a trip out west with her husband.

I have always had a great desire to see the West and I enjoyed the journey very much. Dont think I should like to live off on the prairie or in a small place, the cities and large places are very pleasant.

Mr. Tileston went up to St. Paul. He was delighted with Minesota. I went as far as Portage City in Wisconsin, near old Fort Winnebago. I spent a week there with Mrs. Haskell. ...She had a very pleasant home but I fear she will not enjoy it much longer. Her health is poor, fast going in Consumption. There are a good many Vermonters there among them. A family of Waldo's from East Randolph. Portage was the extent of my journey north and Cincinati South, Chicago west. I saw Perkins Bass and Fanny in Chicago. I stoped a day or two in all the places where Mr. Tileston had business, Cleaveland, Detroit, Milwaukie, Layfayette, Indianapolis, Terra Haute, Cincinati and Columbus. So you see I had an opportunity to see considerable. We were away four weeks and found every thing right at home.

On some accounts I would like to live West. It seems to me I shouldn't have the rheumatism so bad as here. I wasn't lame while I was gone but the very day I came home there came one of these awful East storms that stiffened every cord and joint in my body. It was all I could do to get out of the stage and I hardly get over one such time before another comes and so it keeps me a cripple most of the time. I dont know whether it is the weather or work but I guess both have something to do with it and I have come to the conclusion that I dont like East winds or hard work.

Francis, on the other hand, was neither feeling overworked nor having health issues, according to his November 21 letter. Those who had doubted that his stamina and temperament would permit him to succeed as a soldier were being proved wrong. The life of an army private seems to have agreed with him. After suffering from many health problems at home, he was doing well in an environment that had created difficulties for so many soldiers before him. He also appears to have fit in socially with his fellow soldiers better than those who knew him would have predicted.

> *My health is better than I have had any good reason to expect. The weather has been fine for a few days past. My apetite excellent & my duties light. As I am not troubled with indigestion here of course my health is better if I am not worked too hard than at home. Today it is rainy and our camp is fast becoming a mud hole. The prospect of cold and rainy weather is not pleasant. I am glad that I have got along as well as I have but if it had been worse for me I could not reasonably have indulged in any feelings of regret for I can but consider that I was providentially called here. I saw Henry yesterday, had an excellent supper of soft bread, stewed apple, hams & coffee at his tent and took away with me enough raw potatoes for an excellent dinner today. It is much more pleasant for me to have a brother here than it would be if otherwise.*
>
> *I was sorry to hear of the death of Eunice Bass. I wrote to Lorette a few days since & neglected to mention Eunice which I exceedingly regret. The box you sent me will come around in time but not at present. You may send the knife purchased for Henry if it is good for anything. Put anything you please in the next box. I should like some cheese. Anything good that will keep is acceptable when in camp or winter quarters. I would like some camphor gum. I receive all the papers, postage stamps &c you send me.*

Henry wrote home the same day, but with a greater focus on the larger military circumstances at that moment:

> *We expected to moove this morning but in the night it commenced to rain so we remain in camp. It was intended to advance (as near as I can learn). Rations for the men had arrived (eight days) & forage was to be on hand in the morning. The normal reports were circulating. One was the army was going back. Three Corps were to be kept in front of Washington & the remainder to be sent to the south west &c.*
>
> *We had a grand review of the corps by General Sedgwick & a number of English Officers. The Commander in Chief of the English Army was expected to be present but was not. ... The grounds were very rough & hilly so it was not as pleasant marching. Tonight it has commenced to rain very hard & is very cold. The rains have held off remarkably this season. I am very thankful that we did not start the day before the rain storm commenced.*
>
> *I was surprised to learn of Eunice Bass death. I expected she would not live very long still it is a surprise. I am glad to learn she died so resigned &*

hopeful. I would liked to have been home before she died. Must close or not send by this mail. Please send me a toothbrush in a paper.

As popular opinion moved toward the perception that General Meade had missed an opportunity to destroy Lee's army through a rapid pursuit after Gettysburg, Meade was feeling pressured to chase the rebel army now rather than remain in winter camp. Lee had set up defenses across the Rapidan, about ten miles south of Brandy Station. Meade planned to circle behind and attack Ewell's corps, the right flank of the Confederate position, near Mine Run. Orders were issued on November 25 to prepare to move out the next morning. Henry began a letter home before departing. He had also heard that Vermont Governor Smith had requested Federal troops to be stationed in Burlington, due to rumors that the Confederates might launch raids across the border from Canada.

The invasion of Vermont interests me very much. We almost hope it will be of a magnitude enough to have the Brigade called home this winter. I suppose the State Militia have bound themselves to defend their homes until <u>invaded</u>. I understand they are unwiling to be so organized as to be liable to be called into the United States Service.

There is a great deal of hard feeling about the substitutes not drawing the extra seven dollars per month as well as the drafted men. What mater is it to the State of Vermont whether a man has received an individual bounty, it does not concern them at all. It is only wronging the men who have come under the circumstances. They are mostly poor men who need the seven dollars very much. It is about alike the usage of the first three hundred thousand patriots who did not come for money & receive none while others come out, serve a short period of time then go home, receive so great bounty, enlist again & receive still another for being vetrans. We get a surplus of fighting, they of money. The time is coming when their wrongs will have [to be] faced.

I saw George Smith yesterday. He is well &c.We are still on the grounds gained by the battle of Rappahannoc Station. We have been in readiness to moove for a number of days but weather would not permit. Tomorrow morning we expect to leave cross the Rappidan at Jermanna Ford. We expect a desperate resistance. The railroad track is torn up between Brandy Station & Culpepper. In the morning all the Commisary stores are to be removed to Alexandria to ship for some point. Rumor says to two points. One to Acquia Crick another to the White house. Lees army is reported to be in the vacinity of Hanover Court House. A briliant victory before retiring to Winter quarters would be an excellent thing for us. Hope we may have one.

*Three more deserters were branded on the palm of the right hand. I have
at last received the express box. The boots are just what I wanted, just a fit.
Say to Mr Walker he never made a better pair for me before.*

A brilliant victory would require flawless execution of the plan, but the performance fell well short of brilliance. The army was to march over much of the
same territory as in the Battle of Chancellorsville, but in contrast to Hooker's
complex plan, Meade relied on taking the Confederates by surprise with a quick
advance. The Sixth Corps left early on the morning of November 26 and marched
out to meet the Third Corps as ordered. The Third Corps had not yet received
its orders, so the Sixth Corps had to wait several hours for the Third to prepare.
The march then took much longer than expected through difficult and swampy
terrain. When they finally arrived at the river for their crossing, they found that
not enough pontoon boats had been provided to cross the river. More hours were
lost fixing that mistake, and the element of surprise was lost. With time to assess
the situation, Lee sent Ewell's corps out to meet the slowly advancing Union Third
Corps, which the Sixth Corps was following. After scattered fighting at Mine Run,
Meade prepared for a more massive invasion against Lee's position. Several days of
skirmishing followed, but to Lee's disappointment, Meade had second thoughts
about a mass invasion and ordered a retreat back to Brandy Station, ending the
Mine Run Campaign. The army now settled into winter quarters for good.

Henry did not return to his letter until December 4, late in the retreat:

*At an early hour the 26th day of November the final order came for us to
start. We went direct to Brandy Station, crossed the railroad, passed the entire
front of the army & finaly after a long cold march through dense forests &
swamps we arrived at the banks of the Rappidan. Crossed at twelve Jerimi-
anna Ford, formed lines of battle & lay down to get a few hours sleep which
was interrupted by the extreme cold. The ice froze one inch. You can judge for
your self as to our comfort lying on the frozen ground. At four A.M. 27th we
were called up & ate breakfast at light. The 3rd Corps (our advance) started,
soon found the enemy, engaged them & drove them back. The 6th Corps,
the reserve, mooved up within supporting distance. At three P.M. the enemy
made a stand. The 3rd Division 3rd Corps was orderd to charge composed of
new troops, the 10th Vermont &c. The enemy alowed them to advance over
a rail fence then they opened fire on them & charged. It was new business for
the new troops & they broke & ran, the enemy after them. A portion of them
were supporting a batary. They ran & left it to take care of itself which it did.
The gunners stood by their guns until the enemy were within a few yards of*

their pieces then discharged double shoted canister by volies into their advancing columns so well directed that evry thing in front was swept away. Also the timely arrival of the 6th Corps checked the enemy with great slaughter. The 10th Vermont lost very heavily 68 killed & wounded. Among those killed is Gardner Fay. [He]was shot [with] the ball entering the neck severing a vain so he bled to death. Was seen by one of our men that night. Was put into an ambulance but did not live but a short time. He had got a commision in a Negro Regiment. He was an excelent soldier, always did his duty well.

The number of skedadlers from the troop in front was not numberless but a great many more than there should have been. We were formed in line in their rear & stoped them. How the old soldiers did look upon them. Their slang was enough to cause a frightened man to turn back & fight. The shells flew very lively around us but providentialy none of us were hit. A number of men were killed arround us. Had it not been for the timely arrival of the 6th Corps, the 3rd Corps would not have been able to hold them & a large number of prisoners would have fallen into the hands of the enemy. Our 1st Division went forward with a cheer & the enemy could not brake their lines. We held the battle ground. We lost between three & five hundred men. The enemy much more (we left the dead unburied, strange! We had ample time certainly to bury our own. I never wish to have our dead left in their care for the respect shown is limited. It is very probable they will never be buried.)

At one A.M. 28 Nov. we started for Wilderness Church. We marched until seven & finaly arrived at the very spot. How it could be found is more than I can imagine. We never left the woods from the time we started, a distance of twelve miles. Robisons Tavern is a noted place, one large hotell & some negro shanties. At nine it commenced raining and we to advance. Soon met the enemy & drove them back a number of miles. Finaly they made a stand. We did not attack in force but formed our lines & encamped for the night. Were called up at four A.M. 29th Nov & prepared to advance. The enemy during the night entrenched them selves so that it was hard to get at them. Skermished some during the day then formed a new line. All the reserve artilary was brought to the front & preparations made for a grand attack next day. The 2nd Corps was sent to the left to draw their force from our front which [they] did, [Lee] forming his lines in their sight. During the night Lee mooved a strong force from our front (we had not shown our force in our front.) At one A.M. 30 Nov we were orderd up to make no noise what ever not even speek a loud word, were marched into a piece of woods on the enemies extreme left flank to attack at break of day. A surprise moovement.

The 5th & 6th Corps were massed. The choicest troops of the army. It was a desperate moove & the very best troops were choosen. The Vermont Brigade was to lead the attack. The Regulars were on our left but at early light it was discoverd that the enemy had flooded the swamp so we could not waid it. Also driven sharpened stakes in the mud & placed abattis in front of the rifle pits. It was then decided not to attack. The 2nd Corps was to commence an attack on the left, make a great show then the 5th & 6th Corps secreted were to appear from the unsuspected position & carry evry thing before them. I think it would have been done had it not been for the swamp. All that night & day we were without fire. We never sufferd so much before. I was never so badly chilled before. The nights are extremely cold. At day we left the woods for the old camp we occupied in the morning previous, remain all night & next day. Dec 1st we were sent on picket, remain until relieved. At dark we left for the old camp. We left near the ford. Were marched all night & at eight A.M. Dec 2 marched one mile further & encamped for the night. The Brigade was rear guard. The enemy followed all the way. We drove in many straglers & the 2nd burnt evry house. It was all right in our view. Orders were not to burn but no one was left to prevent & so all was burnt. Next morning Dec 3 we marched to the old camp by way of Stephens Burg. Arrived at four P.M. At nine the enemy commenced to cross Raccoon Ford & we were held in readiness to meet the enemy. Dec 4 the enemy have not appeard. We are very tired & resting to day. I lost one man, a conscript, but found him & put him in the guard house where he will be court marshaled.

Frank held out well. Many of the men were made sick. Frank could not be transfered except by the War Department. I think it will be better in a long time to be where he is. A man must learn to live away from home &c. I was anxious to have him come in to my company but when he had been assigned it was next to impossible to change the assignment. The Regiment is a better one to be in than the 4th. ... Our thanksgiving prooved a ball with us attended by one sex. All the moovements were not particularly graceful or agreeable. ... Expect to moove somewhere soon, hope it will be winter quarters.

The next day, Francis described the fighting in a letter home from his less experienced perspective:

Since writing my last we have been on a campaign of eight days & there has been no opportunity to send out letters even if I had found time to write. I will not now attempt to give an account of our late moves respecting which you have no doubt informed yourself from the papers & will receive an account from Henry. What was the object of the move, whether or not it was

accomplished I can not tell. All of us suffered from exposure, want of food &
hard marching. We are now back to our old camp again but do not expect
to remain here long as our camp is hardly the place for winter quarters and
the movements of the enemy may render a change of position necessary. I
was within sound of the battle at Forest Grove. I am told that that is the
name of the place. There were four lines of battle formed in the field where
we were posted, two in front of ours & as they were needed they were called
into action. The two front lines were ordered to the front but night termi-
nated the conflict before we were needed. I saw many wounded born to the
rear. Many shells burst over our heads doing no injury. The cannonading &
musket firing was terrific. The 10th Vermont was called into action for the
first time since it has been in the service and lost between 60 & 70 killed &
wounded. Among the killed were James Stone of Montpelier, son of Deacon
Stone and Corporal Fay of Williamstown, shot through the head. I had seen
Fay once & anticipated many pleasant times in his society. His death must be
a loss to his family as well as to his company. If no mismove had been made
the slaughter of the 10th would not have been so great.

(Gardner Fay left behind a wife and three young sons. While his loss was no
doubt difficult for his family, they all successfully persevered. His wife received a
government pension until she remarried about ten years later. The sons all had successful careers with one even becoming a lawyer and judge in Barre.)

I intend writing as good an account of our campaign as I can for The Watch-
man which you can obtain and read. I have reced no letters or papers from
home for sometime now. This morning's mail, our first, brought me nothing.
... We are not paid off as we should have been & I am in need of money.
Please send me $6.00 in green backs. I limit myself to a certain allowance.
What my necessities seem to require. ... The box came to hand just before
our late move. The cookies & crackers were very acceptable but I was obliged
to eat them as soon as possible. If we were in winter quarters mince pies or
anything would be acceptable. The butter is excellent and I am very thank-
ful to Mother for her attention to my wants. ... The boots and gloves came
providentially as I should have suffered much without them. The boots were
rather tight at first & I could not have worn them with comfort at first with-
out applying the castor oil which has made them soft, pliable & water proof.
I wish you would buy a cheese for me & send part of it in the box you are
preparing for Henry & the remainder at some favorable time. I would be
glad if I had a pair of scissors. A needle book like that which Lorette made for
Henry is what I need. Give my love to all.

Passing these last two letters in transit was a letter from Ebenezer Bass, responding to Henry's letter of condolence concerning Eunice.

At last I seat myself to reply to your two unanswered letters with which you have favored me since you left here for your post of duty in the field. I find you are not ignorant of our late affliction, and of the lonely condition in which we are left. Although we have been called to bid adieu to our loved Eunice, and deposit her remains in the silent grave we have the consolation that we were permitted to have her with us where we could minister to her comfort, and console her in her last distressing days, and smooth her dying pillow and at last close her eyes in death, and lay her remains safely away beside her mother, brothers and sister on yonder Cemetery hill there with her kindred to crumble back to mother earth. We feel that she is at rest, and would not that she were with us to suffer as in her last days. It gives us satisfaction to feel that we spared no pains for her comfort in her weary pilgrimage down to her grave.

It gives me joy to recount the many rides I have taken with her over hill and through dale to relieve her suffering and prolong her days, and we feel greatful to you for your many kindnesses to her during your last stay at home. She enjoyed the many rides with you, but alas, she is gone and we tarry to toil on till the appointed day. Although my cup would seem nearly full and my days on earth well nigh run, yet my lot may not be more grievous to bear than some others and [I am ready]should it fall upon me to lay my all away on yonder hill, there to sleep till the last loud trump shall sound ... three of us are left while seven are gone, and soon we shall go to them. Our bell tolled Friday for Helen only daughter of Z. Walbridge. This morning for Orville his oldest son, both died of Diptheria, both suddenly. Orville was a student in Burlington Colledge. Old lady Staples yet lives while the young die, and all is a mystery to us.

Volunteering in this town drags heavily, but one enlisted and that a boy of sixteen, whom you do not know. We have raised a town bounty of $200 each, and have another meeting warned to raise an additional 100 to each man. Patriotism seems well nigh played out in this town but money enough may revive it. If not the draft will have to come.

After receiving this letter, Henry wrote a short letter home on December 12:

Last night I received a letter from Uncle Bass. ... Am on Court Marshal trying one of Co A's men for Desertion. ... I suppose you are having a snow storm at home today. It threatens here so I judge that it must be snowing at home. All are well. Boxes come direct to the Army now. Sutlers are pleanty & want the usual prices. A plot was discoverd. The sutlers that complained so biterly of the gerrilas were purposely captured & sold their loads to the enemy for green backs. A smart game. Reinlisting is going on quite smart in the Regiment. I fear the people at home will be disgusted with them selves.

People at home also remained concerned that the war might reach Vermont through Confederate raids from Canada. Lucy White, attending school in Burlington, wrote to Henry in December:

We have had a delightful winter so far with the exception of two or three days last week which reminded us that Jack Frost had not left the country, but we have not had snow enough for sleighing, but those who are fond of skating are very well pleased with the present state of the weather for it is very fine skating in the harbor and on the intervale. Everyone that skates thinks it very fascinating sport but for me I am sorry to say it has no charms. I attempted to skate only once and I'm sure I shall not again very soon.

About a month ago, I thought the seat of war would be transferred from the Potomac to Lake Champlain. One evening the news came that the Secessionists in Canada were making preparations to take Fort Montgomery at Rouses Point and from there come down Lake Champlain, burn Plattsburgh and Burlington and get all they could out of the yankees. The people were so frightened that they immediately sent to Washington to have some men sent here. The boats laid over here one day not daring to go farther north. I began to feel thankful that I had friends that lived among the mountains to whom I could flee if it was necessary.

Emma Ainsworth I hear has gone west. I am sorry for myself and Laura to for Williamstown is such a quiet place, but she is one that will make the best of it. There is a ladies relief association that meets every week to sew for the Sanitary Commission but we have been unusually busy for the last month making preparations for the fair at Boston and if it makes the soldiers any more comfortable we aut to bid it "God-speed.".

Emma Ainsworth was the older sister of Henry's fiancee, Laura.

After settling into his first winter camp, Francis wrote home in mid-December:

Since I last wrote we have moved from our old camp about 1 $^1/_2$ miles to a more healthy location where wood is more plenty. The 4th Vt was not moved. I have been very busy the past week preparing my tent for winter. My tent mates being unwell most of the work devolved upon me. We first made a frame work. Then drove down boards & slabs split from logs about four feet *in length leaving an opening on each side for the door, fire place and chimney. The chimney is laid up log house style & then plastered over with mud and usually stoned up in the inside. The mud usually cracks and then another coat must be put on. How these mud chimneys work in the long run I do not know. Our soldiers never made such before. I believe they took their first lessons from deserted rebel camps. The Virginia mud is of a redish color and of about the consistence of common clay. Henry has just called on me. He was summoned to attend a court martial as a witness to brigade head quarters which are near our Regt and so he stopped at my tent a short time. ... I should like to have you procure me a good cheese & put up a box of good butter which you can send with dried fruit & anything else you may think best. If I have more than I want I can easily dispose of it. I do not wish to put you to too much trouble but butter & cheese are highly prized here. The box can be directed to Henry. It is not convenient to carry a heavy box far, [but] it is best to have the box directed to a commissioned officer as it will not be so likely to be opened on the route.*

Let Lorette read Bunyan's Holy War which Henry will send you. It is an allegorical description of the fall of Satan, Man, his redemption from sin and Satan and the contest with sin and Satan in the renewed heart. The walls of the town of Mansoul represent the human body, the fortress the heart, and the different graces, passions, good & evil, divine, human and Satanic are represented or personified as men each having his appropriate name and doing his part in the work.

It is probable that the army will move soon, perhaps tomorrow. This afternoon Lt Col Stone addressed his men when on drill. Said "that he supposed that they all knew that if they were to meet the enemy this afternoon every man who could fire a gun would be expected to be at his post sick or well. That it was harder for the sick to get to the field but it was no worse for a sick man to be wounded than a well man. And the company officers must see that every man kept his place in the ranks. If captured by the Enemy a soldier might tell his Corps division, Brigade and Regiment but the enemy could compel him to disclose no more." These remarks indicate a battle is immediate prospect. I never felt more ready to go forward than now. Pray that I may quit myself like a man. I am in the hands of a wise, just and merciful God who will permit no real evil to happen to me if I trust him. I hope to escape unharmed but whatever occurs give yourself no trouble for all will be for the best.

In late December, Henry received a letter from his close friend and former classmate at Barre Academy, George Ainsworth. He had planned to return to serve with the Christian Commission, but that had not been possible due to the bad health of his brother and other relatives who worked in the family store.

The Ainsworth Store in Williamstown
Courtesy of Williamstown Historical Society

Several weeks ago I received a welcome letter from you and I intended to answer it ere this. I cannot forgive myself easily for an inexcusable delay in replying to letters from our soldiers. And I have felt that if one's correspondence was suffering from neglect it better not be that part connected with those in the Army for they above most of our friends need and deserve letters from their friends. ... When you went away Henry it did not occur to me that I should not <u>weeks</u> <u>ago</u> be with you all out there in the service of the "Commission." ... I have had quite a multitude of things to harass and occupy my mind. They are <u>little</u> trials tho', I feel, beside what you all are enduring & I know they ought not to be mentioned, or thought of hardly. I hope, tho', to get a few weeks to go to the Army this Winter for the Commission. I can go on a short warning for "all things are ready" about & think I may go now in a few days unless something comes up to keep me at home. ... We have watched with much anxiety your movements this Fall, and have heard with sorrow of your many hardships in your last campaign. For <u>your</u> sake we could wish you in Winter-quarters with as much as you could reasonably hope, to make you comfortable, *and give you rest of body, with perhaps furlough to come home and see your friends. Dec Jones we were all glad to see. People think he has improved much. He shows a great deal of modesty which amuses & pleases every one. He calls himself a private but Mr. Lynde says his papers show him a Sergt. I have been amused when people ask him about the number of battles he has been in, he will say that he does not know, he has not kept count, or that he has been in one. He might say __much__ more than he does and not overstep the bounds of modesty, but he keeps very far the other side of the truth about himself. ...*

Of Eunice's death you have heard, probably all the particulars. 'Twas a matter of consolation to all her friends that she was so ready & anxious to depart. I did not think she would go so soon. I was there the afternoon she died, and there seemed more of __heaven__ than of earth about her then tho' I did not suppose she would die that day. Let us all heed her message to her friends "to be ready to meet her in heaven." She was a __lovely__ girl. This afternoon I went sleigh riding with Lorette. We went down past the Springs. We spoke of the very delightful time we had with you and the others there last Summer. How I wish we might or may have many more such in life.

This evening there is a "war meeting" at the Town-Hall. I think there may be some volunteering this eve. Perhaps you will doubtless hear a report of the meeting soon if there is volunteering. We are very glad to hear Frank Martin "stands" soldiering so well. I __greatly__ feared he could not endure it. Give him much love & tell him we remember him and miss him very much, in our "social_meetings." Especially give my love to all our "boys." We were all very sorry to hear the sad news of Mr Fay's death. We mourn his loss and pity the bereaved wife and children left behind. God will not forget them, I am sure, and I trust we may not. (As I am writing here in our parlor, I hear stamping now and then in the Town-Hall which shows some "spirit" over there.) Well, Henry, I must close but let me say pardon my long delay, and write me again if you do not __see__ me soon.

Francis was indeed enduring army life quite capably, much to the surprise of those who knew him well. He affirmed this again in a December 20 letter:

I have had but little leisure of late although I have not been hard at work – I have not yet found the soldiers life an indolent one. Mother need not be worried about my hardships since the last campaign. I have seen some severe times and what awaits me I know not but the present is not a time of unusual hardship or suffering. It is Sunday today and not much like a home sabbath. The necessities of the soldier and the wont of conveniences give occasion for much

*labor for which there would be no call at home ... [but] the majority make no
effort to keep the day sacred.*

*We are now in winter quarters we suppose. There have been rumors that
we should be removed. This will not be done unless absolutely necessary and
we shall probably remain here. The second Vt. is in a camp by itself. Comfort-
abler shanties are built on each side of the company streets and viewed from
a short distance presents a very neat & pleasant appearance often receiving
complimentary comments from officers in other Corps & brigades. I do not
know what my health will be next spring but at present it is better than when
at home. I have an excellent apetite am not at all troubled with dyspepsia and
am steadily gaining strength. I have some rheumatic pains at times to which
I am unaccustomed and which may trouble me in future. Our rations are
good with a greater variety than we have had before often drawing potatoes,
& sometimes dried apples. When I can obtain it I procure condensed milk to
mix with my coffee which makes it – in my opinion – quite as rich and good
as that we have at home. The coffee which is issued to the Soldiers is probably
superior to any that we get at home. ... The boys are constantly receiving boxes
from home. I hope you will send me the box I requested you to in my last and
put in as much butter and cheese as you think best for I can easily dispose of it
at 50 & 60 cents per pound. Please send a bunch of envelopes.*

Coffee had become a very important commodity in the Army of the Potomac.
Paul Zeller relates that during that long and difficult march to Mine Run, soldiers
of the Sixth Corps, who had been marching for many hours without a pause, began
chanting the word "coffee," ignoring the repeated objections of their officers.
Finally, the officers relented, and a coffee break was permitted. Also, Henry mentioned in an earlier letter that when a flag of truce was offered between the enemy
combatants, they would often trade coffee for tobacco. Some historians have even
maintained that the coffee and tea helped the soldiers avoid water-borne illnesses
since the water was usually boiled. As for the condensed milk, Gail Borden had
only recently, in 1856, been granted a patent for his process of creating it. The War
Department evidently saw it as a safe way to provide a dairy product to the men
with less likelihood of spoilage. The soldiers immediately found it to their liking
and, upon returning home, praised its qualities to family and friends. Condensed
milk began producing great profits for Borden.

Christmas was approaching in the winter camp of the Army of the Potomac,
but the army was becoming even less merciful towards deserters. Henry wrote
home about an incident on December 21:

Last friday was an unlucky day for two deserters, who were shot to death by musketry. One was from the 2nd deserted in presence of the enemy at Gettisburg & sold himself a number of times as a substitute, was finaly caught, & tried by General Court Marshal & sentenced to be shot. Two thirds of the court in favor of shooting. The man from the 5th was a rascal & has met a just fate, the ceremonies I mentioned in a letter to Lorett a few days since. Perhaps you may not see it so I will give a description of the ceremonies of an execution. Just so much of the Division was to be present as could be without damage to the service. At the appointed hour the Division was marched to a place where a grave had been dug & all could see were formed on three sides of the grave. Then General Howe & staff took position in the center of Division & waited for the guard to bring the prisoners. Finaly the ambulances appeared containing each one man & his coffin, were carried oposite their grave. There they left the ambulances, placed the coffins beside the grave, the prisoners taking position at the head of the grave & coffin. The chaplains prayed, their sentences were read & then the men were ordered to kneel on top of their coffins facing the Division. Targets of white paper were placed uponst their hearts, their hats taken off. All being ready the guard was marched so as to front the deserters. The guard was into two squads each numbering ten men. Next came the execution. The command was given, ready aim fire. Both instantly fell, pitching forward off their coffin. One died instantly. The other lived nearly thirty moments. It was an awful sight, worse than any battle. I think it will have an excellent effect on men meditating desertion in the future. One of my men was tried for desertion but plead not guilty & the court did not find him guilty of desertion but absent without leave & sentenced him to forfeit one months pay, to pay the thirty dollars cost of arrest, pay for all government property lost which amounted to twenty eight dollars. Also to serve one month after the expiration of the term of service of the rgt. Finally to stand on a barrel in a conspicuous [place] in the regiment for ten days, two hours in the fournoon & two in the afternoon. Rather humiliating sentence but a cheep one. All deserters are deserving the full finality of the law. How about the enlistment at home. Is your quota full? Why don't the towns raise more money. Three hundred dollars is no account. The nine months men have the same bounty offered as the old men who have served two years & received nothing. This looks very wrong. Old soldiers to shed their blood for love of liberty & family & in defence of their homes without pay. They can do it, have done it & at this present time the old men are reenlisting by hundreds. It looks well but is doing injustice to their breathern at home. They want a chance to serve their country & should not be prevented by any of the old men taking their place.

I never saw men more dispirited when they learned what the people at home were resorting to to get volunteers &c. &c.

Many do not think this war can continue two years longer & it does not seem to me. If Grant gets to Atlanta Lee is placed in between two fires & must retreat. If we can hold them this winter their sufferings will be so great that it will be almost impossible to hold their army together. Davis says every man must bear arms to check the advance of the union armies. The Richmond Enquirer says Davis has virtualy proclaimed himself a dictator. They think that to be more than they bargained for when they commenced the war. I never before saw such signs of destitution as on the last campaign. All that was found in the rebel haversacks was corn and a little hard bread. The prisoners said it was issued to them the same as to the mules but corn will make a good soldier. He can live on it & grow fat. Still it looks like rather hard times. Certainly our army would think it so & they would think right.

We expect to move camp in a few days to better convenience for wood & water. Both are scarce here. The ground freezes every night. The new men think it very cold. We tell them that we were campaigning until a month from this date last year but we suffered very much. The fall has been very favorable for soldiers. Very little rain has fallen so the mud time has not come. We expect it every day if we do not have it this fall we expect it in the spring. I see by the news papers that campaigns are planned to commence next February. Rather too early for successful movements. Past experience has taught every general in the army of the Potomac that it is of no use. Co. B have an excellent detail and a busy one too. Captain Pratt is now recruiting from the Brigade. The inducements held out are $409.00 dollars government bounty, the bounty their respective towns are paying, also the state pay & thirty days furlough to serve three years from the time they are recruited. Many enlist just for the thirty days furlough, so anxious are they to get home. I fear they will repent the day they took so inconciderate a step, but they are old soldiers, have had a long experience & know what they are enlisting for and let the hardships be what they may they must not grumble. ... About thirty of Co. A have reinlisted, will go home this week.

Henry wrote one more letter before the year ended. This one, on December 30, was addressed to the army:

Sirs, I have the honor to express my willingness in compliance with General Orders War Dept. to continue in the U.S. Volunteer Service three years or during the war after my present term of service expires.

The year 1863 had come to an end. The war, however, continued to rage.

Chapter 13

THE HANDSOMEST CAMP
ANYONE EVER SAW

In Williamstown, on New Years Day, 1864, people opened their newspapers and saw what by now had become a familiar sight. A dispatch had arrived from "Conscript," dated December 21, from "Camp near Brandy Station, Va."

Mr. Editor:—The descriptions of life in camp commenced by your correspondent in his last, have already been interrupted by one of those episodes which, in time of war, are not of uncommon occurrence, and which should have been presented to the readers of the Journal ere this, had not other duties of more immediate importance prevented.

On the 24th of November, before light, we received orders to pack up all but our tents and hold ourselves in readiness to move at day break. Morning dawned upon us, ushering in the day with a drizzling rain, our knapsacks were packed, the mules harnessed and hitched to the supply wagons, and the army in readiness to move, but at 10 A.M., the order was countermanded and not repeated until Thursday the 26th. Then we were roused at 4 A.M. and at 8 o'clock A.M., turned our backs upon our camp, bidding it, as we supposed, a final farewell, and moved further onward towards the heart of rebeldom. Our march was slow and tedious, owing to the frequent and long stops we were obliged to make to allow the trains to come up. At midnight, we crossed the Rapidan at Jacob's Ford, ascended the heights on the opposite side, and at 1 A.M. spread our blankets and camped down for the night, having made only about 12 miles. At 3:30 A.M. we were awakened by the revielle, and had hardly time to kindle our fires and cook our breakfast before we received orders to advance. Our march, like that of the day before, was slow, with frequent rests. Before noon we halted in the woods, a few miles from the river, where we remained the greater part of the day, awaiting further orders. Cannonading and musket firing on our right front were heard during the entire day. Late in the afternoon, it became heavier and more incessant, eliciting the remark from a comrade that "death and glory were busy." Long lines of infantry, and now and then a battery, passed us on their way to the front, but our turn did not come until about 4 o'clock, P.M. Then we advanced out of the wood into an open field, within hearing distance, though not in sight of the battle-ground of Orange grove; – a place which was receiving its baptism of blood and must henceforward be of historic importance.

Here the new men began to see for the first time some of the realities of war. Shells were constantly traversing the air, some bursting in front, some in the rear, and some overhead. The burning fuse told us when they were coming, and this was followed in a few seconds by the explosion. Wounded men, borne on stretchers, or, if not too severely injured, assisted by one or two of their comrades, or making the best of their way alone, were constantly passing to the rear. The firing, both of cannon and musketry, was terrific. Three times we heard the cheers of our men as they charged upon the rebels posted behind a stone wall, as we afterwards learned.

Three times they were repulsed, when our batteries opened, speedily demolishing the rebel works, which were then easily carried. We stood in line of battle, anxiously watching the progress of events. Once, when a lot of pioneers, musicians and stragglers came double quick to the rear, we feared that our forces were being repulsed; but as the sound of the battle constantly grew more distant, we concluded that the enemy were being driven. There were two lines of battle in front of us, both of which were called into action; but night put an end to the conflict before our turn came. After dark we began to build small fires, which our officers first commanded us to extinguish, and then permitted us to keep them up until our suppers were cooked, when we spread our blankets – some of us upon the damp ground, but others including myself, upon rails, which we laid out for that purpose – and slept soundly until 1:30 A.M. when we were called up and marched a few miles through the woods to the open country, when we halted and breakfasted at daybreak. Then we moved on a few miles through fields overgrown with weeds and briar vines, or covered with young pines. A constant fusilade was kept up by the skirmishers, and continued through the day; now and then we heard a report, or succession of reports, from some of our batteries. As we neared the pine woods from which the sound of firing proceeded we formed in line of battle, and then advanced into the woods, where we halted, stacked arms and remained exposed to a drizzling rain until dark, when Co. F was ordered on to the picket line. We lay with the reserve through the night and until 2 o'clock P.M. the next day, when we were ordered forward to the picket line, divided into reliefs, and posted when our turns came. I was on the first relief posted behind a tree and was instructed to shoot any man that I might see coming from the rebel side, and then, if necessary, fall back to the next tree. A few rods in front was a road concealed from my sight by bushes, which, however, were of insufficient height to hide passengers. I was told by my Sergeant that possibly, though not probably, I might see horsemen moving up or down the road, and that "unless I was very sure that they were friends, I must fire on them." I remained at my post some time, hearing and seeing nothing, but presently I heard the clatter of horses' hoofs coming down the road, and soon an officer, wearing the United States uniform, rode past. Being very certain that he was not a rebel, I did not fire, and soon after I learned that he was our Adjutant. My next relief was from 10 o'clock P.M. until 12. After coming back from my post I wrapped myself in my blanket under a shelter of rails covered with fine boughs with my feet to the fire in front, and endeavored to obtain much needed rest but soon received the order from our Lieut. to be ready to fall in and go out on the skirmish line. The regiment was spread out as it advanced, the men being posted at distances of five paces. The first took their stations in an open field on the outskirts of the woods we had just left. Here, we afterwards learned, the rebels first became aware of our movements. Our company was stationed behind a rail fence on a hillside overlooking a meadow extending about three-fourths of a mile to the hills on the opposite side. Our orders were "to keep awake and lay as still as possible that the rebels might not get knowledge of our position." The night was bitter cold, and getting thoroughly chilled, we first wrapped ourselves in our blankets, and kept up a continual thumping with our feet to keep from freezing. This proving of no avail, one after another left his post and commenced double quicking to and fro inside of the fence. At daybreak a rifle ball from a barn about three-fourths of a mile distant whistled over our heads, and we at once received orders to fall back to our posts and to lie low. The first shot which was fired struck an Italian belonging to our company, making a slight flesh wound, giving him much alarm, and causing him to give utterance to his most common expression "plenty, plenty." Most of the balls fell short, striking the ground just below our heads. One whizzed directly over your correspondent, causing him to dodge involuntarily with his active body, an effect which had never been produced by a shell. It was very annoying while laying in the cold, to see the rebel sharpshooters retire to a house in the rear of the barn where they were posted, to warm themselves, and then return and keep us quiet by a constant fire. Soon we were drawn back into the woods *in the rear, a little to the left of our old position, where we remained without fires, and many of us without rations, through the entire day. Cannonading was heard in the morning and more or less musket firing, but the anticipated battle failed to come off for reasons with which you readers must already be acquainted. After sundown we moved on a few miles and encamped in a pine forest, where we remained until sundown the next day. Then advancing about four miles at 10 P.M., we encamped for the night. At four o'clock the next morning, Wednesday, Dec. 2d, we resumed our march, recrossing the Rapidan at Germania Ford, at 10 o'clock A.M. moved on past the deserted rebel works, turned into the woods in the afternoon, where just after dark rations of fresh beef were issued to us, the more acceptable because there were but few of us who had not consumed their supply of hard tack, and had been marching for the day past on the strength of coffee without sugar. We left our camp the next morning at 7 o'clock A.M. marched rapidly past Brandy Station, and arrived at our old camp again, after an absence of eight days.*

Your correspondent soon found the site of his old tent, with the charred and half consumed back-log in front, ready to form the base of another fire, whose cheerful blaze and genial warmth with a cup of hot coffee and a dinner eaten with a soldier's appetite, soon drove away the remembrance of past hardships and aroused the home feeling, which even the soldier enjoys when he feels that a campaign is ended and sees his old camp again.

The foregoing is a very imperfect account of the part borne by your correspondent in the late campaign. Many interesting incidents have been omitted for want of time, but as your readers have borne with me thus far, pleading their charity again, I subscribe myself, CONSCRIPT

On that same New Year' Day, Henry received a missive that must have seemed like a belated Christmas present:

Head Quarters 6th Army Corps
January 1st, 1864
Special Orders No 1

In accordance with Par 2 Sc 331 A of P the following named Officers of the 4th Vermont Vols will accompany the reenlisted men of their Regiment to the State of Vermont and return with them at the expiration of their furloughs.

2nd Lieut. Wm H. Martin
by Command of Maj Gen'l Sedgwick
(signed) Maj T. McMahon

Francis also wrote home on the holiday:

Yours of December 21st has been received. I am now looking for the box which will probably come through soon for all the Express does now. It is not at all likely that we shall move from here before Spring. There was some talk of moving because so many of the reenlisted men in the old regiments would go home on furloughs that enough would not be left to sustain our present line & it would be necessary to fall back to Warrenton or Centerville where the lines would be shorter. Our officers did not like to move the men after they were once established in comfortable quarters and this with unfavorable weather probably prevented the contemplated change. As it is we shall have more of picketing and guard duty to do than if we had moved. The location of our camp is said to be unhealthy but I do not know as there is an unusual amount of sickness in the regiment and my own health is as good as usual. I am quite fleshy as is usually the case during the winter season.

I have been coppying the descriptive list of the reenlisted men for Liut Bailey for a few days past but have finished the job. I think that I should prefer such work to picketing and the like but do not know whether it would be as well for my health or not. ... I have not seen Henry Smith yet. When at Cedar Mountain I saw John Green at Henry's tent and was intending to go over to his Company the next morning if we did not move but we were under marching orders during the day & our retreat was made the next night. Afterwards camp duties & the like usually kept me in my Company and when I went over to the 4th to see Henry I never had an opportunity to see Henry Smith without going over to the other end of the regt as Co A occupies the front & Co B the rear. Henry has never called to see me and the principle reason why I have not taken more pains to see him is because I should be likely to meet Charles Lynde & John Green there and it is unpleasant for me to meet either of them. Mother asks if I have no religious society here? I do not know as I have met with more than one religious or even moral man – (Mr Fay whose company was a treat for me) since I came out. Better men than myself may find opportunities for doing good here but the subject of religion is one to which I seldom wish to make allusion here. Our Soldiers are not ignorant on this subject but they do not care to talk on it nor do they wish to govern themselves by the precepts of the Bible.

Only two days passed before Francis wrote again, this time thanking his mother specifically:

I have just received the box you sent me and now will endeavor to make some expression of my gratitude which I hope will in part repay you for your kindness and for the trouble it must have occasioned you to prepare so many delicasies and comforts for me. It is not probable that we shall leave this camp before the first of April next and were it not for doing picket and guard duty, the good rations which are issued to us, the articles we receive from home and our warm houses would make our situation both comfortable and pleasant. Our camp seen from the neighboring hills with its regular and clean streets and houses with thier white canvass roofs presents a beautiful appearance and many say that "it is the handsomest camp they ever saw." None of these things make the army seem like home but they make the soldiers condition more pleasant. I am much oblijed to Lorette for the present she made me. It is what every soldier needs. All the articles put up by you are very acceptable. The jelly, honey, dried apple cookies and bread are as good as I could ask for. The butter is excellent and packed as it is will keep sweet and last me a long time. The cheese is good. The pan cakes were just what I was wishing for. ... I send you a bag of our Army coffee which I have on hand. It may need burning a little but I think you will find it superior to that you have been accustomed to use.

Henry's visit will no doubt be a surprise. I hope it will be a pleasant one for you all. Henry's position in the army is a good one, and I think that there are none who will not say that he fills it well. If my health improves, I presume that I shall have an easier & better place some time but I am in no haste for I wish to do nothing which I cannot do well. I have endured many extreme hardships since I joined the army but cannot say that I am sorry that I came. Though deprived of many priviliges, especially religious priviliges, there is no need of a man's suffering in a moral point of view, while the more manly traits of character and all the common sense that he possesses is drawn out, he need not be the less refined and moral. In my own case, if I find health here, then it is the place for me for I could not obtain it at home. How this will be time alone can determine.

Besides his army duties, Francis was also busy working on another Conscript article, this time describing in precise detail how they built their winter quarters. It was published in the *Vermont Watchman* on January 22.

Camp Near Brandy Station, Va.
Jan. 7, 1864.

Mr. Editor.— Many of the regiments on their return from their last campaign across the Rapidan, were allowed to re-occupy their old quarters, where they could prepare for winter, finishing what they had begun, or enjoying the benefit of what they had already completed; but the 2d Vt. owing to the unhealthy location of its camp, its contiguity to other regiments, whose united wants for fuel and building purposes would too soon exhaust the already scanty supply of timber in their immediate vicinity, and perhaps for other and weightier reasons not known by your correspondent, remained at the old camp no longer than was necessary to look up a more favorable location; this was found about one and one half miles eastward, and at 9 o'clock A.M. the 5th of December, with well filled knapsacks, and loaded with articles of convenience or comfort which could not be packed inside our knapsacks, for we were going as we supposed into winter quarters, and it was no longer necessary as upon previous marches, to divest ourselves of every superfluous weight, we moved to the place chosen as the site of our new camp. Immediately on our arrival we received instructions from the Colonel to build our shanties at least nine feet in length, at distances of four feet, with their sides facing the company streets, doors in front and chimney in the rear. After making selection of building spots, those who had axes commenced cutting poles or splitting out slabs; where poles were used they were laid up log house style, and the interstices filled with mud, but the split slabs were usually driven perpendicularly into the ground. The former way is the most expeditious, but the latter, all things considered, is to my mind preferable. An opening was always left in the rear of the shanty, generally opposite the door, for fireplace and chimney. The dimensions of the fire place differ of course according to the ideas of their different architects, but they are usually about two feet wide and extended about two and a half feet outside the shanty. A frame work of split slabs or small logs laid up and locked together log house style, is made extending as high as the eaves of the shanties, and here the chimney begins, which is laid up in the same style to any desirable height, growing smaller and smaller toward the top, which is often surmounted by a barrel. The inside is well plastered with Virginia mud, first worked over until it attains the consistency of good mortar. Two or three coats may be required, as it cracks in drying; when dry it is as hard as stone, and fire proof. Many use nothing but mud for the inside of their fire places, and for this reason where the mud cracks, it is no uncommon thing for the wood work of the chimney to take fire. The safest way is to line the fire place with stone. To secure a good draught, the fire place should be laid up perpendicularly about three feet and then drawn in five or six inches. When the house is finished and covered with its canvass roof, and a warm fire blazes in its fire place, the soldier has but little reason to complain on the score of comfort, while the pure air he inhales is healthier by far than that of the close overheated rooms of home.

The above description is prefatory to the account of my own first experience as a house builder. When we arrived at our new campground, the Orderly pointed out a spot at the front end of the Company street, where he said I could build. Soon one of my tent mates was detailed on fatigue duty for one of the company officers, and the other went back to the old camp to obtain some articles which had been left behind, while I remained to take charge of our knapsacks, accoutrements &c., and to make observations and do what work I could. As I had no axe of my own and of course could not borrow one so long as its owner stood in need of its services, all that could be done was to pitch my shelter tent, and be in readiness to improve the first opportunity that might present itself. The next day I was detailed to carry timbers for the Captain's tent; in the meantime the best timber in the immediate neighborhood of the camp was fast disappearing, while some rheumatic pains, and a severe cough occasioned by lying on the ground and exposure to the night air, warned me to make such preparations as the increased severity of the weather required, without delay. Still no axe could be procured, and the stock of building materials we obtained with our hatchet was limited to a few poles for posts, plates and string pieces, and the bed, with a few boards and slats taken from a picket fence; with our poles we made the frame work of the house, consisting of four posts four feet in height, with plates nine feet and string pieces six feet in length but without sills. Our boards were then cut in lengths of about 4 1/2 feet, driven into the ground six inches, and nailed at the top to the plates and string pieces. These with the pickets covered the front side and one end. At last we were fortunate enough to procure an axe with which we split out slabs what we needed, and carried them on our shoulders to the camp – no small task. We now began to set the time when our house would be completed, but were doomed to be disappointed, for it extended about one-half its length beyond the range of the shanties at the end of the Company streets, which arrangement was dissatisfactory to the Colonel, who gave orders for its removal. This was irritating; we did not like to lose our labor, nails were scarce and we hardly knew where to look for more to refasten our stockade, but a little consideration showed that it would be unnecessary to undo much of our work. The posts only needed loosening, a few of the stockades were knocked off, and then after running two poles across the ends underneath the plates, with a little extra assistance we carried it safely to a vacant spot on the same side and about middle way, or one half of the distance of the street. Our trials did not end here; sickness deprived me of the assistance of my tent mates, and the bulk of the work devolved upon me. Still persevering under difficulties, the work progressed, and on the night of the 14th I had *the satisfaction of lodging in a shanty which for neatness, convenience and comfort, would bear favorable comparison with any one in the Company. If any of your readers doubt this, let them come and see for themselves.*

On a clear day, seen from the neighboring hill, the Camp of the 2d Vt., with its regular and well policed streets and neat canvass roofed houses, presents a beautiful appearance. Strangers often mistake it for a Brigade Camp, and all concur in declaring it one of the finest camps they have ever seen.

I have perhaps described some things too minutely for the patience of your readers, but the world is made up of little things, and I offer no apology.
CONSCRIPT.

Winter quarters at Brandy Station, VA 1864
Courtesy of Library of Congress

A few days after his article was published, on January 26, Francis wrote home:

I have just reced yours of the 4th also one from Henry beering date the 19th. I am glad to hear that he is having so pleasant a time at home. I had been looking for a letter from home for some time and had begun to have some feelings – not eaxactly of anxiety – but such as one will have when expected and desired letters are delayed. ... On many accounts I should like to be at home. There is of course less of danger and better opportunities to recruit one's strength after undergoing necessary hardships to say nothing of the quiet that we always associate with the thought of home and the fact that the assistance of a son is needed by you. I have never regretted joining the army. I think it was the best thing for me that I could have done, though the necessity which called me forth is to be regretted. I have indeed endured remarkably and *am now more fleshy than, or at least as fleshy as I usually am at this season at home. This is to be accounted for by the fresh air, plain food, and on the whole, lighter work I have had. Whether I shall endure the warm season and the hardships of the coming campaign time alone will determine. It may be my lot to fall on the battle field, for this I should be prepared, and suffer no uneasiness, for do what we will we are only accomplishing our destiny and if we have the assurance that if we are <u>God's</u> children, we may rest satisfied that these same fixed events which go to make up our destiny whatever be their present character are still for our own highest good. Charles Lynde called to see me yesterday. We had quite a pleasant interview. I would write more respecting it if I had room on this sheet.*

(After the war, Francis and Henry's cousin, Charles Lynde, returned to Williamstown and married Alice Martin, who was also their cousin. Within five years after the marriage, Charles contracted small pox and died in 1872. Alice died eight years later at the age of 36.)

If Henry thinks best he may bring me my hat when he returns. I am out of envelops & for some time have borrowed all I have used. My corespondence is not very extensive but I have other than home letters to write, and had rather not get envelopes at the sutlers as they cost 25 cents a bunch. I would like a box of Ayer's Pills. I do not often take medicine of any kind but at this season it is sometimes needed & I do not choose to call on the surgeon. I would also like some two cent stamps so that I can send papers home if I choose. The weather is pleasant now. The mud is fast drying up & it seems very much like April in Vermont.

February arrived and Henry began making preparations for his return, contacting the Tilestons in Hopkinton and arranging to visit them on February 6. Francis wrote a letter home on that day:

I have just received a letter from you. Also one from Henry. I am always glad to hear from home. I have not as you expect left Virginia yet and have only once heard that there was any probability of our moving at present. I am told that General Humphrey said not long since that while we were liable to move at any time, we might remain here until next July. At this season I would think anything like a long march out of the question. The ground is not dry enough for the transportation of artillery, supply waggons &c. I am glad that Henry had so pleasant a visit and am sorry that he should be obliged to leave you at all. If I could be to you all that a son should be I should choose to be at home with you rather than in the army. I seemed to be called here by divine providence and do not regret the call but the war which renders this necessary is to be deplored. The good which is to be accomplished by it is chiefly for those yet unborn and many who take part in the strife doing what God will accept as their duty will not receive the reward of their labor here. That man is happy who so lives as to receive a reward in the world to come.

I hope you will be able to carry on your business without working too hard. What do you do with the willows you cut last fall? I have answered this sooner than I should to let you know that I am here. I hope that Henry will yet return to his home to relieve you of your burdens and to enjoy that home you & mother have labored so hard to prepare. As for myself, I hope to see home again but never until I deserve the name of a wise, brave & good man & Soldier. Without this I never wish to see Vt again. Henry has already earned this.

We have recd marching orders this morning. Where we should move, I do not know.

While Henry was back in Williamstown, Francis composed his next newspaper article which was published in early February. He began with a long quote that he had seen recently concerning the enormous power felt by any soldier on picket duty, greater than "any monarch on a throne." Francis chose to show the more practical reality of this duty.

CAMP NEAR BRANDY STATION, Va.,
    January 1864

Although I acknowledge their truth, I cannot say that I have ever been wrought up to that sublimity of feeling which would produce thoughts of a corresponding nature. The more immediate wants of the soldier—the events which transpire around him—his comforts and discomforts, after the novelty of the thing is gone, usually occupy his mind to the exclusion of ideas of a more abstract and elevated character. In cold or stormy weather he associates with the mention of picketing, recollections of the temporary loss of dearly purchased comforts in camp, too short but tiresome marches through the mud or over rough-frozen ground—long dull hours on post, nights of exposure on the support when sleep only comes by snatches, and perhaps it is the part of prudence not to sleep at all, while a severe cold, possibly, fever and a season in the hospital terminate the vista, or when the weather is favorable, a few days of comparative freedom from military discipline, and rest from camp duties. I do not know the exact distance of the picket line from our camp; it is variously estimated by the boys who are called out, the generality thinking it about three or four miles, probably three and one-half is a correct estimate.

A detail of four privates is made from each company in the regiment for three days; they are notified in the evening, and the next morning at 8 o'clock are marched to the relief of those previously detailed. Your correspondent can tell but little of picket life from actual experience, having been detailed but three times, and only once on three days picket. As his turn drew near, some feelings of an unpleasant character in prospect of a disagreeable duty with which he was as yet but little acquainted very naturally presented themselves, but both the dictates of wisdom and the desire of happiness requiring that they should not be entertained, they were promptly dismissed. In due time the Orderly appeared at the door of my tent with the words, "picket at 8 o'clock to-morrow morning, three days ration," and then closing the door, went on to notify others. I, at once, packed enough for three days in my haversack and knapsack, a little more perhaps than Uncle Sam's allowance, of eleven hardtacks and a piece of beef or pork per day. In the morning I was up earlier than usual, and after cooking and eating my breakfast, folding and packing a rubber and woolen blanket inside my knapsack, and strapping my overcoat on the top, I was ready for the order, "picket fall in." A new soldier, though less efficient, is usually more faithful and conscientious than one who has seen more service, at least he has a more nervous apprehension of being behind in any duty. At the command I and another were in the street—"hurry up, men," brought out a third, but the fourth man did not appear—"come, hurry up, hurry up" said the Orderly, "I'm in a terrible hurry." "I'd like to know who's in a bigger hurry than I," was the reply. "Stop your fooling and come along," said the Orderly. "Come along!" I guess I shall pack up first, if it takes from now till next Thursday, said the soldier, who did not intend to be cheated out of his sleep, breakfast and necessary provisions, or be left behind, as he came out of his tent fully accoutered and fell in with the rest. We then joined those detailed from other companies, in front of the Colonel's tent, come to a front, counted off by twos, and at the command "right face, march," took our places and marched to the brigade headquarters where we were joined by details from other regiments, and then proceeded to the picket line. Arriving at our place of destination, as many of us as were needed were left in companies of four at the different posts; from each post a vidette is sent out who is relieved by another after standing two hours. The vidette is instructed to allow no one to cross the lines with a pass except the *officer of the day, and to salute commissioned officers. While walking my beat but one event occurred to attract my attention. The command "Sentinel, face to the front, and stand to attention with shouldered arms," aroused me from a reverie to make the customary salute to the officer of the day accompanied by a captain, as they rode past. "That will do, sir," said the captain, as soon as the order was obeyed, and I resumed my walk. On post my time was occupied cutting wood for the fire and peeling a hickory stick for a tent broom. After remaining at the post 24 hours, we were relieved and went back to the support, where we passed the remainder of the time for which we were detailed. At the support, where the reserves are assembled, one has a better opportunity for forming acquaintances from other companies and regiments and of seeing them in their intercourse with one another, than in camp where his circle of acquaintances does not extend much beyond his own company. Here the different classes of men who compose the army are well represented and he meets with some serving in the ranks, or as commissioned and non-commissioned officers, of good or superior abilities, and in their conversation evincing more or less cultivation of mind. There too are those just emerging from boyhood— some just commencing soldier's life and others who have been with the army since its organization and tho' hardly out of their teens, may justly claim the title of veteran soldiers—associated with grey haired men already past the prime of life, almost invariably fine looking, fine appearing, intelligent men. Some having received their early training in schools, others supplying the lack of book learning by native shrewdness, observation and that experience in life with the same disposition which at last brought them into the army, in previous life called into exercise and gave opportunity for development, and all having acquaintance with human nature, a degree of independence, composure and self-command, which is not often acquired in any school than the army with its discipline of enforced obedience and of trial in camp on the march and battle-field.*

    Conscript.

By February 11, Henry was back in camp and wrote his first letter home:

I am once more seated at my table which I left five weeks since. Evrything seems as when I left. Was detailed Officer of the day the first night I arrived in camp. The Officers have had a hard time since I left for home having all our duty to do and they were glad to see us on that account if for nothing else.

    I have not seen Frank yet. I have been so full of business have all my returns to make out for the time I have been away. The Captain is not in

Command so I have all the work to do alone as before. Shall be very busy for some time to come.

The men are re-enlisting very fast in the 2nd Vt. also through the Brigade. Henry Wilson enlisted today & a number of others.

(Henry Wilson survived the war and returned home to Williamstown but contracted tuberculosis and died in 1867.)

Had a very pleasant visit at Hopkinton & a pleasant journey to my post of duty. Spent one day in Washington with Mr. Smith. On the tenth I went to the front. All was quiet. The men said they had escaped one march, some consolation. On the late reconnisance to ascertain whether the enemy had left or not, it was found that there were rebils enough to fight certainly one big battle. The forces that forded the river came very near being anihialated.

Mr. Smith thinks Vermont stock would be better for me. ... He will inform me soon what it is best for me to do &c. Mr. Ainsworth said that there was a chance to invest in the State loan at six percent. If so perhaps it would be best to invest a little there and not have my business so far from home. ... My expences were 4.50 ticket to Boston, 2.50 lodging meals, .50 cents for transportation about the City, .50 transportation to the Depot, 2.05 ticket from Hopkinton to Springfield, .25 ride to Cordsville Depot, Amount 10.30. Had better success then I expected. The man [Charles Asp] is in a law suit . ... I urged hard & he finaly paid one hundred. I think him an honest man.

Mr. Smith is trying to look up my lost check. Will write soon concerning his success. The weather has changed & is quite cold. All are well. Kind regards to all my friends. I think of nothing more to write this evening so good night.

Francis wrote home again on February 13:

I suppose that it is very lonely for you and Mother since Henry's return. I saw him this morning and received from him the pie that Mother sent. It was very nice. I have seen nothing that would bear comparison with it since I left Vt. I do not wish to be understood by this as conveying the idea that we do not have plenty of good and wholesome rations in the Army for this is not the case. What we miss most is butter & cheese and when in winter quarters the soldiers are seldom without either, obtaining them from home or from the Sutlers. You are probably aware before this that we have not moved from our camp yet and do not expect to at present.

I fear that you are working too hard for your health or comfort. I would do no more than is necessary. I would not peel the willows this year. If I were at home it would make a difference. The profit may be less, if you send them to Waterbury than if you have good luck in peeling them yourself, but this is of no account at all in comparison [to] the labor and trouble it will occasion you and I advise you by all means to send them to Waterbury and make the best disposal of them there you can.

I hope Mother was pleased with the letter I wrote her for I would wish it to excite pleasant rather than sad feelings. Mother believes in predestination and though I am the responsible agent, my past life is still the accomplishment of the divine purpose. A divine providence has placed me where I now am for my highest good if I am a child of God. With the belief which I entertain and situated as I am I cannot look with indifference on the dangers of the campaign and battle field & to meet them calmly and with the assurance of a good conscience, I must be ready for death or whatever may await me. I cannot like many say that I have a presentiment that I shall live or die but I hardly expect to return to my old home again. Henry may and I hope he will if you ever stand in need of him. While we are absent I advise you to make your work as easy as possible and if you need assistance from either of us we will gladly render such as we can give. I inclose my Ambrosetype which I presume bears some resemblance to though it may not be a perfect picture of myself. Give my respects to Mr. Carleton & say to him that I thank him for the present he wished to make. Write often.

Francis's health remained remarkably good despite the cold weather, as he indicated in his next letter, on February 20:

I have just received your last. I have just returned to camp from three days picket. It was very cold for Virginia the first two days and the third night but I have not taken cold and am not much the worse for my extra exposure. My general helth has been better since I joined the army than when at home and if I could get rid of that feeling of wearyness which has troubled me for years I could do better for myself here than in any other place. Whether I shall ever recover all that vigor of body and mind which all ought to possess at my age I cannot even conjecture.

I have lately attended a bible class a few times, held in a tent belonging to the Christian commission located at a battery camp not far from our own. So far as obtaining instruction, other than one will naturally obtain from reading the bible carefully with others, I cannot say that I have received any. The gentleman who presides is a presbyterian and orthodox enough in his sentiments to satisfy you I think. Some of the members of his class have entertained a hope for years, others have just obtained a hope. Some are well informed and others have comparatively no learning but all exhibited that desire to know the truth & that trust in God's word & in his people which characterizes Christians especially those who are just commencing a Godly life and have not learned to distrust almost every one. The second time that I attended a clergyman from a neighboring camp was present. While there a boy came in and our teacher informed the minister that he was a drummer boy who had attended his (the clergyman's) meetings and had found the Savior and then asked if he knew him but he did not. Thus a work of grace can [go] unperceived. I enjoy myself in the society of Christians. It is not known in my Company that I entertain a hope & I suppose that a discloseure of my real sentiments would render me very unpopular.

Two days later, Henry began a letter home:

Up to this date I have not received a letter from you. I feel confident that you have written & that it is delayed on its way to the army. Not being busy this evening I thought best to write a few lines. I have not seen Frank since I wrote you. I have had no chance to see him. I have not been very well since my return. My visit was as pleasant, thus it may be I visited too much. ... It seems to be the experience of all that have returned. You can immagine for yourself how we may feel. We are released from the army for a certain number of days to leave all our cares there & go home to see welcome friends who seem to be glad to welcome you to their homes & do everything in their power to make your stay pleasant. The above is my experience. I never enjoyed thirty days more pleasantly etc.

There is a variety of rumors circulating as usual. One that the corps is to go to Tennessee the 10th of March next. Another tonight that our brigade or the 3rd is to go to Ohio. Time will decide. I would not object.

I feel that I was very lucky in getting the $100 at Boston. I always thought him an honest man & would pay if he could but you are aware that such people cannot at all times pay their debts let them be ever so honest. He says he is worth about five thousand dollars but was doing a business that required an investment of more money so he said. He could not at all times pay as he ought.

Please tell Lorette that I have not seen George Ainsworth yet so I have not delivered the bundle. ... Had a Corps review today. Governor Smith was present. I was a spectator. It was a very fine review. George Ainsworth was one of the civilian spectators.

While much remained quiet on the eastern front, the ongoing saga of Henry's missed paycheck and the army bureaucracy continued. He received a letter from J. O. Mason, Paymaster of the Vermont Brigade, dated February 23:

> In answer to yours of the 18th, inquiring what course to pursue with regard to a lost check, I would say that you had better write at once to John J. Cisco Assistant Treas at N.Y. describe the check and order payment stopped. If in answer he says that it has not been paid, I can then issue a duplicate.

A letter finally arrived from home in which Henry's parents asked for more information about his visit with the Tilestons in Hopkinton. On February 24, Henry described the visit and also added some information on camp:

> Last night George Ainsworth stayed with me. We had a pleasant visit. He is to return to Vermont next week, is visiting the Williamstown friends in the army. You little imagine how much the men who did not re-enlist [now do so]. ...
>
> We expect an early campaign. Lee is in motion maneuvering. He is expected to try his luck in giving us another attack so they say at Corps Hd Qrs. The army is to [be] consolidated in to three Corps. The 6th to retain its number. It should. It is called the best in the army & feard most by the enemy (so they say).

Henry found that he needed to rush off another letter two days later after learning that they were to move out of camp as part of cavalry leader Judson Kilpatrick's audacious, if ill-conceived, plan to launch a surprise winter raid on Richmond.

> Tomorrow morning we expect to start to take part in a raid. General Averil & Butler is to make a raid to Richmond. We are orderd to be in readyness to moove at light in the morning with five days rations. The weather is very cold & we must suffer some.
>
> I was over to Corps Hd Qers & was told that the Corps would go to the Rapidan, perhaps cross & go somewhere & meet someone on the Peninsula, to occupy Lee's attention, while others are doing what I hope will prove a success. The 2nd & 3rd Corps have relieved our picket & will hold our line while away. Only a part of Hd Qers will leave. Only a part of Co. B. will leave camp. ...
>
> Dexter Jones returned to camp last night. Frank Sancry has just been promoted a corporal. Governor Smith arrived in camp this afternoon. The 4th Regt. had the honor of going to the Station & escorting him to Hd Qers. The Brigade was in line & received him with military honors.

*All are well. I received a letter from you & a paper on the 22nd. I answer
sooner than I should if I were not expecting to moove in the morning. Please
answer soon.*

Kilpatrick had already gained the sobriquet "Kill Cavalry" for his aggressive
actions, and reckless loss of soldiers' lives, in earlier battles. Under this daring new
plan, Kilpatrick and Ulric Dahlgren were to attack Richmond from two directions
while George Custer attracted Confederate attention with a raid towards Charlot-
tesville. The Sixth Corps was to follow behind Custer to offer support if needed.
As the defenses close to Richmond were believed to be very thin, the intention was
to break through and quickly release the prisoners from the Belle Isle prison camp.

On the morning of February 27, the Sixth Corps marched out of camp. The
travel was very difficult over the next two days as they moved toward the Robert-
son River. On March 1 they were ordered to return to Brandy Station, facing an
even more difficult two-day march that included an ice storm. The cavalry raid on
Richmond failed, partly because Kilpatrick arrived earlier than Dahlgren and also
because the forces defending Richmond were stronger than anticipated. After some
early skirmishing, Kilpatrick was pursued by Wade Hampton, but was able to make
it to New Kent where he was protected by General Butler's forces. Dahlgren was
killed during his separate attack. A new controversy then arose as a result of papers
supposedly found on Dahlgren suggesting a plot to assassinate Jefferson Davis.
Northern civilian and military leaders all disavowed any knowledge of this plot.

Neither Henry nor Francis viewed this venture as the fiasco it was, and neither complained about their useless winter march in their letters home after their
return to Brandy Station. Francis described the foray as follows:

*The object of the movement seems to have been to occupy the attention of Gen-
eral Lee and enable Genl Killpatrick to move on Richmond and if possible
capture the city, destroy the public works and release the Union prisoners.
The object of the expedition so far as the 6th Corps was concerned was accomplished. The order to move came very unexpectedly to us. We marched in the
direction of Robinson's River and arrived at our place of destination about
noon the second day after leaving camp. Here we remained two days hearing
some cannonading in front but not being called into action ourselves. After
remaining there two days we were joined by our Cavalry under Genl Custer
who had crossed the river advanced some distance into rebeldom, taken some
prisoners and destroyed a good deal of rebel property. The next morning we
started for camp again and arrived there just before dark having marched a
distance of twenty-five or twenty-seven miles. Henry has been a little unwell*

but is now as well as usual. ... I suppose that we shall not remain in camp much longer. We may move at any time. How I shall endure the summer weather and hard campaigning I cannot tell. I had no great difficulty making the last march. My boots were to small for me. The heels got jammed over so that they blistered my feet. Coming back my boots were well worked and so did not trouble me. I have just thrown the boots away and drawn a pair of shoes.

Please send me by return mail a box of Ayers Sugar Coated pills.

Henry's account was more descriptive about the area through which they marched:

An advertisement for Ayer's cathartic pills, which provided relief for "constipation, indigestion, dyspepsia, headache, dysentery, and a host of other ailments."

Last night I received your welcome letter written one day after we had started for Madison Court House. We left camp with five days rations & marched to James City a small place two or three houses & lots of little white negroes, whiter than many of our dark complexioned people at home. We marched in plain view of the enemy so that their forces might be compelled to moove toards us to protect themselves from a flank movement. Sunday we marched to our destintation, drove in the enemies pickets killing one & capturing a number. At night General Custer & fifteen hundred chosen men passed to cut the communication between Lee & Richmond. He traveled all night & part of next day. At four he made an attack but could not cut his way through so as to accomplish what he desired but it was not expected that he would be as successful as he might desire. The object of his attacking that point was to draw their attention in that direction so then Kilpatrick could make his anticipated successful raid on Richmond. He has been heard from Williamsburg. He could not get into the city but has done good work. Even if he has not destroyed the city he has destroyed railroad bridges & telegraph wires extensively. We had a pleasant time. Went into a country that had not been occupied by union troops. The people are rank sesech. The rebils are conscripting evry man. Our Cavalry brought in a New Yorker who had left a family behind. It was a favord opportunity for him to escape even if he had to leave all behind. It was most interesting to see the contrabands come in. Some traveled forty miles with the Cavalry to get free. Hundreds availed themselves of the opportunity much to the dissatisfaction of their masters. Some took their masters teams so had a ride. It rained all day Tuesday & we sufferd some without tents but the day passed & we are feeling more pleasant. Wednesday at 7 AM we started back for camp some over twenty miles from Brandy Station but we were anxious to get back so we did but how tired we were. Hardly a man fell out. It speeks well for the discipline of the troops. We had no fighting to do. The enemy seemed very clever. We were in easy range of their cannon when we returned. Perhaps they did not wish to waste ammunition. We are back again in comfortable quarters & hope not to leave until warm weather. Many of the rebils vetrains are home on furlough. A number were captured at their homes. They are very much disgusted with the service but their pride over rules reason so they continue to do wrong.

I have just heard from my check. I have written first to the Pay Master General, then to the assistant Treasurer in New York & the Pay Master &c have learnt that it has not been received & they will issue a duplicate at the expiration of three months which will be tomorrow. So I hope not to loose the hundred dollars. I expected it had been presented & paid. ...

I am well again. Captain has left for Vermont this morning to be absent some time. His wife has been here for some time past. He accompanies her back.

Before leaving, Captain Pratt asked Henry to start working on a new form to be used to better distinguish between veterans and new recruits for the purpose of paying out bounties. With the Sixth Corps back in winter camp, it must have seemed as if nothing of great significance was happening in the eastern war theater, but a momentous decision was occurring in Washington, D.C., where General Ulysses S. Grant arrived on March 9. Chauncey Smith wrote Henry two days later:

Have no city news except the arrival of Genl. Grant, who I see by the papers is now with you on a visit. He attended the President's levee last Tuesday evening, where we all saw him.

Grant was named supreme commander of the Union armies. He also planned to take personal command over Meade's Army of the Potomac.

Chapter 14

DEATH IN
THE WILDERNESS

General Meade had performed better than Hooker or Burnside in his first major encounter with Lee, but he had then allowed a defeated army to escape to safety. After the victory at Vicksburg, President Lincoln could no longer ignore the fact that Ulysses S. Grant, while somewhat nondescript and unimpressive in appearance, had a commanding presence on the battlefield. Grant had a record of suffering high casualties under his command, yet he also displayed a willingness to do whatever was necessary to totally defeat the enemy. According to Henry, the soldiers of the Army of the Potomac saw the wisdom in this change in leadership. Defeating Lee and ending this long war was so desirable that the soldiers preferred greater risk of injury or death over prolonging the war under more timid leadership. As Grant was in the process of assuming command, Henry wrote home on March 13 from the camp near Brandy Station:

> Yesterday I returned from three days picket. The first day was unusually pleasant but before next morning the clouds were full of rain & preparing to shower it upon our heads. As luck would have it I was in command of the Center reserve & had some very agreeable officers with me so all joined in making comfortable quarters of boards torn from the secesh fences for floores & our shelter tents for covering. After all was completed we found comfortable quarters for a picket line. At an early hour it commenced raining and continued until the morning [when] we were relieved.
>
> It would interest you to see how rapidly the little cricks are converted into large streams. The soil is red clay so all the rain that falls collects on the surface & runs to the nearest ravine & forms a nice little river. It was not so bad as you would supose at home. If one gets wet he does not mind it but gets dry the best he can. One thing is in our favor the weather is becoming quite mild. ...
>
> While we were on picket there was a report circulating that the 8th Corps

was being brought to the front & we were to take their places to be stationed at Baltimore. Would it not be pleasant for a short time? (I mention the above to show you what rumors are circulating in our lively camps.) General Grant has been down to the front accompanied by the President. We expect him down in a week or two to review the Army and we expect some thing will follow. The army is willing to fight under anyone & desperately too if they can only be lead to victory. We are ready to fight under Grant, Meade, Sedgwick, or any other true loyal man that will make his blows felt when he strikes. One hundred thousand men have been killed & wounded (says the records of the army) since the commencement of the war in the Army of the Potomac. It has been a whole sale butchery on both sides. So true have the men been that amid the almost numberless reverses they are still determined to put their best shoulder to the wheel & keep it there until the war is brought to a successful termination. Even if we have had untrue leaders to commence with we trust the end will be accomplished & the rascals, traitors, copperheads & evry man having a spark of disloyalty in his heart will be shortly punished (all wrong is punished in time).

Colnel Stroughton has resigned [and] is now studying law in New York. His vacancy cannot be filled. We are lacking 17 men of the number required to make a Colnel. It does not seem right but the Government has passed such laws & they must be obeyed. The object of Captain Pratts going to Vermont was to try & raise the number of men. He expects to get a Lt. Colnecy if he succeeds. Our Major (Pingree) will not accept a promotion because of the general order. If a man is promoted he has got to be mustered into the service for three years from the date of his muster-in. So he is determined to leave the service & will not be bound for a term that will not expire next June.

I have received a paper from Mrs Tilston. The NY Observer. She said she would continue if I wished. Of course I accepted.

Another of our men have returned from desertion. He feels very penitent. I have preferd charges against him but his trial will be as light as possible. He has to pay $30.00 for being arrested besides his equipments camp & Garrison equipage [so] he will not find it a paying job.

I have just returned from services. Chaplain Roberts preached to quite a full house. There were two officers besides my self present. All the ladies now with the army are ordered to leave by next Thursday. Rather unexpected to them. It is all right as it would take half of the Ambulances in the army to transport them about.

You have but a slight idea how the wind blows today. Tents not well put up do not stand long. The sun shines warm but the winds come all the way *from Vermont consequently are rather cool. The mud disapears very fast. It is like the snow when exposed to the South wind. It makes the camps look very neat & holsom. ...*

Henry Smith has been promoted a corporal. He had a call from the Non Commissioned officers of the company & a speech was delivered by him & Patriotic toasts by the visitors. I am glad he has been noticed. The men from other towns say that there is but one more Williamstown man left so they will stand a chance soon.

Francis's letter of about a week later showed more interest in the growing religious spirit among his fellow soldiers. He was particularly pleased with ministers from the Williamstown area who had come to preach in the camp.

We are still in our winter quarters and expect to remain here four or five weeks longer. Last week we received marching orders as the rebels were attempting to cross the river but they were soon countermanded. For my part I choose to remain where we are for the present. ... It is quite cold today & there are some snowflakes flying.

I have seen Mr. Barnard several times. He is interested in his work. Enjoys it and will no doubt both do and get good. Mr. Parker leaves us today. I suppose his meetings have been well attended and very interesting as you may judge from the fact that he can say as he did last evening that he never enjoyed meetings before as he had these, will indicate their character to you. They are never characterized by the lifelessness of some of our home prayer meetings nor by any extravagance or undue enthusiasm. I do not think that our churches could have put their pastors to a better use than to send them here for a short time. They will not only benefit the soldiers but receive an impulse themselves which will enable them to labor to better advantage when they return to their homes. I saw Henry Smith today. He is corporal now. Henry was over to the 2nd last Sunday. We called at Mr. Barnard's tent together but did not find him there.

Tomorrow there is to be an army service if the weather will permit. President Lincoln & General Grant will probably be present.

Pliny Barnard was the minister of the Congregational Church in Williamstown; the Reverend C. C. Parker was from the Congregational Church in Waterbury.

Henry wrote home the next day, March 23, and further expressed the optimism being felt in camp over Grant's ascension:

We have had some very severe weather of late today in particular. The north wind was unusualy severe. About three P.M. it commenced to snow & continues this evening. It has fallen to the depth of three inches. Rather cold for those on picket but before tomorrow night it will all be gone & then the weather will be lovely. Tomorrow the army is to be reviewed by Lieut. General Grant, the President & a large number of the prominent men from Washington. The entire force is to be present. All to look very slick, the men to ware white gloves. I have purchased $18.00 worth for Co. A. All are anxious to attend so that they may see the hero of twenty seven battles. It is intended to be one of the most magnificent reviews ever held in the Potomac Army. I think it will be.

Last week I received a call from Mr. Barnard & Parker. Both are well received & I trust they will do good. It will certainly help them. It is quite a privilege to visit the army & not be nesesarily connected with it. They visited Co. B. [and] were introduced to General Sedgwick. [They] were much pleased with his look & appearances. Mr. Parker thought him superior in looks to Meade. ...

I went to see Frank, found him well & enjoying himself. From there I went to call on Mr. Barnard but he was not in. Had gone to the 10th Vermont to preach. His station is near the 2nd Vt. in the reserve artilery. I also called on Captain Platt, met his brother Col. Platt of the Regular Army. He thought the army would not moove before the middle of April, that a strong column was to moove on Richmond by the Peninsula Theater & capture [it]. Lee is determined to maintain his position on the Rappidan which he will not do if he retreats to follow. All think that Grant is to do wonders with this army. It was never in better condition than today. We are to receive all the vetrans from Ohio & other States. We are to have a large army, a vetran army. The rebils are concerned about their chances with Grant at its head. [There is] considerable talk about the President but generaly in favor of him. [With] Grant in the field the next four years, [and with] Lincoln in the executive chair then they think this war will be carried to a sucessful termination [and will] then give Grant the next Presidency. The soldiers do not want peace except unconditional surender & will fight until they get it if they can have their own way. They do not feel as many do at home to have peace under any circumstances. Now [that] it is commenced they wish to let the south know that they cant trifle with the Yankies.

The snow continued to fall, and the scheduled review by Grant and Lincoln was cancelled. Francis, who had not submitted a newspaper installment for almost two months, explained this situation in his next article:

Camp near Brandy Station, Va.
March 26, 1864

Mr. Editor, —Too much time has already elapsed, since your correspondent last appeared in your columns; his only apology is disinclination and the pressure of other duties more imperative in their demands, for be it with others as it may, since he entered the service he has seldom found his time unemployed. Our last expedition might have furnished him with a theme, but anything like a detail of its events, now so often and well described by others, would fail to interest your readers. Suffice it to say that the order to move came unexpectedly, and supposing that something like the late reconnaissance in force at Morton's Ford was afoot, the most of us expected soon to meet the enemy, and had occasion for the exercise of those feelings which naturally arise in the breast of a soldier at such times.

The following verses which I find in a newspaper so well describe the events which usually precede a battle, and the emotions of brave men when called to the post of danger, that I think they cannot fail to interest such of your readers as may not have met with them before.

> *Our van had pressed onward the whole weary way;*
> *The boys were all hopeful and some few were gay;*
> *As we neared the thick wood which covered the foe;*
> *We battled at last,*
> *And pulses throbbed fast*
> *As each felt the cold dread*
> *That before the day fled*
> *Some one of our number in death might be low.*
>
> *Soon the artillery passed by at full speed;*
> *Soon followed the horseman urging his steed;*
> *Then, while we at the front stood waiting the sign;*
> *Up rose the soul's prayer,*
> *"O God! My life spare!"*
> *Now shoulder to shoulder*
> *Each brave heart grew bolder,*
> *As "forward" came thundering along the line.*
>
> *We had heard the same order the long march through,*
> *But now it was freighted with import anew,*
> *The onset was ours: who the end could foretell?*

All death fear was gone,
All thought of self flown,
And not a step faltered,
And not an eye altered
As we closed in the track of our pioneer shell.

How the next command thrilled us, "Advance and fire!"
With the enemy's shot whizzing faster and nigher,
One sole duty was ours—to hear and obey.
We charg'd and we fired,
We loaded and fired,
My good limbs did their part,
But my spirit dispart
From the terrible conflict sped far away.

I was with you, dear friends, in the old hallow'd spot;
I trac'd each lov'd feature, each scene unforgot;
You were sad, my heart was o'erflowing with joy—
My smiles met your tears—
Hopes mingled with fears;
You dream'd not, dear brother,
Dearest father and mother,
That near you was hovering your own soldier boy!

On the 2d of March, the fifth day of our absence from camp, we received orders to return, which we did, between sunrise and sunset, marching (many say) a distance of twenty-eight miles, but I should judge twenty-five miles to be nearer the truth. Again in camp, its old round of duties are resumed with but little to vary or break their monotony.

Last Tuesday the 22nd, we made preparations for a grand army review, to take place at Brandy Station the next day, but it was prevented by the heaviest snow storm that has visited Virginia this winter. The ground was covered to the depth of five or six inches, and afforded every facility to those who were fond of snow-balling. During the day our boys received a challenge from the 6th regiment, which was accepted by a squad of about thirty; these deployed as skirmishers advanced opening upon the enemy with a volley of snowballs, who replied with spirit and soon drove our boys back to their support, where they rallied, formed in line of battle, and with the accession of a reinforcement from camp, advanced again, driving the enemy before them, *but they in turn being reinforced charged and compelled us to fall back. At this juncture our officers appeared with a reinforcement from camp, when we at once assumed the offensive, charged, and the enemy being unable to withstand our onset, were driven before us. From this time we had it all our own way; the enemy rallied and charged upon us repeatedly, but were unable to break our lines or make us give ground, and finally were driven into camp leaving us masters of the field. Five of their officers, the Major, Adjutant and three Lieutenants were taken prisoners, and released at the close of the action. The following is a correct estimate of the causalities: Killed, none; wounded slightly, all; severely, a few whose black eyes still show that even play may be carried too far*

Thinking of nothing else that would be likely to interest your readers, I subscribe myself, CONSCRIPT

In the following week, the snow stopped but the weather remained far from agreeable. Henry and Francis did receive some pleasant news from home, however. Lorette Bass, no longer burdened with caring for her terminally ill sister, had agreed to marry their friend George Ainsworth. Henry wrote to his parents on March 30:

We have been having a very unpleasant time for the past two days. Yesterday morning it commenced to rain & continued all night clearing up this P.M. The country about Brandy Station was afloat with water. Many of the mens tents leaked so that they were very uncomfortably situated. To cap their discomforts they could not keep any fires because they persisted in smoking. Day before yesterday I visited Frank, found him well as usual. He had just received a letter from you so he read it to me. ... Have you learnt when George & Lorett intend to be married? What did Uncle Ira say about George [Smith]? I have not seen George since my return. He is so far from our camp that I can't get away that length of time required. You must excuse poor writing as I have sprained my wrist so I cannot hardly hold a pen. It will be better soon. I gave Mr. Barnard a call this week, found him well enjoying himself & doing good. It must be quite an interesting vacation to him.

There is not much news to write. We are making ready for our Richmond campaign. All are expecting Grant is in earnest. He is increasing the army by ordering the men away from Washington as he should. Fifteen thousand are to come at once. Two heavy artilary Regts & one Brigade have arrived. They look very slick but the shine will be taken off soon. It is said Grant wants two hundred thousand in the Potomac army. He should have them. Capt. Pratt

*has returned but not to his company. I dont care so much as I should if he
did not give me the extra ten dollars per month. We received four recruits last
night not enough to fill the Reg much. Col Foster has received his commission
as Colnel, but no major can be elected until the Regt is full. We lack only
twelve. Capt. Pratt will undoubtably be our next. Col. Grant is expected to
be our Brig when Smith's promotion leaves one vacancy which will be filled
by him. He ought to receive it. He has commanded over a year & in some of
our greatest battles.*

*We expect the 10th Vt is to be put in our Brigade. Hope they will. If any
more Regiments are added there is to be six Regts in a Brigade under the new
organization.*

Under the new organization to which Henry alluded, the First and Third
Corps were eliminated, and their regiments were distributed among the remaining
three corps. The Second Corps was under General Hancock, the Fifth under
General Warren, and the Sixth, including the Vermont Brigade, remained under
General Sedgwick. General Burnside's Ninth Corps, although independent from
the Army of the Potomac, was to act in concert with it in the upcoming campaign.
The Vermont Brigade's commander was Lewis A. Grant, and the brigade was part
of the Second Division, under the command of George W. Getty.

After a two-month gap in his newspaper correspondence, Francis now waited
only one week before sending his next article. News of George Ainsworth's engagement
to his cousin may have prompted Francis to devote an article to the work of
the Christian Commission.

Camp near Brandy Station, Va.,
April 2, 1864

*Mr. Editor.—Perhaps some account of the work of the Christian Commission
in this department may interest a portion of your readers. It is well known
that military life often exerts an unfavorable influence on the character of
those whom necessity or inclination engages in it. The actual change wrought
in the character of the individual may not be as great as it appears, as much of
his conduct is not from disregard of those principles which at home are cherished
as the safeguards of society, but rather from the removal of restraints
and exposure to temptation. Someone speaking on this subject, "The type of
army wickedness," and disposed to show the largest charity to the soldier, says:
"It is not that hopeless beating out of all the good of the soul which is needful
to degrade a man to all these sins amid the restraints and moral influence of*

society, home and religion; but rather the wildness and recklessness of men outside of all the compulsions and restraints to which they were wont, which are necessary to the order of society anywhere, and to fence in from sin the souls of most men. The soldier just appears what the unrestrained impulse of most men would make them, not at all what the man is who defying the order of open society, does just the things which the soldiers do. There is little in his wickedness of that set perversity which overrides all difficulties in the way of evil, burns up in the flaming of its passions the thousand hindrances, and goes through troops of safeguard virtues. His is that vice which runs carelessly in at open doors, which practices itself in mainly unrebuked, uncondemned sin, against which the average conscience in his vicinity, i.e., the common feeling of the army, does not revolt. Most of his evil ways are sins into which he falls because there is no prevailing opinion against them, or vices into which he falls in that way and for the reason that there seems at hand no innocent substitute for them. He will come back to society, not hardened by resistance to and defiance of its influences, but very keenly alive to every one of them all. Home powers for good have not been trampled on, but only unfelt in absence from their sphere."

To meet the wants of the soldiers, both moral, intellectual and physical, to bring social and religious influences to bear upon him, and thus so far as possible to arrest the progress of evil, to induce those who suffer from its influence to take such a course as will not only preserve and benefit themselves, but render them useful and honorable members of society when they return to civil life, and to confirm and strengthen those whose purpose is to so live, is the object of the Christian Commission. Its agents are ever ready to minister to the wants of the sick and wounded, rendering assistance and supplying comforts which cannot be obtained through other channels. If I am rightly informed the Commission has thirteen stations in the Army of the Potomac. At each station is a large Chapel tent, capable of accommodating from one hundred and fifty to two hundred persons. One station is at the camp of the 2nd Vermont. The tent is on the right and in rear of the Regiment. Another station has its location at the Artillery reserve, about 1/4 of a mile to the southeast of our camp, and others are located in our neighborhood. The agents or delegates of the Commission are often clergymen who have tendered their services gratuitously for a short period; two usually remain at each station; conducting religious services in the Chapel tent, where meetings are held every evening, and a bible class at some hour during each day, distributing newspapers, tracts, &c., and doing any other work that devolves upon them. Rev. C. C. Parker (of Waterbury), assisted by Mr. Baker of Greensboro, was first with us and remained six weeks. Both were earnest, active and good men, whose memory will be cherished with gratitude, respect and esteem, by many a soldier.

Mr. Parker evidently possessed in a high degree those traits of character and other qualifications which are indispensable to a good and efficient army chaplain, associating with the soldiers with a familiarity and freedom which only true friendship and regard for their welfare could inspire, winning their confidence and imparting that instruction which education, observation and experience enabled him to give. As an instance of his faculty of illustrating his ideas, or the truths he wishes to inculcate, by instituting comparisons with the events of every day life: thus presenting them with the greatest possible clearness, and at the same time commanding the respect of his hearers by the evidence of his acquaintance with the customs and characters of the different classes he is called to address, I give the following: On one occasion, wishing to show the necessity of watchfulness and prayer, and the uselessness of each without the other, he said in substance, "that a body was composed of many members, each having its special office which the others could not perform, and each dependent for its efficiency on the cooperation with and harmonious working of all the others; that he had just returned from a visit to the picket line, where he saw sentinels posted at regular intervals, and within hailing distance of each other, walking their beat, and he supposed that the line extended around the entire army. These sentinels, he said, were the eyes of the army, and to be efficient they must exercise constant vigilance and be always at their post. He supposed that we apprehended no immediate danger of an attack from General Lee, or from a raid by Mosby's guerrillas,—but still near us was a watchful foe, a foe so watchful as to know of all our doings as well as we know them ourselves, and of our anticipated movements, almost as soon as they were planned. And in view of this what would be the result if those eyes should fall asleep, or in other words if the sentinels should all leave their posts? Our artillery, baggage wagons and army stores, and perhaps the entire army, would soon be captured. Our strength would avail us nothing; if we were surprised and unable to use it. Again, we cannot be all eye; the fact that we are surrounded by a picket line does not make us secure; the pickets have but little strength of themselves, and if they were unable to obtain assistance from some other source, they might be easily outnumbered and captured. But he was informed that within hailing distance was a support or reserve to which they could signal for aid at any moment, and if that was not *sufficient, communication could be made with the main body of the army, which in a very short space of time could be concentrated at any given point and render any needful assistance. Well, as it is with the army so it is with the Christian: he too has foes, numerous, vigilant and powerful, so watchful as to let slip no opportunity of assailing him, and so strong as to render his own strength of no avail in resisting them. Then he must always watch or in an unguarded moment he may be overcome, and when assailed he must pray, or call for aid, and the arm of the Almighty, which is his support, will be used in his behalf. The fact that we have such a support is not of itself sufficient. It must be called upon in time of danger, or it is of no avail to us, and we must ever be watchful or the danger will steal upon us unawares and we shall be powerless to overcome it: so both watchfulness and prayer must be exercised, that either may be efficient."*

With kind regards to those of your readers who peruse my letters, I sub-scribe myself, CONSCRIPT.

The wet and unseasonably cold weather continued at the Union camp during the first week of April. The camp was also greatly expanding as new recruits arrived continually. Henry started a letter home on April 3:

This evening I am the glad recipient of a package sent by Mr. Wilson from you to myself and Frank. On opening it I found its contents full of sweets. I need not tell you it is a luxury you can judge for yourself. It has been nearly two years since I have seen anything of the kind in the army.

Troops are daily arriving at Brandy Station. It looks right to us. I have been on court marshall nearly all day on a deserter case from my company. ... It is raining this afternoon. We expect it every other day. Snow fell last night two inches. ... Cannot do anything as long as it continues storming. ...

He continued the next day:

It is snowing today or would say half snow. Strange weather. Fortunately I am where it is comfortable. Please send me a skein of silk. We have just been paid. I sent you by express $325.00. One hundred is a check which I lost last December. I have decided to try expressing my money. Of the two ways I think the later, the safest. Our chaplain takes the money to the station and starts it on its way.

Captain Pratt lost his pants last night. As he was retiring for the night he hung them on a chair near the tent. He had not got asleep before he heard someone cut his tent stake out. His pants "done in an instant" & run off. He

tried to pursue him but could not so lost his pants. It was one of our substi-
tutes after money. He was suposed to rumage in a jacket full of money. As it
happened there was no money so he got the pants, a knife, comb etc. Two or
three other tents were riped open but no money was to be found. The lackeys
of the cities are very skilful. A man was stabbed by one of them not long since.

Our chaplain says there has been quite a number of conversions with regt.
Quite encouraging for us I think.

We are now rid of the Stoughtons entirely but their examples are still
followed.

One of our officers in speaking of McClellan said he was an admirer of
his Generalship but when he forsook his country for his political ambition he
could not do otherwise than drop him. Although he might have been misused
if he had been a patriot he would never have forsaken his country & joined
the Valendynmiks nor permitted Jeff Davis' friends to cheer him. George
Ainsworth is mistaken. The army are not all McClellan men. I admit a
great many but only a fraction part. Grant is the favorite of the army &
almost super human efforts are expected of him this summer.

McClellan had by this time become one of the candidates seeking the Democratic Party's nomination to oppose Abraham Lincoln in the 1864 election. While
McClellan was not running expressly as a "peace candidate," the Democratic Party
included copperheads such as Clement Vallandigham (whose followers Henry
described as "Valendynmiks"). At the convention, Vallandigham had enough support to put a plank in the party platform declaring the war effort a failure and
calling for an immediate end to the fighting. McClellan received the nomination
but publicly disavowed the platform's position on the war. Nevertheless, he was
certainly associated with a less forceful pursuit of the war objectives than was
Lincoln.

For Francis, life at winter camp continued to be agreeable both physically and
spiritually. This seems particularly surprising since Francis was known to have displayed both health problems and a melancholy temperament at home. He wrote
to his parents on April 8:

I have received two letters from you bearing dates March 21st and 29th with
stamps inclosed. I should have answered the last before but have been out on
picket for the last three days. But little occurs in camp now out of the ordinary
course of events. I do not know when the Spring campaign will commence
but it cannot be far off and will probably be a vigorous and hard campaign
but I hope that good enough will be accomplished to pay the cost. Henry has

probably written you that he is not on duty now being laid up with a sprained wrist. We have more duty to do now and of course less leisure time than usual. With the exception of Saturdays when we have other work to attend to and Sundays we have three drills each day. One company or squad drill in the manuel of arms and bayonet exercise from eight to nine A.M. Then company or skirmish drill from ten to eleven A.M. Next in order Battallion or regimental drill from two till three P.M. For the last drill brigade drill, division or Corps review or something of the kind may be substituted. Still the work we do here while lying in camp bears no comparison with that to which I have been accustomed at home. If I should consult my own comfort and pleasure I would be well satisfied to spend a year or two in the army doing garrison or camp duty which would be more beneficial to my health than any other kind of life I could in my circumstances lead but when it comes to campaigning then our powers of endurance are thoroughly tested and home people know little of the hardship, exposure and dangers to which the soldier is subjected.

Our meetings are still interesting. Those who take an active part seem more zealous and wide awake than the majority of professors at home. Last Sabboth the Sacrament of the Lord's Supper was observed some partaking of it for the first time. As there was nothing which could be considered objectionable I presented myself as a candidate for examination and as I expected was accepted but was providentially hindered from accomplishing my purpose as I was detailed to go on picket the Saturday preceding the appointed Sabboth and could not procure any one to take my place. The sugar cakes &c came duly to hand. Please accept my thanks. They were very nice. Hoping to hear from you soon.

Henry started a letter home the next day, describing more features of camp life:

It is raining as usual now a days. We have been favored with two pleasant days this week. Either we are to have a late Spring or all the raining is to be done at once & have a dry summer. Rain is not very acceptable on a campaign. We are to be all ready by the 16th Grant and Meade haveing not left for Fortress Monroe. You little think how encouraged the soldiers are to see Grant take the field & superintend in person. If he stayed in Washington as Hallack has we might be as well, yes better, without him.

A new soldier came to camp this week dressed in heavy artilary mans uniform inquiring for a certain soldier in Co. D. He was found & to his surprise the artilary man was his wife. She had been very anxious to see him

& resorted to strategy & got passes & transportation undetected. A tent has been built for their accomodation but she will not be permitted to stay. Quite a resolute woman, she is.

Maj. Pingree has re-enlisted. Capt. Laird has been court marshaled for selling liquor to soldiers. His sentence has not been published yet. Hope he will be cashierd in disgrace from the Service. One of our Corporals received his sentence for deserting in New York – to be reduced to the ranks, to forfeit all pay due from time of desertion to receiving of sentance & serve three months after the expiration of his term of service. Rather hard sentance.

One of our men who by accident cut off three of his fingers on his right hand oweing to the negligence of the Doctor has got to have his hand amputated.

Have you received my money yet? My wrist is not well yet.

Henry continued on April 10:

Captain Pratt was saying today that when the Army mooved that all the troops now guarding the Rail Road to Washington were to be withdrawn & thus will we be cut off from all communication. We expect Grant has planned a successful campaign. Perhaps it will be well not to be subject to Head Quarter orders as in time past. It does not rain today but the clouds indicate another storm.

Abraham Lincoln has been nominated by sixteen States through their legislatures for re-election to the Presidency. Hope he will get it. I have just returned from service held at the Chapel. The Chaplains remarks were very good. He gave many gentle hints about reading novels &c. He is doing good. A number have made a profession of religion. Not many attend services. It is raining again. ... There are but seventeen old men to be discharged in June. from Co. A.

[Glued at the letter's end was the following newspaper clipping]

"Tom Thumb retires on a quarter of a million says the Court Journal and adds: This is but a fair illustration of the strange freaks of fortune these topsy-turvy times. It seems much easier to make a fortune by littleness than by greatness."

Francis also wrote home on April 10, sending one of the few letters from either brother specifically addressed to their mother:

The thought of home just suggested to me the affection I have for those who are there and is the reason why I write you at this time.

You will be pleased to hear that for the past few weeks my opportunities for religious services and instruction have been nearly or quite as good as I have been accustomed to enjoy at home. Religious newspapers and tracks have been distributed in abundance. The newspapers are the best that are published so that I have had more reading matter of that kind which most interests me, than I ever did at home. Mr. Parker was first here associated with a fine young man by the name of Baker who is studying for the ministry. Since they left, their places have been filled by Mr. Taylor, a clergyman from Pennsylvania and another clergyman from Connecticut, a Scotchman by the name of Smith. ...

Preparations are now being made for the Spring campaign. When it will commence I can not tell. I dread its tiresome marches, the exposure and the conflict with the enemy, still I am not sorry that I am here and only wish for that wisdom, courage and strength which I need to discharge my work honorably, faithfully acceptably to God and all reasonable men. If we so discharge our duties that God accepts of the service as the best we in our weakness can do, it is enough but it is important that we honor him before men giving them no just occasion to despise us for any folly or weakness which resolution or divine grace might enable him to overcome.

Night before last seven men deserted from the Regiment and I understand that they have been captured. One from my Company has been branded on his hand for previous desertion.

Henry further confirmed how well his brother was adjusting to army life in an April 12 letter:

We had a review by our new Division General Getty. He was very observing. Spoke to two men for not having their equipment on just right.

I called on Frank. Found him well & enjoying himself. Mother need not feel concerned about him more than that he is in the army & in danger with all of never returning. I do not wonder you feel concerned as to our safety. You must pray for us. Frank seems to enjoy himself better than at home & is respected.

I called on Mr. Barnard. He is laboring hard. Has preached everyday in the week & four times a sunday. He has plenty of hearers.

The mails have been delayed three days owing to the bridges being washed away. It has rained a little today. I have just seen John Green. He says his brother Darwin has sold out in New York City for Thirty five thousand dollars & gone into business with another man who invests one hundred thousand dollars. ... I am glad to see him prosper.

I am exceedingly sorry that Ian has purchased the old place. It will be poor property for him & is ruining to you. Help is so scarce that you will be troubled to get your work along. ... I hope some way will be provided to help you along. The willows will be a burden to you, I fear.

I suppose the box is at Washington for the 6th Reg arrived last night. Alby Hayden is in the third Reg & as a teamster. We have arranged with him to furnish us with apples & other fruit as we want it at a reasonable price. It is very esential that we have fruit to prevent Skervey. The sutlers charge enormous prices & some make ten dollars a dz., I have been told from good authority & I don't doubt it.

Although the soldiers of the Army of the Potomac were expecting to leave winter camp, as of mid-April they had gone nowhere. Francis wrote home on April 17:

There have been a good many hopeful cases of conversion attending the work of the Christian Commission here and I have derived much satisfaction, comfort and strength from the same myself. The tent is to be taken down tomorrow. Mr. Barnard is now assisting Mr. Smith while he remains with the Regt. He will soon return to Williamstown. I shall send a book by him ... [and] a number of excellent articles. I do not suppose that you have much spare time, still I know that mother will be interested in many things she will find and so I send them.

Everything indicates an early move and we all look for hard marches and bloody battle fields. It is evidently the path of duty and we do not wish to turn back. Still we need support and I desire your prayers that God may give me all needed grace for he is ever ready to do this for all his creatures who trust in Him. His will is to be chosen rather than our own and doing his will in his strength we do not live in vain.

The army drilled as it awaited its marching orders, and rumors circulated around the camp as Grant met with his other generals and made plans. Henry described the situation in an April 20 letter:

Monday we were reviewed by Lt Gen Grant. I was not on duty so I had an excelent chance to see him. He did not look as I fancied he would. He is about 5 feet 8 inches high, light complexion but not so smart looking as Meade, Hancock or Sedgwick but his deeds mark him out a smart man. Not very gay, wares three stars on each shoulder, rides a beautiful horse with saddle decorated with gold lace & stars. After the review all the Generals went to

Sedgwicks Hd Qrs, took some thing, talked with the Generals about an hour. Then said he could not spend more time there, shook hands with all & left with Gen. Meade. His countenance does not indicate strong drink. Genl Meade looks as though his cares were heavy. He has grown quite gray within a few months. So has Sedgwick & Hancock. They are noble looking men. They have great responsibility resting on their large commands. The 6th Corps numbers 45,000 men. The two others are still larger. Our army will be very large when we start & will meet a large army of rebils. It is reported that the south western army is reinforcing them. It is credited here.

The sick are being sent away today. No citizens are allowed in the army. If any are found they are to be put to hard labor on fortifications. Culpepper is being strongly fortified & files of siege guns are being brought to the front.

It continues to storm every other day. We have three drills a day. The men make a fine appearance. Practice of a few years gives them a second nature for the business. ... Rumor says we moove Saturday. I doubt it. ... Captain Laird was cashiered sent home & never permitted to join the service again. One of our Corporals cut off his toe yesterday.

When Henry wrote home on April 24, it was becoming more evident that the army would be moving soon. Also, apparently his parents now knew of Henry's plans to marry Laura.

Yours of the 20th was received today. Thinking my time will be employed on the march very soon perhaps Tuesday or Wednesday I thought I would answer at once. The weather has been favorable for a moove for the past week. The winds strong & dry, drying up the mud. Evrything seems to be in readiness to moove. Its rumored that the 2nd Corps has started all ready to join the Peninsula force by way of the lower Rappahannoc. There is not much news of late. A number of deserters are to be shot on the 29th, none from this Corps. Col Grant has received his appointment as Brigadier & is now arrangeing his staff. There is a number of our Non Commissioned officers receiving appointments for Negro Regiments.

Concerning the ring, I have it with me & intend to keep it & tell Lorett I can take care of my own rings &c. ... I wish Mother would become acquainted with Laura Ainsworth. I think she will like her.

I am sorry to learn of the prices of articles rising so fast. It looks like the Southern prices. If the gold can't be brought down, we shall be in the same fix. As it is our Soldiers are working for half pay. They should be paid in specie.

There has been a great interest taken of late in religion. Quite a number of very profane men have experienced religion.

We are having three drills a day. I am on duty now. I have not been for the past three weeks. [My wrist] was very badly sprained, nearly broken they think. The bone was fractured but it is so I can do duty. Another of our men have cut himself so he will not do duty for some time. Has Mr. Barnard arrived? He carried my sword home for me.

The next day, April 25, Henry received the following orders from Colonel Foster:

Lieut. W. H. Martin Co "A" is hereby detailed for Picket and will report at these Head Quarters at 8 oclock AM tomorrow. His detail for Regimental Officer of the day is revoked.

Henry then added a few lines to his letter:

I have just received a detail for picket for three days so I will have this letter mailed before I go out. We expect to moove next Wednesday. Burnsides expedition has sailed & we are to moove when he arrives at a certain point.

Francis also wrote home on April 25, concurring that departure from winter camp was finally at hand:

There is little news, other than that we expect to move our camp to Culpepper this week, perhaps we shall move tomorrow, but there are other subjects which are more interesting to a Mother and not the least of these is the welfare of her children both temporal and spiritual. Yesterday I united with the church at the 6th Regiment of which Mr. Webster, formerly of Northfield, is Chaplain. ... This connection can be dissolved at any time should I choose to unite with any other church or church organization and such will doubtless be my wish should we have a chaplain in this Regiment. I have felt it to be my duty to unite with God's people and partake of the sacrament of the Lord's Supper and feel myself blessed in the cause I have taken. ...

If you reced my last you read a note that accompanied the bag of articles I reced through the Commission. A sheet of paper and a stamped envelope for an answer were inclosed & I wrote what I ought to write under such circumstances. A short time since I had a few pictures taken but they were such poor representations that I then thought I would not send any of them to my acquaintances but after I had written the letter the thought struck me that there would be no impropriety in sending one to her [one of the women who sent gifts and letters of support to the soldiers] as I did not wish to throw it away. I did so and received the inclosed answer and likeness which I do not wish to carry with me and so send it home. I knew that it would be a gratification to her to know who received the bag and thought I might possibly be instrumental in doing some good to her.

This nineteenth-century form of social networking, undertaken by the Christian Commission, was clearly not an easy process for Francis to participate in.

As for the next phase of the war, after taking over from Halleck, General Grant had devised an overall plan to end the war. It called for the North to employ its advantages in manpower and industrial strength to now overwhelm the South. Rather than being overly concerned with taking and holding strategic locations, five Union armies were to now simultaneously invade the Confederacy, causing disruption and a loss of food and material supplies, as well as soldiers, for the South. In the western campaign, General Banks was to lead an army from Louisiana to Mobile, Alabama, while Sherman marched from Tennessee toward Atlanta. The eastern campaign included a small army under General Sigel moving into the Shenandoah Valley and another small army under Butler marching toward Richmond from the south. Grant would personally lead the massive Army of the Potomac, numbering 120,000 men, as it tried to defeat Lee north of Richmond. All five Union armies were directed to commence in the first week of May. The Vermont Brigade received its orders on May 3 and departed early the next morning. Henry and Francis both wrote home before breaking camp. Francis, as usual, focused on the more spiritual side of this undertaking:

This afternoon all have received orders to be ready to move at four o'clock tomorrow morning and then the ease of camp life must be exchanged for the hardships of the campaign. Of our destination I am not yet informed. It may be to meet the enemy or only to change our quarters. It is thought by some that the 6th Corps is to be kept as a reserve and that it will not see much fighting. Others have different opinions, but it is not wise for you or myself to seek to divine our comforts from sources which are liable to yield disappointment only. The grace of God is sufficient for us in all places and conditions and without it there can be no true strength or peace. Pray that God's grace may abound towards me, enabling me to do his will wisely, efficiently and joyfully. The thought of the approaching campaign in itself considered affords me no pleasure but in view of seeming necessities I do not regret the step I have taken nor wish to turn back. If anything befals me do not be troubled about it. Trust in God, obey him, and you will be satisfied with his disposal of events. I have enjoyed much for the past few weeks. As often as circumstances would permit professing Christians have met together for prayer and conference. Since the removal of the Chapel tent the meetings have been held in the open air and we all feel that they have been productive of much good. Since I have been in the service I have seen many hardships but have had much enjoyment. The cause in which we are engaged is worthy of the sacrifices we make and we hope will be at last crowned with success. I think, with Mr. Parker, that the noblest type of a man is the Christian Soldier, engaged in the cause of justice and truth. One who faithfully serves his country and his God in doing, enduring or daring. A Soldier is always an intense Man, and if his heart is thoroughly imbued with gracious influences, the trials and dangers through which he is called to pass will produce a religious character of singular earnestness, decision, wisdom and beauty. Most loose much of their piety here but there are shining examples of the power of grace to keep, sustain and sanctify even when surrounded by all the evil influences which are always so active in the Army. (In a purely worldly point of view with good and established health, my prospects of future success & usefulness would be far more hopeful in the army than elsewhere. As it is I presume that I can accomplish more here than at home but it is vain for me to make any reliance on my own strength for only the result can prove how I will endure.) Open air, plain food and light duties have been steadely improving my health and strength but I have not yet that constant vigor which every man at my age should have and do not know how the campaign will affect me. But I know from experience that God's grace is sufficient for me and I have only to put all my trust in him to enjoy as perfect satisfaction as I can expect on Earth.

I was much interested with the letter Mr. Smith sent me. I suppose that you read it. He asks if you, Father, have an interest in Christ's Kingdom. I should not be discharging my own duty nor obeying the dictates of true affection if I should neglect to urge you to obtain a sure evidence of pardoned sin and a hope of salvation. Give your heart to Christ who waits to save you, receive him to your soul for he seeks admittance. Trust in him and he will save you.

Henry, with more military information at his disposal and more to prepare before departing, wrote a more succinct letter about their mission:

We have just received orders to be in readiness to moove at 4 A.M. tomorrow morning with three days rations in haversacks & three in knapsacks & ten extra rounds of cartridges. We expect to go to Mine Run again if possible to

gain the ground before the enemy. Hooker is in the Shanandoa Valley to pre-
vent a flank moovement of the rebils into Maryland. I have got the unpleasant
job of commanding the Company. I had hoped the Captain would be back &
take his place.

We expect to see trying times when we march. Mine Run has not a very
good reputation with us. Still we hope for success. Burnside has arrived at
Brandy Station with fifty thousand men & relieved the 3rd Corps so the
Potomac Army has got the fighting to do after all. I think of no more news
& my haste compells me to close without finishing my sheet. Pray for your
children in the Army.

Those words ended the last of the wartime letters that Chester and Betsey would receive from their younger son.

Getty's Division led the Sixth Corps out of its comfortable winter quarters at 4 a.m. on the morning of May 4 as scheduled. The army had been split in two in order to more efficiently get across the Rapidan. The Sixth Corps, along with the Fifth, marched to Germanna Ford where they crossed on a hastily constructed pontoon bridge. By afternoon the Sixth Corps was across the river and made camp about two miles south of the river on Flat Run. The Fifth Corps had crossed the river earlier and marched to Wilderness Tavern. Grant anticipatied being able to bring his entire army back together to attack Lee's defenses at Mine Run, but Lee now saw another opportunity. Even though he was still awaiting the arrival of Longstreet's corps, by attacking the Federal forces in the Wilderness area he could diminish many of the Union advantages. The thick underbrush and tangled vines would make it difficult to move troops as well as limiting cavalry and artil-lery movements. If Lee could stop the Union advance within the Wilderness area, Longstreet's corps could be expected to arrive later in the day to perhaps finish off an entrapped and exhausted Union army. Lee thus ordered Ewell's Second Corps and A. P. Hill's third Corps to advance toward the Wilderness.

Early on the morning of May 5, General Warren, commanding the Fifth Corps, began receiving reports of Confederate infantry approaching. Although the Sixth Corps was in support of the Fifth, Meade ordered Getty's division, including the Vermont Brigade, to advance to the intersection of the Orange Plank Road and Brock Road. They were to hold the intersection until Hancock's Second Corps could arrive to secure it. Getty's division moved quickly and arrived just before General Henry Heth's division of A. P. Hill's corps came down the Orange Plank Road. Unfortunately for Getty's division, Hancock did not receive his orders immediately, and Getty's men were left to hold this position on their own for about two hours. Warren's Fifth Corps held off Ewell's attack on the Confederate left, while Getty's division at the Orange Plank Road–Brock Road intersection stopped Hill's advance. Aided by the arrival of Hancock's corps, Federal forces began to make inroads against Hill on the Confederate right, forcing Lee to send in more of his reserve forces. The situation changed dramatically with the arrival of Longstreet's corps the next morning along the Orange Plank Road, but Federal soldiers were able to hold onto the crossroads.

The fighting that ensued around the Orange Plank Road–Brock Road intersection, starting around noon on May 5, was some of the most ferociously intense and chaotic of the war. Unable to see far ahead as they tried to maneuver through the thick underbrush, enemy combatants would suddenly come across each other. Smoke filled the air, not only from the muskets but from small brush fires that began to break out, adding to the agony of the wounded and the confusion of the combatants. Soldiers from the Vermont Brigade, which had moved ahead of the other brigades around them, fell in numbers they had never before witnessed, yet they would not fall back. Among the wounded, Henry, leading his company because his captain had not yet returned, was shot in the chest. Francis was shot along the side of his neck, but his injury was not life-threatening. Henry was brought back for medical attention, but in the confusion Francis did not find out about his brother's situation until the next day, when Charles Lynde found him. Francis found his severely wounded brother and remained with him as Henry was transported to a church, probably Salem Church, which was being used as a hospital. Henry passed in and out of consciousness, occasionally conversing with his brother, over the course of the next several days, and died on May 8. Francis then continued on to Fredericksburg, where virtually all large houses and buildings were being used for the wounded, to attend to his own injury.

Fighting continued throughout the Wilderness for several days. The intersection of the Orange Plank Road and Brock Road was one of the most important crossroads of the war. Without control of it the Union army would have been unable to proceed, and Grant, like Burnside and Hooker before him, may have been forced to retreat north of the Rapidan. The Vermont Brigade fought for two days at that intersection, losing a staggering 1,234 men on that spot. Overall, Grant's forces suffered 17,500 casualties to Lee's 10,000. When the fighting was over, however, Grant could stand at the pivotal intersection and point the army south. It would not retreat this time as it had done so often before. At the intersection today stands the Vermont Brigade Monument, commemorating the sacrifice of those who gave their lives in this momentous battle to preserve the Union.

Chester and Betsey Martin heard that their son had died from newspaper accounts of the battle. Two weeks later, on May 22, Chester wrote a letter to Francis:

> Yours informing us where you are is just received & I write you immediately. We have heard nothing from you before since you left camp near Brandy Station. The papers inform us you have had hard fighting & that the loss was very heavy in the Vermont Brigade. That Henry was wounded on Thursday the 5th & died on Sunday the 8th but we could not give up all hope that it was not so. Mr. Smith has just received a letter from Henry [Smith] saying he feared Lieut. W. H. Martin was dead, so we concluded it must be so.
>
> We wish you to give us all the information you can. The particulars respecting him & whether his body can be obtained. He sent the sword presented him last winter by Mr. Barnard. I presume you can anticipate in some measure the sad feeling which Henrys death must produce upon us but we hope & pray that your life may be spared that we may not be left childless. May this affliction be the means of preparing us to meet in that better world where we hope & trust he has gone.

Francis wrote back from Fredericksburg on May 28:

As no mail has come to this place for several days of course I have received no answer to my last in which I informed you of the death of my brother. I am sorry that I cannot hear from home now but do not expect to again until I join the regiment. All the wounded are now on their way to Washington and the nurses & those who have sufficiently recovered from the effects of their wounds will join their regiments as soon as possible. So if you have addressed a letter to me at this place it will be lost. If I could choose for myself, to say nothing of the danger, I would rather be a hospital nurse than a soldier – not that I would turn back where I should go forward but although the work is hard it is less wearing for me than campaigning. It is very sad to loose Henry and I feel deeply for you at home and wish that I might be able to do something to comfort you and to lessen your burdens about the work at home. I cannot now advise as I am not acquainted with your situation. The best I can do is to advise you to seek the aid of Him who is Almighty and infinite in mercy compassion & goodness. Our trials are severe but let us put our trust in Him.

Francis apparently sent a letter home describing Henry's death that was never received. Betsey particularly wanted to know what his final hours were like and his final thoughts and words. After much prodding, Francis finally wrote such a letter, months after Henry's death, on September 12:

Mother expresses a wish to know whether Henry spoke of his home and friends before his death and for her satisfaction I will relate a few particulars which I think I have not mentioned before. After being wounded myself I went to the rear & there to the place where our division hospital was located. This was in the rear of the right wing of our army. The next morning being <u>exceedingly</u> tired, I went to an old building and slept until Charles Lynde found me and informed me that Henry was wounded. I then went to him and remained with him while he lived. Henry first said "I want you to take care of me. I do not wish to have strangers handle me." He was very weak and conversed only at intervails. He knew that the chances were against him but neither he nor I gave up hope and I said nothing to extinquish the hope he possessed feeling that he was prepared for death and seldom indevered to induce him to converse at all unless he manifested some such desire. He was weakened more by his wound than men usually are. He said that as soon as he was shot he tried to walk back to the rear but was so weak that he was unable to go more than two or three rods. He said that if he ever recovered he should be contented to spend the rest of his life at home but said nothing about his parents or friends (that is but no <u>special dying</u> message to them *not from disregard or indifference but because when he was able to talk his attention was to a great extent necessarily occupied with other things as you will see after I have given some further account of the situation in which we were then placed). The ground was covered with wounded men. We could hear the battle raging in front. Towards night the rebels drove on toward our right flank and it was feared that we could not hold them & that they would be down upon us where we lay. During the night the wounded were moved as fast as possible and being unable to get carried in the first ambulance train he was anxious lest the ambulance should be unable to return and that the wounded left behind would fall into the hands of the rebels. (A good many were finally left behind and were not sent for until just before the Fredericsburg hospital was broken up). About daylight the ambulances returned and Henry was taken to the place where the other wounded men have been removed. The confusion of that night, the anxiety which he must have felt in some degree and his weakness would naturally prevent his thoughts from turning homeward as he was compeled to think of other things. The next day when we arrived at a place of comparative quiet he was exhausted and slept most of the time. In the afternoon he revived again and from time to time conversed for a few moments. Until the last moments he manifested but few signs that his mind wandered. It was like this – he was too tired to keep a train of thought in his mind any length of time and would soon forget himself and fall asleep. Although I can transmit no messages from him to you I can testify to his noble manly and Christianlike appearance and assure you that but few regard their friends with such deep affection as he did. I am very thankful that I was with him although it was no common trial to me and I could seek sympathy from no one for where I most derived sympathy & need I did. I of course could not be understood by those who were around me for they were strangers to like feelings.*

Francis might have provided additional comfort to his mother by stretching the truth in his recount and saying that Henry's last thoughts were of his love of home and family, but he clearly chose to maintain a scrupulous honesty.

William Henry Martin died at age twenty-five. Born in Orange County, Vermont, fewer than twenty miles from the state capital of Montpelier, he met his fate in Orange County, Virginia, believing that he was fighting to preserve the vision of the nation's Founding Fathers. He died fewer than twenty miles from the home of one of those Founding Fathers, James Madison, and his family estate, also named Montpelier.

Chapter 15

RETURN TO DUTY

Leading his company into battle, William Henry Martin had been one of the first casualties in what Abraham Lincoln referred to as the "terrible mathematics" of Grant's Overland Campaign. In General Grant, Lincoln had found a strategist who understood as he did that the war could be won only through a war of attrition, with enormous losses of soldiers on both sides. Ultimately, the Confederates would have insufficient numbers of troops to defend their nascent country. Grant displayed the determination to pursue this type of campaign despite the casualty rate. The North could draft more soldiers; the South would be hard pressed to do so.

Rather than retreat after taking such heavy losses in the Wilderness, Grant continued on toward Richmond as if he had just won a major victory. Lee recognized what Grant was attempting and moved his army quickly to await the Army of the Potomac at the crossroads at Spotsylvania Court House. Eleven days of intense fighting ensued. Grant continually moved his forces to his left, attempting to outflank Lee. The Confederate forces moved to stop each advance. By the end of June the Union army had circled around east of Richmond and was ready to start laying siege to Petersburg, the vital railroad junction supplying Richmond from the south. In order to establish this position, the Overland Campaign sustained approximately 55,000 Union casualties during the months of May and June.

Francis missed most of this campaign after receiving his neck injury on the first day of fighting in the Wilderness. He was moved back with the

Fredericksburg Baptist Church
Courtesy of Library of Congress

injured, including Henry, for medical care behind the lines. Francis eventually reached Fredericksburg, where so many of the buildings and large homes were being used as hospital sites. He was cared for in the Baptist church facility and later served as an aide to help those who had suffered more serious injuries than his. On May 26, a group of those deemed to have recovered sufficiently from their injuries, including Francis, were ordered to march from Fredericksburg back to the army.

By June 2 their long march was over, and Francis rejoined his regiment the next day. He arrived in the midst of the Battle of Cold Harbor, the Union's most devastating defeat in the Overland Campaign. On June 3, the day when Francis rejoined his regiment, Grant ordered a futile charge into Lee's fortified positions. Grant later admitted that this attack was a terrible mistake on his part. The Sixth Corps was now under General Wright, replacing General Sedgwick who had been killed at Spotsylvania moments after his famous taunt that the Confederate sharpshooters "couldn't hit an elephant from that distance." Wright's corps had been heavily involved in fighting at Cold Harbor already but was spared from taking huge casualties during the June 3 fiasco. The Army of the Potomac lost an incredible 7,000 men in just thirty minutes during this debacle. The Vermont Brigade, which had suffered so severely in the Wilderness, lost another 104 men. By the time Francis arrived, they were digging into defensive positions after the failed attack.

On June 6, one month after Francis and Henry had been wounded in the Wilderness, and after the heaviest losses at Cold Harbor had occurred, Francis wrote home from "Camp Near Coal Harbor Va."

My last which I hope you have received and answered ere this, was written at Fredericksburg Va. On the 22nd of May the worst cases were taken from the Baptist Church Hospital and removed to the field hospital in the outskirts of the town where they were placed in large tents. About a dozen nurses, including myself, accompanied them. We remained here four days and there the wounded were all taken on transports to Washington and preparations made for evacuating the place. We hoped to be taken to Port Royal or White House on transports but after two days we were ordered to commence our march. We did not take the most direct road and marched 35 miles according to the general estimate and then encamped about 1 1/2 miles from Port Royal. The next morning we entered the town, encamped and remained until the 31st then marched at 5 A.M. to Bowling Green where we arrived at 1 1/2 o'clock A.M. and camped until 5 o'clock the next morning. We then advanced beyond Hanover Court house. The last two hours exposed to a heavy thunder shower. Just before dark we encamped but had hardly put up our tents before we rece'd marching orders as we were in some danger of being captured. We marched until 5 o'clock A.M. and then encamped in a large yard in front of a hand-some white house. At 6 A.M. we resumed our march and entered our lines at 9 A.M. Before night we were sent to Army head quarters where we remained until yesterday and then left at 4 P.M. for Corps head quarters, then for division head quarters and last of all to the Colonel of our Regt. (Col Pingree).

The regiment is now at the front occupying the Second line of breast works. A constant fire is kept up and the balls strike the trees around us from time to time. How this will terminate God only knows. We expect that Richmond must eventually fall. Pray for us that we may have the divine blessing and protection.

I hope you will prosper in your work at home but I should think that the charge of your farm would be too much for you now and if I should lose my life or remain in the service the remainder of my three years I should think that it would be best for you to let out your farm. I should not like to sell it yet. Please write as soon as you get this directing to me at my regt. and if my life is spared I shall probably receive it soon.

P.S. Have you seen an article in the Vt Chronicle entitled "Predestination not Fatalism."

The reason for the postscript was that this was an article he had recently submitted to the newspaper, following his battlefield misfortunes. In this ponderous article, attempting to make a theological distinction between the two concepts in his title, his point seemed to be that while our salvation is preordained by God, not everything in life is predestined to happen as it does because man still retains free will.

On the same day as his letter, Francis also returned to his role as a war correspondent.

Camp near Coal Harbor, Va.,
June 6, 1864.

Mr. Editor—It is now some time since I last addressed your readers through your paper, and they may reasonably expect in so eventful a time as the present, some thrilling account of personal adventure, but my time has been occupied with the less arduous and dangerous, though perhaps the no less important work of caring for the wounded.

On the 5th of May the second day after crossing the Rapidan, I was wounded in the neck and went to the rear. From the field hospital I went with other wounded men to Fredericksburg, at which place we arrived on the morning of the 9th. Most if not all of the public buildings, and many private residences were filled with wounded soldiers. I was sent to the hospital of the 3d division of the 6th corps at the Baptist Church, where I was detailed as nurse as soon as my wound would admit. The wounded were as well cared for as circumstances would admit, but there must have been much suffering if we had received no aid from the Sanitary and Christian Commissions. As it was there was a scant supply of medical stores, to say nothing of short rations, from which both the wounded and their nurses suffered alike. Many died from wounds which under more favorable circumstances might not have proved fatal. On the evening of the 22nd the worst cases were moved from the Baptist Church to the field hospital in the outskirts of the town, where it was thought that they would have better care, and enjoy the advantage of pure air in the large tents which were there prepared for their accommodation. All this was done with the expectation that the location was to be permanent, but as it proved it would have been better for the wounded to have remained in the hospital in town, as they would have been taken to Washington sooner and their stay at the field hospital was too short for them to derive any benefit from the change. On the 26th all the patients were taken to the landing and carried aboard the transports provided for their conveyance to Washington. The nurses hoped to obtain passage on the transports to Port Royal, but were disappointed. We remained at Fredericksburg until the 28th and then at 7 1-2 o'clock a.m. we commenced our march for Port Royal. By some mistake we failed to take the most direct road, and marched according to the general estimate, twenty-five miles, and then encamped within 1 1-2 miles of Port Royal.

The next morning we entered the town with the expectation of being taken to White House Landing on the transports, but soon all nurses, convalescents, and stragglers were ordered into camp out side of the town. Here we remained until the 31st, and then at 5 o'clock a. m. broke camp and started for Bowling Green, where we arrived at 1 1-2 o'clock p.m., and encamped until 7 o'clock the next morning, when we resumed our march, forded the Pamunky at 11 o'clock a.m., then rested until 3 p.m. when we received marching orders again. We had hardly started before a heavy thunder shower burst upon us, in which we marched for nearly three hours and then pitched our tents about a mile beyond Hanover Court House. This was hardly done before we received marching orders again, as it was considered necessary to make a forced march to escape an attack from the rebels who were hovering about our rear. This night's march in almost inky darkness, at times through mud twelve inches deep, with apprehensions of an attack from guerrillas, will be remembered by many as one of the severest in their *experience. At 3 o'clock a.m. we arrived at a handsome white house with a large yard in front, and our men at once spread their blankets under the trees and shrubbery with which the grounds were adorned. I was so fortunate as to secure a place in an out building, where after taking off my shoes, well filled with mud, I wrapped myself in my blanket and slept soundly for three hours, when we received orders to resume our march. We entered our lines at 9 a.m., and were conducted first to Burnside's Headquarters, where the 9th corps men were assigned to their respective regiments. Late in the afternoon we were taken to the Army Headquarters, where we remained under guard until the 5th when we were examined and those who could give a satisfactory account of themselves accompanied with sufficient proofs were sent to the Headquarters of their corps, Division, Brigades and last of all their regiments. I found my company at the front occupying the second line of breastworks. Upon which the rebels kept a constant fusilade of musketry, many of the balls striking the trees around us, but doing us no harm. At 12 m, we were ordered back to the rear, and with the exception of the front parapet, all of the lines of breastworks were vacated, to give place it is said for large siege guns now on their way from White House.*

Hoping that this campaign may reach a successful termination, and that I may be spared to write many letters for your paper, I subscribe myself,
CONSCRIPT.

By the time of Francis's next letter, two weeks later, Grant had abandoned the Cold Harbor attack and moved the army around Richmond toward Petersburg. During the first week of fighting there, the Federal troops endured another 7,000 casualties, but the Vermont Brigade was this time held back in reserve. From that vantage point, it witnessed an impressive showing by the soldiers of the United States Colored Troops on June 18 when they successfully charged a Confederate defensive position. Francis wrote from "Camp Near Petersburg, Va Sunday Morning June 19th 1864":

You have probably learned from the papers before this time that Grant has abandoned his works at Coal Harbor and is now threatning Richmond on the south side. Yesterday there was hard fighting through the day in front of Petersburg. The advantage was on our side but I suppose that we did not gain much ground. The 2nd Vt was not engaged. The night before we were on picket. In the morning we were deployed as skirmishers & advanced about a mile before we found any signs of the enemy. Then we lay quiet about two hours when we were relieved by another line of skirmishers who advanced &

were soon engaged with the enemy. We retired to a road which lay between to high banks or rather in a ravine which sheltered us.

Burnsides negroes were called into action and behaved themselves well. The negroes are animated by a better spirit than most of our men. This is acknowledged by all who are acquainted with the facts as they are. There is less confidence in the early triumph of our cause in the army than elsewhere. The rebel soldiers are as good as ours. Their Generals probably better and they have the advantage of fighting behind strong fortifications on their own ground. When our men charge on their works the loss of life is fearful and we are seldom able to hold their works when taken. Whether this campaign will end the war or whether it will be indefinitely prolonged no man knows. For myself I have little to say and no complaints to make. I have tried to do my duty and I do not think that any other man in my company has had a harder time than I. How I have gone through it all I cannot see. Since the warm weather commenced I have been growing stronger. Open air in good weather agrees with most men. The term of service of the old boys of the 2nd expired today. There are many reasons why I should like to be one of their number.

As the fighting intensified and Union forces attempted to cut off railroad lines entering Petersburg, Francis wrote from "Camp Near Petersburg Rail Road June 26th, 1864":

Last week we were moved to the extreme left where we are now covering the left flank of the army. By Tuesday night just after we had commenced making preperations to encamp we were ordered to fall in & then the brigade was massed as we supposed for a charge. The 1st and third divisions were in front of us and we could hear their cheers as they charged on the enemy lying between us and Petersburg railroad (the road from Petersburg to North Carolina). They found but few rebels and met with but little opposition. They advanced to the railroad and the following day a few miles of its track was destroyed. The next day they were driven back by a superior force of the enemy's and four companies of the 4th Vt and 400 men of the 11th Vt were taken prisoners probably owing to the bad management of their officers. Our regiment advanced to a line of breast works from which the enemy had been driven and halted. We remained there during the next day taking no part in the fighting to which I had made allusion. Just before dark we heard firing. Our men were being driven in so we were at once ordered to throw up breast works and in an hour they were completed and we in readiness to meet the enemy from whom we expected a charge every moment. They approached within 400 yards, encamped for the night and withdrew the next morning. About midnight we were relieved and went to the rear where we still remain. Tonight I suppose that our regiment will go on picket as it is our turn. The weather is very dry and hot. There is plenty of good water here, no small consideration. The men are in good health and spirits. Company F will probably be broken up and divided among the different companies in the regt. We have but few commissioned officers now.

For the next several weeks the Vermont Brigade was involved in skirmishes south and east of Petersburg, particularly around the Weldon Railroad. Francis wrote again from "Camp Near Fredericksburg Rail Road" on July 1:

We have just returned from a raid. Day before yesterday we unexpectedly received marching orders and advanced 8 or 10 miles I should judge to the Petersburg R.R. About a mile of its track was destroyed and then we returned. I suppose that our men intended to hold the position, as strong and well finished breastworks were thrown up. Why they were abandoned I do not yet know. Our regiment was ordered into the skirmish line. Our cavalry was skirmishing ahead of us and we expected to be called into action but were not. ...

I hope you have received another letter from me giving an account of Henry's death. If not I will write it again. Any unconciousness after receiving his wound was occasioned by weakness and weariness. It was nothing of the stupidity or delirium produced sometimes by disease. Henry had many noble traits which none but a brother would have opportunity to discover. I did not expect that he would be killed in this war for it seemed that with his health, disposition, and ability his work could not be done. In loosing him I lost one of my best friends. I cherish his memory with feeling of esteem, love, and gratitude as well as sorrow. Still, I can find no feelings of irreconciliation at his loss. After assisting in his burial I went on satisfied that I had been with him and well discharged my duty to him. I believe that he has gone to rest & joy and if we could look at this event aright I believe that while we sorrowed at our loss, we should rejoice at his gain. All our cares are sent to wean our affections from this world and to teach us to lean upon our heavenly Father for support. I do not know anything about his sword. Perhaps it was lost on the field. I found his pocket pen knife but the blades were broken. He told me of his connection with Laura Ainsworth and Lorette lately wrote me respecting it. When I first saw him he said that if he ever recovered he should be contented to stay at home. I will try and collect the notes you sent me. The best way to procure his pay will be to employ some lawyers. He was last paid on the 29th of Feby. and died on the 8th of May. His pay cannot be drawn here. I am glad to hear that you get along as well as you do. Perhaps this war may end and I may live to be with you another year but rely on no such prospect.

I lately sent a paper home inclosing a bunch of <u>Trumpet Creepers</u> which I picked from a vine covering an apple tree. I presume that they were destroyed before they reached home so that you could form little idea of them. Yesterday I saw the finest morning glories I ever met with growing wild in a field. I see many fine fields of corn and wheat fit to cut. Virginia would be a beautiful state in the hands of Northern men. It is mountainous but while the land is rolling it everywhere abounds in table lands of great extent on which mowing & reaping machines could be used to good advantage. Fruit abounds, apples, peaches, cherries, and berries. With much love for you both and desiring to hear from you.

Francis had gotten so carried away with the flora of the land that he forgot to request some needed supplies, forcing him to rectify the omission the next day:

Yesterday I wrote you. Today I think of some things which I had failed to mention & as my letters do not always go directly I do not wish to postpone writing them longer. I would like to have you procure & send in a newspaper to me a small India rubber pocket inkstand, the top to screw on, the price will probably be 50 cents. If you cannot procure one to answer the description I do not wish to have you get any. Perhaps you had better send me a few sheets of paper & envelopes when you write again. I suppose that we shall not be paid again for two months. At this season one – myself certainly – requires some luxuries such as lemons & the like. Please send me $10.00 when you receive this. There is some risk but I do not wish to be out of money.

As the fighting continued around Petersburg, Francis found time to update his readers on this phase of the war:

*Camp near Petersburg, R.R. Va.,
July 1864.*

Mr. Editor— My stay at Coal Harbor was of seven day's duration. A little more than half of that time was passed in the trenches behind the breastworks, and the remainder resting at the rear. At the front we were comparatively safe if we kept down behind the breastworks; although a rebel shell exploding in our immediate vicinity occasionally warned us that even then we were not out of the enemy's reach. But curiosity, indifference and necessity, often causes our boys to expose themselves, and sometimes one was hit. The rebels must have had sharpshooters in some of the pines overlooking our work, and when a detail of men came in from the rear with boxes of hard tack on their shoulders, the balls which struck the surrounding trees above and on each side in quick succession, showed that they were not unobserved.

In going from one part of the lines to another most of the men crouched to obtain as much protection from the breastworks as possible, but others from a spirit of indifference or bravado, walked upright as usual. One man was the object of special notice to many, never bowing his head, never accelerating his pace, never hesitating to expose himself when exposure was necessary for the accomplishment of his purposes, always cool, yet never doing anything to attract attention, and never I should judge, exposing himself for the excitement which a certain amount of danger often produces, still in one instance when he attracted the attention of the rebel sharpshooters, and a half dozen balls struck the trees within a yard on either side, the love of life for the moment predominated, and he dodged like others and hastened out of danger. Our cooking was done over fires a few feet in the rear. These were usually extinguished at night. In one instance a party who had just returned from picket and had been without coffee through the day, without heeding the warnings of their comrades, commenced preparing that beverage which every soldier prizes so highly, but their work was hardly done before the report of a gun and the sound of a shell directly overhead, made it necessary to scatter the fire brands as soon as possible. At the rear we have opportunity to move about, wash ourselves and obtain needed rest; but even there a long-range ball occasionally found its way from the front, sometimes striking a man. There was no safety from the enemy's shell within range of their guns. Some came from a long distance, so that the first and only warning was that peculiar sound which a nearly spent shell makes in passing through the air. For a few seconds we would hear this, then followed the report as it exploded scattering the fragments all around. Up to Sunday night, June 12th, the breastworks were manned, firing kept up, and fatigue parties detailed to work on the fortifications. At 9 o'clock P. M. we received the order to pack up and fall in. We then advanced a mile and formed in line of battle behind a breastwork, where we remained to guard against a possible attack in the rear, until midnight, then we advanced about eight miles I should judge, and halted to prepare and eat our breakfast at 4 o'clock A.M. Through the remainder of the day we marched rapidly, though with frequent and long rests, often occasioned by the state of the roads, crossed the Chickahomany at 8 P.M. and encamped for the night at 9. The next morning we were on the move again at 5 o'clock, advanced about four miles in the direction of James River, where we encamped in an open field, threw out pickets and remained two days.

On the morning of the 16th we moved forward another mile nearer the river, which we crossed in the evening of the same day on a pontoon bridge not far from Charles City Court House and then pushed on towards Petersburg although at the time we supposed City Point to be our destination, the 1st and 3d divisions of the 6th corps were conveyed to City Point on transports. I am informed that Gen. Niel then in command of the 2d division offered to bet twenty barrels of whiskey that he would get his division to Petersburg, ahead of two which were carried to City Point on the steam transports. Our men fatigued with the march, and seeing no prospect of immediate rest, gave out to their feelings of irritation by such expressions as are common among soldiers at such time, one exclaiming when the column was compelled to halt for a moment by some obstruction in the road; "Oh! don't stop," or "don't stop because you think I am tired, for I ain't," and soon, with variations according to the disposition of the speaker. Soon our rests were so frequent and long that they were almost as tiresome as continuous marching. By a night march the heat of the day is avoided, but a slough hole in the road which by day would soon be passed over, will check the progress of the entire column for a long time. A rest of fifteen or twenty minutes to the mile is very acceptable, but those long stops at night, when the soldier cannot spread his blanket, and does not wish to fall asleep, lasting until he is thoroughly chilled, and then giving place to a forward move of a few rods in a state of semi-consciousness are anything but pleasant. Many of our boys turned into the woods, and overtook their regiments in the morning. The division halted at 3 o'clock a.m., having made ten miles perhaps. At 6 o'clock a.m. we advanced again, and at 10 a.m. encamped within five or six miles of Petersburg, confident in the belief of the report which had several times reached us, that Petersburg was in our possession, a pleasant illusion soon to be dispelled by cavalry men coming from the front who informed us of the actual state of affairs. At two o'clock p.m. we advanced a mile, the heat was intense and many of the men with difficulty kept their place in the ranks. After resting an hour, we moved on again and halted near the first line of works captured by our forces from the enemy.

At sundown the 2d Vt. regiment was ordered on picket. We deployed as skirmishers, advanced a quarter of a mile in a northerly direction and relieved the pickets who were stationed along side of a wide and deep ditch. Here after posting the videttes, we spread our blankets and prepared for a *night rest, but were aroused by the sound of musketry on our left. It was the heaviest firing I had ever heard, and as it seemed to be drawing nearer we concluded that the enemy were driving our men. Soon our batteries opened and for about twenty minutes the heavy reports of the large guns following each other in rapid succession, blended with the rattling volleys of musketry, and then, with the exception of an occasional shot, all was still again through the night. At day break the front rank skirmishers were ordered to advance. We crossed the ditch, moved across an open field , then crossed a road whose well shaded sides we thought might possibly cover the rebel skirmishers, but finding nothing to arrest our progress we continued our advance through a wheat field, towards a line of trees, from which we expected to receive the fire of the enemies skirmishers, but no rebels were there, and arriving at the line of trees, half a mile from our starting point we found ourselves on the thickly wooded banks of Appomattox river, which flowed some ten feet below the left. Up the river could be seen a portion of the city of Petersburg. Directly in front on the same side was a deep ravine. Here we halted, our left wing being stationed on the bank of the ravine our right fronting the river and waited the approach of our rear rank men who soon joined us.*

As anything like a complete description of the events embraced in my plan when I commenced this letter will be too lengthy for one article, I will defer the conclusion until I have time to write again. CONSCRIPT.

Within the week, he had the needed time to continue his account of this campaign:

Camp near Petersburg & Weldon R.R.
July 9, 1864

Mr. Editor.—My last left us on the skirmish line near Petersburg. We did not advance, but at 9 o'clock A.M. were relieved by the 11th Vt., who at once crossed the ravine and were soon engaged with the rebel skirmishers on the opposite side, while we retraced our steps back to the road we had crossed coming out, followed it about forty rods in the direction of the city, where it passed through a ravine, halted and stacked arms, protected on either side by a bank about eight feet in height. Here we remained through the day (the 18th of June) taking no part in the conflict, which was continued with little intermission until dark.

Some of our boys witnessed the charge made by Burnside's negroes, whose gallantry won golden opinions, often from unwilling lips. While their bravery was well worthy of the praise it received, the humanity displayed in their care for the wounded, both black and white, though a less brilliant attribute of heroism, was no less worthy of commendation. A colored chaplain made himself conspicuous by his intelligent conversation, gentlemanly appearance, and the active and efficient aid he rendered to the wounded, working as a stretcher bearer until all the wounded were removed from the field. His patriotism, if his words were its true index, was of the highest order. He was sorry that the regiment to which he was attached suffered so severely, but would rather have seen the last man fall, than to witness them driven by the enemy.

At dark we went back to the Brigade Headquarters in the rear and remained there during the succeeding day. Here those who remained of the men who were with the regiment at the time of the organization left to their homes, their term of service having expired. For faithfulness, fortitude and gallantry in action, they have won a reputation which will last while deeds of heroism had admirers. Ever ready to obey the commands of officers in whom they confided, never willing to give up an advantage once obtained; still they were not renowned for foolhardiness and were guiltless of the foolish declaration attributed to them by so many of the newspapers – "That they would never leave the rifle pits which they had just taken from the enemy, although ordered back, without permission to make the next charge." It is true that they were unwilling to give up the work and offered to hold it if they could be supported with ammunition; but though ready to make a charge if necessary, they never coveted the privilege.

At dark the regiment was ordered back to the front. We lay on one side of a ravine through the following day as a reserve, receiving no orders until sundown, then we were marched about a mile to the left and posted behind a line of breastworks at the front. As usual there was a picket line beyond this, protected by good breastworks. The firing was kept up by the pickets only. To describe the day passed by us in the trenches here, would be a repetition of previous accounts; it was unmarked by any extraordinary incidents, and no casuality of any account occurred. Just before sundown the smoke of one of our fires or the crowd clustering around it, drew a succession of shots from the enemy, driving us back behind the breastworks. This roused the ire of some of our boys, who at once reinforced the pickets and calmed their excited feelings by firing ten or fifteen rounds each at the rebel works.

At 10 o'clock P.M. June 21st, we were relieved and marched a few miles to the extreme left. The next day the 3d division was engaged skirmishing with the enemy, but contrary to our expectations we were not called into action. At sundown we commenced throwing up a breastwork, but our work was soon suspended, and the 1st and 3rd divisions were formed in lines of battle, and *massed for a charge many of us supposed. Cheers could be distinctly heard from the 3rd division advancing in front of us, and soon the different regiments fell into their places, and we followed in the direction of the Petersburg and Weldon Railroad. From the wounded we met returning to the rear we learned that there were but few rebels in front, who did not attempt to offer much resistance to our progress. We advanced two and half or three miles and then halted for the night. The next day nothing occurred to disturb our quiet until sundown, when the approaching sound of musketry indicated to us that the rebels were driving our men in from the front. We were at once ordered to throw up a breastwork, and in an hour it was finished and of sufficient strength to enable us to withstand any attack if the rebels had been disposed to come on. The firing grew more and more distinct, and long range balls occasionally striking near, warned those who were at work or outside with their spades that it was time to come in.*

A picket detail was made out from the regiment and advanced about two hundred yards in front to skirmish with the approaching enemy. We lay in our places ready to resist the expected charge. Our pickets kept up a constant fire upon the wood, about six hundred yards distant, which covered the rebels. This lasted two hours, then the firing ceased, and the light of distant fires showed that the rebels had gone into camp. At midnight we were relieved and went back to the rear where – excepting an advance on the 29th to the railroad, to support Gen Sheridan, from which we returned on the 2nd of July – we have remained guarding the left flank of our army before Petersburg, until the date of this letter.

In writing the above I have not attempted to give a complete account of all the movements of the army in which I have borne a part, but rather to relate some incidents, with a sufficient account of our movements to give connection to the narrative.

For the Vermont Brigade, the siege of Petersburg now came to an end. The Sixth Corps was reassigned to Washington, D.C. They were on their way to being deployed in the Shenandoah Valley. Francis added one more paragraph to his newspaper submission:

Fort Stevens, Washington, July 13.

Last Saturday (the 9th) we received marching orders at ten o'clock p.m. marched to City Point, where we arrived at sunrise. Embarked on transports in the afternoon, and arrived here yesterday. There was skirmishing through the day yesterday, the advantage on the whole, being on the side of the rebels. Just before dark we took one hundred and fifty prisoners, and more are coming in this morning. The rebels left the position they occupied when the fighting ceased, and retired under the cover of night, further to the rear. CONSCRIPT

Chapter 16

IN THE SHENANDOAH
VALLEY

In the summer of 1864, with the presidential election approaching, Abraham Lincoln's political advisors were not overly optimistic. Lincoln had put his trust in Grant to finally win the war, but Grant's overall strategy did not seem to be working out as planned. General Banks was slowed down in Louisiana and never made it to Mobile as Grant had intended. Benjamin Butler came up from the south toward Richmond but, after facing stiff resistance, fell back into a defensive position. In his march toward the railroad junction at Staunton in the Shenandoah Valley, Franz Sigel met defeat at New Market in May. General Sherman had initially moved well against Johnston's retreating army, but he was now stalemated facing the Confederate defenses outside Atlanta. Grant himself was demonstrating the tenacity to fight to the end, but he too seemed bogged down outside Petersburg. Furthermore, the staggering casualty rates resulting from Grant's strategy were not going over well with a war-weary public.

After Sigel's defeat at New Market against Breckenridge's forces, joined by eager cadets from the Virginia Military Institute, he was replaced by David Hunter. In early June, Hunter both took control of Staunton and exacted revenge against the cadets by leaving VMI in ruins as he moved through Lexington. However, when he attempted to take Lynchburg in mid-June, Hunter found his supply lines cut off. After two days of fighting that did not go well for Hunter, and overestimating the strength of Jubal Early's forces, he retreated into West Virginia. With the Shenandoah Valley now clear of Federal forces, Early used the opportunity to advance all the way to the outskirts of Washington, D.C. Although it never appeared that he could break through Washington's defenses, Early's raid caused widespread panic in the capital. As Lee had hoped, Grant was obligated to send a part of his invading army from Petersburg to the Shenandoah Valley. General Wright's Sixth Corps was sent to track down Early.

Part of the Sixth Corps had already been dispatched to support Hunter when the Vermont Brigade received its orders to depart for Washington. The brigade left late on the night of July 9 and arrived by steamers on the afternoon of July 11. President Lincoln, underscoring the Vermont Brigade's reputation, arrived for the specific purpose of welcoming them. With Confederate forces just five miles away, the Sixth Corps was greeted with cheers and celebration by a nervous citizenry as it marched through the city. The weeks that followed included much marching and occasional skirmishes as the Sixth Corps chased Early's forces.

Francis wrote home on July 21 from "Camp Near Leesburg Va." Seeing the President must not have impressed him, since he did not mention it in his letter. It would be hard to imagine Henry failing to highlight the Vermont troops being praised by Abraham Lincoln as he greeted them at the landing.

> *It is hardly two weeks since I left Petersburg and since that time I have been in the defenses of Washington, marched through a portion of Maryland, forded the Potomac at White's Ford, entered the Shenandoah Valley at Snicker's Gap – forded the Shenandoah River and reforded it the same day and am now on my way back to Washington again. It is not probable that we shall remain there long – though we may be kept in that vicinity. I presume that we shall be transported back to Petersburg again. … We have had some hard marching and we are all very tired.*
>
> *A part of the 19th Corps has been here with us. The 8th Vermont belongs to this corps and lay near us not many days since. Frank Staples came over to our regiment and I told him to send Charles and Milton over. They came during the day. There is but little alteration in their appearance.*

Frank Staples had a horrific adventure ahead of him. He had become a corporal one month prior to this visit with Francis and was promoted to sergeant just a month later. In October, however, he was captured and ended up at Salisbury Prison Camp in North Carolina. In the wretched conditions of this camp, where the prisoners lived in the open air without even a blanket, he witnessed the deaths of all the other prisoners from his regiment. Close to death himself, he finally consented to fight on the side of the Confederacy in order to be released from the camp. Once placed in the Confederate Army, Staples immediately attempted to escape but was captured and returned to the prison camp. Already malnourished and suffering from scurvy, chronic diarrhea, and head lice, he was sentenced to a series of sadistic punishments. One involved being suspended by his thumbs, causing one thumb to be pulled out of joint. Another punishment resulted in several teeth being knocked out. Eventually a sympathetic guard aided his escape. After two weeks of walking, he made it back to Union lines near Petersburg almost a year after meeting with Francis. His weight had dropped from 171 pounds to 73. Staples was discharged and received a government pension until two decades later, when a government bureaucrat discovered that he had enlisted in the Confederate Army and canceled the pension. It took several years of struggle but Staples, never one to give up, finally had his pension restored.

Francis's letter of July 21 continued:

The country through which we have passed is pleasant – especially Maryland. The inhabitants were harvesting their wheat and getting in their hay. The treatment we receive from the people here is very different from that to which we have long been accustomed. In Virginia if we are not treated coldly we receive no encouragement. In Washington everyone seemed to take an interest in us. And where opportunity was offered many offered substantial tokens of their regard in the way of eatables. In Maryland the citizens greeted us with smiling faces and the children appeased us with a peculiar respect as though they had been taught by their parents that we were their defenders. However, while we are glad to give all credit to any one for any expressions of regard, we have learned to distrust the sincerity of appearances ...

He concluded the letter four days later:

We are now near Fort Gaines a few miles from Washington. I hope we shall remain here but expect we shall soon be ordered back to Petersburg. I have just reced two letters from you. ... The paper containing the ink stand I think must have been lost but I may yet receive it. Have you sent me the Chronicle containing the article I wrote? I would like to have you send me a fine comb, some pins and a few postage stamps. I shall be sorry to return to Petersburg for we are all tired and need rest.

The troops had returned to Washington because Wright believed that Early had left the area to rejoin Lee at Petersburg. Upon their arrival at the capital, the soldiers received four months of back pay. Francis sent a very short letter home on July 28 from "Camp near Rockville, Md.":

We have just been paid and although I may have to send home for money before we are paid again, I do not care to keep much by me and so send the inclosed $50.00, the rct of which please acknowledge. The paper containing ink stand has been recd.

As it turned out, Wright was wrong in thinking that Early had rejoined Lee's army and the soldiers were wrong in thinking that they were about to return to

Petersburg. In order to stop the transfer of the Union troops back to Petersburg, Early successfully attacked George Crook's Army of the Kanawha in the Second Battle of Kernstown (just outside Winchester) on July 24. He followed this victory with a raid across the border into Pennsylvania and the burning of Chambersburg on July 30 in retaliation for Hunter's destruction of VMI. Grant responded by reassigning the Sixth and Nineteenth Corps to remain in the Shenandoah Valley under the command of Philip Sheridan.

After several intensely hot days of hard marching through parts of Maryland, Francis wrote on August 5 from "Camp near Buckeystown Md.":

Since we have commenced our Maryland Campaign the mail has failed to come to us with the regularity it did when we were before Petersburg. Although we are now nearer Washington than then – I receive all or nearly all of your letters I think. I try to write every week and some of my letters may be lost or long on the road. I think that you must be getting along with your work very well. All things considered I do not suppose that a substitute for a soldier in the field would be accepted. I would like on many accounts to be with you, but see no immediate prospect of it, and whether I ever shall is known by God only.

My situation is not without benefit to myself. To learn to be a man in all places is no contemptible acquisition and I hope that I am daily acquiring some of that spirit.

In my last I inclosed $50.00 I did not wish to keep much by me since when I need it had rather send home for it. After a long march one finds himself so thoroughly tired and hungry that it is hard to recruit himself with mere army food. I do not wish to be extravagant but there is no one left – besides yourselves – in our family – but me – and it is not best to deny ourselves what we need and can afford. I return the note you sent me for collection. Co. A was captured by the enemy and of course I could not collect the note. At some future time I may have opportunity to do so. I have lost my pocket knife & cannot get one here for a reasonable price. Would like to have you get me one – not too large & send it to me in a paper. Some of the boys have tea sent them from home. I should like to have you send me 1/2 lb of the best green tea you can obtain – unless you have to pay letter postage on it. I can get good black tea here.

We have had much hard marching since we came here but no fighting as yet. How long this war is to continue it is useless to conjecture. It is easy for God to defeat our best plans and to continue this scourge which desolates both North and South. Still progress has been made & in time I presume the North will triumph.

The Army of the Shenandoah that had been crafted together for Sheridan consisted of about 35,000 men. Early, who was awaiting more reinforcements, had fewer than half that number and therefore tried to avoid a major engagement until more troops arrived. Only small skirmishes occurred as Sheridan pursued Early south of Winchester toward Early's base at Strasburg. To defeat Early would be of great political value because Lincoln was desperate for a victory somewhere with the election approaching. Moreover, the Shenandoah Valley provided much of the food for the Confederacy. Grant therefore ordered massive destruction of crops and livestock in the valley to support his war of attrition. During the pursuit, Francis wrote home on August 15 from "Camp Near Strasburg, Shenandoah Valley Va." Some of the skirmishing that had just occurred was on what became the Cedar Creek battlefield two months later.

> Last Friday we left Harpers Ferry and advanced up the Shenandoah Valley. On the 13th we overtook the enemy near the place from which this is dated. The 19th Corps & part of one division of the 6th Corps were first engaged. The enemy soon retiring further into the gap (Manassas gap).
>
> Last Saturday I was detailed for picket and remained until this morning. The first night our line was drawn back a few miles. Yesterday firing was kept up along the right of the line between the cavalry pickets who are always posted in advance of the infantry pickets. Just before sundown the line was advanced. The left remaining in nearly the same position & the right swinging round. For a short time there was sharp skirmishing with the rebel pickets who retired before us. Capt Wales of this regt was wounded in the head mortally I suppose – another man was wounded in the shoulder. Our regt has but few good officers now – most of the old officers having been killed or leaving at the expiration of their term of service. Last Saturday it is reported the enemy captured a lot of waggons belonging to the cavalry supply train – the hundred day men who acted as guards offering no resistance at all. The weather is very hot. Our work very hard – a good many have died on the march. I am very tired myself. In future I intend to get excused from duty when I feel unable to perform it if possible. The Shenandoah valley is a very fertile and beautiful country abounding with fruit and abundant harvests.

With supplies running low, Sheridan decided that he could not remain at Cedar Creek at this time. The army moved back through Winchester, and Francis continued his letter on August 20 from "Near Charlestown, Va.":

> We are now returning from the valley. I suppose that we shall stop at Harpers Ferry. There has been no opportunity to send out this letter before this

morning. An army does not need to stop long in any place to make it desolate. Fences disappear before it. Orchards & corn fields are striped – and in many cases all that the inhabitants have for subsistance taken from them. To a certain extent this is necessary and inevitable but it is always carried too far.

There is a rumor in circulation this morning that we are going back up the valley again. I hope not for I would like to be where we could get some rest and regular mails. Captain Wales was not seriously wounded and is now with his company. Have you seen any of the returned soldiers?

This time the rumor of their movement was correct. Confederates followed closely as the Federal army moved down the valley. On the morning of August 21, Early's forces attacked. In a scene reminiscent of Antietam, much of the fighting took place in a field of high corn stalks. The rebels were pushed out of the cornfield by the charging Vermont Brigade and reformed on a ridge behind the field. Francis described the fighting on August 22 in a letter from "Camp Near Harpers Ferry, Va.":

Yesterday morning – Sunday – we were roused by the sound of firing at the front. The rebel skirmishers had attacked our picket line. To all it was a complete surprise. The brigade at once received orders to pack up. The order to move soon followed and we were taken to the front & deployed along the line with intervols of two paces between the men. The Second Vermont lay on the side of a knoll over whose crest we kept up a constant fire at the rebels who lay behind another ridge about three hundred yards distant. The skirmishing continued until dark. At midnight we drew back as quietly as possible and retreated to the heights we now occupy. Our position is a strong one and I do not think that the rebels will attempt to drive us from it although they have pressed closely in our rear and now the sound of skirmishing can be heard. I am told that two hundred wounded were taken to the hospital from the brigade. A number were killed from our regiment. One man wounded out of our Company. The exact loss of this regt I have not yet learned. As usual a good many officers were shot. I think it probable that the rebels suffered as severely if not more so than ourselves. A large house on our line was occupied by two Companies of the 11th Vt. A number of shell struck the house after the rebels got range. Two men were killed by the explosion of a shell in one of the rooms but the house was not demolished. A shell would hardly strike the house before shots would be fired back through the hole made by its passage. I take but little satisfaction in witnessing such scenes or taking part in them. Still if necessary I wish to do well and not to shrink from my post. We all must die but we shall live our appointed time.

Francis concluded the next day:

We have just received marching orders again. Whether we are to go out onto the front line again – or going over into Maryland again I do not yet know. I write because I wish to get my letter in without waiting for anything new to transpire. Yesterday we rested in the rear. The rebels kept up a skirmish fire at the front making no other development of themselves simply holding their position. I lost my fine comb yesterday & cannot well do without it. Please send me another.

When he wrote again two days later, little had changed:

We are still occupying our position on the heights near Harper's Ferry. Breast works have been erected and are in process of erection to make our position as strong as possible. A little firing is kept up by the pickets but as yet no important move has been made on either side. Of the attack last Sunday of which the 6th Corps bore the brunt, I have already written you.

For a few days past I have been suffering from an attack of jaundice, a common complaint here from which but few escape. I have taken medicine which gives me some relief. Whether permanent or not time will determine. I am used to this kind of sickness as you well know.

Respecting volunteers, substitutes &c only strong able bodied men should be sent. Boys who are not too young or delicate are better than those who are liable to be overtaken by the infirmaties of old age, for they usually grow into the work and make good soldiers. Invalids are not wanted here, but I see no reason why boys like George Bruce might not do well enough.

(Seventeen-year-old George Bruce had enlisted a week before Francis wrote these words. A few months later he was injured when part of a tree fell on him while his detail was cutting firewood. He also displayed heart problems but remained in the army until the war was over.)

Henry's pay cannot be collected here. He was paid up to the 29th of February and from that time to the date of his death, May 8th it is due. State these facts to some good lawyer and he will take the matter in hand and for a consideration collect the money. Perhaps I may be able to do something about it. I will see. I reced the knife, also the tea. I would like to have you send me a little green tea every time you send a paper. ... I cannot live with anything like comfort with nothing but our army rations when on a campaign. Milk and fruits can some times be obtained and I wish, without being extravagant, to make myself as comfortable as possible if it takes all of my little wages. ... Can *you give me the address of Mr Asp of Boston, again, and the amount he now owes me. Henry collected $100 of him the last time he saw him.*

Skirmishing continued but the Union and Confederate positions changed little in the weeks that followed. Francis wrote home from "Camp Near Berryville, Va." on September 12:

> *Yours of the 4th containing ten dollars ($10) has been received also the newspapers you sent and their contents. It is very kind of you to attend to all my wishes so promptly. ...*
>
> *The soldiers have had an easier time of late, no long marches and plenty of rest. Last night there was a thunder shower. The rain fell in torrents but it soon soaked in to the ground which has been very dry of late. I was well protected by my tent.*
>
> *The pen with which I write is not a good one. I think that Henry's was better & suppose that you have it. ... I have considerable writing to do and had better send for Henry's pen rather than to buy another.*

One use for that pen would be to continue his war-time correspondence. The next Conscript article appeared in mid-September.

CAMP NEAR BERRYVILLE, Va.,
September 15.

Mr. Editor—After oscillating backwards and forwards between Washington and Harper's Ferry, and up and down the Shenandoah Valley, for the past two months, I will again attempt to renew my correspondence with your paper, which I have failed to keep up since I left Fort Stevens. Our marches have been hard, many of them needlessly so, I should judge, and conducted with an utter disregard to our power of endurance. As a natural and inevitable consequence, men were overpowered with heat and exhaustion, often fainted and sometimes fell out of the ranks, and died, while straggling became the order of the day. Strict orders were given for no man to leave the ranks, but to no purpose, until, without relaxing the strictness of the order against straggling, regulations for giving the men rest at stated intervals, with ample time for cooking and eating food, &c., were adopted, and to some extent carried out. In Maryland we were greeted with smiling faces, and that sympathy was extended to us, which must have had its origin in real love for the Union, and regard for its defenders, though quickened, no doubt, by the realization of the fact, that we were the protectors of their own lives and property, from the ravages of an invading enemy. This treatment, so unlike the cool civility, or ill concealed dislike, which had been our experience heretofore—was appreciated by the soldiers, and the officers had no difficulty in enforcing any orders against foraging.

Near Strasburg, a portion of the 2d Vt., who with details from other regiments were doing picket duty for the first time since leaving Petersburg, had a brush with the enemy. Our line advancing, the left wing swung around and flanked the rebel pickets, who discharged their pieces a few times, and then fell back. A few were wounded on our side. On the 21st of August, while lying near Charleston [West Virginia], we were surprised by an advance of the rebel skirmishers upon our picket line. The 2d division was ordered out to their support, and sharp skirmishing continued with little intermission through the day. In the left of the ground occupied by the 2d Vt. was a large dwelling-house from which our sharpshooters annoyed the enemy and soon drew shell from their batteries. The first shell which struck hit the chimney, throwing up a cloud of brick dust. Others exploded in the yard, the fragments striking the house, and a few passed directly through it. One exploding inside instantly killed two men. The soldiers manifested no disposition to leave their position, and a hole would hardly be made in the side of the house by a shell before one or more muskets would portrude and answer back again with a death-dealing fire.

After dark we drew back as quietly as possible, and reached the heights near Harper's Ferry the next morning where breastworks and other defences were thrown up, and we remained until the 28th. Then we advanced again, marched through that strong secesh town, Charlestown, to the tune of "Old John Brown," whose chorus of "Glory! Glory! Hallelujah! his soul is marching on," must have been refreshing to the citizens. We encamped about a mile beyond, where we remained until the 3d of the present month and then advanced to the camp we now occupy. Day before yesterday, the 13th, the 2d division of the 6th corps, in connection with a division from the 19th, also one from the 8th, made a reconissance, advancing to Opequan Creek. The result was the discovery of the enemy in sufficient force to hold us, the loss of a few men, and the capture of the 8th Georgia regiment numbering over two hundred men. The weather is now cooler, with frequent showers of rain. The health of the regiment is good, and its numerical strength daily increasing from the accession of recruits, and the return of convalescents from the hospitals. CONSCRIPT.

Grant arrived in Charlestown at about this time to confer with Sheridan. Grant reviewed and approved Sheridan's plan to take the offensive against Early. Federal forces soon moved out. Early, mistakenly believing that Sheridan was trying to avoid a major engagement, was caught by surprise at the Third Battle of Winchester on September 19. With an army of 40,000 men, Sheridan could more easily withstand his 5,000 casualties in this battle. The Confederates suffered 3,600 casualties with an army of just 12,000. As a result, they were forced to retreat further into the valley, enabling Sheridan to wreak further destruction among the civilian population in the area.

In the weeks that followed, the economic damage caused Lee to believe that it was necessary for Early to attack so that supply lines to Lee's beleaguered troops at Petersburg could be reestablished. A Confederate attack against Sheridan might have had a greater chance of success had Early not been so successful in initiating a rumor. Believing that Early was in no position to attack, Sheridan had been planning to send the Sixth Corps back to Petersburg. To stop that kind of troop movement, Early made it known that Longstreet's corps would soon be joining him in the Shenandoah Valley. The news made Sheridan sufficiently concerned that he kept the Sixth Corps with him.

Francis wrote on October 11 from "Camp Near Front Royal, Va.":

Yesterday we left Strasburg and moved to this place. It is said that we are here to repair the railroad which runs to Alexandria. Whether this is so or not I do not know. It would require a large force to guard the road from guerillas if finished & put in running order. We are either stopping here for that purpose or to build bridges for our troops to cross and to prevent the rebels from occupying Front Royal for when we drew back from Strasburg before, we did so because Front Royal was occupied by the rebels. When we commenced our march down the valley again the rebels pressed our rear closely but were driven back to Mt. Jackson with the loss of from 500 to 700 prisoners, 11 pieces of artillery & thirty army waggons. Last night I was detailed to go and work on a bridge. I did not feel much like work after my days march but as I was obliged to go I went doing no more work than I was obliged to but loosing a nights sleep. With the health & vigor of some this kind of life would be easier for me. While out some of the boys burned a barn and saw mill. This was sheer mischief and entirely unauthorized. The weather is getting to be quite cold at times. I shall need a pair of gloves soon. ... I suppose that this regiment will not be paid until another pay day as the rolls were not sent in as soon as they should have been. The rest of the brigade have been paid. I may want some money but will not send for any now as I do not like to be asking so many favors. I inclose a letter which I have just received from a man to whom I applied for assistance about collecting Henry's back pay. Very likely you will receive the necessary papers from him. ...

We have all suffered severe trials for the past few years, and experience many disappointments but let us hope that they may not prove of no benefit to us. And let us pray that we may yet meet on earth under more favorable circumstances.

Sheridan's forces were positioned between the Confederate army and Winchester, starting at Cedar Creek. Although outnumbered, Early believed he had found a way to rout the Union army. A narrow pathway had been left unguarded. John Gordon's division was sent on a difficult night march along this path, reaching Cedar Creek in the early morning fog on October 19. The other two divisions marched along the turnpike and joined the attack from further west. Union forces were taken completely by surprise. The Eighth Corps was hit first and quickly defeated. Then the Nineteenth Corps fell. The Vermont Brigade had thought it was just hearing some skirmishing along the picket line, but as retreating soldiers began running past their camp, they realized that something more significant was happening. The Sixth Corps quickly formed its lines and moved out to face the Confederate onslaught. When one of his comrades fell, Francis stopped to try to assist him. Seeing that he could do nothing to help, Francis started moving over to rejoin his own company but, before he could do so, was struck by a Minié ball in his left leg just above the ankle.

The battle was going very well for the Confederates initially. General Sheridan, who was in Winchester when the early morning attack began, rushed to Cedar Creek. He arrived at about 10:30 and found his army in disarray. Fortunately for the Federals, however, the rebel army, long deprived of supplies, paused in the attack to pillage the Union camps. Sheridan had time to rally his army to withstand the next Confederate attack and then to initiate a successful counterattack, turning what had looked like certain defeat into a Union victory.

For Francis, however, there would be no turnaround; his ordeal was just beginning. He related the story of what he endured in his last Conscript entry.

Ward 2 Patterson Park Hospital
Baltimore, Md., Dec. 24th, 1864.

Mr. Editor:—The 19th of Oct., now of historic note, was an episode in my life ending my career as a soldier, and necessitating me to act for the remainder of my days in a sphere entirely different from what I should have chosen.

It was a chilly, foggy morning, and the men turned out reluctantly to fall in under arms at reveille. As usual we were only detained long enough to stack arms in the company street, and then permitted to prepare for breakfast. A scattering fire of musketry could be heard on our right which we supposed to be picket firing which we heard every morning, but it soon extended along the lines to the left, growing sharper and shorter, and before we had fairly kindled our fires we received orders to pack up and fall in. Our brigade was marched to the extreme left, formed in line of battle, and every odd numbered man ordered to bring rails and throw up a slight breastwork. This work was just finished when we were ordered to advance. We moved a few rods, then halted and went back after our rails to throw up a breastwork in our new position. We had only time to commence the work before we were ordered to advance again and crossing a small creek we took up our position on the opposite side. A few moments rest and then came the order "about face," and we recrossed the creek – some of us, including myself, wetting our feet thoroughly – moved back, and took our new position behind the crest of a low hill or ground swell. Here we first saw the rebels who followed us closely, coming within a few rods of the hill behind which we were lying. We expected them to make a charge every moment, but they drew back to a hill some five or six hundred yards distant, and commenced shelling us from their batteries. We replied with our rifles, and fired away the greater part of our cartridges when the order "about face" was given again, and we fell back to take a new position. Moving across an open field we entered a wood where I was struck by a musket ball in the left leg a few inches above the ankle. I at once divested myself of my knapsacks and accouterments, and endeavored to use my gun as a crutch, but failing to make progress in this way, I accepted the proffered aid of two soldiers who helped me along about three miles before we found an ambulance. At length we found one belonging to the 19th corps in which I was conveyed to the 19th corps hospital at Newtown.

Here my wound received a partial examination, was bandaged, and I was then taken to 2nd division hospital of the 6th corps, where I was left on the ground with no blanket or covering of any kind to protect myself from the severity of the weather. During the night an acquaintance shared his blanket with me, but neither this nor the fires which were kindled the latter part of the night were sufficient to overcome the chill I had received. A short time before sundown on the following day my case was attended to. It was thought necessary to administer chloroform in examining the wound, and when consciousness returned I was lying on some straw inside of a tent with no covering at all, shivering like a leaf, and minus my wounded limb. I was unable to procure a woolen blanket, but a wounded man gave me his rubber, and a piece of tent, under which I lay until morning suffering from the severest cramp in both legs, and doing my best to keep as quiet as possible.

Early the next morning, the 21st, I was deposited in an ambulance with two others and conveyed to Winchester. Owing to long halts, we did not reach that place until dark, and then were supplied with bread and coffee and ordered on to Martinsburg. Through the entire night we were tossed about over one of the roughest of roads, arriving at Martinsburg at daybreak where we were left at a hospital until the 24th when we were conveyed in the cars to Baltimore, where for the first time I experienced anything like the treatment a wounded soldier needs. My leg was examined, and the amputation found to have been performed in the worst possible manner. For a number of days it received the best of care, but a bone which was not cut as short as it should have been began to show itself rendering a second amputation necessary. This was successfully performed by Dr. Kempster, of whose skill, caution, attention and kindness I cannot speak in terms too high. I am now doing well, and hope soon to be on my crutches.

The above is a brief and unexaggerated account of my experience since the 19th of October last, and many a wounded soldier can testify that it was substantially his own. I might give the name of the surgeon who amputated my leg the first time, but perhaps it may be as well to withhold it. Here he receives the severest censure, and they say that it ought to cost him his diploma.

As this is probably the last of my series of letters as an army correspondent, I will say in conclusion, that while I regret the casualty which has befallen me, still it is only the fortune of a soldier, and I do not regret that I responded to my country's call, nor feel that I have served to no purpose in a just cause. Though I have never done all I could wish as a soldier, still I have endeavored to do my duty, not shrinking from danger or hardship when called upon, and I am satisfied. If others wish to engage in the same service, I would say to them that the chances are that their lot may be similar to my own, but the cause is worthy of the sacrifice, and I would bid them go forward. CONSCRIPT.

The war had turned decisively in the North's favor, with Jubal Early's army defeated and the Shenandoah Valley firmly in Union control. Adding to Lee's difficulties, General Sherman had recently broken through the defenses outside Atlanta. For Abraham Lincoln, these two victories assured reelection in November over the Democrats and their peace proposals. The war would continue under General Grant, but Francis's service was completed.

Chapter 17

RECOVERY

Following his amputation and appalling reamputation, Francis recuperated for several months at an army hospital in Baltimore. The Minié ball that struck him had entered about two inches above his left ankle. The bone was fractured so severely, however, that the amputation ended up taking place only five and a half inches below his knee joint. As the new year approached, Francis began to talk of relocating to a hospital closer to home. Letters from well-wishers arrived, and, not recognizing the severity of his injuries, some of them hoped that he would be in good enough condition to visit others on his way home to Vermont. Ebenezer Bass wrote on January 8:

Francis Martin
Courtesy of Special Collections,
University of Vermont Libraries

In the first place I have to say I wish you a happy new year and sir may we not reasonably expect, extraordinaries excepted, that 1865 will be to you a far more happy year than was 1864. I trust this may verily be so, not withstanding the many sorrowful hours you may have while reflecting upon the bloody scenes you and your lamented brother Henry have passed through. We trust and pray that within the year 1865, this unnatural, unholy, and bloody strife may be healed, and we once more be at peace. If this should be so, would it not indeed be a happy year to all loyal liberty loving patriots who survive, not withstanding they mourn the loss of kindred and loved ones. Sad indeed it is to reflect upon the misery, woe, and bloodshed, which this cruel rebellion has brought upon our once happy nation. Not withstanding we would that things could have been otherwise, and this expense of blood and treasure saved, yet at whatever cost, we (as in duty bound) must and will defend the star spangled banner and bear it aloft to a final triumph over despots and traitors, and if this but be done in 1865 it must truly be said to be a happy year then let our nation strain its every nerve.

John Green has been here on a visit. His visit was more particularly with Ann Martin, Lyman's Daughter. He left for N.Y. Thursday morn. His address is No 59, Lewis Street N.Y. I thought you might like to see him as you came home.

John Green was mustered out of the Fourth Vermont a few weeks before the Battle of Cedar Creek. Six months later he married Ann Martin, one of Francis and Henry's many cousins. Another cousin, Emily Tileston, wrote to Francis from Hopkinton, Massachusetts in mid-January:

When you first went into the hospital I thought I should write you immediately after learning your address – but my own miserable health and many infirmities this winter must be my apology. I had no inteligence respecting you for some weeks and expected to hear that you were at home some weeks before this. I am sorry indeed to hear that your confinement is likely to be still more protracted. Truly these are days of trial and discipline, public and private, individual as well as national.

I have no dear ones to send to the war, to give life or limb to their country, but I have watched for years you know, over a dear little sufferer who will never know again the free and joyous movements of health and strength. Who would wear this crown must bear the cross & God grant that we may <u>so</u> bear the one as to win the other.

(Emily's children, Ella and George, were born just before the start of the Civil War. Ella lived to age 66 but never married and, based on census reports, appears to have never been employed. One of Emily's descendants indicated that Ella may have contracted polio. Emily's son, George, was employed first in a brokerage house in Massachusetts. At a young age he moved west and started the very successful George Tileston Milling Company in St. Cloud, Minnesota. In 1895, as a 36-year-old father of three, he was leaving the mill in his buggy when his horse became frightened and plunged into the mill's canal. Unable to swim, and with his shoulder injured in the fall, George Tileston drowned in the ten-foot-deep water as the horse dragged the buggy out onto land.)

I had discontinued the papers to you thinking you might have left the hospital. I send a Boston paper. You may be interested in reading the remarks at the funeral of Mr Everett. ... If you know any thing of Mass. politics you know that Mr. E. was almost the only one of the old Daniel Webster school who heartily sustaind the government in opposing this rebellion.

I am sorry to hear that Gen Butler is under a cloud just now. He has taken a strong hold upon the hearts of the people and I do hope he will be able to make his record clear yet. ... I should be very glad to hear from you directly if you are able to write and when you go home you must certainly take Hopkinton in your way.

Edward Everett, the former Whig senator and Governor of Massachusetts, as well as featured orator at the Gettysburg dedication ceremony, had died on January 15. On that same day, Benjamin Butler testified before the Joint Congressional Committee on the Conduct of the War. Grant had finally been able to relieve Butler of his command of the Army of the James, based on Butler's disobedience of Grant's order to attack Fort Fisher in North Carolina. Butler used his political connections to appear before the committee and defend himself. He presented to the committee numerous reports and studies proving that the fort was impregnable. In the midst of his testimony, word arrived that the fort had fallen to a small force under General Terry.

In early March, Emily wrote another letter:

I received your letter in answer to mine some weeks since and have heard nothing from home in relation to you since that time. I thought there was no better way than to write you again. I hoped then that we should see you here before this time – I want you to be sure and come this way on your return home We are two miles from the Cordaville Depot on the Boston and Worcester rail road, and stages run to and from there three or four times a day.

What are your plans for the future? Do you think of retiring to the old home? I saw in a paper within a few days an account of a man who wears a Palmer artificial leg, who can dance and skate. This is certainly encouraging to you as showing that a man is not so much disabled by the loss of a limb as would at first appear.

We have just been getting up an entertainment for the Soldiers Aid Society. The first evening they took $130. It was repeated last night by request – the result I have not learned. The whole thing we regard as a great success. But when all is done that is doing through the country how little it is toward relieving the great suffering and agony. What cause for thankfulness & joy in the prospect that this terrible war is drawing to a close. I like the suggestion that

the day of the Inauguration should be one of thankful rejoicing through all the
loyal land.

While Francis convalesced in Baltimore and later in a Montpelier hospital, he and Chester tried to resolve several financial issues. One concern that continued to bother the Martins during this time was the long-standing debt owed by Riley Mardin. Francis wrote to Mardin, who was now residing in Randolph, on August 1:

I suppose that you can now easily settle my account against you of $20.85
as you were paid at your discharge. I have never been hard with you. The
money has been due for a long time but I will charge no interest if you will
remit the above amt at once. Awaiting your reply.

October arrived with no reply from Mardin. The next step was legal action. Francis received the following from J. K. Parish of Randolph:

Yours yesterday is before me. In reply I am sure R. H. Mardin could pay a
claim of $20. ... I am not a Justice of the Peace & therefore refer you to Phi-
lander Perrin. He will collect it I have no doubt. And surely if Mardin resists
payment Judge Perrin knows him well & you may need an atty. Any thing I
can do for you will be cheerfully performed

Judge Perrin wrote to Chester in December:

I wrote Mardin at Brookfield supposing he had gone there to reside, but he
had not. He consequently did not get the letter for some time. However, some
ten days since I received a letter from Mardin in reply saying that he was then
so unwell that he could not come to see me & that he would do so as soon as he
was able to ride, but that he did not know as he owed any person by the name
of Martin. ... I do not know whether the like can be collected or not.

Back pay issues with the army bureaucracy were another unresolved concern. On March 14, Chester wrote to "the Honorable J. B. Page, Treasurer":

I inclose a Blank order for allotted pay due Wm. H. Martin of Co. A. 4 Regt
also a blank recpt. For the interest of his allotted pay while in Co. B and Co.
A. as I wish to close it all up. Please send your check on a Bank at Montpelier.

Francis did receive payment from the army for his past service, but the amount was far lower than he had calculated, based on his detailed records, leading to an exchange of letters with a colonel in Washington. Concerning the matter of collecting a future pension, in May he received a reply to a letter he had written to the U.S. Sanitary Commission Protective War Claim Agency in Philadelphia.

> *Men who have lost a single limb in the Service receive a pension of Eight dollars per month. I have reason to believe that this pension will yet be increased, but no Act of Congress to that end has yet gone into effect.*

Since early in the war, Governor Holbrook of Vermont had been an avid proponent of building hospitals for injured Vermont soldiers back in their home state. Lincoln and Secretary of War Stanton had rejected the idea, due to concerns that transporting injured soldiers could result in unnecessary deaths. Also, if the new facilities were not military hospitals, desertions might ensue. Holbrook addressed their objections and convinced them that soldiers would recover better in the healthier conditions of these new hospitals and by being close to friends and family, so Stanton agreed to try the idea. Before the war was over, 192 such hospitals were created in the North, including the 500-bed Sloan General Hospital in Montpelier. Francis was transferred to Sloan in spring 1865.

Sloan General Hospital
Courtesy of Vermont Historical Society

By this point, the war was finally coming to a conclusion. After the long-awaited fall of Petersburg, Grant closed in on Lee's beleaguered and badly outnumbered army. On April 9 Lee, recognizing the futility of continuing to fight, surrendered at Appomattox Courthouse. It was now time, as Lincoln had said a month earlier in his second inaugural address, "to bind up the nation's wounds; to care for him who shall have borne the battle." The nation needed to be made whole again, but so did thousands of soldiers who had suffered devastating wounds. For Francis, that wholeness could be assisted by an artificial leg.

Among the major U.S. producers of prosthetic limbs was the Palmer Artificial

Limb Company. Benjamin Franklin Palmer had received an award at the 1851 London World's Fair for creating a more natural-looking artificial leg with springs at the knee, ankle and toe joints. A representative of the Palmer Company wrote to Francis on April 11, two days after Lee's surrender:

> *Your favor of yesterday is at hand. In reply have to say the cause of its taking six weeks to make an art. leg after the order and measures are recd is that we are full all the time with orders for limbs at least six weeks in advance. We enclose a blank for Measure. Also one for your Surgical Statement. Both of which you will please fill out and return to this office with your* <u>*Govt. Order*</u> *for the leg. If formed correct your name will be entered and in due time you will be notified to report in person to be fitted.*

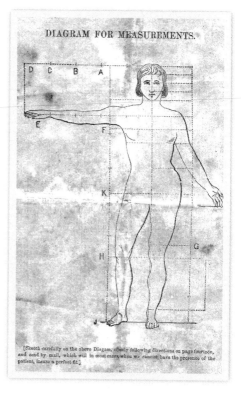

DIAGRAM FOR MEASUREMENTS.

[Sketch carefully on the above Diagram, closely following directions on page fourteen, and send by mail, which will in most cases when we cannot have the presence of the patient, insure a perfect fit.]

A blank form (part of the application for receiving an artificial limb from the Palmer Company) that Francis retained.

Francis was apparently shopping around to get the best possible prosthetic leg for his money. On the back of the Palmer Company form, a competitor, George Kimball, wrote a message saying that he would like to meet with Francis at his office in North Randolph. As of June 6, when Francis wrote home, he appeared to have made his selection:

> *Yesterday Mr Kimball visited this hospital but as he has no Government contract and as there is no certainty of his obtaining one, I do not think that he took any orders for his legs or arms. I think that it will be best for me to take one of Palmer's legs. Mr. Kimball says that Palmer can manufacture a first rate leg but perhaps does not take much pains with the leg he makes for Soldiers. I presume it will not be very durable but it will not be the best policy for me to try Kimball & Co. leg when I can have one furnished by the Govt free of cost. I think that it will be best for me to get my discharge as soon as I*

can for although I shall loose some pay which I might be drawing and may be at some extra expense in consequence in obtaining my leg, still it is much better for me to be at home and what money I might save by staying here will not counterbalance the disadvantage. Anything like real good health I never expect to enjoy and I ought to make myself as easy and comfortable as I can consistently. I am sorry that is so but do not see as it can be helped.

The cost issue to which Francis referred was explained in a *New York Times* article on September 9, 1862:

Mr. B. Frank Palmer, the inventor and manufacturer of the artificial limb, which bears his name, has recently tendered to the Government his services, with the free use of his time and abilities, for the assistance of the halt and mutilated of our armies.

Congress, it will be remembered, passed an appropriation of $15,000 for the purchase of artificial limbs for such; and Mr. Palmer, whose invention is recognized by the various scientific bodies of Europe and America as infinitely beyond that of any other, desirous that the soldiers should have none but the best, has generously offered to take the sum specified, and to apply it, without profit to himself, to the construction of as many of his artificial limbs as the amount will pay for.

Such an offer, at a time when selfishness and avarice might reasonably look for a vast fortune to be made from the necessities of our wounded men, deserves the highest commendation, and Mr. Palmer should receive, as he deserves, the thankful recognition of the public for this promotion of the national good and of much individual happiness.

On June 14, Francis wrote to his parents from Ward 8 of Sloan Hospital:

My stump has not been measured yet although the Dr. has been intending to come in and do it for several days but having other work to attend to has neglected to do it. I think that he will get around to it today or tomorrow. Then I can send my order to Boston and after receiving an answer obtain a pass & go home if I think best. If I wish to have you come down after me I will drop you a line. It will probably be two months or more before I get my discharge as I do not expect to go after my leg until four, five or six weeks after sending my order. Then some time will be spent in getting it and three or four weeks in getting my discharge after my return. This will be rather unpleasant for me but I suppose that I should in this case consult profit rather than pleasure. ...

I have just sent 30cts to pay return postage on a small sample bottle of fine apple cider which will be sent to your address and which I wish to have you keep for me. If it will do me any good I should like to use it although I do not like the practice of using medicine where diet and exercise will supply its place.

I would make that present [the ring] to Laura Ainsworth as soon as I could ...

The leg measurements were taken and Francis sent them to the Palmer Company. A reply dated June 21 came from the "Office of the American Artificial Limb Company" in Boston:

Your favor with measure for an art. leg is at hand. As a great many orders have come in for art. limbs <u>this</u> month we may not be able to reach your case for some weeks. Will let you know when wanted.

Francis informed his parents of the situation the next day:

My measure has been forwarded to Boston and I have just recd the inclosed reply. If you would like to have me come home when it is convenient come down to Montpelier, do your business and call for me about three o'clock P.M. and I can probably get a pass. I think that this will be better than for me to go home in the stage.

With the war over, Chester decided that it was also time for Henry to come home. He enlisted the services of John Roberts, who had been the Fourth Vermont's chaplain at the time of Henry's death, to locate his body and return it to Williamstown. Roberts was also searching for the body of another Fourth Vermont soldier, Henry Smith (cousin to Henry Martin). Smith managed to survive the Wilderness but was killed two months later outside Petersburg. Roberts was to search for both bodies and share the expenses between Chester and Oren Smith. On December 8, having already located Henry Smith's body, he sent a very detailed list of expenses incurred up to that point. The combined bill already exceeded $200.

Chester was apparently not pleased with the expenses. He wrote a sarcastic rebuttal on the back of the bill in which he altered many of the expenses to reflect what he believed were more realistic charges and made up a list of expenses that he could charge

John Roberts
Courtesy of John Gibson Collection

to Reverend Roberts. But the letter that he actually sent to Roberts in early January 1866 was far more cordial:

> *Yours of Dec 8th to Mr. Smith I have examined, & paid him ... I dont know as I fully understand all your charges. Will you not soon be through our town, if so please call & I presume you can give a satisfactory explanation.*

Roberts replied on January 18 with another detailed account of the expenses and an update on his progress:

> *I am now on my way to Fredricksburgh & having been informed since I saw you that your son must have been buried above Salem Church (you will recollect the church) I have written to Mr Paine to have him look for your sons grave & should it be found I shall be much happy to inform you or do any thing in my power for you. I may not return to Vermont for a year or more.*

Francis received his discharge on August 25, 1865 and finally returned home to Williamstown. He had applied and been approved for a pension of $8.00 a month. What he really hoped for was a chance to show that he could still be useful in some way on the family farm.

Chapter 18

EPILOGUE

Wednesday, October 11, 1865

The two farmers stared dejectedly at the large boulder in front of them. For a long time Chester had wanted the rock removed to provide more usable farmland. He felt that he and Francis together could accomplish it. They had dug a large hole and intended to flip the boulder into the hole, but found that they could not budge it. Francis, fewer than two months removed from the hospital, was experiencing difficulty adjusting to farm labor on one unsteady leg. After struggling for most of an hour on an unseasonably warm autumn day, Chester finally concluded that the job was too difficult and dangerous for them to complete on their own. He suggested that they go back to the house, get some additional workers to help them, and return later.

As Francis watched his seventy-year-old father leave in search of assistance, he felt depressed about his inability to be more helpful on the farm. He thought about the large boulder. "They say that you could move the world if you had a large enough lever," Francis said to himself. "I should be able to get under it enough to move it." He began to imagine the looks on the faces of his father and the helpers when they returned and found the boulder out of its long-established resting place and buried in the ground. Francis would be sitting next to it and grinning at them. How amazed they all would be! The newspaper had recently written a story about a double amputee who had surprised people by being able to dance an Irish jig. "When word of this gets out, maybe I'll get my own newspaper story," Francis mused.

VERMONT WATCHMAN AND STATE JOURNAL
OCTOBER 20, 1865
SHOCKING ACCIDENT

Francis S. Martin, son of Chester Martin of Williamstown, and known to our readers while in the army as "Conscript," and who lost a leg at the battle of Cedar Creek, was killed on Wednesday, Oct. 11th, under the most appalling circumstances. Being desirous of getting rid of a very heavy stone in the lot adjoining his house, Mr. Martin, assisted by his son, had excavated a space with a view to sink the stone, and having done all they deemed safe was temporarily left, for some safer mode of completion. Subsequently, during his father's absence, Francis went to the field; not returning as soon as expected his mother became alarmed and sent for him, when he was found with the exception of his head and shoulders buried beneath the huge rock, with body and limbs completely crushed. Help was immediately procured, but not until after two hours of incessant labor was the body extricated. Judge the agony of those parents, with hearts already bleeding from the loss of a noble son in his country's service, now so suddenly and terribly bereft of this only remaining child, an ornament to the community over which deep gloom is cast.

The date the article was published, October 20, 1865, was one year to the day since Francis's leg had been amputated at Cedar Creek.

Chapter 19

AFTERWORD:
FAMILY CONNECTIONS

lthough Williamstown is just a small village, several of its residents had wide-ranging impact during the years after the Civil War. Of particular note was the Bass family, which was related to the Martins. Although several Bass households lived in the area, Ebenezer "Uncle Bass" and his daughters were mentioned the most in the Martins' letters. Ebenezer Bass lived in the large farmhouse, which still stands today, across the street from the Martins. In one of her letters, Emily Tileston wrote to Henry that she had gone to Chicago recently (we were continually amazed by how much Williamstown people traveled around the country) and had visited one Perkins Bass and his sister, Fanny. On a whim, I put Perkins Bass and Chicago into a search engine and found that a Perkins Bass Elementary School was still operating there! That convinced me that there was more to research about the Bass family.

I discovered that the grandfather of Uncle Bass, also named Ebenezer, was a direct descendant of John Alden, and had served during the Revolutionary War as a first lieutenant on the galley *Trumbull* on Lake Champlain. One of the older Ebenezer's sons, Joel Bass, married Polly Martin, an aunt of Chester Martin, and Perkins Bass was among Joel and Polly's grandchildren. Perkins graduated from Dartmouth in 1852 and began practicing law. In 1854 Perkins and several of his siblings moved to Chicago. Besides being a lawyer, Perkins was very successful in real estate and other business ventures. He also served as principal of the Dearborn School, the first district school in Chicago. Perkins was later elected to the Chicago Board of Education and then the State Board of Education, resulting in the present-day school that bears his name. He managed his friend Abraham Lincoln's second presidential campaign in Illinois, and Lincoln reciprocated by appointing Bass as U.S. District Attorney for the northern district of Illinois. After Lincoln's assassination, Andrew Johnson removed Bass from office, viewing him as an ally of the Radical Republicans.

Perkins Bass and his wife, Clara Foster Bass, eventually retired to their family estate in Petersborough, New Hampshire, where they established a family dynasty that would influence New Hampshire political life for the next century. Their son, Robert Perkins Bass, attended Harvard and then was elected to several terms in both houses of the New Hampshire legislature and, in 1910, as governor. The New Hampshire Republican Party became badly split in 1912 when Bass aligned himself with Theodore Roosevelt's "Bull Moose" challenge to President Taft. As a result, Bass was later defeated in two U.S. Senate elections.

Robert P. Bass's son, another Perkins Bass, was also elected to several terms in both chambers of the state legislature, and then to four terms in the U.S. House of Representatives beginning in 1954. In 1962 he was the unsuccessful Republican nominee for the U.S. Senate. His son, Charles F. Bass, has continued the family's political legacy, also serving in the state house and senate and then, following his election in 1994, seven terms in Congress.

Among Joel Bass's many children, his son George suffered a particularly tragic set of misfortunes. He married Laura Poole and had two sons who both died as infants. They then had two daughters, Laura Ann in 1840 and Sarah in 1842. But his wife died in 1842 and then, two years later, George was kicked in the head by a horse and killed. With many uncles and aunts living in Williamstown, the two girls were raised by relatives. By 1860, Laura Ann was teaching school and living with relatives in Illinois, and Sarah was going to school in Massachusetts. Their departure helped to cause Lorette Bass's lament to Henry, in one of her letters, of her loneliness because all the young people were leaving Williamstown for one reason or another. Neither daughter ever moved back; Laura married an accountant and spent the rest of her life in Illinois, while Sarah married into a wealthy family in Massachusetts. Her son, Clinton Aaron Strong, was known for his extensive collection of antiques, many of which were unfortunately lost when a fire consumed his Southampton, Massachusetts residence in 1935.

Ebenezer ("Uncle Bass"), a general in the state militia and a state senator, was one of Joel Bass's children who remained in Williamstown. He became a prominent and successful figure in the community but also faced his share of sadness. He married Eunice Parish in 1826, and two sons were born over the course of the next several years. One son died at age nine, and the other lived only two years. Next came the two daughters, Eunice and Lorette, who corresponded often with Henry and Francis during the war. Ebenezer's wife died in 1838 at age 31. Ebenezer then married Betsey Martin's sister, Lucy Smith, and they had one more child, Lucy Ann, who died at age 16 in 1856, shortly after graduating from Kimball Union Academy. Daughter Eunice had a long struggle with consumption, to which she finally succumbed during the war at age 29. After her death, Ebenezer wrote a letter to Henry in which he referred to the graves of his deceased family members "on yonder hill." Standing at the Ebenezer Bass memorial today, surrounded by all those graves, one can still look over the community and see his home on a hill at the opposite end of Williamstown.

The only remaining child, Lorette, later married George Ainsworth, another close friend of Henry and Francis. Ainsworth was one of more than 5,000 volunteers who served during the war with the United States Christian Commission, an organization offering religious support and other services for the soldiers. (Louisa May Alcott was probably the Commission's most famous volunteer.) George and Lorette then lived in the farmhouse across from the Martins and took care of Ebenezer in his old age. Ebenezer died in 1888. Lorette, his last surviving child, died in 1890, at age 55. George Ainsworth continued to live in the house until his death in 1910.

Around the time of the Civil War centennial, a journalist named Robert Duffus wrote a book, *Williamstown Branch*, about his boyhood memories growing up in that small town. Duffus recalled that, during the late 1890s, his family rented a section of the enormous "General E. Bass house" from what the author perceived as a very elderly George Ainsworth. The world was changing rapidly at that time. For example, Duffus remembered the first horseless carriage that came to town, and that George Ainsworth had argued that it should not be called an automobile because that word would improperly combine a Greek prefix with a Latin root. Yet despite changes occurring all around them, the past was not totally forgotten. Duffus recalled that the neighborhood children would sometimes secretly gather at night behind the farmhouse across the road to tell ghost stories while sitting on a boulder that had supposedly long ago fallen and crushed a man to death.

Henry's fiancée, Laura Ainsworth, a cousin of George, had a very interesting life. In 1867 she married another more distant cousin, James Edward Ainsworth. He was a Norwich University graduate who had fought at Shiloh as a captain in the 12th Iowa Infantry, where he enlisted because he had been working in Iowa as a civil engineer for a railroad company. They then lived in Iowa and Nebraska as James Ainsworth designed construction projects for the railroad. The town of Ainsworth, Nebraska is named for him. The two later returned to Williamstown, where James died in 1909 and Laura in 1925. The Ainsworth Public Library, which still operates in Williamstown today, was established by Laura, who also provided the town with a new, fully equipped fire house and high school. Ainsworth Hall, on the Norwich University campus, is named for her as well. Laura also donated the land for what is today the 905-acre Ainsworth State Park, located between Williamstown and Brookfield.

James Edward Ainsworth
Courtesy of Williamstown Historical Society

Laura Ainsworth
Courtesy of Williamstown Historical Society

Chauncey Smith, an older cousin of the Martin boys, figured prominently in the letters by befriending Henry when he was camped near Washington, D.C. and by showing great concern for the well-being of the other Williamstown boys. As a widower, he had enjoyed taking Henry out for a night on the town and reminded him often of the young women they encountered. Chauncey served as a bond and register clerk for the Post Office, where his responsibilities included receiving and recording all appointments within the postal service, receiving and filing employee bonds and oaths, and issuing the commissions for all postmasters. Chauncey remained with the Post Office after the war and became the head of its Bond Division. He also was active in the Masons. After his death in Washington in 1882 at age 80, the *Evening Star* (later the *Washington Star*) noted that "his host of friends throughout the city will be grieved to learn of his sudden taking off. His life was devoted to acts of genuine charity and kindness." Chauncey's death even received a news obituary in the *New York Times*, apparently due to his high position within the Masonic order.

Chauncey's son, Nathan, had been prepared for college in Washington, D.C., and then returned to Northfield, Vermont to attend Norwich University in 1850. After college he became a lawyer in Green Bay, Wisconsin. With the outbreak of the war, he became a first lieutenant in the 12th Wisconsin Infantry. Nathan resigned his commission due to health problems in August of 1862, but later reentered the army as a first lieutenant in the 32nd Wisconsin Infantry. Immediately after the war, rather than returning to his law practice in Wisconsin, he followed in his father's footsteps by accepting a job with the Post Office in Washington, D.C., where he eventually rose to his father's old position as head of the Bond Division. Nathan continued in that position until his death in 1900.

Nathan A.C. Smith

George W. Smith

George Wilkins Smith, another cousin from the Smith side of the family (Chester's wife, Betsey, was the daughter of Levi Smith), also provides an interesting story. During the war he served in the 17th Infantry of the regular army. At times he is mentioned in the letters when he was camped near the Vermont Brigade, and he corresponded with the Martins by mail when apart. George was the son of Ira Smith, another one of Levi Smith's children. He had been born in Williamstown in 1840 but spent some of his childhood in Lebanon, New Hampshire. He attended Kimball Union Academy in Enfield, New Hampshire, as did Francis, Lorette, Perkins Bass, and many others from Williamstown. In 1861, Smith entered Norwich University. With the outbreak of the war, he enlisted in the army after just one year as a cadet. During his first year in the Army he was promoted to corporal, then later to sergeant, second lieutenant, and first lieutenant. He commanded a company of men at Second Bull Run, Antietam, and Fredericksburg. At Gettysburg he was brevetted captain for "gallant and meritorious service." Smith was wounded at Spotsylvania but remained in the service. After the war, he commanded military posts in Brenham and Seguin, Texas. General Sheridan, who also served in Texas after the war, once referred to Smith as the "right man in the right place" as a result of his success against Indian scouting parties. His wife, Ella Dearborn Smith, later said that Sheridan's comments were in reference to several "hair-breadth escapes from death." In 1869 he resigned from the army but remained in Texas and became a colonel in the state militia. He also served as aide-de-camp to Texas Governor Edmund J. Davis. In that position, Smith was involved in implementing Reconstruction policies. He is also credited with establishing the first public schools in Texas.

Through Ancestry.com, I was able to locate a great-great-granddaughter of George and Ella Smith. As it turned out, she was in the process of sorting through many boxes of documents and photos of family history from her own parents' attic. Her additional information showed that George had wanted to settle down in Texas, but that Ella was not happy living there. They agreed that he would run for political office in Texas, but if he lost they would return to the East. Ella then secretly worked behind the scenes trying to convince people to vote against her husband! George lost the election and they moved back to Philadelphia in 1873. Smith then began working in the furniture-making business for James W. Cooper.

In 1876 George and Ella attended the Centennial International Exhibition in Philadelphia. Of the more than ten million people who attended this World's Fair, most were no doubt primarily interested in the new technological advances being displayed, such as the telephone, typewriter, and electric lighting. George and Ella, however, were most impressed with the hand-carved furniture at the German exhibit, and George recognized the potential market for such furnishings among the newly emerging wealthy class of the Gilded Age. He convinced some of the men at the German exhibit to remain in the United States and work for the newly founded George W. Smith & Company, which expanded rapidly and ultimately became renowned worldwide for the high quality of its furniture and hall clocks. George traveled extensively through Europe, purchasing statues, bronzes, porcelains, and tapestries that he would then resell through his company. Wealthy families of the time, such as the Vanderbilts, were known to make purchases through him, especially through his display room in New York City. George Smith died in 1896 and one of his sons took over the company. By the turn of the century, the Smith family was listed in the *Social Register* as one of the most prominent families in Philadelphia.

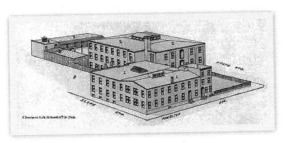

George Smith's furniture factory in Philadelphia
Courtesy of Map Collection, Free Library of Philadelphia

While I enjoyed researching my ancestors' often fascinating histories, I remained puzzled for quite a while by one question: why were all these letters in my father's attic in Pittsburgh when I found them in 2002? The long story of solving this mystery, which takes up the remainder of the chapter, extends in many directions far beyond the Civil War era. As such, it will likely only be of interest to those with a broader interest in both history and genealogy.

My father, William E. Young, had never shown any great interest in the Civil War, nor had he mentioned any family members who were in the war. William had grown up in Barre, Vermont, just six miles from Williamstown. He attended the University of Vermont, majoring in mechanical engineering, and, after graduating in 1941, accepted employment at a Westinghouse research laboratory in Pittsburgh. On December 7, 1941, he attended a dance and met Betty Fraker, who would become my mother (he often joked that the day he met her was a day that would live in infamy). Having earned a pilot's license in college, he expected the Air Force to commission him once the U.S. entered the war, but instead he was assigned to continue working on research projects at Westinghouse, including what would become America's first jet engine. The Westinghouse axial flow design varied in many ways from Frank Whittle's British design and later proved superior to Whittle's centrifugal compressor; however, the British had their planes in the air during the war and they, along with their German counterparts under Dr. Hans von Ohain, were credited with developing the first jet engine. The Westinghouse model did not become functional until a year after the war ended. William Young was also assigned to one aspect of the Manhattan Project, developing a centrifuge for U-235 isotope separation, which would be needed to create an atomic bomb.

William E. Young with the Blue Goose "Gas Turbine Locomotive" in 1951

After the war, this group of engineers began looking at the possibility of applying their turbine technology to high-speed passenger rail service. Many adaptations were made, and by 1950 the "Blue Goose" was ready to begin some trial runs. Its speed and power amazed many of the locomotive engineers who tried it out. On one run it reached 125 miles per hour while pulling a full train of freight cars. Despite the success of the trial runs, however, Westinghouse executives decided that the company's future was in consumer appliances, not jet engines or locomotives, and the Blue Goose project was scrapped.

My father earned his Ph.D. in engineering and spent most of the remainder of his career researching and developing alternative energy systems such as coal liquefaction and magnetohydrodynamics (mhd) power systems, the technology that Tom Clancy chose to power his fictional submarine in *The Hunt for Red October*. But his death in 2002 left me with questions that only he could have answered concerning the box of old letters in his attic. Questions such as: how was I connected to these soldiers, and what were their letters doing in my parents' attic? My father, knowing my interest in history, could have said, "By the way, I have hundreds of Civil War letters up in the attic that you might want to take a look at some time." Since Williamstown is so close to Barre, where my father had grown up, I felt certain that the letters had come from his side of the family. I was aware that my New England ancestry consisted of the Young, Herrick, Waugh, and Harvey families. But who were the Martins?

This entire project created a new interest for me in genealogy. I had always believed that I was part of a very small family structure, with no close cousins, because my mother had one brother who never married and my father (or so I thought) had just one childless brother. I now have created a family tree with thousands of names extending back over five centuries (the Young/Herrick family tree located on Ancestry.com), and I have connected with many relatives of whom I was previously unaware. I was greatly aided by the work that one relative, Edward Arthur Herrick, did more than half a century ago. He had combined a history of the Herrick family with genealogical tables that he had collected, as well as personal anecdotes that he had heard from his older relatives. My father had given me a copy of all of this research back when I was in college, and although I had never paid much attention to it, I still had it stored away in my own attic and could use it to begin my research.

From this work, combined with information from Ancestry.com and other Internet sites, I learned that the Herricks had been a prominent family in England. Sir William Herrick (1557-1652) served as Teller of the Exchequer under both Elizabeth I and James I. One of his sons, Henry Herrick, was an early American colonist, arriving in Salem, Massachusetts in 1629, and one of Henry's sons (also named Henry) was a juror in the Salem witch trials of 1692, even though this juror's daughter and son-in-law testified as witnesses for the prosecution. Ironically, it turns out that, through the Martin family of Williamstown, I am also related to one of the defendants. Chester Martin was a direct descendant of Susannah Martin, a widow and mother of nine children who strongly defended herself against the better-educated and more experienced prosecutors. When the teenage girls accusing her fell to the floor in hysterics, Susannah responded with laughter and dismissed their antics as childish foolishness. She was subjected to a demeaning physical examination of her body, but no clear signs of being a witch were evident. During the proceedings she flawlessly recited scripture verses, an act supposedly impossible for a witch. Nevertheless, she was convicted and was one of the nineteen people hanged. A few years later, Henry Herrick signed a statement, along with several other jurors, asking for forgiveness from those who had suffered because they now realized that they had been "sadly deluded and mistaken" in their judgment.

Many of the Herricks remained in Massachusetts, particularly in Salem and Beverly. One branch of the family settled in Penobscot County, Maine. About a century and a half later, another Henry Herrick left Maine for the lure of gold in California. Henry Jacob Herrick's mother had died when he was an infant and his father was lost at sea when Henry was still a child. He was raised by an uncle, Captain Samuel Herrick, with whom he traveled around the world as a cabin boy on his ship. In his early twenties, Henry set sail for California, arriving in the late 1850s. He left behind a young girl, Harriet Harvey (my great-great-grandmother), telling her he would send for her after he was settled and successful. A year later Harriet, although still a teenager who had never been far from home, started out by herself, traveling to Boston, then by sea to Panama, then overland across Panama, and finally boarding another ship on the western side that took her to California. By the time Henry located her at a San Francisco hotel, she had already turned down three marriage proposals, attesting to the scarcity of women in California at that time. From there came the most difficult part of the journey, traveling for over fifty miles on foot or on a mule, with no roads, to his cabin in the mining town of Douglas City. Displaying such tenacity and courage at a young age seems to have been a Harvey family trait. Harriet's grandfather, James Harvey, fought at Bunker Hill at age 14 and remained in the Continental Army for the duration of the Revolutionary War. Standing six feet, seven inches tall, in that era he must have been a very inviting target for the British soldiers. He not only survived but in 1842, at age 80, he returned to Boston to attend the dedication ceremony for the Bunker Hill monument. In his famous address at the dedication, the gifted orator Daniel Webster specifically singled out James Harvey as one of the few defenders of Bunker Hill still alive and able to attend the ceremony.

James Harvey's granddaughter, Harriet, and Henry Herrick married and remained in California for five years. Harriet began teaching school for three months a year to children in the mining towns, receiving $100 in gold a month as her pay. Henry continued prospecting, and—despite many dangerous adventures involving thieves and claim-jumpers, Indians, bears, and rattlesnakes—they survived and prospered. (I have evidence they found gold, because I own a gold belt buckle that Henry made and brought home with them.)

Harriet's sister, Ellen Harvey, traveled even further west. Her husband, Lawrence McCully, graduated from Yale in 1852 and later joined Henry at Douglas City. Failing to find his fortune in California, he decided to try building a life in the Hawaiian islands. He began practicing law and, in 1860, was elected as a representative to the Hawaiian legislature. Soon he was chosen Speaker of the House, and in 1877 King Kalakaua appointed him to the Hawaiian Supreme Court. While in that position, McCully authored *Statutes of the Hawaiian Kingdom*. The McCullys also served as ambassadors to Spain and England, where Ellen developed an intense dislike for Queen Victoria.

After Lawrence McCully's death, Ellen returned to Maine and married John Hamilton Higgins. Having grown up poor in Charleston, Maine, Higgins had traveled at age 15 to New York City to work for an uncle in the carpet industry. When the Civil War began, he was exempt from the draft as the company was providing blankets for the soldiers. After the war, Higgins proved to have a very astute business mind, devising a way to produce high-quality carpet at a far lower cost than under the earlier process. By his early thirties he had risen to the top of the company and had become quite wealthy. But to his uncle's dismay, Higgins believed that he was being called to the ministry and left the company. He returned to Maine and became an itinerant preacher for the next seventeen years. In 1891 he purchased Charleston Academy, where he had gone to school, and redesigned its curriculum as Higgins Classical Institute. Two new buildings were added at a cost of over $100,000. While the buildings were being constructed, his wife died. Around the same time, the recently widowed Ellen returned from her years in Hawaii. The two married and Ellen moved her ornate furniture, some of it having come from the palace of Queen Liliuokalani, into Higgins Classical Institute. Higgins wanted his residential school to keep tuition low and use work-study programs to provide a high-quality education for those who otherwise could not afford one. The institute was originally intended primarily to serve as a preparatory school for Colby College. Hollywood entertainer John Davidson, whose full name is John Hamilton Davidson, is the great-grandson of John Hamilton Higgins.

Another of Harriet's sisters (there were 14 children in the family), Elonia Harvey, also traveled to California and married Henry Herrick's mining partner, Stephen Thayer. Elonia and Stephen settled in Douglas City and remained in California for the rest of their lives. As for Henry and Harriet Herrick, after the Civil War, with the building of the transcontinental railroad, they decided to return to their hometown of Levant, Maine and use their earnings on a business venture. As John Sutter had done several years earlier along the American River in California, they built a sawmill. Although the Penobscot River yielded no gold, the Herrick family did make a fair living working there. Through an arrangement with a shipping merchant, they began to specialize in wooden slats that were exported to Italy and then assembled to make crates for fruit. Henry and Harriet had four children, including my great-grandmother, Edith Herrick, who remained in Levant and married Elwin Fremont Waugh. Their daughter, Ada Waugh, attended both Higgins Classical Institute and Colby College. She later moved to Barre, Vermont to teach school. There she met and married William James Young, my grandfather, a widower who had been born in Canada.

Through researching the Herrick family, I was surprised to discover a connection to another rather famous figure from American history. The mother of both Harriet Herrick and Ellen Higgins, and the dozen other Harvey children, was Abigail Dexter. The Dexter family had long been established in New England. Thomas Dexter was one of the original Puritan settlers in Massachusetts Bay, arriving in 1630 along with John Winthrop and John Endicott, the early leaders of the colony. When Dexter got into an argument with Endicott a year later, Endicott struck him in the face and, under a court order, Dexter received ten pounds as compensation. Dexter later built a grist mill (which has been rebuilt as a historical site in the town of Sandwich on Cape Cod) and the Dexter family ultimately became very prosperous and prominent in colonial New England. Abigail Dexter, Harriet Herrick's mother, was a descendant of Thomas Dexter's son, William. A descendant of Thomas Dexter's daughter, Frances, several generations later married a French immigrant named Apollos Riviore. Their son, named for his father, anglicized his name to Paul Revere.

So at this point I had discovered family connections to several prominent New England families and to one of the most famous figures in American history. Paul Revere, according to the resources provided by Ancestry.com, was my fourth cousin, six times removed. But still there was no link to the Martin boys. Perhaps the connection came from my grandfather's side of the family.

This branch of the Young family can be traced back to Ephraim Young (1753-1841), who was living in Gouldsborough, Maine (near Bar Harbor) at the time of the American Revolution. He sided with the loyalists and decided to move to Canada rather than fight against the British. Together with a fellow loyalist, John Hanson, who had served in the British army and had fought under General Wolfe in the Battle of Quebec, they departed for an unsettled region of Canada. They first spent some time on Campobello Island, which Franklin D. Roosevelt later made famous, and then continued on to New Brunswick on a whaling ship. In 1777 they became two of the earliest settlers at St. Andrews, which consisted of just a small trading post operated by two trappers who traded with the local Passamaquoddy Indians. Young and Hanson settled on a small island in the bay called Chamcook Island (later known as Minister's Island). They brought in their families, built homes, cleared farmland, and lived there without incident for the next six years. However, they had no true legal claim to the island, and this became a major problem for them when the British decided to relocate a large group of loyalists to St. Andrews in 1783. The island was handed over to Captain Samuel Osborn, who commanded the warship *Arethusa*. When Young and Hanson initially refused to recognize his claim to the island, Osborn began using the island for target practice for his ship's 38 guns. Although forced to flee, they then appealed to Governor Thomas Carleton. In his appeal, Young claimed that he had been loyal to England and had suffered "severe hardships" as well as greatly improving the property on which he had lived. He asked that he "not be dispossessed of this dear-earned fruit of his labors and reduced with his family to the distress that such a measure will subject him to." Carleton ruled against Young (I assume my parents were unaware of any of this when they named me) and Hanson, although both did receive a monetary payment from Osborn for improvements made to the island. Both then resettled nearby at Bocabec in Charlotte County, and both had many offspring. By the time of his death in 1841, Ephraim Young had 13 children, 108 grandchildren, 140 great-grandchildren, and 3 great-great-grandchildren!

One of Ephraim's sons married a daughter of Hanson. As the families expanded through the years, several Youngs and Hansons married each other. Also, a granite quarry was dug out of a section of Hanson's farmland, launching a prosperous career for some family members. Multiple quarries were started by both Hanson and Young family members to dig out the red and black granite in the region. However, many of the quarries played out rather quickly.

Several Young family members also became active in the merchant and trade professions. Abraham Young, one of Ephraim's grandchildren, became a prominent merchant. One of his three-masted sailing ships, the *Cyprus*, built in 1878, is still celebrated in a walking tour in Bridgetown, Nova Scotia, as the largest ship ever constructed in its shipyards. One of his sons, Clarendon Young, became a ship captain, but was later lost at sea. A much younger son in this maritime family was my grandfather, William James Young. When William was twelve years old, his uncle, Captain William Wallace McLeod, was also lost at sea when his ship went down near Indonesia. Not surprisingly, William Young decided to move away from the dangerous seafaring life of New Brunswick, going to Vermont to work in the newly expanding granite quarries located between Williamstown and Barre. Barre was already a leading producer of granite, but Williamstown was developing its own granite industry due to a recently completed railroad spur line.

So my grandfather had a connection to Williamstown, the hometown of my two Civil War soldiers and their parents. However, my grandfather was born in 1872 and didn't move to Williamstown until 1890, a decade after Chester Martin's death and a quarter-century after Henry and Francis had met their fate. As I learned more of my family history and extended the family tree further out, still there were no Martins. It was time to make a trip to Williamstown.

In summer 2003, our five-person team of Edd, Nancy, Bill, Carol and me began by touring the University of Vermont, where my father had once attended and my nephew was enrolled at the time. After exploring Special Collections for answers to some of our questions, we set off for Williamstown. We drove into the small town and immediately noticed the large Civil War monument at the center of the town. We stopped and read the names of the Civil War soldiers who were honored there. No Martins were listed. This was another mystery, but one that was at least partially solved several years later. I found a historical record that indicated that there had been some controversy when the town voted on building the monument in 1868. It was to be only "to the memory of the officers and soldiers who counted on Williamstown's quota in the war of the Rebellion and fell in battle or died of wounds or sickness received in aiding to put down the Rebellion." Henry had enlisted before there was a draft and Francis joined as a substitute in place of a resident of Randolph, so neither one met the criterion. Since the marginal cost of inscribing names would be so little in relation to the cost of the monument itself, it seems likely that a political dispute within the town had caused the names on the monument to be limited in such a way.

Beyond the monument, we found the building for the Williamstown Historical Society. There we were greeted by WHS president Adam Boyce, who proved to be a delightfully eccentric and witty New Englander. His business card read: "Adam R. Boyce, Native Vermonter, Humorist, Historian, Fiddler, Composer." We had hoped that perhaps we would walk into his building and find a large display about the Martin family with pictures of all our people of interest. No such luck. Nothing seemed to relate closely to our soldiers or their family. What Adam Boyce did offer, however, proved extremely valuable. He informed us that he was familiar with the cemetery sites of Henry and Francis because he decorated the graves of all the veterans every Memorial Day. He also explained that Chester Martin's

Civil War monument next to the Congregational Church attended by the Martins
Courtesy of Williamstown Historical Society

old farmhouse could still be found along the main street at the south end of town, and that it was now part of a nursing home called The Gardens.

We were not quite sure what to expect as we approached the home of our two soldiers, but what we found amazed us. The beautiful old Federal-style brick farmhouse still stood near the street. The back walls of the house had been removed and a long nursing home had been built out onto the back property. We walked in to find that the original section of the house had been restored with a nineteenth-century appearance and was now serving as a lobby for the nursing home. We had an eerie feeling of familiarity as we walked from room to room. We had been immersed for so long in the letters of this nineteenth-century family, and now here we were actually in their home, which in all likelihood had looked much the same when they were here. The upstairs bedrooms were where our two soldiers had grown up. In the living room, most likely, each of their letters was read. The kitchen was the place where food items were prepared to be boxed and sent to the brothers. And somewhere in this house the letters themselves had been boxed and stored after the death of both soldiers, as the parents clung to these final ties to their sons.

We finally dragged ourselves away from the house and headed for the large cemetery on the north side of the town. There we found the graves of my grandparents and my uncle, Henry Sibley Young. "Uncle Sib" was my father's half-brother and was named for his mother, Bernice Sibley. Through earlier research I found that she had been born in Kansas, although that just served to confuse the family history even further. When I asked Adam Boyce about the name Sibley, he informed us that Benjamin Franklin Sibley, who I knew to be Bernice's father, had driven the town hearse at one time. He also explained that the graves of the Martin family we were seeking resided in the much smaller West Hill Cemetery. We drove there and began reading names on the graves. As we did so, we noticed, at the opposite end of the cemetery, an ornamental iron railing around some very large grave markers. We began ignoring other headstones for the time being and worked our way towards this one imposing structure. Upon reaching it we discovered, to our amazement, what we had come so far to see. We had found the graves of Chester and Betsey Martin and their four children.

Despite our sense of closeness to this family, we still had no idea why their letters had been in my parents' attic. Still working on this puzzle, we next made our way to the state capital of Montpelier and began examining

The Martin house today

historical records in the government offices. We divided ourselves up, trying to find more information on our people of interest from wills or birth, marriage, death, and military records. After several seemingly fruitless hours, Carol, who had been concentrating on the marriage records, suddenly yelled out, "I've got it. Here's the connection. It's through Bernice!"

We learned that by the late 1860s, Chester and Betsey Martin had buried all four of their children, two having died young and our two soldiers dying during the war. Betsey Martin died in 1870, leaving Chester alone at age 75. With his wife and all his children gone, Chester started over, in a sense. He married a widow, Audelia Wood Hill from Westford, in 1873 and invited her children to live in

the large farmhouse in Williamstown. In particular, Benjamin Franklin Sibley, who had married Audelia's daughter Lucia, returned from Kansas where they had gone to try to make their fortune. Ben ran the farm for the aging Chester, who died in 1880. Walking through the Sibley section in the upper

The Martin family plot at West Hill Cemetery

corner of the large cemetery in Williamstown today is a heartbreaking experience. One can only imagine the anguish of the parents who lost so many children to fever and disease in the years after their return to Vermont: Delia (b. 1874) at age two, William (b. 1877) at age eleven, Arthur (b. 1882) at age six, Hiram (b. 1884) at age two, George (b. 1892) at age one. In one day of unimaginable sorrow, they returned home from the cemetery where they buried one child only to be told that another child had died while they were gone. Two daughters managed to survive childhood. The oldest child, Bernice, born in Kansas in 1872, grew up in the Martin farmhouse in Williamstown and in 1895 became the first wife of my grandfather, William James Young, who, as mentioned earlier, had moved across the border from Canada to work in the granite quarries. They remained in what was now the Sibley farmhouse and had two children: Henry Sibley, whom I would see often as a child and knew as Uncle Sib, and Katharine, whom I never met.

After outliving so many of her childhood siblings, Bernice died in 1915 at the age of 42. A few years after Bernice died, my grandfather then married my grandmother, who was from the Herrick side of the family. Ada Waugh, as mentioned earlier, was the granddaughter of Henry and Harriet Herrick, who had sought their fortune in California during the gold rush. Ada was a teacher at Spaulding High School in Barre. (Barre Academy had declined in reputation and enrollment after the death of its founder and leader, Jacob Spaulding. It closed down and Spaulding High School was built on its site in 1891. Today that impressive brick and granite Romanesque building, overlooking the city of Barre, is the home of the Vermont Historical Society.) After marrying, William Young and his two children, who were only a few years younger than his new bride, all moved to a house in Barre. By the time my father was born, his half-sister, Katharine, had already married and moved to New Hampshire. Consequently, they seldom saw each other. Sib remained in the area longer and continued to see his much younger half-brother through the years after both had moved far from Vermont.

As for the Civil War letters, I can only conjecture now how they ended up in the Pittsburgh house where I grew up. As a young girl, Bernice perhaps established a close relationship with the elderly Chester (she was eight when he died). Perhaps he entrusted the letters to her, or read through them with her and talked about his sons. For whatever reason, she must have valued the letters and held on to them. After she died, they remained with my grandfather. When he died in 1946, my grandmother moved back to her family home in Levant, Maine. She must have taken the box of letters with her and placed them in the family attic, mixing them with the remaining Herrick mementos. When she died in 1980, my father, her only child, went to Maine to clear out her house and sorted through her possessions, quickly deciding what to throw out and what to bring back to Pittsburgh. Presumably, in all that chaos he came across the box of letters and considered it worth taking home and looking at more carefully at his leisure. The box was then relocated to his attic and soon forgotten. Now, after so many decades of being packed away, they were being read once again.

For my wife and me, there would be one more New England trip of some interest. I had been looking through an old scrapbook of my grandmother's one night and noticed a faded old newspaper clipping from the 1930s about a high-school student named Priscilla Gilchrist receiving an award from the Daughters of the American Revolution. As explained previously, Katharine, who grew up in the Martin-Sibley house in Williamstown as the daughter of Bernice Sibley and William Young, was only five years younger than her father's second wife. By the time my father was born, Katharine had married Maurice Gilchrist and moved to Franklin, New Hampshire. Priscilla was their daughter, and if she was still alive and if I could locate her, she might have information that could help us concerning the letters. Also, although I had never met her, she would be a first cousin and therefore one of my closest living blood relatives. In an Internet search I found an address for a Priscilla Gilchrist in Franklin, New Hampshire. I wrote a letter explaining what we were doing and waited to see if I would get a response. A few days later she phoned me, and we had a pleasant conversation in which she remembered having met my father when she was younger and shared her memories of our grandfather, who had died before I was born. Concerning the Mar-tins and Sibleys, she explained that she was very familiar with that part of the family line and had many old family photographs. She also added that she and a niece had particularly become interested in Francis and Henry Martin recently and had been researching their military records. "We have some of their letters," she added, "and we also have Henry's sword." That was enough for us to plan a trip to New Hampshire.

We met at their cottage on a small lake near Lake Winnipesaukee. Priscilla had been the middle child in her family. Her brother and sister had both died within the last decade, but both had children and grandchildren still in the area. Priscilla had returned to New Hampshire after living an adventurous life. She had joined the WAAC's

Bernice Sibley

during World War II and then chose to continue her military career as a physical therapist. As a result, she made many moves around the country as well as experiencing two more war settings, in Korea and Vietnam. Now she was back at her family home and sharing the lake house with her nieces and their families. Together with one niece, they had begun researching the Martin soldiers because they had five letters that had somehow been separated from our collection long ago. They also had a drawing of the Battle of Fredericksburg that showed where the Second and Fourth Vermont were positioned during the battle. For the occasion, they unveiled Henry's sword—a beautifully decorated ceremonial sword in excellent condition, with "W. H. Martin" clearly engraved at the top.

As for photographs, Priscilla had pictures of all the Sibley and Hill family members going all the way back to Chester Martin's second wife, Audelia Hill. Together with the photographs we had found of Henry and Francis, what had once been just voices from the attic now had real faces attached.

I had always believed that I was part of a very small family; now I recognized myself as part of an enormous one with many memorable people, both living and deceased. The Chester Martin family line may have come to an end with the death of his four children, but the much larger family of those related to them has influenced the world far beyond tiny Williamstown.

ACKNOWLEDGMENTS

This book would never have been possible without the help of many others who gave generously of their time. As mentioned in the Introduction, Edd and Nancy Hale, Bill Lutz, and my wife Carol deserve much of the credit for the transcribing of the letters, researching, and writing of the chapters. I especially thank Carol for her interest in and contributions to the project as well as for her continued support through its long duration.

We made multiple journeys to Vermont to conduct research on the protagonists and their friends and family members in more depth. There we received invaluable help from many people. At the University of Vermont, Jeffrey Marshall, Director of Research Collections in the library's Special Collections section, graciously assisted us and located many items for us to peruse despite having to address a family member's urgent medical situation that day.

The staff at the Vermont Historical Society—which is located on the site where Henry Martin once attended Barre Academy—were also very helpful. The current building had been Spaulding High School, where my grandmother was a teacher and my father was a student. When I explained who we were, one of the volunteer receptionists promptly telephoned her husband, who had graduated from Spaulding with my father. The accommodating and supportive staff helped us find many photographs and information concerning Barre Academy and several of the soldiers in the Vermont Brigade.

For the information on George Smith and the many other Norwich University graduates who appear in the letters, thanks go to Norwich's Special Collections staff. Kelly Gonzalez and, later, Gail Wiese were particularly helpful in applying their research skills to collect this information.

At every battlefield that we visited, National Park Service rangers were highly interested in the battle descriptions contained in the letters and happy to share information and take us to the relevant battlefield locations. Special thanks are due to National Park Service historian Francis O'Reilly, who met with us twice at Fredericksburg.

I would also like to acknowledge Ancestry.com. Not only was it a valuable tool for researching many of the people named in the letters, but its messaging system enabled me to meet and share information with many other members. Some of those with whom I exchanged messages even turned out to be distant relatives, and we remain in contact as a result.

I have relied extensively on two excellent works by historian Paul Zeller. *The Second Vermont Volunteer Infantry Regiment, 1861–1865* provided much useful information about the Vermont Brigade's movements throughout the war and its military engagements. Another of his books, *Williamstown, Vermont in the Civil War,* is full of fascinating vignettes about the Williamstown boys who went off to war. Many of those stories have been summarized in this book when they pertained to people mentioned in the letters. Paul's interest in Williamstown has led him to relocate there, where he hosted us and gave us more leads to pursue. He has also written *The Ninth Vermont Infantry: A History and Roster* and is actively involved with the Vermont Historical Society.

BIBLIOGRAPHY

A History of Williamstown, Vermont, 1781-1991. Williamstown, VT: Williamstown Historical Society, 1991.

Benedict, George C. *Vermont in the Civil War: A History of the Part Taken by the Vermont Soldiers and Sailors in the War for the Union, 1861–1865.* 2 vols. Burlington, VT: Free Press Association, 1888.

Burton, Brian K. *The Peninsula and Seven Days: A Battlefield Guide.* Lincoln: Univ. of Nebraska Press, 2007.

Catton, Bruce. *Glory Road.* Garden City, NY: Doubleday, 1952.

Catton, Bruce. *Mr. Lincoln's Army.* Garden City: Doubleday, 1951.

Catton, Bruce. *A Stillness at Appomattox.* Garden City, NY: Doubleday, 1953.

Chambers, Doreen. *Williamstown.* Charleston, SC: Arcadia, 2012.

Coffin, Howard. *Full Duty: Vermonters in the Civil War.* Woodstock, VT: Countryman, 1993.

Coffin, Howard. *Nine Months to Gettysburg: Stannard's Vermonters and the Repulse of Pickett's Charge.* Woodstock, VT: Countryman, 1997.

Coffin, Howard. *Something Abides: Discovering the Civil War in Today's Vermont.* Woodstock, VT: Countryman, 2013.

Duffus, R. L. *Williamstown Branch: Impersonal Memories of a Vermont Boyhood.* New York: W. W. Norton, 1958.

Ellis, William Arba, and Grenville M. Dodge. *Norwich University, 1819-1911, Her History, Her Graduates, Her Roll of Honor.* Montpelier, VT: Capitol City, 1911.

Foote, Shelby. *The Civil War: Fort Sumter to Perrysville.* New York: Random House, 1958.

Foote, Shelby. *The Civil War: Fredericksburg to Meridian.* New York: Random House, 1963.

Foote, Shelby. *The Civil War: Red River to Appomattox.* New York: Random House, 1974.

Gallagher, Gary W. *The Wilderness Campaign.* Chapel Hill: Univ. of North Carolina Press, 1997.

Lewis, Thomas A. *The Guns of Cedar Creek.* New York: Harper & Row, 1988.

Lowry, Thomas P. *The Story the Soldiers Wouldn't Tell: Sex in the Civil War.* Mechanicsburg, PA: Stackpole, 1994.

Marshall, Jeffrey D., ed. *A War of the People: Vermont Civil War Letters.* Hanover, NH: Univ. Press of New England, 1999.

O'Reilly, Francis Augustin. *The Fredericksburg Campaign: Winter War on the Rappahannock.* Baton Rouge: Louisiana State Univ. Press, 2003.

Parker, Francis J. *Genealogy of the Ainsworth Families in America.* Boston, MA: 1894.

Rogers, Lynn, and Patricia Pickard. *Levant, Maine: A History.* Levant, ME: Levant Historical Society, 1995.

Rosenblatt, Emil, and Ruth Rosenblatt, eds. *Hard Marching Every Day: The Civil War Letters of Private Wilbur Fisk, 1861-1865.* Lawrence, KS.: Univ. of Kansas Press, 1992.

Sears, Stephen W. *Chancellorsville.* Boston: Houghton-Mifflin, 1996.

Sullivan, David. *Minister's Island: Sir William Van Horne's Summer Home in St. Andrews.* St. Andrews, New Brunswick, Canada: Pendlebury, 2007.

The History of Brookfield, Vermont. Brookfield, VT: Brookfield Historical Society, 1987.

Tracy, Ann Blaisdell. *Higher Ground: A Memoir of Higgins Classical Institute.* Camden, ME: Down East, 1988.

Vermont Chronicle. Vermont State Library, Montpelier, VT.

Vermont Watchman. Vermont State Library, Montpelier, VT.

Ward, Eric, ed. *Army Life in Virginia: The Civil War Letters of George G. Benedict.* Mechanicsburg, PA: Stackpole, 2002.

Warden, William A., and Robert L. Dexter. *Genealogy of the Dexter Family in America; Descendants of Thomas Dexter, Together with a Record of Other Allied Families.* Worcester, MA: Blanchard, 1905.

Watson, Elliot Burnham, and Alven Martyn Smith. *George Martin of Salisbury, Mass., and His Descendants.* South Pasadena, CA: A. M. Smith, 1929.

Williamstown My Own: The History of Williamstown, Vermont, 1781-2012. Williamstown, VT: Williamstown Historical Society, 2012.

Zeller, Paul G. *The Ninth Vermont Infantry: A History and Roster.* Jefferson, NC: McFarland, 2008.

Zeller, Paul G. *The Second Vermont Volunteer Infantry Regiment, 1861-1865.* Jefferson, NC:McFarland, 2002.

Zeller, Paul G. *Williamstown, Vermont in the Civil War.* Charleston, SC: History Press, 2010.

PEOPLE IN THE STORY

Martin family

William Henry Martin – A second lieutenant in the Fourth Vermont Infantry who went by the name Henry. He wrote most of the letters used for this book.

Francis Smith Martin – Henry's brother, sometimes referred to as Frank, was a private in the Second Vermont Infantry.

Chester Martin – Frugal Williamstown farmer and the father of Henry and Francis, as well as two other children, George and Caroline, who died at young ages.

Betsey Smith Martin – Chester's wife.

Carlos Martin – One of the "Williamstown boys" (and one of Henry's many local cousins) who fought in the Eighth and Twelfth Regiments.

Henry Martin – Older cousin of Henry who joined the Sixth Vermont as a paid substitute at age 34. He was promoted several times before leaving the service. After the war he became a very prosperous farmer in Williamstown and served in many political positions including state legislator.

Bass family

Ebenezer Bass – Uncle of Henry, often referred to as Uncle Bass.

Lucy Smith Bass – Betsey's sister, married to Ebenezer Bass. Their large house was across the street from the Martin house.

Lorette Bass – Henry's cousin (Ebenezer's daughter) who often wrote letters to Henry.

Eunice Bass – Henry's cousin (Ebenezer's daughter) who was slowly dying from consumption during the war.

Ainsworth family

George Ainsworth – Served in the Christian Commission, aiding the soldiers in various ways. After the war he married Henry's cousin, Lorette Bass.

Laura Ainsworth – Young woman from Williamstown (George's cousin) who secretly became engaged to Henry.

Smith family

Levi Smith – Betsey Martin's father.

Ira Smith – Henry's uncle (Betsey's brother).

George Wilkins Smith – Henry's cousin (Ira's son), who left Norwich University after just one year to enlist in the regular army rose to first lieutenant in the 17th Infantry Regiment.

Jane Smith Davis – Henry's cousin (Ira's daughter), who married Mahlon Davis and joined him when he was stationed in Florida with the Seventh New Hampshire Regiment.

Chauncey Smith – A much older cousin of Henry who had a high-level Post Office position and was residing in Washington, D.C.

Nathan Smith – Chauncey's son, initially a first lieutenant in the Twelfth Wisconsin Infantry.

Henry Smith – Williamstown boy (and another cousin of Henry) in the Fourth Vermont who was wounded and died late in the war during the siege of Petersburg.

Sally Smith Pride – Another of Betsey's sisters and the wife of Darius Pride.

Emily Pride Tileston – Henry's cousin (Darius and Sally's daughter), whose husband, James Tileston, had extensive business dealings in the Midwest.

Lynde family

Major Isaac Lynde – Henry's uncle, who was blamed for an early Union defeat in New Mexico.

Fred Lynde – Henry's cousin (Isaac's son) and one of the Williamstown boys in the Fourth Vermont. He survived the war and then remained in the army for a military career.

Helen Lynde Dent – Henry's cousin (Isaac's daughter) and the wife of Brigadier General Frederick Dent.

Mary Lynde Fitzhugh – Henry's cousin (Isaac's daughter), who traveled south to be with her husband, Major Norman Fitzhugh, Assistant Adjutant General to General Jeb Stuart.

Charles Lynde – Another of Henry's cousins (Isaac's nephew) and a Williamstown boy in the Fourth Vermont.

Lucy Lynde – Teenage sister of Charles who corresponded with her older cousin Henry.

John Lynde – Older brother of Charles and Lucy. He became a second lieutenant in the Second Iowa Regiment.

Ellen Lynde Bass – Older sister of Charles and Lucy who married Walter Burnham Bass, a nephew of Ebenezer Bass, and was living in Illinois.

Judge John Lynde – Father of Charles, Lucy, John, Ellen, and several other children.

Dolly Smith Lynde – Wife of Judge John Lynde and sister of Chauncey Smith.

Leading officers

William F. "Baldy" Smith – St. Albans native and West Point graduate who rose in rank until he eventually commanded the Sixth Corps after Antietam.

John Sedgwick – Replaced Smith in commanding the Sixth Corps after the defeat at Fredericksburg. He later became the highest-ranking Union officer killed in the war.

Horatio Wright – Norwich University graduate who took over command of the Sixth Corps after General Sedgwick's death at Spotsylvania.

William T. H. Brooks – Although an Ohio native, became the initial commander of the First Vermont Brigade (or Old Brigade) consisting of the Second through the Sixth Vermont Infantry regiments.

Henry Whiting – Was given command of the First Vermont Brigade in 1862 when Brooks was promoted. Some Vermont soldiers believed he acted in cowardly fashion during battles.

Lewis A. Grant – Commander of the Fifth Vermont Regiment who was given command of the First Vermont Brigade in 1863 when Whiting resigned.

Edwin Stoughton – Young colonel and recent West Point graduate who initially lead the Fourth Vermont. Returned home to Bellows Falls for health reasons after the Peninsula Campaign but later returned as a brigadier general commanding the Second Vermont Brigade (the 12th through the 16th Vermont Infantry regiments) until he was captured in his bedroom by John S. Mosby.

Charles Stoughton – Brother of Edwin Stoughton and Norwich University graduate who rose from adjutant to command of the Fourth Vermont when his brother was promoted. He remained in that position until being seriously wounded, along with Henry, at Funkstown.

George Stannard – Replaced Edwin Stoughton as commander of the Second Vermont Brigade. After the war he served as doorkeeper for the U.S. House of Representatives.

George P. Foster – Promoted several times during war, he eventually became the final commander of the Fourth Vermont.

Stephen Pingree – Started as a first lieutenant in the Fourth Vermont and was promoted several times, eventually to lieutenant colonel, although Henry believed that he was elevated due to his political connections rather than merit. After the war he returned to his law practice and became a state legislator.

John Pratt – Started as a corporal in the Fourth Vermont and was promoted several times, eventually to lieutenant colonel.

James Platt – Norwich University graduate who started as a captain and remained in the Fourth Vermont throughout the war.

Other Vermont soldiers

George Bruce – Williamstown boy in the Eighth Vermont who enlisted late in the war at age 17 and was injured at Petersburg.

Martin Burnham – Williamstown boy in the Sixth Vermont, captured during the Peninsula Campaign.

Truman Blodgett – Williamstown boy who remained in the Fourth Vermont throughout the war, but died two years after returning home.

Newell Carleton – A friend of Henry in the Fourth Vermont, he was the first of the Williamstown boys to die.

Chester Clark – Williamstown boy in the Fourth Vermont, injured at Fredericksburg.

Lewis Clark – Williamstown boy in the Fourth Vermont (brother of Chester Clark) who died from injuries at Fredericksburg.

John Clough – Williamstown boy in the Second Vermont, injured during the Peninsula Campaign.

Frank Cosgrove – Williamstown boy in the Fourth Vermont, sent home early in the war for health reasons.

Charles Davis – Williamstown boy who served in the ninety-day First Vermont and did not re-enlist.

Henry Davis – Williamstown boy who served with his younger brother Charles in the First Vermont. He later re-enlisted as a second lieutenant in the Twelfth Vermont but was discharged as a result of charges of excessive cruelty toward his men.

Fred Doyle – Williamstown boy in the Sixth Vermont, killed at Chancellorsville.

Nelson Farnham – Williamstown boy who served for a year in the Twelfth Vermont. He returned home and married Martha Benedict, a local girl who had earlier shown an interest in Henry.

Newell Farnham – Williamstown boy and younger brother of Nelson who served for a year in the Twelfth Vermont and later re-enlisted.

Gardner Fay – Williamstown boy in the Tenth Vermont, killed during the Mine Run Campaign.

Willard Fay – Williamstown boy (younger brother of Gardner) who remained in the Fourth Vermont throughout the war.

Frank Flint – Williamstown boy in the Fourth Vermont, sent home early in the war for health reasons.

Reuben George – Enlisted in the Fourth Vermont at age 37. He died of disease during the war, and Henry helped to procure a pension for his wife and children.

John Greene – Williamstown boy who remained in the Fourth Vermont until his term of service was over in September 1864.

William Holden – Corporal in the Thirteenth Vermont from Barre.

Wilson Hopkins – Williamstown boy who had moved to Potsdam, New York just before the war and enlisted in the 16th New York Infantry.

Dexter Jones – Williamstown boy who remained in the Fourth Vermont throughout the war but had many health problems in the years that followed.

Riley Mardin – Private in the Fourth Vermont from Brookfield who borrowed money from Henry early in the war and showed little interest in ever repaying his debt.

Eli Mayette – Williamstown boy in the Fourth Vermont severely injured at Fredericksburg.

Donald Nichols – Williamstown boy in the Fourth Vermont, captured during the Peninsula Campaign.

John Roberts – Chaplain for the Fourth Vermont who later offered his services to Vermont parents and wives to search in Virginia for the bodies of their loved ones.

Frank Sancry – Williamstown boy who remained in the Fourth Vermont throughout the war. He was promoted several times, eventually to first sergeant.

Charles Staples – Williamstown boy who remained in the Eighth Vermont throughout the war, being promoted to corporal.

Frank Staples – Williamstown boy in the Eighth Vermont (cousin of Charles) who was captured at Cedar Creek and placed in a prison camp but survived the war.

Milton Staples – Williamstown boy in the Eighth Vermont (older brother of Frank) who remained in the army throughout the war.

Eldon Tilden – Williamstown boy who remained in the Fourth Vermont throughout the war, then returned home and married Henry's cousin, Lucy Lynde.

Charles Whitwell – Sergeant in the Fourth Vermont who was killed during the Peninsula Campaign.

Elijah Williams – Williamstown boy in the Eighth Vermont, killed in the Battle of the Wilderness.

Clark Wilson – Williamstown boy in the Fourth Vermont, killed at Fredericksburg.

Henry Wilson - Williamstown boy (younger brother of Clark) who remained in the Fourth Vermont throughout the war, but died from consumption two years after returning home.

For more information on Williamstown,
the Martin family, Civil War battles, and the letters,
visit our website:

www.martinletters.com

Made in the USA
San Bernardino, CA
16 March 2018